THE **DENAZIFICATION** OF
Germany

A HISTORY 1945–1950

THE **DENAZIFICATION** OF

A HISTORY 1945–1950

PERRY BIDDISCOMBE

TEMPUS

First published 2007

Tempus Publishing Limited
Cirencester Road, Chalford,
Stroud, Gloucestershire, GL6 8PE
www.tempus-publishing.com

British Library Cataloguing in Publication Data.
A catalogue record for this book is available from the British Library.

ISBN 978 07524 2346 3

Typesetting and origination by Tempus Publishing Limited
Printed in Great Britain

CONTENTS

PREFACE

Five years ago, Jonathan Reeve, my editor at Tempus, suggested that I write a general history of the denazification process in occupied Germany. The only English-language title was a dated and rather problematic effort by Irish-American intellectual Constantine FitzGibbon, and a German text by Justus Fürstenau had never been translated into English. There were also area studies by a number of historians, mostly in German, plus more general works by Tom Bower and James Tent, both of which included the word 'denazification' in the title, but focused primarily on other aspects of the occupation experience (war crimes trials in the first case, re-education in the second). Thus, there seemed a gap worth filling. In tackling the project, I hoped to mesh older writing about denazification in the American and British zones with more recent revelations about the purges conducted by the French and the Soviets. In particular, the new scholarship created the possibility of treating occupied Germany in its totality – rather than as an entity about to bifurcate – and it suggested denazification as a phenomenon that affected the entire country, often in similar ways, and despite zonal boundaries. Thus, denazification seemed a perfect topic for study in the reunification era, when people have once again begun to think about German wholeness and continuities in German history.

I also have a longstanding fascination with matters of moral ambiguity, and denazification encompasses many such issues. Was it, for instance, more important to serve the cause of justice or to keep Germans alive and fed by ensuring administrative efficiency? Was the nature of the Nazi movement the fault of its leaders or of its followers, and how should blame have been apportioned? Was it fair to treat Nazis who had joined the party for opportunistic or professional reasons in the same fashion as true-believers? And was it necessary to segregate Nazis and arrange for their exclusion from German civil and economic life, or was it wiser to rehabilitate and reintegrate such elements? These are difficult questions with no easy answers.

This book was always intended as a synthesis of existing scholarship, which is scattered through a large body of literature, and throughout the course of research and writing, I have tried to assimilate the most important studies of the topic. As my work got underway, I also found it possible to add a few original tid-bits, particularly since I had explored American occupation planning during my MA studies, which yielded some insights, and I had continued to gather primary source material as I spent years in the archives working on related projects. Thus, on matters such as the Morgenthau Plan, the SHAEF denazification letter of 23 February 1945, denazification of the coal mining industry and the U-7 conspiracy, I have tried to cast new light.

Some of the book's themes have been germinating in my mind for twenty-five years, so my thanks must extend to people who influenced my early think-ing about the American occupation, particularly Peter Kent and David Beattie. Talking with Bronwen Magrath, one of our department's MA students, as well as reading Ms. Magrath's MA thesis, helped me develop a fuller appreciation of the background for French occupation policy. My profound gratitude also extends to the archivists at the *Bundesarchiv*, the Imperial War Museum, the National Archives of the United Kingdom and the U.S. National Archives, and to the librarians at various institutions, particularly McPherson Library, who have facilitated access to the materials that provide the basis for this study. And finally, thanks to my family, who have always steadied my course and have provided the foundation on which I have been able to build life as a scholar.

Perry Biddiscombe, Victoria, BC

THE DENAZIFICATION DEBATE

In post-war history, few terms have evoked such intense feeling as 'denazification'. The very word 'Nazification', preceded by a negative prefix, suggested that the Nazi 'coordination' of German society in 1933/34, the notorious *Gleichschaltung*, could be reversed, although even the most ardent supporters of denazification admitted that the malicious impact of the Third Reich could never be wholly undone. In order to accomplish this herculean feat, Allied authorities introduced 'the most extensive legal procedure [that] the world had ever witnessed', or at least that was the description provided by John McCloy, the U.S. High Commissioner in Germany. The military governor of the U.S. zone, Lucius Clay, called it a 'program ... almost without precedent in the history of the world'.[1] And those descriptions were justified by the numbers involved: throughout occupied Germany, nearly two million Nazis bore one form of punishment or another (mostly job dismissals and fines) and more than 400,000 spent a period in internment.

The word 'denazification' was used in 1943 by post-war planners in the Pentagon, although the first such reference was connected to schemes for the forced reform of the German legal system.[2] In fact, the word can be applied to the full range of Allied/Soviet reform and punishment measures in occupied Germany, and is still occasionally used in such a sense.[3] As early as 1944, however, 'denazification' was usually employed to describe the specific liquidation of the National Socialist Party (NSDAP) and the elimination of its influence, particularly through the arrest and incarceration of the party's senior personnel, plus the purging of party members from the German Government and the business management structure. This is how most historians have interpreted the topic and it is the specific meaning that will be explored in this text.

It is worth noting – at least parenthetically – that U.S. and Allied planners slotted a number of subsidiary initiatives under the rubric of denazification, particularly the elimination of Nazi propaganda and literature, the banning of Nazi regalia, the closure of Nazi museums or monuments, and the renaming of streets, parks and public buildings.[4] Amongst the Allies, there was some debate about the propriety of seising and destroying National Socialist books, which summoned up the horrific image of book burnings, and the term 'Nazi' was sometimes defined rather loosely, covering works by Heinrich von Treitschke, Oswald Spengler and Knut Hamsun. There was also a concern in the British Foreign Office about the necessity of destroying stone memorials and statues, and also some doubt about suppressing the use of swastikas. 'The less the Allies insist … on the total elimination of these emblems,' said one memorandum, 'the more rapidly they will likely in fact disappear…' Labour Party ministers in the British Government insisted, however, that a ban on *all* such insignia be strictly enforced.[5] The Germans themselves debated whether pictures of Junker warhorse Paul von Hindenburg should remain on the walls of public offices,[6] but for the most part, the elimination of the cultural and symbolic aspects of Nazism seemed so commonsensical that it elicited little debate. Since it was thus a straightforward policy implemented with few deviations, it merits none of our further attention.

As for the purging of Nazi Party members, this central function of denazification was subject to many twists and turns in implementation, and has since given rise to significant controversy. The first generation of historians treating the occupation was comprised mainly of people with direct experience in military government, particularly Harold Zink, the semi-official historian of the U.S. occupation. Many of these writers dealt primarily with the evolution and execution of American policy, perhaps because of the predominant influence exercised by the U.S. in world affairs, perhaps because its policies were models for the other occupiers,[7] although historians such as Wolfgang Friedmann, Michael Balfour and Constantine FitzGibbon attempted studies that covered all four zones of occupation. The first German historian of denazification, Justus Fürstenau, tried to deal with the three western zones. With the exception of work by Zink and Fürstenau, these early efforts were highly impressionistic and poorly documented,[8] and FitzGibbon's *Denazification* (1969) was particularly heavy on rhetorical musings and exposition, while being correspondingly light on narrative detail or presentation of archival evidence. Such works depicted denazification as a necessary evil conditioned by the *Zeitgeist* of 1944/45, but almost bound to fail because of the scale at which the project was attempted. According to this interpretation, the policy of the Western Allies was originally influenced by a perception of German 'collective guilt', plus a desire for vengeance, an intention to 'appease' the Soviets and high hopes for imposed reform in Germany, although all these assumptions supposedly diverted the Allies from undertaking more positive initiatives. This critique suggests that denazification was finally undercut in 1947/48, mainly by the re-emergence of a more humanitarian approach and by an allegedly more realistic assessment of Germany's position and capabilities in a world dominated by power politics, a realisation that was in turn prompted by fear of the emergent Soviet threat. Such a view emphasized the supposed lack of coherence in denazification measures: an initial overstatement of objectives was followed by a wrenching swing in policy.[9]

Such 'liberal-conservative' interpretations did not fully monopolize the field amongst early writers. John Montgomery, a social theorist at the University of Chicago, drew heavily from a collection of operational research reports compiled by the occupation authorities – in fact, he had collaborated with Fürstenau in the development and exploitation of this data – and upon this base he developed his view of denazification as the fundament of a laudable 'reformist' strategy. Montgomery described the American goal as an 'artificial revolution', a sensibly moderate programme of change fostered by a power traditionally shy about endorsing either imperialism or Marxism. Thus, denazification seemed like a good idea, although Montgomery developed a detailed critique of the programme's implementation. 'Reformist' military government was also described by Montgomery as the first stage of 'a continuous assault on totalitarianism as an ideology', although he conceded that this achievement was curtailed in a hurried effort to contain communism by restoring Germany as an anti-Soviet bulwark. Nonetheless, he claimed, 'revolutions cannot achieve perfection, and this flaw in the design was probably unavoidable. It was certainly not fatal.' According to Montgomery, the final result of denazification was the Bonn republic, which he portrayed as restored version of Weimar 'not unacceptable to the Allies', although he was not yet willing to vouch for the long-term stability of the new state's liberal-democratic character.[10]

In Germany, two sharp polemics were published in response to denazification, both at the opposite pole to the 'reformist' interpretation. One, Ernst von Salomon's *Fragebogen* (1951), was the personal account of a former *Freikorps* officer and German nationalist who was angry about having been interned by the Allies. Blaming Nazism on the impersonal forces that characterize modern life, von Salomon pointedly asked whether the Americans had reached such a level of democratic achievement that they could afford to teach lessons to others. Running along somewhat complementary lines was Caspar von Schrenk-Notsing's *Charakterwäsche* (1965). It attached great importance to supposed socio-political attempts to change German 'national character', allegedly influenced by German émigré advocates of psychotherapy, such as Wilhelm Reich and Erich Fromm.[11] In turn, Schrenk-Notsing claimed that the work of such men was an essential precondition for the development of the 'collective guilt' doctrine, despite the lack of evidence that psychoanalysts exercised any direct influence on the formation of U.S. or Allied policy.[12]

Thankfully, the 1960s and 1970s also saw the publication of several more balanced assessments. Work in the United States reflected the new spirit of the

Kennedy-Johnson era, which encouraged systematic and logical appreciations of policy-making, and it also profited from public access to the records of U.S. military government. The result was a literature with a new recognition of the importance of pragmatism, a trend pioneered by such professional historians as John Gimbel and Earl Ziemke. Gimbel, in particular, established a reputation as the most important and most prolific historian of the U.S. occupation. Such 'pragmatists' disagreed with the prevailing consensus that there had been wild policy swings in the American occupation, noting instead that the *de facto* agenda was often set locally by U.S. military government in Frankfurt or by military government detachments in the field. These forces allegedly did what they thought was necessary to deal with practical, short-term problems, such as widespread privation and the desperate need for reconstruction of German infrastructure and industry. Confronting such matters emphasized the need for a degree of continuity. In this view, U.S. military government undertook a schematic form of denazification largely because it had an acute sensitivity to American public and congressional opinion, which originally favoured a radical purge, although the negativity of the programme did little to foster the rise of a new, reform-minded German elite. Never comfortable with the programme, U.S. military government eventually gave up on such goals in an effort to get the German economy back into working order.[13] Gimbel also took issue with the notion of an 'artificial revolution', arguing that it was not the methodology of the occupation that had failed to produce a radical shift of German elites, but an inherent failure to reconcile the United States' primary political goals.[14]

Running on a parallel track was the 'Left Revisionist' literature of the 1970s and 1980s. The most important figure of this school was a young German historian named Lutz Niethammer, whose study of denazification in Bavaria is sometimes cited as the most important contribution to the literature. Niethammer's work certainly influenced the direction of all subsequent scholarship.[15] Niethammer was much influenced by Gimbel's arguments about continuity in American policy, and like Gimbel, he bore an antipathy toward the idea of an 'artificial revolution', rather unfairly charging Montgomery with having made unsubstantiated claims about the revolutionary successes of American reformism.[16] He also drew heavily from the 'New Left' historiography of the Cold War and from the 'restoration' thesis, a then-fashionable notion suggesting that a broad-based shift in the German social order had been blocked by Western intervention, and that this intercession had led to a reassertion of economic and social frameworks that had been discredited – at least briefly – in the eyes of most Germans. Such new themes in the scholarship reflected the impact of the Vietnam War, supposedly the archetypical manifestation of an over-extended brand of American imperialism, as well as the increasing *rapprochement* between West and East Germany, which created a greater willingness – at least among intellectuals – to entertain a Marxist critique of the political and economic order in the Federal Republic. In

Niethammer's view, denazification failed in the most meaningful sense because its U.S. architects abandoned its potentially revolutionary assumptions and thus failed to co-operate with German leftists seeking social change. Moreover, Niethammer put great stress on the continuity theme, arguing that U.S. policy had long been anti-communist as well as anti-Nazi, and that the rehabilitative aspect of denazification was always implicit within its germ. The superficial vetting and processing of large numbers of Nazis, he contended, had always been intended as a pre-requisite to restoring such people to German economic life, and was the most characteristic feature of the programme. Thus, the system of German denazification boards, or *Spruchkammern*, was supposedly 'a conservative invention ... designed to avert the dangers of [both] fascist illegality and anti-fascist democracy, and to secure the continuing leadership of the bourgeoisie'.[17]

British muckraker and BBC presenter Tom Bower also hammered home such themes, arguing that the Americans, instead of fostering revolution, treated denazification as an administrative matter, although they had neither the machinery to carry it through nor the heart to impose it if it threatened principles of order and efficiency. In Bowers's view, the fate of denazification was supposedly sealed when it was sloughed off on the Germans in March 1946, after which the occupiers convinced themselves – despite all evidence to the contrary – that the programme was working. The final result was the evolution of a deeply flawed Federal Republic that shared the chief weakness of its Weimar predecessor: its financial, business and educational institutions were supposedly never swept clean of elements that despised pluralism and democracy.[18]

Yet another school of thought also emerged in the 1970s and 1980s, although it was sharply at odds with the 'pragmatic' and 'Left Revisionist' interpretations. 'Libertarian' historians, such as Edward Peterson and James Tent, returned to the older contention that Allied objectives had originally been punitive but that policies shifted radically, although they did share with the 'pragmatists' an intense interest in bureaucratic problems and in low- and mid-level decision-making. Fusing post-Vietnam realisations about the limits of military power together with a neo-conservative suspicion of 'big government', Peterson and Tent argued that an originally optimistic set of plans for interfering in German civil life – the product of an emotionally-charged wartime climate – were eventually retracted when American administrators realised that such measures would not work without consent from the German people. Peterson echoed a theme popular among German conservatives by claiming that denazification was hardly necessary at all, 'Germany was in large part denazified by Hitler, because Nazism was based on success and Hitler failed'. Moreover, most party members had not been active Nazis, but apolitical. What passed for denazification was an uneven campaign of authoritarian repression that dissolved into a mess because military government had eroded the German administrative system, its only practical mode of operation. Eventually, U.S. administrators abandoned authoritarian interventionism, a 'retreat to victory' in Peterson's phraseology, not because of a dawning recognition of the alleged Soviet threat, but because American officials had become hopelessly overextended and bogged down in paperwork.[19]

In the last quarter-century, the main research agendas have been shaped by the release of documents from the British and French archives, as well as by the flood of data made available by the collapse of the Berlin Wall and the end of Soviet dictatorship. In the 1980s and 1990s, many 'contemporary' historians also began calling for a more thorough understanding of the immediate post-war period, the investigation of which had previously been derided as 'journalism'. Rather than having colleagues continue to root around the nineteenth and early twentieth centuries in an attempt to understand the nature and eventual appeal of National Socialism, they argued that the passage of the Nazi regime – and the attitudes behind it – were surely as significant as its origins and prehistory. Indeed, they said, it was the duty of historians to sort out whether 1945 had actually marked a 'new beginning', as had often been asserted, or if that key year was actually followed by a 'restoration' of traditional centres of power and attitudes.[20] Given the fact that Niethammer had already laboured on denazification in Bavaria, and that his empirical work was regarded as definitive (if perhaps not his conclusions), the ground for fresh inquiries seemed to lay in the former British, French and Russian zones of occupation. Indeed, as early as the 1960s, Justus Fürstenau had recognized that there were significant variations between the denazification programmes in the various zones, and the depth and extent of such differentiation has now become fully apparent.

Historians have long realised that the British had attached less importance to denazification than the Americans, a point conceded by the official historian of British military government, S.F.V. Donnison.[21] This salient fact alone, as Ian Connor notes, 'may partly account for the absence of a major academic study of their policy'.[22] Recent historians of the British zone, such as Ian Turner, Jill Jones and Barbara Marshall, have produced some well-documented and sophisticated interpretations of the British zone experience, but they have also reasserted the basic claims of their predecessors, at least with regard to denazification.[23] A German study of the implementation of denazification in North-Rhine Westphalia, Wolfgang Krüger's *Entnazifiziert!*, was based solely on German archives and reinterpreted Niethammer by claiming that the rehabilitation of Nazis was not only necessary, but the greatest achievement of the denazification programme![24]

Until recently, the French zone was largely *terra incognita* – its 'silk curtain' was the western counterpart to the 'iron curtain' – but the opening of the French archives in 1986 began to peal away the mystery and led to many changes in interpretation.[25] Klaus-Dietmar Henke, a disciple of Niethammer, had already produced an excellent study of denazification in South Württemberg (1981), but access to the archives yielded important works by Rainer Möhler and Reinhard

Grohnert, the first covering the Rhineland-Palatinate and the second South Baden. This scholarship suggests that the French too varied considerably from the American paradigm, although there is an on-going debate about the degree to which the French denazification process was centrally planned and executed. Henke argues that French denazification policy was characterised by discordancy and was 'instrumental', that is, important only in the sense that it facilitated larger goals; Möhler and Gronhert tend to see more evidence of consistency and they argue that French military government saw the policy as a principal mechanism for the organisation of a democratic Germany. Henke's book on the French-occupied portion of Württemberg illuminated the one significant attempt, at least in western Germany, to let German leftists conduct the purge.[26]

As for the Soviet zone, historians carrying out area studies of Soviet denazification policy – specifically Helga Welsh, Timothy Vogt and Damian van Melis – have recently provided new insights, although all three suggest that there was considerable unevenness and variation between the zonal *Länder*. And again, there were significant differences between the Soviet and American patterns. Welsh and van Melis see the Soviet version of denazification as part of Stalin's larger desire to change the nature of society in eastern Germany, although Vogt's study of *Land* Brandenburg suggests that Soviet goals, at least in the early phase of the occupation, were less revolutionary than has long been assumed.[27]

After fifty years of scholarship on denazification, it is perhaps an opportune moment to take stock, and such an exercise is the primary purpose of this book. In the following pages, I shall attempt a synthesis of the existing accounts, stressing the common points in the literature – that is, the general agreement about denazification's faulty inception and design, its over-extension, its inconsistent application and its ultimate failure – while at the same time pointing out where there is still disagreement. In navigating such choppy waters, I have used my judgement and my discretion in choosing certain lines of argument over others, and I have supplemented the discussion with insights provided by my own research in primary sources, particularly in addressing where there have been gaps in the existing record. The result is not pleasant reading for statists who put faith in bureaucratic problem-solving or for idealists who believe in the power of well-intentioned reform. Neither is it edifying for anyone who hopes that true justice was meted out to Nazi activists and troublemakers. What this chronicle does provide, however, is a salutary lesson for readers interested in how *not* to approach the reform of totalitarian societies, a topic that remains as relevant today as it was in 1945.

1

A Perfectionist's Plan

Denazification arose from a synthesis of trends that influenced American policy-makers and then radiated outwards to shape the policies of the other occupying powers as well. These tendencies have often been depicted as 'soft' or 'hard' versions of occupation doctrine, although they actually reflected a number of more fundamental approaches to policy formation – liberal idealistic, pragmatic, Marxist, 'realist' – that implied 'soft' or 'hard' outcomes. In addition, a number of larger-than-life personalities, such as Franklin Delano Roosevelt, Henry Morgenthau, Franz Neumann and Herbert Marcuse, had a profound impact on the policy that evolved. The process of combining diverse ideas promoted by different schools of thought and policy-makers was the work of several senior bureaucrats in the U.S. War and State Departments. The names of these men – John McCloy, John Hilldring, David Marcus, John Boettiger, Edgar Allen, Freeman Matthews, James Riddelberger, Emile Despres – will not ring familiar, but they played a crucial mediating role in creating occupation policy.

In the broadest sense, denazification was embedded in an American tradition of foreign policy idealism. Born of Puritanism, the American Enlightenment and the democratising influence of the frontier and the melting pot, this idealism had motivated nineteenth-century ideas of 'Manifest Destiny', as well as informing the peculiar form of American imperialism popular at the turn of the twentieth century. Most importantly, it endowed American wars with a messianic aspect, framing them not merely as struggles of national interest, but as campaigns to reshape the international order, particularly through the promotion of a liberal doctrine of self-determination. In such a conceptualisation, even the enemy could be reformed. The Declaration of Independence, the Emancipation Proclamation and the Fourteen Points were all products of this moralising zeal.[1] The Atlantic Charter, a high-minded wish list for the re-establishment of international harmony, expressed the same spirit. It was issued jointly by the United States and Great Britain and was meant to provide the anti-Axis coalition with a set of ethical objectives, including a promise to destroy 'Nazi tyranny'.[2]

This approach suggested reform more than punishment, and its truest champion was Vice President Henry Wallace, a Midwestern progressive who was the first major figure of the Roosevelt Administration to speak publicly about Germany's future. Wallace was deeply influenced by the writings of leftist German émigrés and he was also familiar with Thorstein Veblen's classic *Imperial Germany and the Industrial Revolution*, which he had read as a young man and then reread in 1940. He willingly accepted the existence of a 'good Germany', the antithesis of the negative side of the country then bearing its fangs, and he hoped that Germans would mete out justice to their own 'Nazi overlords', negating the need for denazification from abroad. Rather, he laid stress on providing encouragement and external direction for Germans 'steeped in the German liberal tradition and the ideals of Scandinavian cooperation'. He expected that such elements, particularly educators, would lead their own country away from 'Prussianism' and Hitlerism. A cleansed Germany would then have a key role to play in Wallace's dawning 'Century of the Common Man'.[3]

Unfortunately for idealist reformers, Wallace had little institutional say in postwar planning and his boss, President Franklin Delano Roosevelt, was not cut from the same cloth. Many historians have portrayed Roosevelt as a Wilsonian internationalist, but one with realist and even hawkish tendencies behind a liberal exterior.[4] Roosevelt's prescriptions for the peace were usually more harsh than magnanimous, although he also dithered unconscionably about making postwar preparations. Nazi Germany's defeat could be foreseen as early as 1943, but Roosevelt was allergic to the idea of setting detailed occupation policy before the situation had matured even further. In fact, he was hard-pressed to make the most fundamental decisions. In early 1943, he pledged the Western Powers to achieving the 'unconditional surrender' of Germany and to 'the destruction of the [Axis] philosophies … based on fear and hate and the subjugation of other peoples'. He also privately conceded that the failure to occupy all of Germany in 1918/19 had been a mistake.[5] During the same year, he agreed – in accord with Churchill and Stalin – that Germany deserved to be overrun totally and administratively divided into three zones of occupation, each governed by one of the Allied Powers. He also indicated vague approval for partitioning the country and subjecting it to various industrial controls and sanctions, and he declared that 'all dangerous elements of the population [should be] forcibly removed'.[6]

Roosevelt, however, ventured little beyond these basic assumptions, and since he arrived at the Teheran Conference – the first of the 'Big Three' conclaves – in a policy fog, Stalin dominated the proceedings with very tough rhetoric. With the subtlety of a booming cannon, the Soviet dictator recommended dismembering the Reich, destroying German industries, and detaching Germany's eastern provinces.

He also 'joked' about executing thousands of German officers.[7] Teheran, however, provided merely a forum for an exchange of opinions, and as Treasury Secretary Henry Morgenthau later observed, none of the president's advisors ensured that the spirit of these exchanges took shape as specific policy directives.[8] Liberals of the Morgenthau stripe were also offended by the drift of policy at lower levels. They chided the U.S. Army for the supposedly reactionary curriculum of a school for military government officers, which had been organised in Charlottesville, Virginia, and they noted that in French North Africa, American officers and administrators had left Vichy French officialdom in place, which seemed a poor precedent. Sour memories of this so-called 'Darlan Deal' resurfaced in 1944, when its architect, diplomat Robert Murphy, was appointed as the American political advisor in General Eisenhower's Anglo-American command structure, the Supreme Headquarters, Allied Expeditionary Force (SHAEF).[9] The Allied occupation of southern and central Italy also proved a disappointment and offered few valuable precedents. Bradley Smith later called the Italian precursor 'a constantly shifting series of improvisations centered around the idea of preventing "disease and unrest"'.[10]

While Roosevelt dawdled and liberals seethed, the policy vacuum was filled by action below, particularly in SHAEF, which had responsibility for planning and executing the invasion of north-western Europe. Soon after SHAEF's formation in February 1944, it established a civil affairs section called G-5, plus a German Country Unit (GCU) for occupation planning, which was based at Shrivenham, near Oxford, and came under G-5's purview. Although G-5 was run by a succession of British generals, its authoritative second-in-command was an American, General Julius Holmes, and since British personnel were in short supply, the GCU was disproportionally American in composition, with some areas of work handled by staffs that were entirely American. The GCU's primary function was to prepare the *Handbook for Military Government for Germany*, the necessity of which was inspired by a similar volume that had proven invaluable in Allied-occupied Italy. Work began on 4 March 1944 under the direction of Colonel Edgar Lewis. The importance of the *Handbook* was that if the Big Three failed to agree on occupation policies or to properly specify those policies for subordinates, the *Handbook* would become the chief policy guide for occupied Germany, if only by default. In fact, the eventual chief of American military government, General Lucius Clay, later observed that the actual form and method of the American occupation was similar to the policies originally envisioned in the *Handbook*.

Operating largely free of critical oversight, *Handbook* drafters reflected traditional military attitudes toward occupied territories, particularly the 'welfare of the governed' school of thought, which was inculcated in the Charlottesville training programmes and through military field manuals such as FM27-5 (1940). The 'welfare of the governed' theme was a nineteenth-century concept that assumed the bulk of the enemy population was a passive body requiring normal patterns of administration, particularly since such procedures would ensure relative quiet along Allied lines of communication and help the conquerors complete operations at the front. A 'hearts and minds' approach was also suggested by memories of the U.S. role in the post-First World War Rhineland occupation, particularly in the way that this experience was reflected in the works of Colonel Erwin Hunt, whose 1920 report on the occupation had formed part of the background for FM 27-5. Thus, performance expectations for U.S. military government elements were functional, rather than political, and they reflected the speed with which occupiers could restore utilities, public health and the labour supply system in any given area. Trainers at the Charlottesville school assumed that the Allied theatre commander would abolish the Nazi Party but would otherwise leave the German administrative structure intact, although he would be able – at his discretion – to make limited removals of undesirable personnel. Such precepts were also in strict accord with international law, which prohibited foreign occupiers from changing the legal or social structures in areas overrun as a result of military operations. In addition, many army officers were essentially engineers, and military government officers, in particular, often came from civilian backgrounds in business. In the very fibre of their being, the main impulse of these men was to restore public utilities and communication systems and to prevent the outbreak of contagious diseases. It was in this sense, in particular, that the military technocratic ethos was superimposed upon a New Deal interest in public works and infrastructure development. Such an approach cannot justifiably be described as 'soft' – in fact, GCU planners regarded their plans as suitably tough and the fact that members of their forward office in London had to dodge German buzz bombs did nothing to encourage Germanophile sentiment. Nonetheless, their set of priorities suggested working *with* indigenous elites and administrative structures rather than replacing them, and this establishmentarianism reflected the conservative inclinations of many military officers.[11]

GCU planners backed away from the intention of COSSAC, SHAEF's predecessor, to make open use of Nazi organisations and corporate institutions, such as the Reich Food Estate,[12] but they nonetheless proposed to rename such structures and then exploit them. In fact, British military experts advised GCU planners that abolishing such institutions was outside normal legal practice – they could only be suspended – and they further suggested that 'utmost use should be made of the existing (German) organisations and personnel, eliminating only those officers found to be incompetent or non-co-operative'.[13] Even by August 1944, however, British officials in the Foreign Office realised that such assumptions were no longer tenable. After examining a draft of the *Handbook*, they warned that they too had planned to make use of Nazi organi-sations, but that such hopes had already been dashed by 'British Ministers'.[14]

Of course, *Handbook* drafters realised that they would have to address the power and influence of the Nazi Party, but this responsibility was so far outside the traditional boundaries of military government that the GCU lacked a specific staff section with which to treat the issue. Its internal bureaus were each devoted to plan-ning for the customary responsibilities of military government (that is, oversight of local administration, the civil service, the economy and the legal system). The first two mimeographed editions of the *Handbook*, which were circulated in the spring of 1944, made no mention of liquidating the NSDAP or corralling Nazi officials, although the issue was eventually addressed by the GCU's Board of Editors, whose job was to harmonize the work of the various GCU staffs, and by its planning section. The key personnel assigned to the issue – O. W. Wilson, Thomas Hall, Keith Wilson – were largely jurists or former policemen, and it was they who advanced a legalistic/bureaucratic approach, even adopting the British police term 'Special Branch' as the name for military government's denazification force. After such work got underway, the third issue of the *Handbook* (June 1944) called for the liquidation of the NSDAP and the seizure of the party's assets and records, although it provided only for the incarceration of senior Nazi leaders, and even this was regarded as a security issue rather than a means of changing the nature of the sociopolitical order. The drafters of this document had considered either suspending *all* officials, pending screening, or retaining *all* officials, pending screening, but they finally decided that such stark alternatives were impractical on political and administrative grounds. Rather, they eventually decided to leave much discretion in the hands of the theatre commander, who was encouraged to dismiss 'even the lesser Nazi officials', although he was left plenty of room to make exceptions 'on the grounds of expediency or administrative necessity'. This formula had already been used in occupied Italy, although even there it was proving troublesome. GCU planners also lacked detailed data on the Nazi Party's patterns of organisation, using the British Foreign Office's area guide for Germany – the so-called 'blue book' – as the source for whatever knowledge there were able to glean about the Nazi Party's structure or the Nazification of the German civil service. As a result, their provisions for release categories or purge criteria remained vague.[15] As a means of extracting detailed information from the Germans themselves, Major Aldo Raffa, who had drafted a questionnaire for use in Italy – the *Scheda Personale* – drew up a similar document called the *Fragebogen*, which was to be distributed to all German government officials and elicited detailed information about Nazi affiliations. An early draft of the *Fragebogen* was printed and circulated for discussion in May 1944. The main task of Special Branch would be to collect and process the *Fragebogen*. It was calculated that the time needed to perform this function would be about six months, a time frame that later proved to be wildly optimistic.[16]

Admitting some of their conceptual limitations in identifying Nazis, GCU officers called upon the services of the CIA's predecessor, the Office of Strategic Services (OSS), whose Research and Analysis Branch (R&A) had already provided the Pentagon with a series of detailed studies on German society and government. On 18 March 1944, Sinclair Armstrong, a member of R&A's Central European Section, arrived at Shrivenham as OSS liaison, and the denazification issue was literally farmed out to Sinclair's associates in Washington.[17] Who were the Central Europeanists toiling away along the Potomac? Many were brilliant young Ivy League academics (H. Stuart Hughes, Sherman Kent), while others were German social scientists and historians who had been forced to flee their homeland in the 1930s, either because of their leftist political orientations or their Jewish faith. Amongst the émigrés were Felix Gilbert, Hajo Holborn, Carl Schorske and several scholars from the famous 'Frankfurt School', especially Franz Neumann, Herbert Marcuse and Otto Kirchheimer. The Frankfurt School looms large in our story because its members had developed a neo-Marxist methodology called Critical Theory, which attempted to recapture the fluid and critical aspects of Marx's work, particularly the early Marx of the 1840s, when a form of Left Hegelianism still deeply influenced his thinking. This critical Marxism was aimed at a pervasive 'false consciousness' that prevented otherwise revolutionary elements from pushing for the creation of a more egalitarian and democratic society. In particular, the emphasis on Hegel implied the importance of negation and contradiction, crucial elements in the famous Hegelian dialectic. Such ideas proved crucial in shaping the American strategy for denazification.[18]

The Frankfurt School also developed one of the first theoretical appreciations of Nazism, which was presented in Neumann's magnum opus *Behemoth*, published in 1943. Neumann and his cohorts were among the few, outside the Comintern, who could claim a coherent understanding of the force that they were intending to destroy. They argued that National Socialism was not a true political philosophy, but a deceptive and self-conscious rationalisation for the domination of a few groups that controlled power. In fact, they claimed that the Third Reich was not a state at all, but a political condominium in which four centres of power (the Nazi Party, the army, the bureaucracy and the capitalist business elite) were loosely coordinated by the *Führer*, who exercised ultimate control by dint of his charismatic authority. The strength of the system, but also its potential weakness – note the Hegelian contradiction – lay in its propaganda and derivative 'ideology', which mollified Germans with pseudo-socialist and faux egalitarian ideas. In other words, Nazism provided Germans with a pervasive form of 'false consciousness'. Sooner or later, however, the technocratic and working class elements of German society would see through this mirage and demand genuine social justice. 'Even false egalitarianism,' said Neumann, 'will leave indelible impressions,' and there were already signs of discontent because the system was compulsively producing instruments of war instead of delivering adequate material benefits. According to the Frankfurt theorists, however, Nazism could only be defeated if Germans were allowed to exercise a spirit of criticism grounded in the country's cultural and philosophical tradition. 'Thought of any kind…,' they contended, 'must inevitably have a critical and revolutionary impact', although what they really hoped to encourage was a renewed sense of political engagement by labour unions and the socialist movement. As one of their colleagues later recalled, they were 'decidedly pro-Social Democratic'. In the opinion of the Neumann group, however, the ultimate irony was that an Allied invasion could prevent a revolution by 'freez[ing] the social situation at the point reached at the beginning of the occupation period'. 'This is the perplexing dilemma that the Allies face,' noted an R&A position paper: 'In order to make sure of their victory and to remove the German danger, they will have to move into Germany to occupy her, but in doing so, they will probably prevent the anti-Nazi reaction of the progressive forces then coming to its fulfillment, and thereby will prevent a solution of the German problem which would probably give a better guarantee of future peace than any peace treaty could provide.' Thus, the failure of the 1918/19 German Revolution would be repeated.[19]

Some German exiles in U.S. Government service suggested simply allowing anti-Nazi disturbances to unfold, despite the violence and disruption, and certain elements in the OSS were preparing to send socialist émigrés into Germany in order to support such a revolution.[20] However, the U.S. War Department opposed such plans for a violent 'self-cleansing', mainly on the grounds that it might fail and that it would exceed the degree of tolerance allowed to an occupying power under the Hague Convention.[21] In any case, the Central Europeanists in R&A had an alternative that they felt was the golden mean: it was more realistic than proposals aimed at inspiring wholesale unrest, yet it was in accord with American idealism – the exiles regarded the New Deal as the ultimate fulfilment of Wilsonianism – and it was not overly draconian.[22] The Neumann School was also influenced by the old-fashioned 'Spoils System' of their new homeland, which – despite its undeniably odious character – was sometimes rationalized as a democratic circulation of elites.[23] The answer to existing problems, suggested Naumann and his cohorts, was to remove the repressive weight of the Nazi Party and its placeholders, which would allow a flowering of opposition and support a process of creative renewal. The job of crafting this policy was left largely to Neumann and Marcuse, the latter still a little-known philosophy professor, although he would one day become the intellectual guru of the sixties youth movement. They introduced several key innovations. First, they drafted black and grey lists specifying Nazi personalities who would be subject to arrest or removal from office, plus white lists of acceptable replacements. Black lists were comprised of the names of senior bureaucrats, war criminals, and high echelon members of the party and its affiliates, all of whom were subject to *mandatory* dismissal. Grey lists named lower rank administrators, civil servants and members of the party and its paramilitary auxiliary, the SA, who were subject to *discretionary* removal. White lists designated persons 'whose character, professional standing, experience, and political reliability render them especially suitable to be placed in positions of responsibility'. These three types of lists, Marcuse later recalled, were 'based on exact research, reports, [and] newspaper reading', although the officers who later used them in Germany found that they were spotty. In addition, Neumann and Marcuse drew up lists of Nazi offices and positions, the holders of which would be automatically arrested or dismissed. Bradley Smith suggests that some of the information necessary to assign these categories was gleaned from a U.S. Army manual on the *Wehrmacht* and its auxiliary forces, which had been published in 1941 and was out of date. Nonetheless, the important thing to note is that many subjects of the prospective purge became accountable because of their membership or appointments in various Nazi organisations, rather than on the basis of individual actions. Conversely, many people guilty of malfeasance, but outside the bounds of the NSDAP, would be relatively safe from punishment, particularly if they were not part of the business elite. Many German Freemasons, for instance, were strident nationalists, but since they had been excluded from the Nazi Party owing to Hitler's anti-Masonic bias, they were now potentially free of the sort of targeting encouraged by a schematic approach. Marcuse later cited his black and grey lists to argue that his studies were more than mere exercises in quantification, but his greatest impact was to suggest dealing with broad categories of officials, specifically some 220,000 to 250,000 placeholders who would be arrested and then interned, appropriately – it was felt – in concentration camps that the Nazis themselves had created.

In addition, other centres of power in the Nazi system would be affected. Neumann and Marcuse named 1,800 business leaders deserving incarceration, and Kirchheimer provided position papers calling for a thorough purging of the bureaucracy and civil institutions. According to Marcuse, the reasoning behind such measures was that 'denazification, in order to be effective, must be more than a purge of personnel and an abolition of Nazi legislation … it must strike at the roots of German fascism by eliminating the economic foundations of the anti-democratic policy of German big industry'. Only in such a fashion – or through such a 'negative moment' – could the instruments of Nazi oppression be wholly removed, thus allowing the re-emergence of the sort of critical thought that drives the Hegelian dialectic and encourages progress to unfold.

Since the R&A plan suggested treating people mainly as categories rather than individuals, ascertaining who belonged to the categories was imperative. Obviously, collecting such intelligence would prove difficult, but the prescription of the Central Europeanists was to ask the Germans themselves, as officers in the GCU were already proposing to do with their *Fragebogen*. Every adult who expected to work or collect a ration card would be expected to fill out a 131-point questionnaire, which would elicit information about party membership, official appointments, military service, writings or speeches after 1923, income, travel and other details of a personal nature. With such data in hand, Allied military governments would supposedly be able to segregate the population into different blocs, each meriting separate standards of treatment. Complaints would be directed toward appellate tribunals staffed by military government officers. Of course, there was the rather glaring possibility that individuals might lie in their responses to the questionnaires, but Neumann and Marcuse argued that after a few hundred initial offenders were punished, the remainder of the population would get the requisite message.

Finally, the neo-Marxists in the Central European Section saw little value in the marketplace of ideas so prized by liberals, and they believed that such a notion had no place in a society emerging from totalitarianism. Rather, the Nazis had so contaminated the German consciousness that there could be no 'level playing field', at least intellectually or politically. Thus, the proper task of Allied military government was not only to eliminate the Nazis as a state party, but to prevent similar groups from re-entering the fray once German political life had been restored. Repressive measures were also appropriate in order to crush the potential threat of a Nazi underground movement.[24]

The problems with this programme were manifest. Constantine FitzGibbon later called it 'a perfectionist's plan', while Tom Bower derided it as 'a bureaucratic solution to a political problem'. Kurt Tauber described it as 'a revolution by administrative ordinances and official forms in triplicate'. Almost all Germans have since concluded that it 'totally overlooked the reality of National Socialism'.[25] Guidance on whether Nazism should have been treated as an idea, a movement or a party could have helped to specify more about the type of people meriting removal from positions of responsibility. In particular, the schematic nature of the Neumann-Marcuse system – despite the obligatory *mea culpas* – implied an Allied focus on party members rather than on individuals who had benefitted from the Hitler regime but were never officially part of the Nazi movement. In addition, the use of questionnaires was likely to fail as a device for identifying Nazis, if only because social chaos and the eventual lack of Allied manpower would probably hinder the accompanying investigatory process. However much the Central Europeanists sneered at technical problems, it is also legitimate to ask how the occupiers were supposed to find the skilled personnel needed to run the government and economy in a situation that was bound to put a premium upon administrative ability? And the numbers would be substantial: the German civil service was larger than that of any other western or central European country and was almost the size of its American counterpart, although the U.S. population was twice the size of Germany's. As early as June 1944, the U.S. Army Medical Corps was already criticising R&A's plans for cleansing the German food distribution system, noting that 'consideration must be given to the number needed, and possible shortage of, adequately trained personnel to replace pre-existing personnel… Such numbers of competent personnel are not easily obtained.' And finally, one must wonder what was to happen to the millions of dismissed, jailed or disenfranchised Nazis? Presumably, they could not be locked up forever, or even indefinitely excluded from public life.[26]

Despite such problems, the Neumann group did offer the first comprehensive approach to denazification. For readers who appreciate irony, there are several rich examples in these developments. First, it was Germans themselves, albeit exiles, who introduced the idea and methods of denazification that would later become so roundly reviled in many quarters of German society.[27] In particular, Marcuse helped develop the all-encompassing form of denazification that would later ensnare his own graduate supervisor and onetime mentor, Martin Heidegger. Second, the government of the world's foremost capitalist nation had empowered

Marxists to develop one of the largest legal programmes and social engineering schemes in American history, although Barry Katz is right in noting that other agencies of the government did not necessarily subscribe to R&A's interpretation of Germany's ills or to its faith in revolutionary socialism as a remedy.[28] In the State Department, showing favouritism toward any particular German faction was regarded as a strategy likely to discredit the party in question, as well as providing possible cause for a falling out among the occupying powers, who might not choose to back the same German elements.[29] Finally, Marcuse eventually turned his line of reasoning upon American society itself. While he believed that there was 'hope in the air' in New Deal America, thirty years later he detected 'a militarism and a repression that calls to mind the terror of Nazi Germany',[30] and he argued that the tolerance of U.S. society had become superficial because it preempted the formation of truly radical views. His response was to re-politicize Critical Theory, encouraging another 'negative moment', this time involving students, minorities and the poor. In the 1960s, he called upon this 'counterculture' to confront the prevailing order.[31]

Members of the Neumann group realised that their version of denazification challenged the 'welfare of the governed' theory, although they disdainfully regarded the latter as privileging mere technical or instrumental considerations. They worried that the military governments of the occupying powers would only strip the bark from the Nazi system, leaving the trunk intact. Kirchheimer warned that in replacing dismissed officials, military government should worry about political reliability more than 'technical qualifications'.[32] Of course, such fears were not far wide of the mark. When a preliminary version of Marcuse's denazification memorandum reached England, GCU officers were aghast at the huge numbers of placeholders that military government was expected to purge. The figures included senior and mid-level leaders in the NSDAP and its closest affiliates, plus blanket detentions of everyone in the Gestapo and the SS Security Service (SD). The Shrivenham planners argued that there would not be enough Allied personnel to carry out such arrests and that there would be insufficient facilities to house large numbers of prisoners. An anxious summons to the local OSS station in Britain resulted in the dispatch of Felix Gilbert, chief of the small R&A Central European Section in London. An expatriate German historian, Gilbert was *not* a member of the Frankfurt School but, interestingly, was a pioneer scholar of the role of idealism in American foreign policy, to which he often applied a critical eye. In August 1944, he met with GCU officers and agreed that the breadth of the purge recommended by Neumann and Marcuse was not feasible. As a result, the list of potential arrest targets was pared down to include only senior officials, rather than all the members of key Nazi organisations.[33] In particular, the potential scale of dismissals in the economy was scaled back, thus depriving the Neumann-Marcuse plan of much of its quasi-revolutionary aspect, and the list of 1,800 recommended removals in business and high finance was later ignored in the preparation of automatic arrest directives, which failed to provide even for the detention of leaders in the Nazi economic chambers or corporate groups. British observers also advised GCU that the projected number of internees was too high. Sir John Troutbeck, the Foreign Office advisor on German affairs, suggested that the Allies would not be able to arrest and hold even 200,000 detainees.[34] SHAEF G-5 was also skeptical about the idea of *Fragebogen*, although as one officer admitted, 'we know of no other way of tackling this almost impossible task of eliminating the Nazi'.[35]

While a fight was brewing between the Frankfurt School and the Shrivenham planners, this conflict was overshadowed, and largely subsumed, by several larger bureaucratic battles that broke out in the late summer of 1944. These debates marked the emergence of the 'collective guilt' school of thought, supporters of which always expected the worst of the Germans. 'Collective guilt' is one of the more difficult ideas that came to inspire public policy during the course of the twentieth century. Taken literally, it is an irrational doctrine – how do groups of people bear responsibility for acts that have been individually executed and of which they might have no knowledge? – but many thinkers have posed legitimate questions about the scope of public responsibility for the actions of political and military authorities. Approaching the question from an existentialist stance, Karl Jaspers posited the existence of 'political guilt', which he saw as the corporate guilt of individuals who had complied with an obvious evil, and his onetime student, Hannah Arendt, contended that if 'human wickedness' won public acceptance, it became 'an inherent psychological quality which man cannot choose or reject but which is imposed on him from without and which rules him compulsively'. Arguing from a psychoanalytical perspective, Carl Jung theorized about a form of collective psyche that could be possessed by 'demonic forces'.[36] If Germans were expected to develop the level of self-analysis to deal with such character faults, however, the psychological eradication of Nazism was unlikely because such feats were simply beyond the capacity of most people.[37] Some writers (Karl Barth, Michael Balfour) put great stock in the difference between 'collective guilt' and 'collective responsibility', but it is hard to see why people should bear 'responsibility' for acts of which they are free of blame.[38]

Whether or not the concept of 'collective guilt' has merit, there is no doubt that it was deeply rooted in the Western consciousness. The Old Testament was rife with instances where families or nations supposedly bore guilt for the sins of individuals, and the ancient Greeks and Romans understood the concept. 'Collective guilt' implied 'collective punishment' and punitive war, such as Athens' obliteration of Melos or Rome's treatment of Carthage, the latter of which so devastated the city that it left posterity with the term 'Carthaginian Peace'. Subsequently, the Catholic Church charged Jews with 'responsibility' for the crucifixion of Jesus Christ, and the same type of collective idea undergirded the feuding common in Germanic tribal and medieval society. In modern times, the idea of 'collective guilt' was often applied to armed forces operating outside the 'bounds of convention' (at least as such limits were defined by the imperial powers). When the British encountered bands along the north-west frontier of the Indian Empire or raiders from Arabia, and such groups were presumed to be supported by their tribes, these unfortunate peoples bore the brunt of collective reprisals. And indeed, the Nazis themselves had used 'collective responsibility' as a principle behind reprisal measures in occupied territory, a fact that European Jews, in particular, had painfully come to realise. On the other hand, advocates of 'collective guilt' believed that Nazi Germany was itself an international outlaw and deserved such treatment.[39] Notions of 'collective guilt' also reflected the collectivist spirit of the 1930s and 40s, and as Reinhold Niebuhr trenchantly observed, they constituted an inversion of the Nazis' own race dogma.[40]

The notion of German 'collective guilt' had been evolving gradually throughout the Second World War.[41] The area bombing undertaken by Allied air forces, particularly the RAF, reflected its impact. The official line was that German civilians were the collateral victims of bombing aimed at industrial or military targets, but Churchill tipped his hand in June 1941, when he spoke of making 'the German people taste and gulp each month a sharper dose of the miseries they have showered upon mankind'. Foreign Secretary Eden and Deputy Prime Minister Attlee made similar comments.[42] Although only a minority of the public in America openly subscribed to the notion of 'collective guilt',[43] such ideas encouraged public discussion about the large-scale shootings of Germans, mass sterilisation, deindustrialisation, and the formation of huge German labour gangs for work in foreign countries,[44] all of which laid the psychological groundwork for the evolution of a 'tough' occupation policy.

In particular, there were several events in the summer of 1944 that made the 'collective guilt' doctrine a decisive factor in planning the occupation. Initially, the Allies had expected that a landing in north-western Europe would be followed by a prolonged bout of attritional fighting, perhaps lasting two years, as the Germans were slowly pushed back toward their frontier.[45] It was considered likely that the events of 1918 would eventually be repeated: Hitler would be overthrown and a post-Nazi regime would capitulate. Allied occupiers would then stream into Germany in what FDR called a 'railway invasion of little or no fighting'.[46] However, events did not follow this course. The expected revolt against Hitler occurred on 20 July 1944, but it failed, and the *Führer* then rallied to destroy domestic centres of opposition, apparently with the continued backing of much of the German populace. In addition, the near obliteration of German armies in the Falaise-Argentan Battle meant that the end of the war seemed more imminent than had been anticipated. By late August and early September 1944, decoded German radio intercepts suggested that Germany's western field armies had lost nearly all their heavy equipment and were retreating as a disorganised mass of gutted units and *Kampfgruppen*. There were only twelve intact divisions with which to man defenses along the western frontier of the Reich. Despite the magnitude of this defeat, SHAEF expected the Nazi regime to keep fighting, if necessary by forming guerrilla bands and waging partisan warfare, perhaps with the active support of a quarter of the population.[47] Even as early as 31 July, the head of SHAEF G-5, General A.E. Grassett, predicted that 'there will be no responsible or competent central control of Germany, combat with guerrillas [will] continue after collapse, and disturbances [will] occur among rival factions'.[48]

Such appreciations encouraged draconian views at the most senior pinnacle of SHAEF. By early August 1944, General Eisenhower was predicting 'long and bitter guerrilla warfare', which only reconfirmed his belief that Germans were by nature a warlike nation and that the burden of responsibility for Nazi crimes lay upon the entire country.[49] 'The German people,' he averred, 'must not be allowed to escape a sense of guilt, of complicity in the tragedy that has engulfed the world.' In a famous meeting during this period, Eisenhower told Treasury Secretary Henry Morgenthau that 'prominent Nazis, along with certain industrialists', should be tried and punished, and that 'membership in the Gestapo and the SS should be taken as *prima facie* evidence of guilt'. Even more importantly, he argued that the country's economy should not be bolstered. He would like, he said, to 'see things made good and hard on them for a while'.[50] Thus, Eisenhower turned against the 'welfare of the governed' theory that had guided efforts at Shrivenham, but which now seemed unwarranted when applied to a country that had pioneered modern techniques of mass mobilisation for violent purposes. The main policy expression of this about-face was a protest against Combined Chiefs of Staff (CCS) directive 551, which the Joint Chiefs of Staff and the British Chiefs had provided to SHAEF in April 1944, and which provided for the maintenance of economic and social life in areas of Germany conquered before a final Nazi surrender. Since this directive had advised working through the German administrative structure 'as a general rule', it had prescribed purging mainly German leaders and 'prominent' Nazis. CCS 551 had been available to GCU planners and had helped shape the *Handbook*, but with Allied armies now speeding toward the German frontier, Eisenhower and his civil affairs deputy, Julius Holmes, suddenly lashed out at these policies, refuting both CCS 551 and their own organisation's *Handbook*. In a cable to the CCS on 23 August, SHAEF complained that 'it may well be that the German Army as a whole will never surrender and that we shall enter the country finding no central German authority in control, with the situation chaotic, probably guerrilla fighting and possibly even civil war in certain districts... If conditions turn out to be as described it will be utterly impossible to control or save the economic structure of the country. The structure will inevitably collapse, and we feel that we should not assume responsibility for its support and control.'[51] Holmes later claimed that the draconian approach to planning for Germany originated in SHAEF: 'we were the first,' he noted, 'to become aware of the fact that it would not only be dangerous but futile for us to prop up the rickety economic and financial structure of Germany.'[52]

Even more important was the unprecedented intervention into occupation planning by the Henry Morgenthau, who suddenly emerged as a modern Cato, crying for the destruction of Carthage. Morgenthau's staff at the U.S. Treasury had already encountered 'objectionable' U.S. Army and State Department policies designed to control inflation during a prospective occupation of Germany,[53] but while touring the Western Front, Morgenthau and his deputy, Harry Dexter White, were surprised – and greatly impressed – by Eisenhower's call for 'letting "Germany stew in its own juice"'.[54] Morgenthau had previously blasted the supreme commander because of his role in arranging the 'Darlan Deal', and presumably did not expect much from this quarter.[55] Subsequently, the Treasury Secretary decided to develop Eisenhower's sentiments into a full-scale policy. During a stopover in London, Morgenthau told his British counterpart, 'I have an idea that is purely my own… I think we could divide Germany into a number of smaller provinces, stop all industrial production and convert them into small agricultural land holders.'[56] Once Morgenthau and White returned to American shores in mid-August 1944, they launched a campaign to discredit the existing policy developed in the GCU and thus open a door to their own initiative, a task that Morgenthau called 'the most important thing that I'll ever handle'.[57] His main piece of ammunition was the military government *Handbook*, which had come into his possession via Bernard Bernstein, an ex-Treasury officer who had been serving with the GCU staff and had rightly thought that its tendencies would be offensive to his old boss. The *Handbook*, Morgenthau admitted, was 'worth its weight in gold'.[58] On 25 August, he presented FDR with carefully culled excerpts, which rekindled the president's instinctive Germanophobia and riled his Old Testament sense of justice. Roosevelt then spoke in cabinet of a Germany 'stripped down' of all but subsistence industries, with Germans congregated in soup lines.[59] He even sent the War Department a scathing memorandum, much of which had been drafted by Harry White, but to which FDR added an introductory paragraph and his own signature: 'This so-called "Handbook" is pretty bad,' he fumed. 'It gives me the impression that Germany is to be restored just as much as The Netherlands or Belgium… It is of the utmost importance that every person in Germany should realise that this time Germany is a defeated nation. I do not want them to starve to death, but, as an example, if they need food to keep body and soul together beyond what they have, they should be fed three times a day with soup from Army soup kitchens.'[60] While possessed by this vitriolic spirit, FDR invited Morgenthau to a key Anglo-American summit meeting in Quebec, where the latter exercised a considerable impact, convincing both Roosevelt and Churchill to sign a directive approving the deindustrialisation of Germany, even though Churchill had been warned by his War Cabinet *not* to approve such a policy.[61] With this accomplishment, Morgenthau appeared to stand at the apex of his power and influence.

The interventions by Morgenthau and Eisenhower put lower echelon policy-makers in a difficult position, particularly in the Pentagon. In particular, Roosevelt's memo left such elements 'quaking in their boots' (according to columnist Drew Pearson).[62] In the War Department, the two key figures of note were General John Hilldring, a former combat officer who was the head of the Civil Affairs Division, and Assistant Secretary John McCloy, a Wall Street lawyer and one of the influential 'wise men' who shaped the internationalist foreign policy of the post-war era. Hilldring and McCloy were both acquiescent to the needs of field commanders, who now appeared to have turned against the 'welfare of the governed' idea, and Hilldring, at least, had also been charged by Army Chief of Staff George Marshall with mollifying liberal cabinet officers and members of Congress, thus preserving the army's freedom of action in prosecuting the war. Hilldring was also highly sensitive to press commentary about the forthcoming occupation of Germany.[63] The problem was how to balance these priorities, while at the same time preserving a shred of the 'welfare of the governed' notion and preventing a potentially draconian policy from dragging down the economies of the European countries around Germany. The reaction of Hilldring and McCloy was to find a middle course. They initially showed sympathy for the 'tough' line suggested by Eisenhower and Morgenthau, with Hilldring proclaiming 'war guilt' as one of the 'fundamental principles underlying the War Department's policy'.[64] On the other hand, they could not give up entirely on the 'welfare of the governed' theme, particularly since their boss, Secretary of War Henry Stimson, favoured the recovery of German industry and the reintegration of Germany into the wider European economy.[65] Stimson's idea of Nazism – that it was the product of a criminal leadership conspiracy rather than a consequence of capitalism – suggested the forms of organisational and individual prosecution that would later be used at the Nuremberg Trials. Such a process, he believed, was the most appropriate way to wake-up Germans and address 'the German problem'.[66]

Officials in the War Department had also tried to keep State Department rivals from influencing policy formation, which was done with a great success, although they could not afford to totally ignore the diplomats. Like Stimson, State Department planners worried about Germany's role in fostering a Europe-wide recovery, supposedly a hedge against a post-war recession that could impair the American economy, and a few arch anti-communists were already looking at Germany as a possible bulwark against the Soviet Union. A briefing paper by State's Committee on Post-war Programs rejected saddling Germany with 'war guilt' and recommended the country's 'assimilation into [the] world economy without discrimination other than that necessary for security controls'.[67]

The response to such conflicting currents was a synthesis that became the essence of American occupation policy. The details of this compromise were forged by Hilldring, McCloy and several mid-echelon Pentagon officials, particularly David Marcus and John Boettiger. First, they parried the deindustrialisation proposal, a policy outlier that was too harsh for almost everyone outside the Treasury. Luckily, Morgenthau was vulnerable because of his desire for *rapid* deindustrialisation. Influenced by John Pehle, the Assistant Secretary of Treasury, Morgenthau had assumed that a measure as radical as deindustrialisation would have to occur while the invaders were sweeping through Germany and their blood was at a boil. He felt that after the end of the fighting, demands would be lodged against Germany for restitution and even for current reparations, which would mean treating German industry as a milch cow. In the Morgenthau–Pehle view, complacency would eventually set in and the opportunities of the moment would be lost.[68] In this conception, ensuring deindustrialisation meant altering CCS 551 and the *Handbook*, which were the chief existing policies for the pre-surrender period, but Morgenthau could not accomplish this task. Formally, both CCS 551 and the *Handbook* were collaborations with the British, and the latter vetoed proposals – both by the Treasury Department and by SHAEF – to revise substantially these sets of orders.[69] The failure to amend CCS 551 and the *Handbook* also owed to the fact that one of the chief architects of Treasury policy, Harry White, was skeptical about immediate deindustrialisation – he was convinced that a future Germany should make restitutions of heavy equipment and pay reparations – and he was thus quick to accept War Department pleas about British intransigence in such matters. Yes, he agreed, 'what they do in the actual fighting isn't very important, it is what happens when the fighting stops.'[70] Pehle and Morgenthau thought differently. On 6 September, Morgenthau attempted to get FDR's backing for immediate deindustrialisation and he encouraged Roosevelt to denounce CCS 551, although the president had already reverted to dithering on the 'details' of occupation policy, telling Morgenthau that 'we have got to do this thing gradually'.[71] Thus, the practical implementation of deindustrialisation was largely blocked even before the policy was endorsed at the Quebec Conference, and later SHAEF discussions regarding the immediate treatment of captured German industries made mention only of closing down certain facilities, not priming them for destruction.[72]

Having deprived Morgenthau of the major element in his programme, Pentagon planners were willing to stiffen occupation policy in almost every other respect. Concession, after all, is the cornerstone of compromise. Denazification was one of the most important of these realms. A total rewrite of the *Handbook* was impossible, at least within the few days until the existing edition would be issued to troops approaching the German frontier.[73] However, British representatives in Washington were willing to entertain a few revisions that could be attached as a flyleaf and then included in the text of subsequent drafts. The Americans wanted severe language regarding denazification, which Boettiger admitted was adopted directly from Treasury Department briefs, but the British War Office balked at a phrase prohibiting Allied use of any 'Nazi organisations', insisting that the word 'Party' be inserted in order to further specify the character of such structures. In truth, the British preferred merely a provision preventing 'active Nazis' from holding office, but they were under pressure to accede to American amendments.

The eventual *Handbook* flyleaf provided that 'under *no* circumstances shall active Nazis or ardent sympathizers be retained in office for purposes of administrative convenience... The Nazi Party and all subsidiary organisations shall be dissolved. The administrative machinery of certain dissolved Nazi organisations may be used when necessary to provide certain essential functions, such as relief, health and sanitation, with denazified personnel and facilities.' With their unparalleled mastery of supple formulations, Hilldring and McCloy told the British that all SHAEF was committed to doing was 'to dissolve formally the [Nazi] organisation by its original name, purge it as necessary, and rechristen it'.[74]

Eisenhower was also supposed to adjust public announcements and declarations that had been based on *Handbook* themes. One of the first acts of military government teams was to post Allied proclamations, and an allegedly 'objectionable' SHAEF proclamation had already been placarded in the small sliver of German territory overrun in early September 1944, creating a fear that '[the] press may display an awkward notice'. SHAEF was told to alter the proclamation in order 'to avoid the implication ... that Germany is to be treated substantially like a liberated country. It should stress that both Nazism and German Militarism are to be obliterated'.[75] In addition, Eisenhower made a radio broadcast address on 18 September, in which he told Germans that military government would 'begin the task of destroying National Socialism. It will remove from responsible posts all members of the Nazi Party and of the SS Elite Guard... This process begins immediately on the arrival of Allied armies in each area.'[76]

Such policy statements provided the framework for SHAEF's first detailed instructions on denazification, which were issued on 9 November 1944 as part of the 'Directive for Military Government of Germany'. This document had been prepared in September and was revised in order to cohere with the specifications outlined in the *Handbook* flyleaf, the last official instruction to SHAEF about denazification. The directive decreed the liquidation of the Nazi Party, as well as identifying large categories of people who were subject to mandatory removal, and some to mandatory arrest. In particular, it ordered the removal from public office of all persons who had joined the Nazi Party before January 1933, the date when the Hitler movement had come to power.[77] The use of such a chronological limitation was based on the assumption that Nazi true believers were already in the party by 1933, whereas many later entrants were merely conformists or placeholders who needed NSDAP membership in order to keep their jobs. Of course, it could be argued – and was – that some of the pre-1933 contingent were idealists who were unaware of the measures that a Nazi Government would undertake, while the post-1933 entrants suffered under no such illusions. As a result, the opportunism of the latter could be interpreted as worse than the naive enthusiasm of early supporters, and thus even more deserving of punishment. Whatever the merits of such specifications, there is no doubt that SHAEF's general policy reflected the OSS intention to blanket large categories of Nazis with sanctions, although – notably – the spirit of OSS planning was largely absent. In particular, the 9 November directive prohibited any political activity in newly-occupied parts of Germany, presumably even that of the Left, and SHAEF had given up entirely upon encouraging Germans to revolt.[78] Except for the fact that SHAEF approved limited trade union activity, its version of denazification retained the OSS formula but abandoned the leftist assumptions that provided its original rationale.

This approach eventually provided great offense to the German Social Democratic Party (SPD), not only because it prevented that party's early partici-pation in a distinctively German reckoning with National Socialism, but because it cast it in the same light as middle class parties that had borne a more ambiva-lent attitude toward National Socialism. By denying the SPD any measure of special credit, the occupying powers demoralised re-emerging elements of the party. Opinions about the practical effect of this policy vary: Barbara Marshall argues that it caused the SPD incalculable political damage, but Michael Balfour contends that it unintentionally saved the socialists from the taint of collaboration with the occupying powers.[79]

While the impact of the 'collective guilt' approach was partially contained by British influence in the CCS and in SHAEF, a new battle broke out in Washington over the so-called 'interim directive', the policy statement that would guide U.S. military government *after* the end of conventional fighting but before implemen-tation of the tripartite control machinery that the occupying powers intended to operate. On 1 September 1944, FDR formed a Cabinet Committee on Germany, which consisted of Morgenthau, Stimson, Secretary of State Cordell Hull and presidential advisor Harry Hopkins.[80] This body's mandate was to oversee the development of the 'interim directive', which would eventually be approved by the Joint Chiefs of Staff as JCS paper 1067. It was originally hoped that the 'interim' document could be coordinated with the British and established as a joint Anglo-American policy, but after it became apparent that this was impossible, it was issued solely as the policy guide for U.S. military government.

The initial meetings of the Cabinet Committee revealed a wide breach of opinion over dismemberment and deindustrialisation, which left the cabinet secretaries – and more particularly, their deputies – scrambling to find a few elements of common ground. McCloy, especially, identified denazification as one of these points of conjunction,[81] although even here there were divergences between different schools of thought. Everyone was in accord with the prohibition of the Nazi Party and its affiliates, as well as agreeing with the arrest of Nazi and SS leaders and the apprehension of all members of the Gestapo. However, the War and State Departments wanted only Nazi Party leaders, or 'active Nazis', removed from government service and managerial positions in business.

As for Morgenthau's cohort, they naturally assigned secondary importance to denazification – why deprive the enemy of Nazi bureaucrats when it was more effective to dismember and pauperise him – but to the extent that they did focus on purge measures, their policy was naturally tough. Treasury officials had already reviewed some of the civil affairs guides and policy papers produced at R&A, and they were fully in accord with the schematic method advanced by members of the 'Frankfurt School'. In a letter to Hilldring, White provided a superficially persuasive rationale for this approach:

> It is the view of the Treasury Department that during the initial stages of the occupation, there should be a simple and practicable test for eliminating undesirable persons. Since the nature of the position occupied by a person in any important German organisation or institution constitutes a most reliable clue as to his belief in and support of the Nazi system, the automatic removal of persons who hold certain key or policy-making positions becomes a most practicable technique for eliminating Nazis. Our experience with this problem in other liberated areas has convinced us that the examination of each person's character or reputation during the initial period of occupation not only places an undesirable burden on the Allied Authorities, but is not administratively feasible.

Not only did Treasury officials agree with a blanket proscription of Nazi place-holders, but they wanted such sanctions applied widely, covering not only *all* NSDAP members, but also 'Nazi sympathizers', 'Junkers' and military officers. In addition, they suggested that all such elements be disenfranchised.[82]

Naturally, it was not long before the Treasury complained about the supposedly inadequate denazification requirements put forward by its sister departments, particularly the Pentagon.[83] During this period, Stimson and McCloy were also being 'bombarded' with memoranda from the Neumann group, whose recommendations were – as noted – similar to the Treasury's programme, although they had an entirely different rationale.[84] In response to such calls, the War and State Departments were reluctant to admit the necessity for a purge of *all* Nazi Party members. State's Committee on Post-war Programs argued that even firing members in leadership positions would mean the release of two million people, and that the dismissal of all Nazis would nearly triple that number. Imposing such 'comprehensive disabilities' upon all party members would, State claimed, 'involve undertaking an enormous administrative task and giving the same treatment to the active and incorrigible nucleus of leadership as to a great mass of passive, and by then presumably disillusioned, followers'. McCloy agreed and even thought that the State Department failed to go far enough, arguing that preventing any party member from voting, practicing law or playing a role in government, as suggested by the Treasury, would be impractical and would paralyse the functioning of military government.[85]

Meanwhile, the ground under the feet of policy-makers was shifting. During inter-departmental discussions in September 1944, the War and State Departments were able to turn back Treasury efforts to insert dismemberment or deindustrialisation strictures into JCS 1067. 'The interim directive,' argued McCloy, 'has to be something to keep the situation pretty much in status quo … you can't take a definite attitude, for example, on partition, because you can't take partition until you have worked it out with the Russians and British. There are a lot of things like that…'[86] Stimson and McCloy had to accede to Eisenhower's formula for letting Germans 'stew in their own juices', although even in this regard they inserted a clever 'escape clause' that allowed military government to aid German recovery if such actions were supposedly necessary to prevent unrest or the spread of contagious disease. This formula had already been included in CCS 551. In addition, Roosevelt – in pre-election mode – grew gun-shy after news of the 'Morgenthau Plan' leaked to the press, which elicited a flood of negative commentary and left the president squinting in the unwanted glare of media attention. By late September, he had retreated to his familiar habit of prevarication, and Morgenthau and his associates were increasingly forced to set their sights on long-term policy preparation, which was hardly yet underway and set an unlikely schedule for implementing a policy as radical as deindustrialisation.[87]

However, while War and State Department planners prevented the Treasury from landing its major catch, they had to concede many of Morgenthau's views on denazification, particularly since Morgenthau kept claiming that any attempt to save the German economy would lead to compromises on measures to eliminate Nazi influence. There was also a general recognition that 'defascistisation' policy in Italy had been far too mild, and that its German equivalent would have to be more rigorous. Thus, the political directive in the initial version of JCS 1067 was largely of Treasury Department inspiration. 'It was not the Morgenthau Plan,' as McCloy later recalled, 'but it was still negative.' Essentially, it reasserted the 'collective guilt' of the German nation, which was supposed to suggest appropriate consequences, and it included fourteen expansive categories of German personnel subject to automatic arrest. By one estimate, these instructions meant that the occupiers would likely have to incarcerate 'several million persons'. This original version of 1067 also called for 'all members of the Nazi Party and ardent supporters of Nazism' to be removed from civil service and business management positions. In case supporters of the 'welfare of the governed' theory should prowl the future corridors of military government, the document asserted that 'under no circumstances shall persons be retained in … offices for the purpose of administrative convenience or expediency'. All the War and State Departments could secure was a caveat that Nazi Party members could be retained as clerks or 'non-policy making functionaries'. Even though the State Department gave this draft a reluctant nod of approval, Hull advised the president on 29 September that the Cabinet Committee had failed in its work.[88]

Much of the spirit of the September draft was retained when JCS 1067 was officially issued to Eisenhower's military government specialists in April 1945, but interdepartmental negotiations had dragged on, particularly since policy-makers were endeavouring – without success – to earn British approval for the document. During this continuing tug of war, anti-Morgenthau forces remained active, with

State Department representatives James Riddelberger and Emile Despres arguing that the political directive within JCS 1067 ought to be the special preserve of their own department. In particular, they wanted to water down denazification strictures, trying to introduce 'carefully worked out categories of Nazis for dismissal', although the War Department rejected such arguments, 'for the stated reason that they would not be pleasing to the Treasury Department'. Officials of the Foreign Economic Administration (FEA) also blocked attempts to get more lenient dismissal categories.

State Department bureaucrats finally made progress when they received Roosevelt's authorisation to encapsulate the decisions taken at the Yalta Conference as policy directives. In a memorandum approved by FDR in early March 1945, State Department planners announced that only 'active Nazis and supporters of Nazism' – some two million people – should be removed from public office and managerial positions in the economy. In view of Roosevelt's policy shift, McCloy suggested that JCS 1067 would have to be revised and resubmitted to the JCS, and that such a process would mean reconvening the interdepartmental committee for policy on Germany. Naturally, Morgenthau was outraged, although the State Department's moderation of economic policy and its tendency to treat Germany as a single country provided him with even broader targets than revisions of denazification policy. When Morgenthau complained to the president, FDR, now ill and failing, admitted that he did not even recall approving the State Department's memorandum. Although Morgenthau opposed revisiting 1067, which he claimed Yalta had reinforced, the State Department had wrangled enough of a concession that they were able to force a limited recasting of the document.

The final version of JCS 1067 was a State Department draft approved on 25 March 1945 and signed by Truman on 10 May. It defined the criteria for denazification dismissal as follows:

All members of the Nazi Party who have been more than nominal participants in its activities, all active supporters of Nazism or militarism and all other persons hostile to Allied purposes will be removed and excluded from public office and from positions of importance in quasi-public and private enterprises… Persons are to be treated as more than nominal participants in Party activities and as active supporters of Nazism or militarism when they have (1) held office or otherwise been active at any level from local to national in the party and its subordinate organisations or in organisations which further militaristic doctrines, (2) authorised or participated affirmatively in any Nazi crimes, racial persecutions or discriminations, (3) been avowed believers in Nazism or racial or militaristic creeds, or (4) voluntarily given substantial moral or material support or political assistance of any kind to the Nazi Party or Nazi officials and leaders.

The document then reasserted a need for the release of such persons despite 'administrative necessity, convenience or expediency'.[89] Nonetheless, the final version of JCS 1067 was not as sweeping as earlier formulations nor as comprehensive as the 9 November directive adopted at SHAEF. Specific dismissal categories had been drawn up by Neumann and Holborn of R&A, who had tried to find a middle course between the tough demands of the Treasury, the FEA and the War Department, and the more lenient standards of the State Department.

Potentially, the evolution of American occupation policy would have had importance only for the U.S. zone of occupation, except for the fact that the Americans treated their agenda as a model for denazification throughout the entirety of defeated Germany. Since 1943 there had been agreement amongst the 'Big Three' about the need for coordination of policy in a future occupation regime, mainly through the agency of a committee of the military governors, which was eventually dubbed the Control Council (CC). Despite the fact that American policy-makers were divided amongst themselves, their occupation planning was more advanced than that of their partners, Britain excepted, and they intended to provide form and inspiration to the policies of the other powers. The 'Big Three' conference in Yalta (February 1945) provided an obvious site for policy coordination, but denazification was not officially discussed at the meeting, and the final conference communiqué provided precious little – only a vague commitment to 'wip[ing] out the Nazi Party' and 'remov[ing] all Nazi and militarist influences from public office and from the cultural and economic life of the German people'.[90] However, at the 'Big Three' meeting in Potsdam (July–August 1945), American negotiators introduced the JCS 1067 formula on denazification as a general model for all the occupiers, and this suggestion was entertained by the three foreign ministers (Jimmy Byrnes, Anthony Eden and Vyachaslav Molotov) on 18 July. There was little debate, although Molotov took offense at language specifying that any Germans retained or appointed by the occupiers held office by merit of continuing 'good behavior'. He argued that this wording could serve as a possible loophole for the retention of Nazis in positions of power. Byrnes agreed to drop the sentence, and by the following day it had been replaced by text indicating that persons replacing dismissed Nazis should be politically and morally capable of 'developing genuine democratic institutions in Germany'. This version appeared in the final conference protocols.[91]

As officials in the U.S. occupation zone intensified their own denazification efforts in the summer and fall of 1945, they also pushed for the implementation of a quadripartite policy, arguing that the lack of a denazification procedure transcending zonal borders would cause Nazis in the U.S. zone to flee into neighbouring zones governed by less stringent regimes. American policy, they contended, would thus ultimately fail.[92] After the Control Council began meeting in August 1945, its 'Nazi Arrest and Denazification Sub-Committee' drafted two instructions, CC Directive 24 (12 January 1946), which pertained to job dismissals, and CC Directive 38 (12 October 1946), which outlined appropriate treatment for people falling into the automatic arrest and dismissal categories. Directive 24 was based directly on JCS 1067 and both directives reflected American ideas that had been approved at Potsdam. These two orders comprised the ultimate transition of political principal into policy, although as we shall see, this policy was not always uniformly implemented by the four occupying powers.

CC Directive 24 cited the JCS 1067 criteria for determining 'active Nazis', as well as replicating much of the content of an American military government denazification directive issued on 7 July 1945. In essence, it outlined ninety-nine compulsory removal categories, including war criminals, recipients of Nazi honours, various categories of civil servants and business officials, military officers belonging to the General Staff and the National Socialist Leadership Corps, supervisors and teachers in elite Nazi schools, and NSDAP officials and senior classes of Nazi Party members, as well as people in equivalent categories in Nazi Party affiliates. There was also wide latitude for discretionary removals of career military officers and 'Prussian Junkers', particularly nobles, large landowners and former members of elite university student corps, who were to be retained in management or supervisory capacities only if there was a lack of replacement personnel, and even then were to be kept under scrutiny. Nazis who had joined the party after 1937 also fit into the same discretionary removal category, which meant a shift of four years from the SHAEF cut-off date, perhaps because it was realised that a civil service law in 1937 had made Nazi Party membership nearly compulsory for state bureaucrats. During the deliberations of the 'Nazi Arrest and Denazification Sub-Committee', the British and French had fought hard for concessions to reality, in the process facing a joint American-Soviet front. The British failed to keep mayors and police chiefs out of automatic dismissal categories, but they did insist on inclusion of a clause that permitted zone commanders to postpone dismissals in extraordinary circumstances. Nazis affected by the process were also allowed to plead their cases to the military governments, which were committed to a review process. When evidence suggested that an individual was not a militarist or a 'Werewolf', or was nothing more than a 'nominal' Nazi, he could be 'retained in office in spite of the mandatory clauses contained in this directive', although it is interesting to note that the system worked on a presumption of guilt. Despite such concessions, the Foreign Office was disappointed with Directive 24, arguing that its rigidity would force British forces in Germany 'to ignore the letter of the law and act in the spirit of common sense'. As for the French, they failed to secure formal recognition of the role of German-manned tribunals in denazification, a practice thats was already in use in the French zone of occupation.

CC Directive 38 was meant to resolve the fate of people within the arrest and dismissal categories outlined in Directive 24, and was a crucial document in the history of denazification because it marked the evolution of the programme from a 'cleaning the decks' operation, meant to remove Nazis from office, into quasi-judicial procedure designed to punish – and possibly to rehabilitate – various categories of Nazis. The directive also based on the Nuremberg Trial verdicts, the latter of which were delivered in early October 1946 and provided the legal basis for the treatment of dangerous Nazis and persons hostile to Allied purposes. It provided for the exoneration of relative innocents and established four categories of guilt, which had already been used as criteria for prosecution in the U.S. zone. Both exoneration and membership in the guilt categories could be determined by military governments or by German tribunals, and either of these institutions could also handle trial and review processes. Category one ('Major Offenders') consisted of war criminals, Nazi leaders, officers of the German High Command and members of the SS, Gestapo and SS Security Service; category two ('Offenders') was made up of 'activists', militarists and war profiteers; category three ('Lesser Offenders') was comprised of offenders who could claim mitigating circumstances (folly of youth, evidence of rejection of National Socialism at an early date); and category four ('Followers') consisted of nominal or candidate members of the NSDAP. Different ranges of penalties were specified for each of the four categories. Members of the two lower categories were subject to probation, job demotion, reduction of pension benefits, temporary loss of income from investments or holdings, prohibition of the right to stand for public office and disenfranchisement. 'Offenders' and 'Major Offenders' faced the same restrictions, but could also be interned or jailed for various terms, barred from practicing a profession or from holding a management position, subjected to loss of property or pension benefits, prohibited from joining a business association or trade union, and prevented from holding a driver's license. If a case merited especially severe punishment, 'Major Offenders' could be executed. However, zone commanders enjoyed a considerable range of sanctions that could be applied to members of each category, a necessity because Directive 38 was issued so late that various routines had already been established in the occupation zones. An important loophole was also suggested by the fact that zone commanders, or in some cases German tribunals, could shift individuals from higher to lower categories of guilt.[93]

CC Directive 38 was the last significant brick in the denazification edifice. In subsequent chapters, we will explore how denazification was implemented, but it might be worthwhile expanding on a few points before we move on. In fact, two questions beg asking. First, were the goals of denazification policy worthwhile and were they practical? And second, was denazification policy developed in a responsible and balanced fashion?

With regard to the ethical value of denazification, there is no doubt that in the best of all worlds, firing every party member – or nearly every member – would have been the most just resolution of the Nazi Party's affairs. Most party members, whether they joined the movement before 1933/37, or whether they had signed up after those arbitrary dates, knew what they were supporting. They might not have reckoned upon the Final Solution or upon starting a world war, but they supported a party whose naked worship of power and violence led directly to such results. In this world, however, the perfect is the enemy of the good. Politics and law comprise the practical means for exercising power and maintaining order, and even if they are informed by moral considerations, they cannot be determined solely by such criteria. Moreover, as Jill Jones notes, Allied policymakers never developed planning to the point where they were able to draw distinctions between moral and political criteria, much less defining specific aims in either sense.[94]

In addition, it is clear that risking the total collapse of society in an already bomb-battered country was a chance that most military government officers were unlikely to take, especially given the ingrained nature of the 'welfare of the governed' theory, so any policy that pushed toward such a risk was likely to be implemented in lukewarm fashion. It would have been more realistic to have developed a limited but workable policy, and there is no doubt that eventual problems were foreseeable because War and State Department planners were pointing out various pitfalls as early as the spring of 1944. British planners, as we shall see, were similarly prescient. Marcuse, the chief advocate of a broad and schematic system of denazification, has often been branded as a romantic, a utopian and a philosophical abstractionist,[95] and it is perhaps unfortunate that he and his cohorts were able to exercise such a decisive influence on the formation of policy.

This observation leads directly to a consideration of our second query, which involves the nature of policy development. Although the Neumann group was comprised of undoubted experts on German social and political structure, it was likely that their sweeping proposals would have been watered down, but for the actions of Morgenthau and Eisenhower. In particular, the Treasury Department's intervention into occupation planning set a new threshold for the 'hard' approach toward Germany. It is true that the Treasury's main proposals were defeated, but the extreme nature of Morgenthau's ideas forced competing bureaucracies to 'up the ante'. Accordingly, it was in this atmosphere, amidst one of the most bruising interdepartmental battles in American history, that the Neumann-Marcuse system was sanctioned.

Alarmingly, one of the analytical models that best describes this scenario is the 'functionalist interpretation', which historians have often used to discuss the inner workings of the Nazi state. Scholars studying the political and bureaucratic history of the Third Reich have described how a remote and charismatic leader provided rough policy guidelines and then allowed subsidiary centres of power to squabble over implementation. Radicalisation was one of the principal results of this fractured style of policy-making, as competing individuals and organisations tried to outdo each other in implementing the will of the *Führer*. Although this was not the usual pattern of policy formation in the Western democracies, Roosevelt's peculiar habits, especially his personalisation of executive power and distrust of the State Department, produced unfortunate similarities. It is striking that, as Michael Balfour notes, 'the nation which has shown most enthusiasm for applying scientific methods to the study of human relations should have made so little use of them in this outstanding case history'.[96] In particular, the irritable and increasingly ailing president let the bureaucracies float rudderless until the most radical policy proposal had also become the most compelling. The American brand of denazification was the wild and overindulged child of this process.

2

FROM IDEA TO REALITY

Although the denazification project was largely an American creation, U.S. troops struggled with actually implementing the programme. One initial difficulty was that throughout the fall, winter and spring of 1944/45, there were actually four denazification policies that had some measure of approval: the *Handbook* flyleaf, the 9 November SHAEF directive, an early draft of JCS 1067 (which had been informally provided to SHAEF), and the final version of 1067 issued in April 1945. While these were all variations on a theme, and they all agreed about the need to abolish the Nazi Party and detain large numbers of senior Nazis and SS men, they differed with regard to the key question of dismissing Nazi placeholders from the civil service and business management positions. The flyleaf ordered the termination of all 'active Nazis' and 'ardent sympathizers'; the 9 November directive targeted all members of the party who had joined before 1933; the first version of the 'interim directive' specified dropping all Nazi Party members; and JCS 1067, in its final form, ordered the firing of NSDAP members who were more than nominal participants in party affairs. To further complicate matters, the army groups and armies of the Allied coalition rarely provided their constituent corps and divisions with the original versions of instructions that they had received from above. Rather, they redrafted orders, which in the case of denazification allowed room for even more variation to creep into the process. Military government officers eager to consult the fount of Allied policy discovered that actual copies of the *Handbook*, and of the OSS black, grey and white lists, were scarce. By the spring of 1945, one Allied army group was ordering the arrest of all Nazis, while another had largely suspended the programme so that the stability of German civil society could be maintained.[1]

This lack of consistency was a recipe for disaster, and the potential for scandal loomed in areas where American forces gave the denazification policy a liberal interpretation. As early as October 1944, Secretary Morgenthau was already citing a *New York Times* report on the retention of pro-Nazi elements as mediators between military government and the 14,000 German civilians who had recently come under Allied control. Such situations, he warned Stimson, were bound to raise questions 'in the public mind', and they directly contravened the denazification stipulations of JCS 1067.[2] By November/December 1944, contingents of the OSS, the Counter Intelligence Corps (CIC) and American military government (AMG) were involved in an ugly bureaucratic battle over the nature of German civic governments in several small towns along the American-occupied fringe of the Rhineland. In Würselen, a Nazi Party member appointed as *Bürgermeister* by one AMG detachment was dismissed by a succeeding unit that ran the town; the same sequence occurred in Roetgen, where the Assistant *Bürgermeister* was appointed by one American officer and then dismissed by another. In Alsdorf, accomodationist elements of AMG were more determined. The OSS and CIC charged that the local AMG detachment had retained a *Bürgermeister* who had been in the post since 1934 and had been a member of the NSDAP since 1933. This case was so contentious that it reached the desk of General William Simpson, commander of the U.S. Ninth Army. Lieutenant Colonel Clarence Richmond, chief of the AMG unit in Alsdorf, told Simpson that 'his' *Bürgermeister* had been only a nominal member of the party and that he had been vetted by a CIC unit during the fall of 1944. He refused to revoke the appointment, and so there the matter stood.

Aachen, the first major German city to fall into American hands, provided an even larger headache, particularly because it involved not only the principle of denazification, but the difficult matter of how the occupier should treat replacement personnel who were not Nazis, but traditional authoritarians. Aachen was of tremendous symbolic importance because of its historic connection with Charlemagne and the German crown, which gave the town a cultural resonance that outweighed its limited size and population. Its early occupation by the Americans also provided a crucial test case for AMG. Because of Nazi evacuation measures, less than a tenth of the city's population of 260,000 people was still in the town when it fell to American forces in late October 1944, and since this small cohort had defied Nazi orders to flee eastwards, it was logical to surmise that they had never been keen supporters of Nazism, or at least that they were no longer enthusiastic about Hitler. Nonetheless, CIC and AMG teams were bursting with an initial enthusiasm for radical measures. Nearly all the remaining inhabitants of the city – some 10,000 people – were rounded up and relocated in the Homburg Barracks, a former Belgian Army facility near the border between Germany and Belgium. The purpose was to individually interview and vet all the remaining inhabitants of the city. It was at Homburg, for instance, that American interrogators first developed a technique later regarded as invaluable for interviewing the Catholic inhabitants of western and southern Germany: they gave up asking *if* a subject was a member of the NSDAP and began asking *when* he/she had felt 'compelled' to join the party. This approach created a less confrontational atmosphere and typically elicited a flood of admissions. Even before the Homburg project was completed, however, CIC and AMG were already beginning to realise their limitations. Although the interviews were a goldmine for the CIC and for Allied psychological warfare (PW) specialists, the evacuations strained military transport and provided a windfall for Nazi 'whisper propaganda', which described the evacuation centres as 'concentration camps'.

As the population gradually returned to Aachen, supplemented by returnees who had fled to the local countryside, the town's population began to rebound and there was an obvious need for the establishment of a civic administration. It was the character of this government that first brought the question of denazi-fication to a head. After a brief search for a suitable mayor, AMG officer Leo Svoboda accepted a recommendation from the Bishop of Aachen and submitted the name of Franz Oppenhoff, a local lawyer and businessman. Seeking counsel from the bishop was a natural course for AMG officers because their training had encouraged them to cultivate contacts with the German clergy, thus revers-ing an embarrassingly ineffective policy that had characterised the post-First World War occupation of the Rhineland. Moreover, Catholic clerics were often able to respond to such entreaties because – unlike their Protestant counterparts – they had continuing contact with a large pool of non-Nazi personalities previ-ously in the Catholic-dominated Centre Party, which had played a major role in German politics from the 1870s until the Nazi era. In the case, of Aachen, however, Oppenhoff proved to be problem. He was not a Nazi – indeed, the Nazis accused him of treason and deployed 'Werewolf' assassins who eventually killed him – but neither was he a model Democrat. The new *Oberbürgermeister* was a conservative Catholic who displayed a cold attitude to his contacts in military government and had authoritarian inclinations. He regarded critics as 'dangerous Reds' and threat-ened to send his police chief to the offices of the *Aachener Nachrichten*, the town newspaper, in order to censor stories that were unflattering. His political models were not Hitler and Goebbels, but such authoritarian traditionalists as Pétain and Franco. He hated the Weimar Republic and told the Americans that he would never work to restore the pre-1933 status quo. Instead, his idea of 'true democ-racy' was a Christian '*Ständestaat*', which would lack political parties but represent people's interests through the corporatist organisation of society into functional economic categories. Oppenhoff gathered around himself a clique of like-minded spirits, who served as the section chiefs in his municipal government. Only one of these men was a member of the NSDAP, but they were all from the business or professional class that had profited during the Third Reich and they demonstrated a tolerance of Nazis at lower levels of the administration. Of the seventy-two 'key positions' in civic government, twenty-two were held by Nazis.

Within several months of Oppenhoff's appointment, the same type of dis-pute as in Alsdorf had broken out amongst various factions in the U.S. forces. A large group in the local AMG detachment, led by Svoboda, was comfortable with Oppenhoff. In civilian life, most of these men had been civil servants and businessmen whose opinions, while not as extreme as those of Oppenhoff, were on the same side of the political spectrum. When a local trade unionist circulated a leaflet critical of Oppenhoff in January 1945, Svoboda called for the agitator's arrest on the charge that he was a dangerous incendiary. Cooler heads prevailed. A much more critical group in the local AMG detachment included troops of the 'Special Branch', which had a mandate to organise denazification, plus the Press Control Teams that had authorised the establishment of the *Aachener Nachrichten*. This faction was led by Major John Bradford, an outspoken New Dealer and the deputy chief of the Aachen AMG detachment. Bradford opposed interning Oppenhoff's critics and on 5 January 1945 he submitted a memorandum contending that the detachment had 'a chance to make … history', but that it had to be motivated by long-term considerations as well as the needs of the hour. No one was indispensable, he argued, and requisite course corrections would disturb neither the military effort at the front nor the provision of life's necessities for German civilians. Bradford also wanted a wider spectrum of Aachener society represented in the municipal government, particularly elements from the working class. Outside the offices of the Aachen detachment of AMG, Bradford had allies in the CIC and in SHAEF's PW Teams, led by Major Saul Padover. An Austrian-American historian, Padover had been an aide to Harold Ickes, FDR's pugnacious interior secretary, and had then served in the OSS. The CIC and PW Teams were outside the regular chain of command – formally, they could only observe, advise and warn – but Padover was a master of political gamesmanship and knew the power of publicity. He had a close relationship with Max Lerner, a correspondent for the liberal New York daily *PM*, and he used the threat of press scrutiny as his ultimate weapon. Like Bradford, he prepared a critical report on Aachen, which he submitted to the headquarters of the U.S. Ninth Army in early February 1945. He charged that 'we are setting the example for an "eternally authoritarian" German regime – where no balance of democratic forces will be tolerated'.

The commander of the Aachen detachment was Major Hugh Jones, a former car salesman from Wisconsin. Jones tried to position himself between the two contending factions, although in practice he leaned more to the Right than the Left. Until his transfer in April 1945, he never understood the vehemence of the critique against Oppenhoff. Jones believed that only 'ardent and active Nazis' should be the targets of American repression, and he subscribed to the notion that technical ability merited concessions. 'Where,' he asked Padover, 'would you find competent people who are not Nazis.' Jones also remained acutely aware than Oppenhoff and his associates had stepped forward despite Nazi threats upon their lives, and that they had remained loyal even during the Ardennes Offensive of December 1944, when it had appeared that the Americans might be forced to withdraw from Aachen and its surrounding area. On the other hand, he knew by early 1945 that he was sitting atop a ticking time bomb, particularly with regard to potential criticism from the American press. He launched a modest purge aimed at removing forty-five leading Nazis in the Aachen administration, although Oppenhoff already had proven a master at shuffling such people, rehiring them as contractors or consultants even once they had been formally dismissed.[3]

Leaks to the press in late January and early February 1945 publically exposed Padover's criticism, which in turn prompted negative articles in *PM* and *The Daily Express*, plus captious broadcast editorialising by Eric Severeid and other radio pundits. On 4 February, John Hilldring, who collected a huge file of press clippings, alerted SHAEF G-5 to the critical commentary, prompting what one denazification officer later called a sense of 'pandemonium and panic'. Nervous SHAEF officials denied that the 'Darlan Deal' was a template for the governance of Aachen, which *PM* had quoted one AMG officer admitting, and they immediately launched several investigations into the Aachen regime, all of which found more than a kernel of truth to the Bradford-Padover accusations. Under fire, AMG officers complained that they had received precious little in the form of practical policy guidance, so that if matters had gone astray, it was the fault of senior authorities more than their subordinates. On 21 February, more bad news arrived at SHAEF: a Belgian intelligence report, compiled by an ex-resistance fighter with contacts in the Aachen region, portrayed the entire municipal government as a 'fifth column'. SHAEF ordered the 12th Army Group to launch yet another investigation.

SHAEF's ultimate response was a 23 February circular impressing the need for Allied army groups to stiffen denazification strictures, noting that no 'active Nazis or ardent Nazi sympathizers' could be employed, and that 'no exception will be made to this policy on grounds of administrative convenience or expediency'. On 9 March, a SHAEF letter also warned that nearly 360,000 Germans were candidates for automatic arrest, and it specified the numbers that fell into each category. SHAEF did concede that commanders in forward areas could make short-term use of Nazi appointees if necessary for the success of combat operations, although all such cases had to be justified in written reports. At least one officer in G-5 pointed out that the 23 February document contradicted the first draft of JCS 1067, which called for the dismissal of *all* Nazis, not just the 'active' variety, but nothing came of this complaint. Four directives based on SHAEF's new orders were subsequently issued by the headquarters of subordinate armies and army groups. These varied in tone and severity. The most radical, issued by Omar Bradley's 12th Army Group, called for the dismissal not only of members of the NSDAP, but participants in all party affiliates, even German Labour Front (DAF), the NS-*Lehrerbund* (teachers' association) and the NS-*Frauenschaft* (women's organisation). Since 45 million Germans – the majority of the population – belonged to one or another of the NSDAP's affiliates, execution of this directive would have entailed not only the release of almost every civil servant in Germany, but the exclusion of most potential replacements. This radical document was drafted by Colonel Page, the deputy director of G-5 in the army group, although Tom Bower speculates that it was inspired by Colonel Bernard Bernstein, who had become head of AMG's finance branch and was Henry Morgenthau's unofficial representative in the European Theatre. In army slang, such Morgenthau proxies were known as 'Chaos Boys'.

In addition to issuing new directives, SHAEF G-5 also coaxed Eisenhower's political advisor, Robert Murphy, into finally providing a sense of political direction, since 1067 specified who to dismiss, but not who to hire. This latter issue, it will be recalled, had contributed to the difficulties in Aachen, and the nub of the problem, as Michael Balfour later observed, was that the Allies simply underestimated the strength of illiberal and authoritarian ideas amongst the German middle classes. Nonetheless, within the bounds prescribed by a liberal democratic consciousness, Murphy tried to deal with the issue. In a letter in early May 1945, he warned against relying solely on the advice of Catholic or Protestant clergy as a means of locating potential appointees. Such a policy, he noted, would usually lead to the elevation of relatively conservative elements. It was better to seek out former members of the labour movement, the SPD and the Democratic Party, although ex-members of the Centre Party were to be treated with caution, since one of its wings had been 'anti-democratic'. Former conservatives and right-wing liberals were to be avoided since they allegedly represented nationalist and militarist values hardly distinguishable from Nazism. Many such men had been left in the bureaucracy during the post-First World War occupation of the Rhineland and they later had done little to deter Hitler's rise to power. Within the bounds of these strictures, appointments were supposed to reflect the social and confessional character of local regions. Murphy also advised that jobs be shared among people of different backgrounds in order to avoid the impression of American favouritism toward any particular party.[4]

The practical effect of these new directives was mixed. The 12th Army Group's notion of denazification was so extreme that most AMG detachments ignored it, although there was a stiffening of policy in some areas, particularly those controlled by the Ninth Army. In Aachen itself, there was a furious round of purges in February and March 1945, aimed mainly at 'nominal' Nazis employed by the Oppenhoff administration, although the real sympathies of military government were perhaps revealed by the fact that Leo Svoboda, far from being drummed out of AMG, was eventually *promoted* to the deputy directorship of military government in Berlin. When British military government officers arrived in Aachen in early May 1945, equipped with a mandate to replace their American allies, they noticed that Oppenhoff's successor, Dr Rombach, was in an 'automatic removal' category, and they promptly dismissed him from office. In the industrial town of Mayen, west of Koblenz, AMG accepted the help of a five-man committee of German socialists and communists, who advised the Americans on various appointments. Padover also used his newly-acquired influence to encourage the appointment of surviving SPD activists to the mayoralties in München-Gladbach and Düsseldorf, although he found much AMG resistance to the new reforms. Padover's candidate in München-Gladbach, Willi Elfes, replaced a Nazi holdover publically named in Max Lerner's column as a potential problem. In München-Gladbach's twin city of Rheydt, the hometown of Joseph Goebbels, a local military government officer resented having to fire the Nazi-appointed mayor, whom he judged an honest man, and in Oberkassel, another AMG officer told Padover that sanctions against the employment of Nazis and right-wing national-ists had caused 'one hell of a problem'. U.S. military government officers were not burdened with an extensive knowledge of German culture or social conditions – few knew the language – and they resented having to burrow beneath the surface of society in order to ferret out suitable appointees.[5] In an interview with *Stars and Stripes*, Major General Ernest Harmon pleaded the doctrine of practical necessity, arguing that it was one thing to teach Germans who had won the war, another to let them freeze and starve because the transport and manufacturing systems had been allowed to collapse.[6] An interesting incident at Gütersloh, the headquarters of the Ninth Army, also suggests that the threat of press exposure sometimes influenced appointments, rather than SHAEF directives or matters of conscience. Major Olson, the local AMG officer, wanted to appoint 'a person with Nazi connections' to the mayoralty, but a senior colleague dissuaded him, warning that Gütersloh was an army headquarters town, so 'the glare of publicity was brighter than normal'.[7]

It was the bomb-battered city of Cologne, however, that provided a belated sequel to the Aachen controversy. Upon arrival in the town, the local AMG detachment, attached to the First Army, immediately sought out Catholic clergy-men in order to provide advice on appointments, and the eventual municipal regime was thus comprised largely of Catholic-conservative *Honoratioren* (local dignitaries) led by Konrad Adenauer, the pre-1933 Lord Mayor. However, the AMG detachment commander, Lieutenant Colonel John Patterson, had learned one lesson from the Aachen scandal, which was to talk tough about denazification. In mid-March he announced that absolutely no Nazis would enjoy appointments in the municipal government and that all *Parteigenossen* released from employment would be deprived of pensions. In practice, however, the Cologne regime contin-ued to employ numerous Nazis as workers or as appointees in subordinate jobs, positions for which screening by CIC or the Special Branch was less intense than for senior placeholders. By late April 1945, only 743 of 3000 municipal employees in Cologne had been thoroughly vetted, of whom 318 had been released (a rate of approximately ten per cent). Nearly two-thirds of the city's work force – a group including numerous Nazis – had been given only cursory screening. In May 1945, a report on the condition of Cologne made such problems known to senior echelons, although the author of this document, Lieutenant Milton Chernin, concluded that the AMG detachment had done its best to negotiate a compromise between the imperative of denazification and the need to restore civic life. Chernin's report was subsequently treated like a state secret, but it was impossible to prevent such news from leaking out. On 22 July 1945, a local SPD leader complained to the occupiers about the domination of civic government by former Centrists and about the lack of denazification. By this time, a shift in the spacial alignment of Allied forces had left the British in control of the city. Although they had no objections to a lax denazification policy – in fact, they ordered Adenauer to keep in place 'less-incriminated *Parteigenossen*' – they were sensitive to the narrow character of Adenauer's regime and to the mayor's predilection for 'political intriguing'. As a result, they fired the aged *Oberbürgermeister* on 6 October and at the same time they barred him from political activity. In the long run, however, Adenauer regained the right to organise kindred political spirits, and his rebuff by the British unintentionally provided him with the time to promote the new Christian Democratic Union (CDU), whose Cologne chapter Adenauer joined in December 1945.[8] He eventually became a founding father of the German Federal Republic, although he then carried his autocratic style of governance into the federal chancellorship.

Even more than in Cologne, it was in central and southern Germany that real problems developed, although as American armies approached these areas the war was coming to an end and the supposed need to limit denazification in order to help forces at the front was diminishing. By the time that American troops reached the limits of their eastward penetration in Thuringia, Saxony and Prussian Saxony, almost all regular AMG detachments had been deployed in areas to the west and the occupiers had to rely on 'provisional military government' detachments, which were drawn hastily from combat forces and were comprised of troops who had received only one or two weeks training in military government. Conditions were desperate because of the local congestion of refugees, 'displaced persons' (DPs) and PoWs, and the rationale for a thorough political clean-up was less compelling than in western Germany because these provinces were officially part of the Soviet occupation zone and would eventually have to be given up to the Russians. In most towns in central Germany, the CIC and Special Branch arrested senior Nazis and forced Germans to fill out *Fragebogen*, although the level of vetting was usually superficial.[9] In Eisenach, AMG officer Knute Hannston fired the Nazi *Bürgermeister* of the city, but he allowed village mayors on the outskirts to remain in place, only to discover that they remained uncooperative and were still used the '*Heil* Hitler!' greeting. In Magdeburg, the U.S.-appointed mayor, Otto Baer, pursued a lacklustre denazification campaign and allowed returning *Wehrmacht* officers to join the town police force. On 29 May, British military government assumed temporary control of Magdeburg and quickly dumped Baer, citing his 'mild action' against the Nazis. Baer was reinstated by the end of June and was then kept on by the Russians, although they forced him to release nearly a thousand Nazi municipal employees, which he found a painful experience. In Stendal, AMG actually retained the incumbent *Bürgermeister*, Karl Wernicke, although Wernicke had been a National Socialist since 1933. Upon the entry of the Red Army on 1 July 1945, Wernicke was arrested and sent to the Sachsenhausen internment camp, from which he never returned. Only in Leipzig and its environs did the U.S. occupiers do a credible job: in this district, they cooperated with a local anti-fascist committee in cleansing the public administration, even causing their mayoral appointment, Dr Vierling, to complain that they were crippling the city, and they also launched purges of the private economy and the local university. In one village outside the city, a National Socialist mayor was arrested by the Americans and was then discovered by local civilians in a nearby field, dead from a gunshot wound.[10] In another town, however, the mayor and council were caught issuing Nazi propaganda literature.[11]

In the Saarland, the Palatinate and the southern Rhineland, the military government detachments of the U.S. Third and Seventh Armies had been largely unaffected by the Aachen affair, and the Sixth Army Group was short of Special Branch officers.[12] Sixth Army Group issued its own radical denazification order on 30 March, specifying the dismissal not only of Nazis, but former members of the German Nationalist Party, the *Stahlhelm* and other right-wing groups, but in practice officers at the front continued to employ Nazis in civil service positions, even without filing the paperwork ordered by the 23 February circular,[13] and AMG officers continued to argue that most German bureaucrats were simply 'nominal' Nazis who had been forced to join the party in order to keep their jobs. AMG's main concern was to find billets for U.S. troops and keep the population fed, matters in which they became dependent upon bourgeois technical experts, especially those with knowledge of the English language. Although many of their northern colleagues had become aware of the need to vary municipal appointments between representatives of different parties and classes, military government officers in the Sixth Army Group continued to ignore this imperative. As early as 5 March, while the Aachen scandal was still unfolding, the new AMG chief of Trier, Lieutenant Colonel Speaks, was holding a clubby meeting with neighbourhood wine merchants (Trier was the commercial centre of the Saarland-Moselle wine-growing region). In attendance was a prominent Catholic lay personality, Werner Mühlenbrock, the local head of the relief organisation Caritas. After Mühlenbrock himself declined the post of *Oberbürgermeister*, he recommended wine salesman Friedrich Breitbach, the Hitler-era director of the Trierer 'Citizens' Association. Breitbach was then allowed to choose the section leaders for his municipal government, although this type of practice had already led to severe problems in Aachen.[14]

In the nearby city of Mainz, AMG officers again went to the local bishop in order to get recommendations for municipal appointments. In this case, the individual assigned to the mayoralty was Rudolph Walther, a Centrist and former civil official who was reluctant to pursue German war criminals or even to admit Germany's predominant role in starting the war. Many Nazis remained in important administrative posts, where they continued spreading Goebbelsite propaganda and terrifying the population. Walther also thought that the return of Mainz's Jewish population would prove problematic, since people would resent giving up expropriated property, and he was a devout anti-communist whose misgivings about 'Reds' was exasperated when he realised that Mainz was officially part of the French zone of occupation and would eventually have to host French troops. 'People fear a French occupation,' he grumbled, 'because they think the French will bring communism with them.' Not surprisingly, Walther was dropped from his post shortly after the French arrived in Mainz.[15]

Once the Third and Seventh Armies crossed the Rhine, they encountered intensively Nazified regions such as Franconia. In Nuremberg, the 'spiritual capital' of the NSDAP, the municipal government was more thoroughly penetrated by Nazis than in any other German city. Naturally, denazification proceeded slowly, although the occupiers ignored suggestions from Nuremberg trade unionists, who argued that they could provide capable replacement personnel and thus speed up the pace. Instead, local AMG claimed the need to retain a functional administrative structure, and it even left most *Parteigenossen* in their existing houses or tenements. It also supplied such people with full rations and failed to force them to organise for special labour details. Only in July 1945 did the local military governor organise a radical denazification that cleansed the city administration of a third of its workforce, although even after the beginning of the Nuremberg Trials, which offered the ultimate rationale for denazification, there were still over one thousand Nazis in the municipal administration of the city hosting the tribunal. In 1946, Special Branch recommended dismissing Adam Geier, the Second *Bürgermeister* of Nuremberg, for interference in denazification operations.[16]

In Würzburg, the Americans managed to find anti-Nazis to serve as *Oberbürgermeister* and police chief, but the deputy mayor was Lambert Greck, a *Parteigenosse* who had been 'forced' to join the NSDAP in 1937 – his job was supposedly on the line – although he claimed to despise everything that the party represented. Nonetheless, he continued to spout racist rhetoric, denouncing African-American troops and claiming that the future belonged to an alliance of Western powers pitted against 'Asiatic' Russia. In September 1945, several Germans who had been 'helping' military government were arrested as part of a neo-Nazi cabal that had disguised itself as a club of Freemasons.

In Frankfurt, the new *Oberbürgermeister*, Kurt Blaum, was a former German Army major who had helped expand production at a wartime munitions plant. Under denazification strictures, he should have been automatically barred from public office. Like Oppenhoff, Blaum conducted a vendetta against the local press organ, *Frankfurter Rundschau*, which he derided as 'communist'. Blaum and his police chief showed a preference for recruiting policemen amongst the ranks of demobilized professional soldiers, a cadre that had traditionally been discouraged from holding any political party membership (including Nazi), but were often strident German nationalists. The result was that a secret group in the police department was eventually discovered cooperating with pro-Nazi judges, especially in obtaining the release of incarcerated Nazis and arresting anti-Nazis. The deputy police commissioner was eventually exposed as a disguised SS officer who was distributing counterfeit identity documents to Nazi activists. In January 1946, AMG was forced to restore direct American control of the Frankfurt police in an effort to organise a clean-up. Moreover, in the neighbouring community of Höchst, members of a local anti-fascist group warned that AMG had inadvertently appointed Nazis to the auxiliary police, and that these elements had encouraged looting and chaos, hoping that such conditions would produce a violent nationalist backlash against military government.

The Bavarian capital of Munich offered perhaps the worst case of all. The police chief, *Oberst* von Seisser, had been the deputy commander of the German Army high command's southern branch during the First World War, and the deputy mayor, Fritz Stadelmayr, was a party member who had served as mayor of Würzberg during the NS-*Zeit*. Four of twelve departments in the municipal government were headed by Nazis and one city commissioner estimated that between fifty and eighty per cent of his colleagues were *Parteigenosson*. In the early weeks of the occupation, *Oberbürgermeister* Karl Scharnagl had managed to negotiate a 'denazification moratorium' with the American city commandant, but to his dismay the more senior echelons of AMG would not honour the agreement and Scharnagl was forced to form a committee charged with cleansing the municipal government. Scharnagl's own tendency was to blame the Allies for the rise of Nazism – France had allegedly bullied Germany between 1919 and 1923 – and he advised that unless the Allies wanted to encourage a popular stampede toward communism, their plans would have to be modest. He personally favoured fining Nazis with a reduction in salary and forcing them to undergo a re-education programme in Christian and democratic values. Nonetheless, under Allied pressure he was forced to dismiss a quarter of the city's staff, and eventually he had to release even Stadelmayr, although he wrote him a beautiful letter expressing 'warmest thanks' for his services.[17]

It was the nature and composition of the Bavarian *Land* government, however, that eventually gave rise to a public scandal exceeding even the Aachen debacle. The U.S. military governor of Bavaria was Charles Keegan, a poor choice – given the Aachen precedent – because Keegan's formative experience was as a Democratic Party machine politician and acolyte of the archbishop of New York, Francis Spellman. A New York City alderman until 1942, Keegan had enjoyed an exceedingly close relationship with Catholic ecclesiastical authorities in the Bronx, and his natural inclination was to follow the same mode of operation in Munich. In fact, Spellman provided Keegan with a letter of introduction to the local cardinal, Michael von Faulhaber, whom Spellman counted as a close friend. Unfortunately, while Faulhaber was an outspoken critic of the Nazis and a renowned theologian, he was also a right-wing monarchist with little appreciation of liberal democracy. Rather, he revived the counterrevolutionary motto of 1919, 'Ordnungszelle Bayern', that is, Bavaria – preserve of order, and the Bavarian elite was in a favourable position to create such a state because they were less balanced by reviving working class power than was the case in other parts of Germany (although they certainly feared a mass swing to the Left). Faulhaber's candidate for the Bavarian premiership was the Munich lawyer and civil servant Fritz Schäffer. Keegan was in rush to set up a provincial government – the problems of transportation, food distribution, health and public welfare weighed heavily upon his mind – and on 27 May he obligingly appointed Schäffer as 'minister president'. Unfortunately, Schäffer had a rather difficult background. He was a former member of the Freikorps and had loyally served the conservative-authoritarian governments of the interwar period. In 1922, he helped defeat an SPD motion to ban the NSDAP. 'Thank God,' he had said, 'that the idea of self-defense is not dead... We cannot despise the German youth in whose heart the combat spirit is still alive and who are thinking along militant lines.' As chairman of the local equivalent of the Centrists, the Bavarian People's Party (BVP), he had offered in 1932 to back a Hitler-led government with BVP support, and in 1933 he had enthusiastically supported the Enabling Act, later noting that 'a collapse of the present national government would be a disaster'. Like Faulhaber, he had subsequently run afoul of the Nazis – in particular, he had spent several months in Dachau in the post-July 20th crackdown on conservative opposition personalities – but he shared Faulhaber's corporatist and authoritarian political inclinations.

Schäffer's government consisted mainly of elderly Catholic laymen drawn from the ranks of the professional classes and the business elite, many of whom had flourished during the heyday of the Third Reich. These men worked to reestablish the local Wittelsbach monarchy, which suggested reviving particularist tendencies, but they were also exceedingly malleable in dealing with Nazis, whom they were trying to gather into the BVP in order to reinforce its position against the Left. They also feared that if Nazi placeholders were fired amass, Prussian refugees – presumably less sympathetic to Bavarian conservative values – might flood into the bureaucracy as replacements. Thus, sixteen prominent Nazis continued to be employed in the ministry of agriculture alone, and the Nazi food provisioning system, the 'Reich Food Estate', was left intact in all but name. Schäffer's minister of economics was a war profiteer and a close friend of the former Nazi Gauleiter; his chief deputy was a former general in the National Socialist Transport Corps; his acting interior minister had been head of the 'Association of Germans Abroad', a group that the Nazis had used as an instrument of espionage, subversion and propaganda; and his ministerial director in the Interior Ministry – an individual who had been appointed on the recommendation of Faulhaber – was a Parteigenosse. Schäffer's principal advisor,

Dr Gessler, had been German secretary of war in the 1920s and had helped organise Germany's illegal rearmament and the formation of the *Reichswehr*'s secret reserve component. Since Schäffer knew that the appointment of such a personality was bound to draw scowls from the occupation regime, he used his services informally, although Gessler was always addressed as '*Staatsrat*' and attended all cabinet meetings. It is true that nearly 50,000 Nazis were released from positions in lower levels of administration. Special Branch still functioned at full speed, despite the lack of any support from above, and thirty-five to forty per cent of the school teachers in the *Land* were dismissed, which owed especially to the influence of local AMG's education czar, Edward D'Arms, who was a denazification hardliner. However, Schäffer implicitly advised his most senior associates to lie on their *Fragebogen,* and he stalled the submission and processing of such forms. Shäffer told the Allies that their approach to denazification was too broad – most members of the party, he asserted, had been merely 'nominal' – and he decried the programme's unevenness in application from region to region. In July 1945, he tried to moderate directives forcing *Parteigenossen* into 'less important agricultural work', saying that such measures were tantamount to organising 'slave labour' and that they could be used to defame certain parts of society. He also tried to shield Nazis from loss of their accomodations, arguing that such procedures were sure to open the door to corruption. In late August, Schäffer's Interior Ministry actually set up an employment office for civil servants who had been removed and now needed new jobs.

Meanwhile, Schäffer's state chancellery was already preparing its own measures to replace AMG's denazification programme. These proposals recommended the formation of regional German commissions that would deal with Nazis in a legal but flexible fashion, using supposedly 'objective criteria' to determine those deserving of removal or punishment. Lutz Niethammer sees in this proposal the germ of the eventual '*Spruchkammer*', which he characterizes as 'quasi-revolutionary institutions [that] were supposed to be staffed with counterrevolutionary personnel'. As he notes, certain procedural mechanisms in this suggested system were sure to spare proper, church-going Nazis, whom the BVP were interested in recruiting, while the main thrust, aside from punishing a small circle of Nazi bosses and war criminals, was to reintegrate a much larger mass of personnel otherwise targeted by the Americans.

Rumours about the Schäffer regime soon reached the ears of G-5 and CIC officers in Eisenhower's headquarters, most of which were impossible to verify because the Third Army had largely ceased providing detailed reports to its ulterior chain of command. Investigators sent to explore the situation reported that Keegan was a public relations disaster. Not only was he failing to properly administer the denazification programme, but he seemed unable to advertise any modest successes that he did achieve. One report suggested that the Schäffer regime 'was only a little better than the Nazis it replaced'; another complained about the disillusionment of Bavarian anti-Nazis, who saw 'the establishment of a new kind of German totalitarian or at least undemocratic regime.' 'Morgenthau Boys' in the Finance Section of AMG were especially incensed by the retention of Nazis in the *Finanzamt* of the Bavarian regime. A particularly shocking instance of Keegan's passivity came to light in early July, when American medical inspectors happened upon an asylum in Kaufbüren, where unregenerately Nazi personnel were still engaged in euthanasia killings and experiments for 'improvements in the race'. Local officials had known about the facility but had done nothing to cease its operations, much less to denazify its staff. Understandably, press coverage about Bavaria grew increasingly hostile, especially since the earlier experience of the Spanish Civil War had convinced many American intellectuals that conservative Catholicism was synonymous with fascism. By the late summer, *PM*, *The New York Times* and the *Chicago Daily News* were all ranting about the systematic failure of denazification. On 4 September, Keegan was fired as military governor, whence he flew home to New York and reclaimed his seat on city council.[18]

Sacking Keegan hardly resolved matters. Rather, attention now focused on Keegan's boss, the egomaniacal clotheshorse George Patton, who despite his myriad shortcomings, was the best combat general in the U.S. Army. Unfortunately, Patton's talents were not on display after he was appointed as military consul in the eastern half of the American Zone (which included Bavaria). Depressed about not being deployed to the Pacific Theatre, Patton grew increasingly unstable and his anti-Semitism ballooned to dangerous proportions. In addition, he railed about the 'Mongolian nature' of the Soviets, against whom he wanted to march, perhaps using defeated SS troops as an auxiliary. Never a supporter of the 'collective guilt' thesis, at least as it applied to Germans, his loathing of Jews and Russians fostered a rapidly improving assessment of the former enemy. 'It is vitally necessary,' he confided, 'for us to build up Germany as a buffer state against Russia', and he complained that Jews and communists were picking on German businessmen. While touring the United States during the summer of 1945, Patton read Stimson's correspondence with Morgenthau and Roosevelt, which convinced him that denazification was a nefarious by-product of the Morgenthau Plan. In Patton's reckoning, the programme was worse than unnecessary; it supposedly sanctioned 'Gestapo' methods in order to weaken a potential ally.

Eisenhower, who genuinely believed in the rectitude of denazification, kept urging Patton to initiate the process, finally losing all sense of decorum on 27 August, when he told his subordinate to 'get off [his] bloody ass and carry out the denazification programme … instead of mollycoddling the goddamn Nazis'. In turn, Patton threatened to bring the matter to the attention of Republican newspapers in the United States and he talked of releasing 'automatic arrest' detainees held at Moosberg and Garmisch-Partenkirchen, stating in front of captured SS officers that their internment was 'sheer madness'. At the very least, he increased rations for 'automatic arrest' detainees to a level of 4000 calories per day, which was more sustenance than anyone else in Germany was receiving. In press conferences on 22 and 25 September, he announced that the Bavarian

Government would be more effective if it employed a higher number of Nazis, and that Nazi Party members were tantamount to Democrats or Republicans, and had joined the movement under the same lure of patronage appointments. Patton had actually been advancing this thesis since May 1945, but had previously had the presence of mind to order reporters not to quote him. He also noted that while he had killed many Germans in battle, it was criminal to allow Germans to die of hunger or cold because of the insufficient state of administrative organisation.

This rhetoric comprised a critical mass that set rapid changes into motion. The new president, Harry Truman, wrote to Eisenhower, demanding answers, and the latter began to worry that a scandal was licking at his own heels. Eisenhower's main advisors, chief of staff Walter Bedell Smith, G-5 boss Clarence Adcock, and his special consultant on denazification, a history professor and veteran of R&A named Walter Dorn, requested that the Signal Corps tap Patton's telephone lines and 'bug' his headquarters in Bad Tölz. This eavesdropping soon produced statements in which Patton mused about orchestrating incidents in order to launch a war with the Soviet Union, hopefully with surrendered SS troops playing a role on the American side. If public faux pas had not been enough to terminate Patton's career, these private asides were sufficient. It was not just an issue of what Patton had done, Eisenhower confided, it was 'what he's going to do next'. On 28 September, 'Ike' invited Patton to his headquarters at Frankfurt and asked 'what in hell' the American Army was doing in Germany 'if not to rid the German administration of notorious and conspicuous Nazis? The Russians are killing them off and we are keeping them in office.' He then stripped Patton of the Third Army and of the Eastern Military District, telling him that henceforth he would be shuffled off to an obscure administrative post. After brief visits to Bavaria, Robert Murphy and Walter Dorn reported that press accusations against the Bavarian Government were 'exaggerated', but they nonetheless recommended replacing the entire regime, which was quickly dumped in favour of a coalition government under Bavarian SPD leader Wilhelm Hoegner.[19] However, like Adenauer, who was dropped under similarly unceremonious circumstances, Fritz Schäffer survived to make a political comeback. Although barred for two years from political activity, he eventually helped lead the Christian Social Union (CSU), successor to the BVP, and he too became a founding father of the *Bundesrepublik*, serving as federal finance minister from 1949 to 1957.

The Bavarian imbroglio had a huge impact upon denazification policy throughout the U.S. zone. Fortunately for advocates of denazification, Eisenhower's key deputies sincerely believed in the necessity of the programme, even in its most radical form. These officials included Adcock and the AMG chief and deputy military governor, Lieutenant General Lucius Clay, who was regarded as a firm advocate of the Eisenhower-Roosevelt line on Germany. Certainly both Adcock and Clay were impressed as much by the denazification imperative as by the 'welfare of the governed' theory. Adcock, for one, regarded the purge as the chief reason why U.S. forces had come to Germany. After *l'affaire* Patton, there was an obvious need for bold statements in favour of denazification, although there were only limited possibilities for making the policy even more severe. The liberation of Nazi concentration camps in April 1945 had already been accompanied by a vast publicity campaign that had reinforced the 'collective guilt' thesis. Through camp tours, posters, radio programmes and documentary films, the latter of which German civilians were forced to watch, at risk of losing their ration coupons, the Americans hammered home the theme – 'This town is guilty! You are guilty!' The obvious purpose was to suppress German impulses to resist and to drive home the need for denazification.[20] On 7 July 1945, AMG had already promulgated the strictest set of denazification regulations anywhere in occupied Germany, listing 136 mandatory removal categories (although these instructions also had an ameliorating effect by sparing those who had joined the NSDAP after 1 May 1937, mainly with the rationale that the later generation of Nazi Party members had been forced to join on pain of keeping their jobs). Some *Kreise* (counties) run by energetic AMG officers had already been denazified at a furious pace (although many others were governed by officers obviously convinced of the need to employ Nazis in order to 'get things moving'). By 20 August 1945, 150,000 Nazis had already been removed from public office. In addition, the number of 'automatic arrest' detainees had skyrocketed from 1000 in March 1945 to 80,000 in July (plus 35,000 in PoW camps), and this number was still rising, despite signs of overcrowding at internment camps.[21] Lutz Niethammer rightly characterizes American 'automatic arrest' categories as 'extraordinarily extensive', and he notes that on a per capita basis, the Americans locked up a higher percentage of the population than any other occupying power, even the Soviets.[22] In cities damaged by bombing, Nazis were forced to help in rubble clearance; in the American controlled enclaves of Bremen and southern Berlin, *Parteigenossen* were being mobilized to scrub pro-Nazi slogans off the walls of buildings.[23]

Despite such tough policies, Patton had still managed to stain the reputation of AMG on home shores. According to James Tent, 'all hope of an orderly denazification vanished', replaced by witch-hunts and hysteria.[24] Adcock and Clay tried to assuage public opinion through promulgating Military Government Law Number 8, which was unlike earlier orders or administrative regulations in the sense that it was a legal decree and supposedly bore the extra weight of such a document. It was sketched out in the course of a single day by Clay's legal advisor, Charles Fahy, and was announced so suddenly that many AMG detachments first learned of it over Armed Forces Radio. This decree was also colloquially called the 'Butcher Law', because Clay was said to have been roused to action by rumours of an Augsburg meat vendor who was still favouring fellow *Parteigenossen* in allocating his supplies. American reports had also warned that if the occupiers continued to sweep the public service without a corresponding purge of the economy, many Nazis would flood into the latter realm, where they would retain much of their power and influence. With the problem of Nazis in private enterprise thus highlighted, Law Number 8 extended denazification strictures to include industry and the service sector. Henceforth, no member of the party would be allowed to serve in any management capacity, either private or public in nature. Germans, according to Earl Ziemke, 'reeled under the shock', particularly because German labour exchanges were supposed to provide lists of workers so that AMG could vet the names of job applicants. Meanwhile AMG authorities struggled with finding enough personnel to check German labour lists against captured NSDAP membership records, and they were also forced to prepare new lists of automatic removal categories, although positions in private business were not as uniform – and therefore harder to categorise – than offices in the Nazi Party or the civil service. In October 1945, Brewster Morris, Robert Murphy's representative at the headquarters of the Western Military District, reported that both German officials and AMG officers felt, 'that the recently published Law No.8 ... was unwise and is creating great nervousness and uncertainty among the people'. Allegedly, German communists were the only party to support the law because they saw it creating a vacuum in industrial management that could be filled by workers. Others worried about potential damage to the German economy or, worse yet, the creation of a large body of unemployed Nazis who would be expelled from the labour force with little or no consideration of their individual backgrounds, and who would thus receive the sympathy of German society rather than being ostracised. Dark rumours also swept the zone suggesting that Law Number 8 – and the sacking of Patton – had resulted from the exercise of supposed Jewish influences in Washington, and some Germans believed that the Morgenthau Plan was being revived.

After much gnashing of teeth and the creation of a considerable bureaucratic burden, the actual result of the policy was modest (at best). There was widespread German evasion through various subterfuges, particularly the sale of firms to the sons and wives of affected persons. A Munich civic official advised businessmen, 'People are simply fired, rehired as workers. With a flexible conscience, it's easy to say you've fired a man, and he's now employed as a worker.' Some firms did not even bother firing and rehiring, but simply shifted the formal employment classifications of supervisory personnel who were Nazis. Some *Parteigenossen* recruited partners with untainted records; some based their businesses at home; some collected salaries or payments in cash in order to avoid bank account blocking; some offered large bribes to German officials in order to get party records changed. Worst of all, AMG learned that by exempting firms with fewer than ten employees – a provision included in the text of the directive – they had spared ninety-two per cent of all German businesses. In the end, only 100,000 people were dismissed, which AMG regarded as an inconsequential outcome.[25]

Clay, however, still had several other cards to play. In October 1945, he began focusing his interest upon the German post office and the *Reichsbahn*, the German rail service. Run by the U.S. Army Signal Corps, the *Reichspost* had received little attention from the Special Branch and a 4th August directive for its purging had allowed the rehiring of 'nominal' Nazis at subaltern levels. In the biggest cities of the U.S. zone, less than 2,600 dismissals had been made from a staff of 23,000 employees, and *Fragebogen* were being processed very slowly. As for the *Reichsbahn*, the condition of the purge in that service was even more dire. The theatre command of U.S. forces, which controlled transport, had exempted all but the most senior *Reichsbahn* Nazis from mandatory removal, and neither the 7 July directive nor Law Number 8 were being applied. By late September 1945, only 9,000 of 36,000 mandatory removal personnel had been barred from service, a number that AMG felt embarrassed to publish. Moreover, the Army's Theatre Service Forces had already risked public scandal by nominating seven heavily incriminated Nazis to lead the restoration of zonal rail service. One of these candidates, Albert Ganzenmüller, was a veteran of the Beer Hall Putsch and later, as deputy director of the *Reichsbahn*, had facilitated the Final Solution by helping to organise rail transport for the SS. Only a State Department intervention had secured Ganzenmüller's removal from the list of nominees. The nub of the problem, as John Montgomery notes, came from using army organisations to operate the same services that they were responsible for purging.

Clay soon reacted. On 20 November, he cancelled most of the exemptions made for *Reichspost* employees, and six days later he did the same for the *Reichsbahn*. According to new instructions, the authority to retain Nazi railwaymen, pending review of their cases, would end on 1 February 1946.

In November 1945, Clay also circulated a directive on 'Local Government Codes of Election', which disenfranchised all Nazi Party members in forthcoming *Kreis* elections. In issuing this order, Clay rejected recommendations by a military government advisory committee, which wanted to restrict disenfranchisement to Nazis in automatic arrest categories, and he ignored advice from the State Department, which was comfortable with the exclusion of automatic removal categories, but wanted 'nominal' Nazis on the voting rolls. Critics of Clay's decision argued that lack of documentation made it almost impossible to vet would-be voters, and they contended that such measures hindered the assimilation of Nazis into the new political order.[26]

It is at this point that we reach the ultimate moment of truth for denazification policy. The basic notion, as crafted by American policy makers, had always been overly optimistic in its scope and unrealistic in its method of application, and the consequences of this approach were now apparent. The mere printing and distribution of millions of *Fragebogen* put a strain on AMG resources, but that burden was modest compared with the task of reviewing completed forms that inundated military government offices through the summer and fall of 1945. In fact, finding room to store such masses of paper proved a problem. It is true that officers in the Special Branches and the CIC were aided in their efforts by the capture of Nazi Party files and membership lists, which were gradually collected at a central archive called the Berlin Document Center. The German mania for record keeping, as one Special

Branch officer later recalled, provided an unexpected boon for the occupiers. As a result of such finds, *Fragebogen* responses could be verified against documentary evidence, and the Americans were careful to place notices in German newspapers alerting the population about the existence of such resources. This tactic probably produced more honest *Fragebogen* submissions (although it also prompted respondents who were caught lying to claim that since the occupation authorities already had the evidence they needed for prosecutions, the *Fragebogen* were actually a lure to tempt Nazis into further incriminating themselves). Whatever the case, the task of checking forms against captured records was still gargantuan. Indeed, the review process was time-consuming because it involved assigning each *Fragebogen* personality to one of five categories: mandatory removal; discretionary removal with an adverse recommendation; discretionary removal with a positive recommendation; non–Nazi; and anti–Nazi. Cases of suspected falsification were supposed to be referred to the Policy Enforcement Branch or the CIC. In order to accomplish this task, increasing numbers of personnel were assigned to the Special Branch, but many had only a poor comprehension of the German language or were otherwise out of depth. Some had no more interest in the programme than they, or their immediate predecessors, had demonstrated while the fighting was still underway. As a result, progress was difficult, although American troops did manage to review nearly 1,600,000 *Fragebogen*, and they dismissed nearly 374,000 people. Military government officials also found that denazification was coming to absorb more time and energy than any other assignment, especially in the Legal and Public Safety Branches of AMG. As Harold Zink notes, the political powers in Washington could have spent many millions of dollars in training and deploying a large corps of technical experts capable of running denazification at the scale originally envisioned, but this was never done. In fact, at the precise moment when denazification demanded the most effort by the American authorities, popular pressures to demobilize U.S. forces and 'bring the boys home' was rapidly reducing the manpower levels of the occupation forces.[27] In November 1945, one AMG officer complained that 'good, experienced men were getting harder and harder to find', and that it had become impossible to plug holes in the staff structure.[28] During the same period, military government was forced to withdraw its shrinking cadre of officers from direct involvement in the *Kreis* level of German government, with obvious implications for the denazification programme. Such pressures suggested that unless remedial measures were introduced, the denazification policy would soon collapse under its own weight.

Clay responded to this challenge with a well-established practice for deflecting sensitive political topics: he set up a commission to study the issue. This body, the 'Denazification Policy Board', was created on 30 November 1945 and was entrusted to the chairmanship of Charles Fahy. The man who had first proposed creating such a panel, Colonel Robert Bowie, was put in charge of the board's 'working committee', which did much of its essential footwork. The problems facing the Americans had already become clear.

The CIC had never been enthusiastic about participating in denazification, arguing that – at most – it could handle arrests of suspect Nazis, but that job dismissals were largely the responsibility of military government. AMG personnel complained that CIC detachments were understaffed and were interested primarily in dealing with Nazi 'big shots' rather than 'subordinate civil servants'. In some cases, the application of automatic arrest guidelines was resulting in arbitrary punishments – one observer spoke of a 'small-scale terror' – while at the same time AMG carped that the CIC was often casually releasing dangerous Nazis. In other instances, enthusiastic followers of Hitler – or other forms of anti-democratic reactionaries – were being vetted as long as they were not members of the NSDAP.

The denazification programme operated in fits and starts, swinging back and forth between harsh and lenient interpretations of doctrine, and it was poorly integrated with other AMG operations.

A large pool of dismissed Nazis, numbering perhaps three and a half million people, was festering in isolation, pitied by the remainder of society and providing a potential spawning ground for neo-Nazi extremism. The massive scale of denazification had actually created sympathy for the Nazi die-hards who were its most dogged opponents, an effect opposite of that intended. Thus, there was an obvious need to create a mechanism that could resolve the legal status of minor Nazis and administer final punishment, after which 'denazified' individuals could reenter society with a degree of civil rights.

Terms used in military government directives were sometimes poorly defined. What, for instance, was a 'nominal' Nazi? What qualified as a party 'affiliate'? And with regard to Law Number 8, what was a 'position of responsibility' in the economy? These uncertainties had a paralysing effect on the reorganisation of civil society. U.S. small unit commanders were themselves so unsure of the measures that they routinely contravened denazification employment policies in their own facilities.

The Americans were haunted by the problem of finding adequate replacements for dismissed Nazis, especially since they knew that the optimal course was to find capable young anti-Nazis, rather than just non-Nazis or discredited holdovers from the Weimar era. The weakness of German administrative structures also exasperated a steadily heightening German fear of epidemics and disease, a concern that a U.S. intelligence report described as fully warranted and which the CIC claimed was aggravated by the dismissal of Nazi doctors and physicians.

On top of everything lay the lack of adequate AMG manpower. This was a most pressing issue in the Public Safety teams, which bore primary responsibility for denazification. AMG had been calling since the summer of 1945 for the recruiting of trained policemen and the secondment of FBI agents in order to augment the strength of such teams.

The apparent answer, as recommended by Bowie and as backed by Fahy and Dorn, was to involve Germans in denazification, which could give the programme a German face. In language reminiscent of the R&A planners, the 'Denazification Policy Board' suggested that Germans should participate in the 'political and social revolution' that denazification was supposedly facilitating, and that they use categories of relative guilt – the same categories eventually included in CC Directive 38 – as the basis for prosecutions. As Clay quickly realised, this approach made a virtue out of necessity, and to implement it he turned to the three state governments that had been organised in the American zone by the fall of 1945, each on a coalition basis. In October, Clay had ordered the premiers of these three jurisdictions, Bavaria, Hesse and Württemberg-Baden, to form a *Länderrat* (Council of *Länder*), which consisted of the *Land* premiers and had a mandate to coordinate policy, although it lacked any executive function. Even in the autumn, Clay was already anticipating that the *Länderrat* would provide advice on denazification, and in December 1945 the premier of Hesse, Karl Geiler, proposed that the *Land* governments write a uniform denazification law that could be adopted by all three states and thus establish a German role in the process. Hoegner tried to dominate developments by putting forward a Bavarian proposal that drew partly from Schäffer's prepatory work and partly from a draft devised by Heinrich Schmitt, a communist who served as Hoegner's own denazification expert. However, neither the Hessians – who had a proposal prepared by their own denazification expert, Gottlob Binder – nor the Württemberg-Badeners were happy with the Bavarian draft, at least in its unmodified form. After negotiations in Stuttgart, representatives of the three governments produced their own denazification bill. This 'Stuttgart compromise' drew from both the Bavarian and Hessian proposals, and suggested a modest programme designed mainly to rehabilitate the German administrative *Apparat* and quiet the mounting concerns of the German middle class. This bill provided for denazification tribunals, now called '*Spruchkammern*', that would have relatively lax prosecutorial functions and would impose only a limited range of sanctions. In early 1946, Fahy and Bowie met with the three *Land* justice ministers, and it quickly became apparent that while the Americans were eager to hand over executive functions connected to denazification, they had not surrendered the right to dictate the terms of the programme. Fahy and Bowie demanded that the German draft legislation include the automatic dismissal categories of which the Americans were so fond, and which the Special Branch and the 'Morgenthau Boys' in the Finance Division had insisted upon including in any 'Germanised' form of denazification. The Germans, according to Jim Pollock, U.S. advisor to the *Länderrat*, had not understood 'the full import of Control Council Law No.24'. Fahy and Bowie also insisted on 1937 as a cut-off point for discriminatory measures, although the Germans complained that such a date was arbitrary. Bowie actually sympathised with the German position, but he was unable to talk Clay out of superimposing the Directive 24 specifications upon the new process, development that guaranteed a series of mass trials based on presumptions of guilt. After much internal wrangling, the Germans reluctantly agreed to most of the American amendments, hoping that they could moderate objectionable features of the legislation through its application. The resulting document, the 'Law for Liberation from National Socialism and Militarism', was officially approved by the *Land* premiers on 5 March 1946. Pollock suggested that the signing ceremony take place in Munich, original birthplace of the Nazi movement.

The 'Law for Liberation from National Socialism' became operative in each state of the U.S. zone and created a denazification ministry in each *Land* government. A network of 545 *Spruchkammern* was a further fruit of the legislation. These bodies were organised at the *Kreis* level and assembled a German staff of more than 22,000 persons, each of whom was vetted by officers of the Special Branch. The investigatory process was still focused on questionnaires, although these were now renamed *Meldebogen* and were shorter than the ill-fated *Fragebogen*. As suggested by Walter Dorn and by one of Clay's legal advisors, Karl Lowenstein, the *Spruchkammern* organised prosecutions along the basis of the four categories of guilt recommended by the Denazification Policy Board, that is, 'Major Offenders', 'Offenders', 'Lesser Offenders' and 'Followers'. Respondents could also be completely exonerated. In order to retain the spirit of Military Government Law Number 8, which the new ordnance superceded, respondents awaiting trial were prohibited from holding management jobs, except in small enterprises. These employment restrictions were included at the behest of the Public Safety Division, which was generally critical of the devolution of the programme. In addition, the U.S. turned over official control of its large number of civilian internees, who they instructed the Germans to process under the terms of the new law. At the apex of the new hierarchy were six appellate tribunals, or *Berufungskammern*, which were set up in order to entertain appeals. This entire body of institutions was overseen by a committee of the three *Land* denazification ministers, which met twice monthly, and was supposed to operate under American oversight, particularly that of the 'MG Denazification Coordinating Committee', which was chaired by Walter Dorn and succeeded the Denazification Policy Board. Under this regime, the Public Safety Branch was supposed to perform spot-checks and reviews of *Spruchkammer* decisions, a task assigned to mobile 'Advisory Teams' of German-speakers. U.S. officials had no direct function in the system's daily procedures, but *Land*-level branches of AMG had the right to provide directions to the various *Land* denazification ministries, and they also insisted upon the right to pre-screen *Spruchkammer* personnel, which meant that such persons served – in the final analysis – at the pleasure of regional AMG offices. Perhaps the greatest significance of the 'Law for Liberation from National Socialism' was that it marked the practical end of the 'collective guilt' thesis as a source of policy. Despite a secret AMG report suggesting that less than one per cent of Germans were committed anti-Nazis, the new presumption was that three quarters of the population was unblemished enough to judge a contaminated minority. The Americans also now conceded that the denazification process should encourage rehabilitation, rather than being solely punitive in character. 'The program,' as Clay explained, 'was designed to separate the nominal Nazi from the active Nazi so that the former could regain his place as a citizen.' In addition, the occupiers recognized that denazification should move beyond categorical considerations in order to judge 'the entire conduct of a person'.

The Germans still faced huge numbers of indictable Nazis, perhaps numbering as much as twenty-seven per cent of the adult population of the U.S. zone. Even Clay realised that the programme was unenforceable at such a scale, so he helped out by organising large-scale amnesties. An article in the 'Law for Liberation from National Socialism' already suggested that 'special regulations' could be issued for youthful offenders, and a general or partial amnesty was being considered as early as May 1946. Three months later, Clay decreed that all Nazis born after 1 January 1919, being supposedly too young to have understood the full consequences of their actions, were henceforth amnestied (unless they had played a major role in the Hitler Youth). Even after the Youth Amnesty, Clay still faced a pool of 3,000,000 chargeable people, which promised an administrative lag of 'at least 2 years', and during which period there was likely to be continuing political instability. Thus, at the end of 1946 he also amnestied so-called 'small fry' Nazis – those with annual incomes less than 3,600 *Reichsmark* in the years 1943 to 1945 and property valued at less than 20,000 *Reichsmark* – with the dubious claim that such people had not benefitted from Nazi rapaciousness. Clay decided to use the 1943–45 income levels as a gauge of relative poverty because they had already been reported in the *Meldebogen*. Nazis who were disabled were also amnestied.[29] Almost two and a half million pending cases – nearly seventy per cent of the total – were resolved with these blanket measures, although such expedients were as divorced from issues of personal responsibility as the sweeping categorisations of guilt that characterised the denazification programme. *PM*, for instance, criticized the youth amnesty on the grounds that it provided practical exoneration to thousands of individuals most deserving of some form of punishment.[30] Clay responded that 'actively' Nazi youth were still likely to be incarcerated, '[but] if we punished and made outcasts of all German youth, we would have a huge void in the population which would not respond to democratic teachings'.[31]

Despite high hopes for the 'Germanisation' of denazification, the new system worked even more poorly than its predecessor. In the first place, there was yet another scandal, this time in the universities. In a precursor to the general transfer of denazification to German hands, the U.S. zone universities had already been allowed – even as early as the summer and fall of 1945 – to form 'University Planning Committees' (UPCs), which had preliminary responsibilities for vetting faculty before handing over the process to AMG officers. Some institutions did an adequate job, particularly Heidelberg, where Karl Jaspers insisted on cleansing a Nazi showcase, and where it was possible to recall a strong cadre of professors from the 1920s, when Heidelberg had been a republican bulwark. However, the UPCs claimed to use more sophisticated denazification criteria than the blunt indices favoured by the Americans. They were interested, for instance, in the actual sympathies of faculty members rather than in simple party membership. At Heidelberg, the university's rector, Karl-Heinrich Bauer, was inclined toward 'generous treatment' of former NSDAP members as long as they were not hacks who owed their academic appointments to political connections. Perhaps such discretion signaled a wise approach, but it also created problems, particularly when it was applied by faculty members judging their own colleagues. In addition, the UPCs did little to scrutinize students, mostly *Wehrmacht* veterans, who flooded through the gates as soon as the universities reopened, but then endowed the institutions with a barracks-room aura. Under heavy pressure to get the universities operating, U.S. liaison officers permitted the vetting of students *after* admission. By the time that 20,000 student questionnaires were eventually checked by Special Branch men and military government Education Officers, the 1945/46 school year was nearly finished, although 1,300 students were belatedly dismissed on political grounds.

By 1946, it was becoming clear that the UPCs were often demonstrating a lamentable leniency. At Heidelberg, where the UPC did a better job than in most of its sister institutions, 153 of 272 professors examined by the UPC were released from service. Even here, however, the director of military government in Baden-Württemberg, Colonel William Dawson, accused the university of certain 'irregularities', and in May 1946 the CIC complained about the retention of numerous professors who had been members of Nazi organisations. Clay and Adcock blasted the U.S. zone intelligence czar, Edwin Sibert, for reporting this claim in a widely-circulated intelligence summary, although Adcock privately admitted that 'I have never been satisfied that we opened Heidelberg University in other than a very hurried manner'.

The situation was worse at Munich University, where there was no Karl Jaspers to drive the reform process, and the UPC was concerned mainly with addressing the university's severe physical damage and the prospective lack of replacements for faculty dismissals. The first post-Nazi rector, Albert Rehm, distrusted the scale of American-style denazification; the second, Karl Vossler, was more sympathetic, although his advanced age and fragile health rendered him ineffective. Of 100 professors and technical assistants examined by the UPC, ninety were reinstated (although ten of these were rejected by AMG). Amongst the survivors were Leopold Escherich, who had been in the party as early as 1923 and had taken part in the Beer Hall Putsch, and Theodor Süss, who had been a section leader in the Nazi lawyers' association, as well as having been an officer in the SA-Reserve. This situation comprised a potential public relations disaster. In May 1946, *New York Times* correspondent Raymond Daniell, who had already helped to bring down Schäffer and Patton, published an exposé about conditions at Munich University, which had recently reopened. Daniell and his *Times* colleague, Tania Long, reported that faculty and students were openly opposed to the occupation, and that *Wehrmacht* veterans in a student 'debating club' were planning to attack political enemies, including Wilhelm Hoegner. One professor, Wilhelm von Isenburg, had published extensively on race theory and was allegedly offering a course on the topic. The local AMG re-education chief, Alfred Pundt, denied most of the charges, especially the claim against Isenburg, and was supported by General Walter Muller, the director of military government in Bavaria. Nonetheless, evidence of a similar nature soon came flooding in from other sources, and Pundt was removed from his post in disgrace. Not surprisingly, Clay was outraged. He demanded that the objectionable students be dismissed immediately, and on 25 June he noted that 'these reports re Munich University keep recurring. If even partly correct, something must be done.' Dorn and Muller were ordered to investigate and 'clean house'.

Meanwhile, a similar scandal exploded at Erlangen University. Early in 1946, Evangelical students at Erlangen had insulted one of Germany's leading theologians, Martin Niemöller, shuffling their feet and deriding Niemöller as a 'tool of the Allies' when he lectured about 'collective guilt'. Niemöller himself downplayed the incident, but in February the Bavarian Government ordered the university to re-screen the student body and to expel Nazi or nationalist ringleaders, warning that any further trouble 'could result in the suspension of university operations'. Six months later, nothing had changed, particularly since the university's rector had deliberately made his institution a gathering ground for Nazi educators dismissed elsewhere. A big part of the problem was the theologian Paul Althaus, an ultra-chauvinist who had welcomed the events of 1933 and yet was put in charge of the university's denazification effort, whence he provided indiscriminate recommendations to everyone who came to his office. Faculty and students were involved in the same kind of activities as their colleagues in Munich, as well as bullying the few Jewish students who had returned to the university. 'The day will come when I can take these jokers under my control,' declared one student, a former *Volkssturm* officer, 'and then Auschwitz might be called a paradise.' On 6 July, students tore down and trampled an SPD banner.

With evidence that the cancer in higher education was not confined to Munich, Dorn recommended appointing Edward Hartshorne as the man to run a ruthless purge. A gruff Harvard professor and former OSS and SHAEF PW officer, Hartshorne had once written an influential book about the Nazification of German universities and was felt to have an unparalleled appreciation of the breadth of the problem. In 1945, Hartshorne had supervised the creation of the first UPC at Marburg University and had overseen the relatively successful denazification of that institution, impressing his superiors as an individual '[who can] handle these professors and knows how to get things done'. In the late summer of 1946, Hartshorne began forming a network of denazification teams recruited from the Special Branch and the Policy Enforcement Branch. These units launched investigations at each university and uncovered widespread evasion of the 'Law for Liberation from National Socialism'. They were ordered to give no one the benefit of a doubt and to recommend the prosecution of German officials – and even AMG officers – who had previously allowed Nazis to remain in faculty posts. By mid-November 1946, fifteen per cent of the faculty at the seven universities in the U.S. zone – all previously cleared by AMG, UPCs and *Spruchkammern* – had been fired. Heidelberg University lost seventy-two professors, Munich thirty-three (including Isenburg) and Erlangen thirty, although by mid-1947 Erlangen's losses were up to seventy-six personnel, a diminution that forced the closure of the institution's law school. As a result of these dismissals, institutional morale 'sank to unprecedentedly low levels', and in Bavaria, the system of higher education came perilously close to the point of collapse. In fact, there were elements in AMG that considered formally closing all of Bavaria's universities.[32]

Such actions were deadly serious business, which is illustrated by the fact that Hartshorne never lived to see the result of his purge. A month after he was appointed, the denazification chief was assassinated while driving along the *Autobahn* from Munich to Würzburg. A jeep with two men in U.S. uniforms, plus two female joyriders, pulled alongside Hartshorne's vehicle and an assailant shot Hartshorne through the head, although not firing at his wife or driver. Military Police investigations subsequently revealed that the jeep and uniforms were stolen and that the killer was a German farm boy and *Parteigenosse*, Johann Detterbeck, who was involved in a series of robberies around Nuremberg. Although Detterbeck had told one of the girls that Hartshorne's staff car was 'hogging the road', the fact that the victim was in the middle of a purge aimed at potentially violent elements suggests that the shooting may have had a deeper motivation. The truth may never be known. Four days after the attack, Detterbeck was cornered by the U.S. Constabulary and killed in a shoot-out in the Moegeldorf Forest. In reflecting upon Hartshorne's violent passing, CIC agents thought it interesting that another denazification officer, Lieutenant Morgenstein, had been killed in an earlier incident – an apparent car crash – at the same intersection where Hartshorne had died.[33] One AMG officer called Hartshorne's death an 'accident'.[34]

Even beyond the universities, the 'Germanised' system of denazification showed signs of failing. In Bavaria, the communist denazification expert, Heinrich Schmitt, was appointed as purge minister, mainly on the recommendation of Hoegner, who convinced Dorn that a staunch leftist was needed to balance powerful reactionary forces in the *Land*. However, Schmitt's immediate attempt to politicize denazification exceeded anything imagined by his American sponsors, and this brief flirtation with radicalism was short-lived. Schmitt realised that his original set of denazification proposals had been severely watered down before reappearing – in some fashion – as the 'Law for Liberation from National Socialism', but he still believed that there was enough leverage in the legislation to reduce almost all Bavarian Nazis to the eventual level of wage labourers or low-level functionaries, where he had no objection to their earning an honest day's living. Such an outcome, he believed, would transform the socio-political order. His method for achieving this objective was to make sure that devoted anti-fascists, particularly communists, dominated the *Spruchkammern*, which he had begun to organise. AMG discovered that the nomination lists prepared by Schmitt's five 'special representatives' throughout Bavaria – three of whom were communists – were assessed, and sometimes altered, by functionaries of the Bavarian People's

Communist Party (BVKP) before being sent on to the Special Branch for vetting. CIC agents inserted within the Bavarian Denazification Ministry also found that Schmitt's personnel chief, party comrade Max Holy, was stacking the ministerial investigatory service with communists. In early May 1946, the Americans purged the ministry, 'because it was packed almost exclusively with inefficient and inexperienced delegates of the KPD'. Holy was one of those ousted, and new appointments henceforth had to be countersigned by Hoegner and officials in the Justice Ministry. Naturally, BVKP maneuvres had also drawn howls of protest from the other political parties, which charged that Schmitt took his orders from Moscow, and the minister's position became increasingly untenable as the CSU gradually built up an unrivaled base of support in Bavaria, which foiled his master plan to have all three major political parties secure equal representation – and thus a functioning working class (SPD-BVKP) majority – in the *Spruchkammern*. Resentful of this 'parity principal', the CSU held up the organisation of most *Spruchkammern* and Dorn eventually concluded that despite his personal regard for Schmitt, the communist minister would have to be sacrificed, if only to encourage the growth of a wider consensus behind the denazification programme. After only three months on the job, Schmitt was sacked.

The new denazification minister was Anton Pfeiffer, a prominent Catholic conservative from the Bavarian Palatinate and a longtime member of the BVP. Clay characterised him as 'an old-time reactionary and a strong nationalist', although Pfeiffer was certainly no Nazi: during the war, he had actively cooperated with conservative opposition circles in the *Abwehr*. In 1945, Schäffer had appointed Pfeiffer to the Bavarian state chancellery, and he quickly emerged as a leading figure in the CSU. As noted above, the Christian Socialists had brazenly opposed the 'Law for Liberation from National Socialism', although Muller then informed the CSU chairman that the party risked American resumption of direct control over the programme and that inadequate denazification would threaten the scheduling of Bavarian elections. Officers in AMG privately discussed changing the party's leadership, although this proved unnecessary. In June 1946, the party dropped its official opposition, a concession that Pfeiffer had long been encouraging within party counsels, and Pfeiffer then fought hard to create the ministerial bureaucracy, *Spruchkammern* and *Berufungskammern* necessary to complete the purge, enjoying more success in this regard than Schmitt. In Pfeiffer's view, the 'Law for Liberation from National Socialism' was not a conventional statute – it certainly was not implemented through the regular judicial machinery – but rather it was a 'treaty' between the *Länder* and AMG. By holding up its side of the deal, the Bavarian state could prove its goodwill and its administrative capability, thus perhaps winning back some expanded degree of self-rule. In an attempt to de-politicise denazification, he recruited more jurists for the ministry and *Spruchkammern*, an approach previously opposed by Schmitt, and he also abandoned a Schmitt-devised scheme to rush 'Followers' and less-incriminated Nazis through the system first, a tactic that had aimed to have the franchise returned to hordes of such 'nominals' by the fall 1946 elections, when Schmitt had hoped they might show their appreciation to the BVKP. The Americans had opposed this strategy, although they were hardly more impressed with the way in which Pfeiffer treated Nazis. As a matter of policy, Pfeiffer launched a conscious effort to acquit 'Major Offenders' or have them shifted to lesser categories of guilt, particularly the 'Offender' category. The Americans were shocked by his estimate that only 30,000 Nazis properly fitted into categories one and two. Despite repeated warnings from the Americans, Pfeiffer's *Spruchkammern* also frequently assigned probationary terms of less than two years to 'Lesser Offenders', a dispute that owed to slight differences in wording between the English and German texts. of the 'Law for Liberation from National Socialism'. Pfeiffer snubbed members of a few communist-dominated tribunals and he was 'horrified' by the most 'severe decisions of the tribunals'. Some *Spruchkammern* carped about a lack of ministerial oversight and support, or they complained 'that the attitude of some officials appears to be that of indifference'. Under Pfeiffer's watch, Bavarian *Spruchkammer* reclassified at least sixty per cent of senior Nazis, saddling them only with minor fines, and they also exonerated more than seventy-five per cent of the officials previously dismissed by AMG. On 2 October 1946, Muller warned Hoegner that any case improperly handled by a *Spruchkammer* should be reported to AMG and then retried.

There was also considerable flux within denazification machinery of the two smaller *Länder*. In Württemberg-Baden, the apparatus was formally organised not as a ministry, but as a state secretariate in the office of the minister-president. It was led by Gottlob Kamm, a member of the SPD highly rated by the Americans, who saw him as 'the ablest denazification official in the Zone'. Baden, where the denazification programme was organised with a degree of autonomy, was less efficient than Württemberg and functionaries there were suspected of lacking in determination. The entire system was shaken at the turn of 1946/47 when Minister-President Reinhold Maier, the formal head of the purge process, was himself accused before a denazification tribunal of having supported the Enabling Act. Making this seminal choice, it will be recalled, is one of the charges that had stood so heavily against Fritz Schäffer. After a bitter party squabble, a legislative committee upheld the tribunal's jurisdiction over its own boss, although when 'Maier versus Maier' came to trial, the *Spruchkammer* exonerated the respondent on the grounds that his vote did not prejudice his position as a personal opponent of National Socialism. In the long run, Maier got to keep his job, although Germans noted the hypocrisy: many of the new elite were forgiven for their 'political errors' in 1933, while others not so favoured by AMG were punished for making the same mistakes. The state branch of the CDU then suggested handing the entire programme back over to the Americans.

In *Land* Hesse, the denazification minister, Gottlob Binder, was also a member of the SPD, although his advanced age and ill-health hindered his activities. In addition, his ministry was small and understaffed. Opinion polling suggested that Hessians were more sympathetic to the plight of 'little Nazis' than the inhabitants of any other *Land* in the U.S. zone, and that there was a considerable degree of opposition to the whole idea of denazification. Binder himself revealed that he was flummoxed by the vast scale of the programme, which involved more than three-quarters of a million Hessians, and he admitted that certain aspects of the denazification law troubled him, particularly the 1937 cut-off date. He also asked Dorn why the authorities in the other zones were able to take a liberal interpretation of Control Council directives, while in the U.S. zone they seemed carved in stone. It was a question for which there was no easy answer.

Everywhere in the American zone, the 'Germanised' version of denazification got off to a shaky start, partly because of public indifference toward a programme already discredited by American fumbling, partly because of the difficulty of finding personnel for a new form of bureaucracy. In fact, the Americans were attempting to do something in which only the Nazis themselves had shown any facility, that is, mobilize and integrate individuals who had previously remained outside politics. However, the pool of untainted people, especially with professional qualifications, was limited, and there was a definite shortage of anti-Nazi or non-Nazi lawyers and jurists, especially since a stipulation in the 'Law for Liberation' specified that *Spruchkammern* had to be chaired by judges. Many professional people worried about missing a chance to earn better money in private business or in other agencies within the *Land* bureaucracies. Some Germans willing to cooperate with the Americans preferred to work directly for the occupation garrisons or for AMG, even in positions of menial labour, where they at least earned a guaranteed meal every day, plus better rations and good wages. As the denazification machinery became flooded with clerks and day labourers, many Germans – schooled to respect authority and class hierarchies – saw a touch of the absurd in allowing such people to judge cases of respondents who were sometimes highly educated and socially prominent.

Material shortages were a problem too. Lack of office space and equipment were sometimes dire. In Augsburg, denazification officials were so desperate for office furniture and typewriters that they bartered for such materials, trading releases from denazification with local businessmen. In Aschaffenburg, the local tribunals were late in starting work, partly because personnel lacked vehicles and gasoline.

American liaison officers quarreled constantly with the *Land* denazification ministers, as the latter tried to reduce the scope of the 'Law for Liberation from National Socialism'. The Germans tried to limit the range of job restrictions and they wanted to remove the 'Follower' category from the *Spruchkammer* process. They also argued that *Amtsträger* – officials in the NSDAP and its affiliates – could qualify as *Mitläufer*; the Americans disagreed, thus giving rise to a prolonged and severe dispute. Officers of the Special Branch complained that the *Spruchkammern* were still focused on 'small fry' Nazis, to the exclusion of more important figures, although the Americans had unintentionally encouraged this mode of procedure by blocking the employment of a huge mass of less-incriminated Nazis. Naturally, the tribunals attempted to deal with this problem by denazifying the lighter cases and potentially restoring these individuals to the labour market. In Württemberg-Baden, Justice Minister Beyerle openly encouraged officials to rush less-incriminated Nazis through the *Spruchkammer* process, arguing that his ministry could hardly evade the fact that a shortage of labour was 'affecting the welfare and order of the state'.

Even as matters stood, lack of skilled labour and low-level managers left frantic employers scrambling to provide *Spruchkammern* with testimonials to the good character of their workers – these documents were dubbed '*Persilscheine*', after the name of a detergent that removed 'brown stains' – and German clergymen also worked overtime in turning out such documents. Germans also developed many ingenious methods of avoiding the labour prohibition while indicted Nazis were awaiting hearings. In some places, jobs were left open for Nazis awaiting rehabilitation, a practice that was formally illegal but was widely tolerated. Meanwhile, Nazis pending denazification often continued to perform the same job functions but with different occupational titles, or their wives formally occupied their spots. Despite the shortages of labour, some jobs simply went unfilled until they could be assumed once again by their old occupants. In one incident in 1946, a well-educated Austrian businessman – a veteran of the Tyrolean resistance movement – was stopped by U.S. border guards while trying to cross the zonal frontier into Soviet-occupied Germany. The Americans were reluctant to let such an experienced businessman leave their zone, but he informed them that he had visited a dozen firms looking for work. All these businesses had actual jobs to fill, although the positions had been formally terminated so that they could be recreated when their former occupants were able to resume working. This tactic stopped the *Arbeitsamt* from meanwhile pestering these firms with candidates for jobs that they did not wish to fill, at least not with fresh faces.

Within the *Spruchkammern* themselves, procedures were hardly models of jurisprudence. As a concession to the Germans, who sought to avoid the imposition of *ex post facto* laws, the chambers were not formally legal institutions, but quasi-political bodies, empowered to determine 'responsibility', not guilt, and then to assess proportional reparations, restrictions of rights or fines. AMG officials called them 'courts of common sense'. Prosecutions were usually launched by *Spruchkammer* prosecutors on the basis of *Meldebogen*, although in theory anyone had the right to initiate proceedings against persons otherwise cleared on the basis of their *Meldebogen* submissions. Hearings could either be public, if oral, or private, if based solely on written evidence. Respondents were allowed the right of legal counsel, although German leftists complained that the employment of such expertise gave repondents an advantage over the lay – and sometimes poorly educated – members of the tribunals. Indeed, defence lawyers were allowed to browbeat witnesses with threats of suits for slander and perjury. Final judgements by the *Spruchkammern* were decided in secret by majority vote. They were usually mild and panel members and judges often seemed to act under the duress exercised by surviving Nazis. Special Branch 'Advisory Teams', comprised partly of German Jewish émigrés with strong opinions about Nazism, provided jaw-dropping reports about *Spruchkammer* operations. According to these assessments, many tribunals ignored regulations and others were contaminated by bribes or systematic efforts to whitewash defendants. In Dingolfing, for instance, Special Branch observers rated the *Spruchkammer* prosecutor as disinterested and eager to return to his job as a trucker. He frequently failed to introduce all his evidence on respondents into hearings. The result was a consistent record of decisions wildly divergent from the spirit of the 'Law for Liberation from National Socialism'. Xaver Lang, the Nazi mayor of Reisbach during the Second World War, was found a 'Follower', even though his *Meldebogen* worksheet clearly indicated 'that he was an outstanding Nazi'. In Hofheim, a longtime SA man and Deputy *Blockleiter* was also rated as a 'Follower'. Special Branch advised the Bavarian *Land* ministry to dissolve the entire tribunal responsible for this verdict. In the first five months after the promulgation of the 'Law for Liberation from National Socialism', German tribunals eliminated 530,907 cases without trial, the vast majority of the 583,985 cases that came before the courts. In Heidelberg, Special Branch spot-checks showed that eighty per cent of incriminated persons sentenced as 'Followers' should have been placed in higher categories of guilt. American overseers also objected to the way that denazified 'Followers' were allowed back into the job market, free of any further restrictions, and they insisted on the right to review such cases. Germans argued that such a procedure would add another level of trials that had not been negotiated during talks before the 'Law for Liberation from National Socialism' was legislated.

Military Government fired a shot over the bow of the German authorities with a directive on 21 September 1946, demanding that German officials demonstrate 'political and moral qualities capable of assisting in developing genuine democratic institutions in Germany'. Special Branch had long complained that its attempts to insure 'corrective action' by the *Land* denazification ministries had been foiled by Dorn, who opposed interventions into German control of the purge, and its oversight functions were subsequently expanded particularly through development of the 'Delinquency and Error' (D&E) System, a bureaucratic process for the uniform assessment of all *Spruchkammer* decisions. AMG also bared its teeth by ordering the dissolution of a *Spruchkammer* in Munich – Special Branch had reported that it 'was hearing cases absolutely contrary to provisions of the Law for Liberation from National Socialism' – and by 'cleaning political house' in *Stadt* Giessen, where many top civic officials were removed from power for refusing to comply with the denazification law. Several weeks later, Clay lashed out at the *Länderrat* in a famous speech that encapsulated his welling set of concerns. He revealed that he

was 'sorely disappointed' with the results of denazification, and that he had personally examined 575 'Major Offender' cases put before the *Spruchkammern*, only to
discover that 355 had been reclassified as 'Followers' and that another forty-nine
had been acquitted. He announced a sixty-day review of the tribunals' conduct and
warned that without any sign of improvement, AMG would be forced to restore
direct control over the programme. This threat has often been interpreted as a bluff
– AMG manpower levels were lower than they had been a year before – but there
was a real debate within AMG about the desirability of re-assuming more direct
forms of responsibility for denazification. No one spoke of recovering full control
of the programme, but some of Clay's advisors suggested letting the *Spruchkammer*
continue to impose a range of punishments, although now subject to a form of
micro-intervention by American authorities, while AMG would decide separately
who was fit to assume positions of responsibility in private and public enterprises.
The Public Safety Branch warned that such hair-splitting would not work, and
Clay demurred, announcing on 8 January 1947 that the programme had passed the
sixty-day test. However, Special Branch could now exercise much more pressure
upon the Germans in order to correct the defects mentioned in Clay's speech,
and Clay also forbid the further reinstatement of Nazis who had released by AMG
before March 1946, an order that had the practical effect of putting teeth in the
D&E System.[35]

During 1947, the basic policies undergirding denazification shifted radically.
There were two reasons for this sea change. First, the 'Potsdam formula' had failed
to improve the quality of economic life in western Germany, where the population was facing starvation and severe shortages of heating fuel by the winter of
1946/47. Under the existing regime, Russia was supposed to provide grain and
other staples from its zone, the traditional breadbasket of Germany, while the
Anglo-Americans would reciprocate by returning reparation goods and heavy
equipment. In reality, little food ever arrived from the east, and the Russians had
already undercut the viability of any such exchange by transferring many of the
food-producing regions to administrative control of the Poles. In turn, Clay suspended the eastward movement of reparations in 1946. The ultimate consequence
of this deadlock was that American and British taxpayers were left with the huge
cost of importing food into Germany, merely in order to sustain minimal ration
levels, while the overall economic situation continued to deteriorate. Thrashing
around for a solution, the Americans had already provided official approval for
the economic rehabilitation of Germany, which was expressed in Jimmy Byrnes'
famous 'Stuttgart Speech' of 6 September 1946, and they also moved to implement the Potsdam accord, at least partially, by organising the economic fusion
of the U.S. and British zones, even if the Soviets and French as yet showed no
inclination to cooperate. By the spring of 1947, this initiative had created a new
economic unit informally called 'Bizonia'. As relations with the Soviets grew
increasingly tense, American policy-makers eventually gave up entirely on the

'Potsdam formula' and instead decided to revive Bizonia independently. The main mechanism for this initiative, the Marshall Plan, was announced by the U.S. secretary of state, George Marshall, in an address on 5 June 1947.

This large-scale and long-term endorsement of the 'welfare of the governed' theory boded ill for the denazification programme, which had always privileged ideological purity over the achievement of administrative and economic efficiency, although an AMG study commissioned by Clay in the fall of 1947 concluded that the purge was the least of many factors hindering the recovery of German businesses. In fact, Clay argued that some firms had used denazification as a means of dislodging superannuated management, and that the programme was actually a vehicle for the rationalisation and modernisation of German industry.[36] Lutz Niethammer also argues that the promotion of economic recovery led the Americans to emphasize the rehabilitation aspect of denazification, which they had formally endorsed in 1946. In Niethammer's view, the *Spruchkammern* now justified their ultimate rationale as '*Mitläuferfabrik*', that is 'Follower factories', which were involved in the 'mass production' of superficially cleansed 'Followers' (*Mitläufer*). Or as he expressed it through another metaphor, the *Spruchkammern* 'separate[d] the sheep from the goats', imposing durable disqualifications upon a small minority of Nazi 'activists', but providing practical amnesties to a much larger cohort who were intended to resume their roles in the economy and then contribute to reconstruction. In this sense, a sort of perverse success could be claimed for the policy, at least if it was judged by its own criteria of restoring 'Followers' to the wage-earning labour force.[37]

A second factor bearing upon the policy shift was the rising sense of enmity between the Anglo-Americans and Soviet Russia, which meant that each side increasingly came to regard Germany as an ideological battleground. Obviously, this new state of affairs eroded the harmony necessary to run Germany as a single political and economic unit. In February 1946, State Department official George Kennan drafted his famous 'long telegram', outlining the allegedly hostile motives behind Soviet conduct, and he quickly followed this seminal document with a cable explaining the supposed impossibility of governing Germany within any condominium that included the Russians.[38] In the November 1946 mid-term elections, Republicans won control of the House of Representatives and Senate, bringing a definitive end to the Rooseveltian era, and the Republicans (and their allies in the State Department) increasingly found Marshall, the new secretary of state, lending them an open ear. In March 1947, President Truman issued the doctrine that bears his name, promising help to countries resisting foreign aggression or internal subversion, and during the same period a 'Big Four' conference of foreign ministers in Moscow failed to arrive at long-term arrangements for the joint control of Germany. At the Moscow conference, the Soviets demanded a schedule of reparations from current production, as well as favouring a strong unitary regime for Germany, while the Americans and British wanted economic rehabilitation and the formation of a federal system of government. This impasse was never resolved, and it marked the effective termination of the 'Potsdam era' of attempted quadripartite control.

As for denazification, charges flew back and forth at the Moscow Conference about which side had done the most to undercut the programme. Marshall wanted a Control Council law based on CC Directive no.38, which would potentially apply a uniform version of denazification throughout Germany; Molotov pushed for measures in order to speed up the pace of the programme. In the final conference report, the foreign ministers ordered the Control Council to accelerate denazification and even to study the possibility of setting a termination date, while devolving responsibility for uniform application upon the zone commanders. The Americans also had to endure the insertion of uncomplimentary language about the necessity for discretion by responsible German authorities, particularly the need to avoid an 'indiscriminate trial of the mass of the nominal members of the Nazi Party'.[39]

Even before 1947, elements of the American garrison not under Clay's direct control had already begun fighting the Cold War, which naturally involved flouting denazification. While some CIC officers remained loyal to the denazification dictum, others had begun to provide assistance to *Abwehr*, SD and *Waffen*-SS officers, all of whom were in automatic arrest categories, sometimes even as their fellow agents were still attempting to apprehend such men. This practice apparently began in 1946 with the release of *Abwehr* and Gestapo officers who had been recruited as snitches in internment camps, and were then retained on contract even when they were paroled. The rationale was that Nazi security personnel who had fought communist resistance movements and Soviet spy rings purportedly had contacts and methods of operation now of value to the United States. Klaus Barbie, a sadistic Gestapo torturer who received the patronage of officers in CIC Region IV (Munich), was only the most famous of many such cases. Although Barbie had earned a gruesome reputation as the Gestapo chief in Lyon, France, where he had abused and killed scores of French resisters and Jews, American intelligence officers thought that he could play a valuable role in penetrating the French *Deuxième Bureau*, plus providing the same services against Soviet intelligence networks and the KPD. Indeed, the broader failure of denazification meant that Barbie had access to a network of Nazis and SS officers who were increasingly re-emerging at the head of local police forces, and who proved willing to help an ex-*Parteigenosse* to a much greater degree than they ever would have provided aid to the occupation forces. Thus, the CIC protected Barbie from extradition to France and eventually helped relocate him to South America, along with his family.[40] An equally disturbing story revolved around the figure of Otto von Bolschwing, an SS bureaucrat who had helped draft the guidelines for the seizure of Jewish property in Austria, and then as Himmler's representative in Bucharest, had helped orchestrate the 1941 pogrom in that city. After the end of the war, von Bolschwing was hired by the CIA, which eventually brought him to America and pressured the Immigration and Naturalisation Service into awarding him U.S. citizenship.[41]

Similarly, the U.S. Army protected Nazi scientists and technicians whose recruitment and contributions to subsequent research were rated as essential to national security. As early as 1945, the scientific exploitation programme in Germany, organised as the Field Information Agency, Technical (FIAT), was already redirecting Nazis with technical abilities away from menial jobs and offering them 'common labour' with the agency, although this prompted a complaint from AMG in *Land* Hesse, which claimed that FIAT 'may be violating denazification directives on a large scale'. Senior American headquarters subsequently punted this complaint back and forth, but nothing was done.

Worse yet, several programmes organised by the JCS, dubbed 'Overcast' and 'Paperclip', arranged the transfer of 765 German technical experts and engineers to the United States, often in flagrant disregard of denazification rules. Although these programmes were supposed to screen out objectionable Nazis, lively recruitment competition with the Russians (and the British, French and Argentines) ensured that short-cuts and exploitation of loopholes became the norm. On the other hand, such practices were brought to light at a relatively early date, when they became the object of press scrutiny, and 'Paperclip' was also plagued by the obstruction of liberals in the State Department, who refused to provide visas in a timely fashion. Wanting to regularize the status of its scientists, the War Department eventually asked Clay if he would mind Nazi scientists being tried by *Spruchkammern in absentia*, although Clay responded that they should be either returned to Germany and forced through the regular process or simply kept in the United States illegally. He would not, however, sanction special treatment that would no doubt be made a *cause célèbre* by leftists working within the denazification machinery. After Marshall became secretary of state, he broke the logjam by telling his immigration officers to judge the scientists' visa claims on the basis of national security merit rather than the claimants' prior membership in the NSDAP or its auxiliaries. 'Paperclip' director Bosquet Wev noted that, 'Nazism should no longer be a serious consideration from the point of view of national security when the far greater threat of Communism is now jeopardising the entire world.' Several of the 'Paperclip' scientists were nearly the nefarious equals of Barbie and von Bolschwing. Arthur Rudolph, the onetime operations director of V-2 production at the Mittelwerk facility in central Germany, had systematically abused concentration camp prisoners working at the plant and was probably directly involved in the hanging of twelve foreign labourers on charges of sabotage. Although Rudolph had long been a member of the NSDAP and in 1945 was recommended for internment as a '100 per cent Nazi, dangerous type', he was brought to the United States and later designed the Saturn V rocket that carried American astronauts to the moon.[42]

Within AMG itself there was increased grumbling about Clay's obstinacy in dealing with denazification, partly because it was feared that the Soviets would hurriedly end their own programme and thereby trump the United States. The pace of the purge had actually diminished over the winter of 1946/47, when extreme cold and heavy snow had interfered with transport and the heating of public buildings. In Berlin, denazification panels lacked even the paper necessary to make reports to Allied officials and thus finalize their decisions. Over 200,000 cases had been heard, but another 1.3 million were still on the docket. The CIC warned that widespread resentment of denazification was in danger of mutating into a more general resistance movement. Despair reigned supreme. Perhaps worst of all, a short-term improvement in *Spruchkammer* performance, evident after Clay's November 1946 speech, evaporated after it became clear that Clay did not intend to re-impose direct AMG control. Thereafter, month by month, the categorising process grew steadily more lenient. In April 1947, Walter Dorn suggested that the implementation of a lengthy policy opposed by a large majority of Germans was no longer feasible, at least in unadulterated form, and that the labour provisions of the 'Law for Liberation from National Socialism' were devastating German society. Periodic meetings of the *Länderrat* denazification committee became forums for a protracted battle of attrition between military government liaison officers and resistant *Land* ministers. Worse yet, the German political parties began requesting that their members withdraw from the denazification process. Clay, however, stood firm. As late as 5 August 1947, he was threatening the *Land* premiers with a resumption of direct AMG control over the programme, and he also advised that denazification was a necessary precursor to German economic recovery.[43]

It was external currents that eventually forced Clay to shift his stance. A Cold War atmosphere now came to permeate AMG, and Washington became much more willing to intervene in Germany on a regular basis. As Clay's biographer notes, 'The winds of history had shifted.'[44] While JCS 1067 included six paragraphs devoted to denazification, the directive that superceded it, JCS 1779, included only one sentence, which ordered implementation of the decision taken by the foreign ministers at Moscow.[45] A derivative of the Marshall Plan, JCS 1779 was issued on 11 July 1947 and marked the official end of the 'harsh' phase of occupation. A month later, the new secretary of the army, Kenneth Royall, arrived in Germany with a fresh message for Clay: wrap up denazification as quickly as possible. In fact, Royall would have brought an immediate stop to the process – the Russians had indeed raised the stakes by announcing the imminent cessation of their version of the programme – but Clay was still resistant, arguing that many cases were yet pending and that, in any case, Germans were now doing most of the work (although they were also doing most of the complaining). Clay did agree, however, to launch a drive to complete denazification by 1 April 1948.

On 9 September 1947, only a month after bitterly berating the *Land* premiers about denazification, Clay told the three leaders that he was conceding many of their demands, particularly those introduced in the 'Heidenheim Proposals' of 30 June 1947, upon which all the *Land* denazification ministers were agreed. 'Followers' would now be allowed to work in the private sector while awaiting *Spruchkammer* hearings, and prosecutors could exercise independent initiative in reclassifying offenders, usually from higher to lower grades of guilt, rather than waiting for tribunals to undertake such re-categorising. In addition, charges would henceforth be laid on the basis of evidence rather than categorical pigeon-holing, with members of the SS, the SD and the Gestapo – the groups declared criminal at Nuremberg – providing the only exceptions. These accommodations cut in half the anticipated completion time and reduced the number of cases in the higher classifications from 750,000 to 250,000. On 13 September, Clay also loosened limits on the number of ex-Nazis admitted as students into German universities, a level that had previously been set at a maximum of ten per cent per institution.

By early 1948, denazification was still lagging behind schedule, and a congressional sub-committee of the House Select Committee on Foreign Aid unanimously recommended tying up the programme by 8 May 1948, perhaps by amnestying all 'Followers' and 'Lesser Offenders' and then concentrating on the two worst categories of guilt. Led by Christian Herter, a prominent Republican proponent of the Marshall Plan, members of the sub-committee had toured the U.S. occupation zone in the fall of 1947. Their conclusion was that 'American denazification policy went too far and tried to include too many. Its categorisation was too broad and too rapidly applied…' After 8 May, they advised, the Germans should be given complete autonomy to handle the programme in whatever fashion they chose. Royall pressed these suggestions upon Clay, who finally capitulated in the face of overwhelming compulsion from his political masters. Clay and his advisors then considered several courses of action, including a complete cancellation of denazification and a broad amnesty covering nearly all Nazis. However, they finally decided upon a crash programme that was intended to reach the end of the line within sixty days. In order to expedite the process, Special Branch officers would take a closer hand in the proceedings and would provide transport in order to move suspects to trials.

Most importantly, Clay authorised his Public Safety czar, Theo Hall, to meet with the *Land* denazification ministers and encourage them to bring matters to a hasty conclusion. In a conclave in Stuttgart on 19 March 1948, Hall admitted that denazification had tried everyone's patience and that any public appetite for the programme, either in America or Germany, had disappeared. The denazification ministers had long been complaining of problems that the Americans were now willing to concede, but in an episode that John Gimbel describes as one of the great role reversals in the history of the occupation, the Germans now claimed that they needed more time to finish the programme! In particular, they had dealt with relatively minor – and therefore simple – cases initially, but the proverbial big fish were still on the line, and much preparation had gone into these cases. In addition, they argued that an unseemly dash for the finish line would antagonize a surviving group of leftist activists who had invested much hope in the programme and still hoped for its success. Hall brushed aside such considerations and suggested that pending Marshall Plan aid was dependent on German devotion to the principle of economic and administrative efficiency. After much to and fro, several 'schnell' reforms were introduced. First, German prosecutors secured full discretion in filing charges; second, pre-trial restrictions on employment were lifted for 'Offenders' (although such people were allowed jobs only in the private sector); third, prosecutors were allowed to independently assess fines for 'Followers', thus avoiding a trial; and fourth, Spruchkammern were permitted to limit sentences in consideration of time already served in detention or as a consequence of suspension of employment since 1945. In addition the 'schnell' reforms nearly did away with class III, which had always been a provisional category in which respondents were forced to serve out a term of probation or pay fines before being finally categorised in either class II or class IV (in practice, almost always the latter). Prosecutors could now slot Nazi 'activists' directly into the 'Follower' category, with no intervening probationary period. A sense of how this system subsequently worked is provided by an assessment by two senior AMG officers in Hesse, 'Under the recent acceleration proceedings adopted by OMGUS, many highly incriminated individuals are now being found followers. This is a natural result since the prosecution is not allowed an opportunity to investigate the cases adequately and must grind out follower certificates. This is probably necessary under present world conditions … [but] we must not delude ourselves into thinking that the certificate made such people democrats.'

Despite the 'schnell' reforms, there were still over 28,000 cases of Nazi hardliners awaiting trial on 1 May 1948, and there was paperwork yet to be submitted for a much larger number of cases. AMG was concerned that if the programme continued to drag along, it would embarrass the West German government due to be formed in 1949, but the issue was now felt to fall wholly within the realm of the Land denazification ministries.[46] As denazification staffs and Special Branch teams were dissolved, it became normal practice for Spruchkammern to review hurriedly cases of hardcore Nazis in the 'Major Offender' and 'Offender' categories and then slap such individuals with minor fines, a standard of punishment often less severe than that imposed upon 'Mitläufer' in 1946/47.[47] Naturally, this process created a sense of ill-treatment amongst minor Nazis who had been brought to trial early, and even the U.S. State Department admitted that the lack of substantial punishment for high-level Nazis created 'a threat to the development of democratic processes in Germany'.[48]

Despite such criticism, two good things can be said about the programme. First, many of the 'major' Nazis denazified late in the process had to spend a much longer time than their 'minor' colleagues in internment camps, so that even if eventual penalties were light, they already had considerable 'time served', often in uncomfortable circumstances. And second, the most senior Nazis, such as former *Gauleiter*, *Kreisleiter* and SS leaders, might eventually have secured prosecution in lower categories of guilt, but they were sufficiently proscribed that they later found it difficult to regain positions of significant rank or authority in German society. Studies of the long-term impact of denazification uopn German leadership circles have suggested that political elites were the most affected strata, certainly much more than civil servants or the business management class.[49]

In addition to the problems caused by the last-minute rush, the plan to terminate denazification was bedeviled by the constant trickle of released PoWs and German refugees into the country. As a result, new registrants numbered nearly 14,000 per month from October 1949 to September 1950. Nonetheless, by the early fall of 1950 there were only 1,740 cases still pending, and the U.S. High Commission, the successor to AMG, was pleased when the lower house of the German parliament requested that the *Land* governments wrap up the programme by April 1951.[50]

The total number of Germans registered and tried under the U.S. zone denazification programme looks large, at least superficially, but the impact of the figures pales under closer scrutiny. More than 13 million Germans were registered and five years after the end of the war, 958,000 had been tried. Of this group, however, less than 25,000 were rated as a 'Major Offender' or 'Offender', a number suggesting that an extremely limited cadre had organised the conquest and manhandling of Europe under the Nazi banner! A quantity twenty-five times as large – 595,000 people – were classified as 'Lesser Offenders' or 'Followers', and in another 321,000 cases proceedings resulted in exonerations or were abandoned. Over half a million people were punished, but most – 573,000 – were fined. Until the currency reform in mid-1948, fines could be paid in *Reichsmark* that were all but worthless, while the real wealth of many Nazis was then held in cigarettes or Black Market commodities. According to one AMG estimate, one third of Nazi Party members in the U.S. zone – about five per cent of the total population – had lost jobs at one point or another between 1945 and 1947, usually due to denazification, although nearly all members of this group were employed again by the fall of the latter year. Over 23,000 people were banned permanently from public office, but as we shall see, many people affected by such restrictions regained full privileges after the restoration of West German autonomy. Over 27,000 people suffered seizure of property and over 30,000 were sentenced to community service. After moving through the system, fewer than 10,000 Nazis were detained in labour camps, and by 1950 only seventy-three of these people were still being held.[51]

So what are we to conclude about the American version of denazification? The pattern of the story is not hard to discern: U.S. troops came to Germany equipped with a series of denazification directives that were difficult to implement, but each time bureaucratic resistance – both American and German – undercut execution of these policies, successive waves of public scandal encouraged bouts of radical enforcement. This unedifying spectacle impressed neither advocates nor opponents of the programme, although only the advent of the Cold War was sufficient to bring it to an end.

As for the functional value of denazification, there is no doubt that the initial round of mass incarcerations helped suffocate potential 'Werewolf' activity, and it is likely that the efficiency of German business was not badly harmed – and was perhaps even helped – by dismissals of Nazis from senior positions. It is possible that American devotion to a sweeping programme of danazification demonstrated a laudable dedication to securing democratic goals in Germany, but this was not the impression made upon most Germans. As Harold Zink notes, the final results involved numbers roughly similar to those envisioned in early GCU studies and documents, although the roundabout and obviously dysfunctional means of reaching this goal diminished American prestige and influence. Moreover, the time and energy poured into denazification distracted American authorities from other objectives, many of which were more positive in nature.[52] And finally it can be added that the model of the 'spoils system', much cited in the Special Branch as a means of shifting personnel without undertaking social revolution, ultimately proved an inadequate means of securing the goals that the Americans had originally set for the denazification programme.[53]

3

A MODEST PURGE

If Americans had customarily endowed their wars with a revolutionary or messianic aspect, no such tendency existed among the British. In British domestic custom, there was no recent tradition of forcibly displacing existing centres of authority, and Britain's long history as an imperial power had taught conservative lessons, a fact recognized by the former colonial administrators so plentifully situated through the ranks of British military government in Germany. German socialist leader Kurt Schumacher was only half joking when he said that he feared the independence of India because a mass of redundant colonial officialdom would thereafter descend upon his country. Veterans of empire, however, were well aware that experiments in changing the nature of other societies and cultures, such as attempted by Thomas Babington Macaulay in nineteenth-century India, had often provided negative results, while efforts to govern through existing structures had frequently proven more feasible. British control of the Egyptian legal system and of Indian schools were studied as a possible precedents for practices in occupied Germany, and British military government actually tried (unsuccessfully) to lure away the Government of India's Education Officer and appoint him as its own specialist on school reform. Indeed, one officer in military government later recalled that 'we seemed to have become District Officers on the model of the old Colonial Service', and the very notion of the 'political officer', who in Germany provided the military governor with advice and owed loyalty to the Foreign Office, was an imperial innovation that had first developed in India and was meant to provide a mechanism for cultivating relations with local centres of power. Especially in ruling peoples of European descent, imperial officials had long recognized that tolerance provided superb grease for the machinery of governance, and they took pride in the fact that liberal parliamentarianism had mollified even quarrelsome Boer South Africans and French Canadians. Such cases provided particular models for the occupation of northwestern Germany.[1] And indeed, a few prominent policy-makers, such as Richard Crossman, formerly deputy chief of the SHAEF PW unit and in 1945 a newly-minted Labour MP, argued that north-west Germany ought to be added to the Empire. This idea had some support amongst Germans, particularly the conservatives in the Lower Saxony Party (NLP), who emphasized Hanover's traditional relationship with the United Kingdom, but the latter – increasingly weary of empire and exhausted by six years of war – opted to establish a temporary residence, rule through a form of indirect control and eventually withdraw. As Bernard Montgomery, the British military governor, later noted, 'It would be useless to try to make Germans like unto ourselves, as some people wanted to do; our aim should be rather to turn them into good and right-thinking Germans.'[2]

While Britain suffered under the impact of German bombing, V-1 and V-2 attacks and submarine warfare, the country never experienced the 'wildfire of revenge' kindled in the United States, nor was there a revival of the visceral anti-Germanism that had swept the nation during the First World War. Tellingly, the main British advocate of a harsh peace, Lord Robert Vansittart, was more charitable than his American counterpart, Henry Morgenthau. Vansittart also lacked the institutional power of Morgenthau. Although he had once been Permanent Undersecretary in the Foreign Office, where he had fought the appeasement trend of the 1930s, after 1941 he was merely a retired civil servant with a peerage. Thus, he had to charge the ramparts from the exterior, introducing motions in the House of Lords and trying to sway public opinion through the publication of inflammatory books and press articles. Despite many institutional obstacles, he did have some impact, aided by steadily increasing revelations of Nazi ruthlessness and genocidal barbarity. Once the British public disabused itself of the notion that an anti-Hitler uprising would bring the war to an end – Labour supporters had expected much of the German proletariat, while Tories had once hoped for something from Hermann Goering and the generals of the *Wehrmacht* – opinion on the 'German Question' tended to harden. Although Britons remained little influenced by ideological or moral interpretations of the war, they largely subscribed to Vansittart's claim that Nazism was an intensification of traditional German nationalism and militarism, and that some manner of electroshock therapy was necessary in order to change German 'national character'. Even Churchill publically subscribed to this idea. In August 1944, opinion polling showed that eighty per cent of Britons supported a relatively 'hard' peace, and majorities throughout 1944 favoured the imposition of a post-war reparations bill and the possible partitioning of Germany into smaller countries. Vansittart also promised that while all Germans would be held to account, Nazis would be 'specially remembered' – 'Not just the big shots but the "small squirts" as well.' On the other hand, only one-third of those polled wanted Allied treatment of Germany based upon the principle of vengeance, and Noel Coward scored a hit song with 'Don't Let's Be Beastly to the Germans'.[3]

Official opinion largely reflected this broader understanding of Germany's future, although it was rather more sensitive to practical considerations.[4] Unlike the Americans, the British put lengthy study into the matter and had devoted considerable bureaucratic machinery to its resolution. The Armistice Terms and Civil Administration Committee, a Cabinet-level body to coordinate occupation policy, was established in August 1943, more than a year before its American equivalent, and in April 1944 this panel was reorganised as the Armistice and Post-War Committee (APW). The APW was chaired by the deputy prime minister and Labour Party leader, Clement Attlee, and literally became a foreign policy school for Attlee and his Labourite colleague Ernest Bevin, who was minister of labour. In order to provide bureaucratic support to the APW, a panel of senior civil servants, the Official Committee on Armistice Terms and Civil Administration (ACAO) was also set up, replacing an earlier interdepartmental committee that had been functioning since 1942.[5] The ACAO was organised, chaired and dominated by the permanent under-secretary of war, Sir Frederick Bovenshen, a stubborn and dedicated civil servant who took a special interest in matters of military government and was determined to preserve War Office dominance of this field. Members of the ACAO spent much of their time reviewing papers forwarded by the Foreign Office, the War Office and other government departments, and then advancing approved policy along to the APW. Under Bovenshen's direction, they set the tone for British occupation policy, which was sensitive to the practices prescribed by tradition and by the Hague Conventions, and which was informed by a sense of Britain's dire economic plight and the resultant difficulty of establishing a massive presence in occupied Germany. Planners hoped that Germans would experience a shockingly massive defeat, which would presumably deliver a salutary lesson, and that this short yet sharp process would be followed by a peace of reconciliation. Certain British agencies, like the Chiefs of Staff, were already beginning to worry about the threat of Soviet post-war expansion, which in turn demanded the rapid stabilisation of non-communist Europe and the possible cultivation of western Germany as an ally. On the other hand, British policy did admit an unprecedented need to interfere in the affairs of the conquered enemy, mainly to 'bring home' the failure of Nazism and facilitate 'the abolition of the Nazi system'. It was especially for this reason that the mid-level planners recommended the total occupation of Germany, a proposal then given tripartite approval at the Moscow Conference in October-November 1943.[6]

British planning for Germany reflected many of the priorities evident in U.S. State and War Department schemes, particularly in its concern with the economic, territorial and governmental nature of Germany's ultimate disposition. However, the British also focused on 'political re-education', certainly much more than their American allies. Nicholas Pronoy argues that while the U.S. and the Soviet Union were absorbed with the prospects of materially diminishing German power through deindustrialisation and dismemberment, 'the British alternative … was to go for the mind instead of the body', which meant winning over Germans to a course of philosophical pragmatism, constitutionalism and respect for the rule of law. Academics in the Foreign Office Research Department (FORD) originally launched such planning, so there was a special focus on reforming German universities, particularly by breaking down the class barriers that had limited admission, re-connecting scholarship with social needs and introducing a new spirit of internationalism. The notion of purging German professors figured into such plans – an interdepartmental working party drew up 'black', 'grey' and 'white' lists – but such measures were felt to be far from sufficient in achieving the intended outcome. Along with changes in primary and secondary education, university-level reforms were regarded as the essential method of influencing normative attitudes. Planners in the Political Warfare Executive (PWE) also considered censorship and the reorientation of German media as a means of shaping public opinion. Planning for such projects began in 1942 and had reached APW by 1944, where they were endorsed enthusiastically. Central to the entire effort was a liberal tenet of non-intervention, which was considered more desirable than ramming reforms down the throats of German educators and opinion-makers. 'We should appear,' said a cabinet paper, 'to guide rather than lead, to influence rather than to initiate.' Obviously, this approach reflected principles of indirect rule that had worked so well in the colonies. On 3 July 1944, APW approved a 'Draft Directive on Re-Education', and a month later it passed a 'Memorandum on Control and Censorship of Public Information'. Despite superficial similarities to the American model, the essential understanding of denazification signaled by these directives was distinct. In the British view, true denazification – psychological and spiritual denazification – would result from a change in the German mind rather than from a mere removal of undesirable personnel or a shift of elites.

Despite such high-minded intentions, the British still had to deal with the distasteful reality of purging Nazi placeholders, however much this necessity played a subsidiary role in their thinking. The course of denazification planning was heavily influenced by T.H. Marshall, a professor at the London School of Economics and head of FORD's German Section. Although a socialist who fervently believed that Germany's future lay with democratic collectivism, Marshall had an approach that differed radically from his Washington counterparts in the R&A branch. Because of his instinctive pragmatism, Marshall saw the potential problems of the occupation more clearly than many of his contemporaries. He argued that the Western Powers would not be able to force reforms upon the Germans,[7] and that they might find themselves forced to make use even of Nazi corporatist organisations, such as the Reich Food Estate. Moreover, Marshall pointed out that it would be impossible to replace many Nazi Party members who were equipped with technical skills or administrative expertise, even despite the theoretical desirability of purging such people. In addition, a broad purge policy might be potentially unfair: the average German bureaucrat, 'may have joined [the party] in order to have a chance at a promotion, and latterly he could not have entered the civil service at all without being a party member'. Marshall also added that only senior civil servants were policy-makers; the role of mid-echelon personnel was solely administrative and such functionaries would presumably follow orders provided by any legitimate source of power. Thus, he concluded, there could be no 'exact rules' regarding dismissals. Broad guidelines could be provided, but the best practice would be to leave discretion in the hands of local British officers. Obviously, he pointed out, officials of banned organisations would have to be automatically dismissed, plus the most senior rank of civil servants: state secretaries, Reich Labour Trustees, ministerial directors, provincial presidents, district presidents and *Oberbürgermeister* of major towns. Automatic internment would apply to cabinet ministers and special commissioners, *Reichsleiter, Gauleiter, Kreisleiter* and officials in the party organisation at the level of department head or higher. As Lothar Ketternacker notes, the key question revolved around what categories of German civil servants (*Beamter*) should be suspended, a lively issue because German bureaucrats still elicited some degree of professional respect from their British counterparts.

While career diplomats little appreciated the socialism of Marshall and his colleagues, Marshall's inherent caution deeply influenced the position of the German Advisory Section in the Foreign Office, which was led by John Troutbeck. As early as 1943 Troutbeck warned of an overly extensive purge, which he felt would 'lead us into incurring greater responsibility for administration than is wise or necessary'. One of Marshall's papers on conditions in the post-surrender period was adopted by the German Advisory Section in March 1944, with Con O'Neill, Troutbeck's deputy, arguing that it supplied 'admirable' conclusions to the 'hideously complex subject' of denazification, although even O'Neill did not want to dismiss state secretaries or ministerial directors. 'If there is no Central Government…,' he argued, 'these will be the really key men, and we shall want their cooperation if we can get it without too greatly compromising ourselves.' Edward Playfair, a Treasury official, felt even more strongly in this regard, contending that 'many of these officials are career civil servants but though they may have joined the Party are not necessarily Nazi at heart'. In fact, Playfair opposed even the dismantling of the German Government. Surprisingly, it was the War Office that pushed back: 'We do not want to set up such men merely for the sake of easy administrative or economic convenience. They are unscrupulous opportunists. Their dismissal is necessary to make it clear that a complete break is being made with the Nazi system.' After the various departments had arrived at a compromise – state secretaries and ministerial directors were all to be dismissed, but they could be rehired on an individual basis – Marshall's paper eventually became the basis of War Office Directive Number 7, which was issued in October 1944 as part of a package of thirty-eight orders collectively called *Policy Directives for Allied Commanders in Chief*. Like the American directive JCS 1067, this series was intended to serve the period after the dissolution of SHAEF.[8]

In Britain, bureaucrats in the Foreign and War Offices usually dominated the process of policy formation, operating through a committee system that tended to make policy both rational and representative. However, the tension between mid-echelon planners and political leaders, so evident in Washington, was also a factor, and the same tendency toward 'hard' viewpoints emerged at the political level. Indeed, the opinions of some Labour ministers grew increasingly draconian, particularly those of former anti-appeasers in the 'social patriotic' or 'conservative' wing of the Labour Party. As early as 1940, such elements had largely abandoned hopes for a popular revolution in Germany, although Attlee continued to wonder whether the Germans should be left simply to deal with their own warmongers. By 1944, however, the feelings of some Labour ministers were drifting in the same direction as their liberal counterparts in Washington, such as Morgenthau and Roosevelt, and conservative Labourites represented as much of a 'tough' policy as developed in the senior echelon of the British government. Attlee, for instance, complained that the War Office appeared ready 'to deal with Germans who can "keep order" in the post-surrender chaos', and he griped that the Foreign Office seemed eager to reestablish the prewar Germany. He personally preferred seeing Germany dismembered and he wanted sweeping reforms – a virtual revolution – despite potentially massive economic dislocation. Hugh Dalton, the president of the Board of Trade, had once counted Vansittart as an advisor and had rejected the 'two Germanies' concept as early as 1939. He favoured a reparations policy so harsh that it resembled the Morgenthau Plan. A hardline document drafted by Dalton, which reflected the 'collective guilt' theme and took to task the German people, was adopted by Labour's National Executive Council and approved at the party's 1944 annual conference.[9]

Although such flourishes were usually ignored by mid-level policy-makers, Labour ministers on APW did manage to toughen the wording of War Office Order Number 7. When they reviewed an early draft in June 1944, they complained about Marshall's apparently lenient tone toward dismissals and also observed that there was too much reliance on making use of Nazi organisations. Foreign and War Office planners revised the document accordingly, eventually providing – for instance – for the internment of over 90,000 Nazi officials. However, Anthony Eden, the Foreign Secretary, stanchly defended the direction of planning in his ministry and Troubeck managed to preserve the principle of practical necessity as a means for keeping otherwise suspect individuals in office.[10]

Churchill and his small circle of advisors, many of them former opponents of appeasement, also provided a problem. Unfortunately, the British prime minister shared FDR's dislike of detailed planning for future contingencies, and as Dalton groused, 'recent victories have made him less, rather than more, disposed to think in concrete terms of post-war plans'. The Foreign Office especially resented such vacillation, but by 1943 Churchill's dominance in foreign affairs was diminishing. His penchant for dynamic leadership and inspiring rhetoric had once been crucial, but the heroic phase of the war was now over and new factors were coming to bear, particularly the need to accommodate Labour ministers, as public opinion within Britain shifted leftwards, and also the need to engage the Americans, who were increasingly emerging as the dominant Allied power.[11] At a crucial juncture in 1944, Churchill and some of his counselors, including Minister of Information Brendan Bracken and scientific advisor Frederick Lindemann, backed the Morgenthau Plan, even in the face of bitter opposition by the War Cabinet and the Foreign Office. This experiment in radicalism came close to upsetting existing policies. Warren Kimball is right in pointing out that Churchill's attraction to Morgenthauism was anything but perfunctory, as has sometimes been claimed, and that in addition to endorsing the plan at Quebec, he enthusiastically promoted it when visiting Stalin in mid-October 1944. Fortunately, longtime friends such as Jan Christian Smuts subsequently began talking sense to the prime minister, raising both pragmatic and humanitarian arguments to which he seemed increasingly willing to listen.[12] Nonetheless, British policy-makers momentarily teetered between two courses: a deindustrialised and dismembered Germany that would satisfy Britain's security concerns, or an economically strong Germany that would serve the nation's economic and financial interests.[13] Despite such tensions, however, the development of British policy was never driven to extremes by the imperative of a fierce inter-departmental battle, quite unlike the concurrent drift of policy formation in the United States.[14]

While the attention of certain ministers was captured by shiny baubles and schemes, Whitehall bureaucrats continued to pursue a reasonably steady course. One of their functions was to review the work of the German Country Unit. Until the summer of 1944, bureaucratic snafues often prevented British feedback to SHAEF from reaching its intended destination in the GCU. Despite this lack of coordination, the Shrivenham planners rarely advanced policies contrary to British designs, although Troutbeck had already begun to complain about proposals that challenged a central assumption of British planning, which called for the suspension of Nazi officials and their subsequent reinstatement if investigation revealed that such placeholders were 'acceptable'.[15] However, the real fireworks began after R&A, Eisenhower's office and the U.S. Treasury Department all started having an impact on occupation planning. The ACAO blocked the introduction of radical changes into CCS 551 and also managed to limit the revisions in the SHAEF *Handbook* flyleaf. In the first case, the British resented the 'sweeping denazification' proposal advanced by the Americans, instead favouring restraint 'in the interest of administrative convenience'; in the second, they regarded potential limitations on the use of Nazi organisations as 'too sweeping … and impracticable'.[16] In addition, Churchill may have approved the Morgenthau Plan at the Quebec Conference, but the Americans discovered in the autumn of 1944 that British planning papers continued to lack any mention of 'the elimination or destruction of heavy industry', and that when engaged in conversation, 'British officials seem strongly opposed to sweeping measures of de-industrialisation'.[17]

It will also be recalled that the British refused to accept JCS 1067 as the basis of a joint Anglo-American directive, partly because their policy papers were not as strict about the widespread elimination of Nazis and Nazi sympathisers, partly because they felt that 1067 had lost track of positive objectives.[18] The initial British response was to suggest using the pre-surrender directive – CCS 551 – in the post-war period, although this proposal was quickly rejected by the Americans, mainly because the directive's denazification clauses were not sufficiently comprehensive.[19] The British then devised a draft 'interim directive' of their own making, which was circulated in June 1945 and was superficially similar to the American version, although it contained subtle differences. Obviously, the British agreed to dissolving the NSDAP and suppressing Nazi propaganda, but with regard to purge measures, they declined to define the category of Nazis who were 'more than nominal participants', thus implicitly leaving a great degree of discretion in the hands of the theatre commander or the military governor. In addition, they neglected to include a reference to dropping 'active supporters of Nazism' (although 1067 featured such a stipulation), they made no mention of 'excluding' people from office (as well as 'removing' them), their description of persons liable to dismissal in private enterprise referred only to 'positions of major responsibility' (which was more specific than a U.S. reference to 'positions of importance'), and they refused to reassert the need to denazify even despite questions of 'administrative necessity' (although this point was deliberately stressed in 1067). Finally, they introduced a new provision suggesting that, 'Germans who are permitted to remain in, or are appointed to, official posts (e.g. in the police or the administration) should understand that they hold office only during good behavior'.[20] This language was later picked up by the U.S. State Department, in an apparent attempt to mollify the British, and was included in the American draft directive introduced at Potsdam, where it was promptly denounced by Molotov as a possible loophole for the retention of Nazis.

Despite Whitehall's success in limiting the impact of American thinking upon joint planning, British troops were still subject to SHAEF directives that reflected a U.S. inspired toughness, and their occupation garrison was formally bound by the Potsdam decisions and by Control Council laws 24 and 38. Formality, however, was a different matter than practice, particularly in the case of the quadripartite regulations, which were so long in coming that the British – plus the Russians and the French – had already developed their own *modus operandi*. The British, as Ian Turner notes, lacked 'the missionary zeal of the Americans'. In July 1945, Field Marshall Montgomery denounced the draconian nature of SHAEF regulations, which were lapsing, and British military government also disclaimed any intention of copying the 7 July orders, which had just gone into effect in the U.S. zone, calling them, 'far beyond anything we should regard as practicable'. In fact, the salad days for the British way of doing things came in the summer and autumn of 1945, during the interim between SHAEF and the imposition of quadripartite control. Of course, the Potsdam decisions became operative in August 1945, but these were vague enough to allow a range of interpretation. In the following month, British military government introduced a *Directive on the Arrest and Removal of Nazis from Office*, which was drafted jointly by the Public Safety Branch and Field Security. The *Directive on Arrest and Removal* revived the old Marshall formula, allowing field commanders a broad degree of discretion in arranging dismissals. The number of people in the compulsory removal categories was narrowed, and the number of arrests was also limited by introducing a new category called 'compulsory investigation', which suggested that certain ranks of Nazis merited mandatory investigation, but not necessarily arrest. Such persons, however, could only be retained in office for one month, pending the results of enquiries. Senior ranks of the civil service, which had previously been in compulsory arrest and removal classes, were shifted to the 'compulsory investigation' category. Even once CC laws 24 and 38 were passed, the spirit of the *Directive on Arrest and Removal*, if not its letter, remained the guide for British denazification practice.[21]

As in the U.S. zone, the nature of the people who ran denazification was also a matter of crucial importance. Most of Montgomery's top officers were combat veterans who had been shifted to military government, even including 'sand in the shoes' warhorses who had been with the field marshal since North Africa. 'Monty', recalled one general, 'wouldn't have any non-campaigners in Germany's post-war government.' Fortunately, the most prominent of these men, General Gerald Templer, was a figure of outstanding perception and political sensitivity (he eventually went on to lead the successful British campaign against communist partisans in Malaya). Templer became the functional chief of British military government. However, some combat commanders took actual pride in their lack of civil affairs training or political finesse. Richard Brett-Smith, for instance, later bragged that he and his cohorts were little concerned with 'catching out' a local gas works manager or harbour-master; rather, 'we relied … upon the rule of thumb and common sense, and left Germans who knew their business get on with it'. Like the Americans, the British had organised a college to train specialists in military government – this institution functioned at a former women's normal school in Wimbledon – but few of these men reached Germany, and those who did were often relegated to minor posts. In 1946, there was also a flood of civilians who came to man the control machinery for German industry. However, the combat veterans, the Wimbledon alumni and the civilians were all essentially the same kind of people: conservative, middle class, often bigoted, functionally unilingual and easily impressed by English-speaking Germans who appeared as paragons of *bürgerlich* respectability, but were sometimes Nazis or extreme nationalists. Although intelligence officers tended to take a tough line with Nazis, most British officials worried that German unrest would aid the advance of communism and they suggested that order had to be restored as quickly as possible. Once ensconced in north-western Germany, such men became comfortable with Germans like themselves, and in Westphalia they followed the now-discredited practice of getting help from the local Catholic bishop in choosing officials. Denazification tended to progress faster and farther in locations, such as Arnsberg, where the occupiers found German bureaucrats who were eager to denazify their own ranks and undertook most of the work. In most cases, British officers had established friendly relations with German officials, whence digging into their pasts became an unwanted embarrassment. Since British officers were frequently out of their depth in dealing with transportation systems, public health facilities and utilities, they usually developed a protective attitude toward German technical experts, whose abilities provided the difference between success and failure in performing assigned missions.[22]

A good example of such tendencies occurred in January 1946, when Captain Delaney, a peacetime schoolmaster, berated the fire chief of the British Sector in Berlin because the latter had shown the temerity to sack a Nazi subordinate named Poppek. Although the fire chief was a Social Democrat who had lost his job during the NS-*Zeit* and had spent two years in Oranienburg concentration camp, Poppek had greeted him with a Nazi salute and a '*Heil* Hitler' salutation, which the chief naturally regarded as 'a provocation'. Delaney, however, was outraged by the chief's supposedly 'high-handed behaviour', which had resulted in an unsanctioned firing. 'I'd rather have a smart Nazi than a slovenly run fire station,' he snarled. 'Anyway, what have fire-fighting and politics to do with each other? Poppek ran a tight ship. His station was the most efficient in the whole sector.' Only with the threatened resignation of the fire chief and his district officers did Delaney back down, particularly since he could envisioned negative press headlines and a Soviet propaganda feast.[23]

It is also worth noting that British soldiers and administrators chose to regard denazification as a security policy, which Ian Turner sees as an outgrowth of the 'collective guilt' perception. This reasoning suggests that because nearly all Germans were guilty of supporting militarism and extreme nationalism, it was useless to pursue a significant mass of the population, but made better sense to target a dangerous few who actually posed a physical and administrative danger to the occupation. The deputy military governor of the British zone, General Brian Robertson, conceded as much in March 1947, and another officer with British military government later remembered that security concerns provided the rationale for assigning denazification to the Public Safety Branch of military government.[24] In fact, the chief of the Public Safety Branch, Colonel Gerald Halland, was a highly decorated British policeman and former Inspector of Constabularies. He tried to form a 'Special Branch' that would be staffed largely with British 'bobbies', who would purge Nazis, vet their replacements and then prevent a Nazi revival from installing such people back into power. From a distance, this seemed a reasonable course, although Tom Bower claims that Halland's efforts collapsed within days of his arrival in Germany in May 1945. Although Halland originally approached his task with a great degree of determination, he lacked personnel – British military government was initially short of manpower – and in April 1945 it was estimated that Public Safety Branch elements in Germany were already short by 210 officers, and that police specialists were at a premium. General Eisenhower promised to back 21st Army Group's efforts to get more men, but when Halland arrived in Germany he had just twenty former policemen under his direct command. Moreover, a colleague in military government later noted that Halland's constables, 'worked conscientiously and fairly, [but] were often handicapped by having had little or no experience of German or even continental politics and ways of life'. Due to such pitfalls, Halland was unable to organise Special Branch teams until August 1945, three months after the end of the war.

Halland also botched an attempt to denazify the German police and introduce British methods of organisation for metropolitan policing, being blamed by the Foreign Office for poor supervision of his subordinates and for attempting to export British ideas into an alien culture.[25] Early British failures in this field were responsible for several fiascos. In British-occupied Osnabrück, a German policeman set fire to a gutted department store that was being looted for clothes by Soviet slave labourers; two Russian women died in the resulting blaze. News of this event prompted outrage in the USSR – Ilya Ehrenburg wrote a highly critical article in the Red Army newspaper, *Krasnaya Zvezda* – and Eisenhower ordered Montgomery to launch an immediate investigation, focusing especially on whether the municipal police force had been properly vetted. '[The] press,' he noted, '[are] generally sensative on [the] question of removal of Nazis.'[26] Several months later, a Bremen policeman named Gerdes was caught smuggling arms into Wilhelmshaven, even though all German policemen were supposed to be disarmed, even after denazification vetting. The British suspected Gerdes of involvement in a Black Market ring, although – ominously – he had paid 500 Marks for a list of British officers living in Wilhelmshaven billets.[27] In Aachen, both the Americans and the British found it impossible to rebuild the municipal police force without the cooperation of *Parteigenossen*. As a result, the local *Regierungspräsident* eventually complained that of the forty officers under his direct control, thirty-one had been members of the NSDAP or the SA.[28]

During the initial occupation of north-west Germany, Montgomery's troops often allowed the retention of Nazi elements in municipal offices, usually with the rationale that they were irreplaceable technical experts.[29] The case of Hanover has been well documented and is perhaps illustrative. When American troops entered Hanover on 10 April 1945, the city was a disaster zone. It had been hit heavily by Allied bombers, so three-quarters of the downtown was leveled and sixty per cent of the city's houses were completely or partially destroyed. Electricity, water and sewage systems had failed. As a result, the population had shrunk to 217,000, down from a pre-war total of nearly half a million. Nazi snipers roamed the ruins, and liberated slave labourers had run amok, mobbing the municipal police force, some of whose members the Allies saw strung up on lampposts. In addition, there were no white flags evident, and an officer with the U.S. 84th Infantry Division later noted that 'the mood was much more hostile, or at least cooler, than in the cities and towns west of Hannover'. The first British military government detachment soon arrived on the scene, but this was a pitifully small eight-man contingent, which in the early weeks was out of contact with its ulterior chain of command. The unit was commanded by Major Lamb, and after early June 1945, by Colonel Pownell, both of whom were pragmatists who recognized the extent of the city's peril. Reports from June/July 1945 suggest that military government's tiny and overworked cadre in the Hanover region stood on the brink of collapse.

Given such conditions, it was imperative to find Germans willing to run Hanover, and to locate such people as quickly as possible. While it was usual practice to approach local churchmen or *Honoratioren* for advice, in Hanover a three-man delegation from an anti-fascist group succeeded in reaching the Americans and providing them with a list of credible candidates for major munic-ipal posts. The Americans used this list in appointing *Oberbürgermeister* Bratke, an elderly men with roots in the 'conservative' wing of the SPD. Such a choice seemed suitable since Hanover had once been an SPD stronghold. The British were subsequently impressed by Bratke's anti-communism, but they also realised that although nominally a social democrat, he had marked authoritarian incli-nations. For instance, he described his staff with the Nazi term '*Gefolgschaften*', which implied a belief in the *Führerprinzip*. He controlled all appointments and would brook no dissension from within municipal government. Once a town council was elected, he claimed the right to initiate its meetings and suspend its decisions, at least until he was stripped of these prerogatives in 1946. Lamb and Pownell exacerbated matters by giving Bratke unlimited powers and making him responsible for denazification. Bratke released 861 Nazis from municipal service, but he also retained many technical experts, some at senior posts. In 1945, two department heads – of a total of ten – had been department chiefs in 1943, and at the next level, twenty-five per cent of divisional heads were holdovers who had held the same jobs in 1943. As well, seventy-one per cent of the new bosses were appointments from within the technical bureaus of municipal government. In these kinds of jobs, incumbents had probably held party membership. In one case in June 1945, a lifelong and capable SPD activist serving in the Labour Exchange was actually fired when he quarreled with his boss, who was a Nazi holdover. The British assented. When Eisenhower launched a drive to have *all* Nazis dismissed within SHAEF-administered territories, Bratke issued a 'sharp protest', arguing that implementation of such a measure would paralyze the city's administra-tion. British military government agreed, arguing that it was not their intention 'to dislocate the administrative machine by a sudden holocaust of dismissals'. In fact, when the Reconstruction Committee (RC), a surviving remnant of the anti-Nazi underground, tried to alert the British to the pervasiveness and complexity of the Nazi machine, the latter grew suspicious of the RC itself, and on 2 June 1945 they dissolved the group when they discovered that it was expropriating suburban apartments and allotments occupied by *Parteigenossen*.

In particular, the assemblage of a Nazified police force in Hanover resembled the similar scandal in Frankfurt.[30] Despite the fact that nearly nineteen per cent of the Hanover constabulary was purged on political grounds – 266 of 1,430 policemen – seven of the force's top officers retained a Nazi taint. The police chief, Adolf Schulte, had been a longtime NSDAP member and had served as personnel chief of the German police in the occupied Netherlands, whence he had eventually been sent home because of Black Market dealings. His deputy, Werner Bez, had served as chief of personnel in the SS and Police Main Office in Berlin, and the head of the detectives' school, Pius Wagner, was an '*Alte Kämpfer*', that is, a pre-1933 Nazi activist. In fact, Wagner had joined the party and the SA in 1921. Not only were such men on the job, but they were suspected of promoting fellow Nazis, while at the same time purging men of more democratic convictions.

Although Hanover trade unionists were complaining by the end of 1945, and London also began making noises about re-vetting the entire municipal police force, it was only a protest by Kurt Schumacher that brought matters to a head. Schumacher, whose headquarters were in Hanover, employed a twelve-man police guard. After turning in one evening in mid-May 1946, the socialist leader overheard his guards talking amongst themselves. From what Schumacher could gather, four of the sentries were former SS men, and two were ex-officers, a revelation that Schumacher, who had been tortured in concentration camps, found hard to bear. Naturally, Schumacher complained and via backdoor channels between the SPD and the Labour Party the story eventually reached the ears of Jenny Lee, a Labour member of parliament who subsequently brought it up on the floor of the House of Commons. Officials at the Control Office, which had ministerial responsibility for the occupation, wrung their hands. Their boss, J.B. Hynd, was 'seriously perturbed at [the] apparent state of the Hannover Police' and demanded to know why officials in compulsory removal categories were still in positions of power. British military government reported that local Public Safety Branch officers had already described the Hanover police as completely cleansed, although it also quickly came to light that orders for a second vetting of the department had not been obeyed. To clean up the mess, the British brought in Fritz Kneipe, a genuine anti-Nazi who had left the Hanover force in 1933, rather than join the NSDAP, and had spent the NS-*Zeit* labouring as a textile worker. A special 'Denazification Panel' was also set up and the seven most senior Nazis were fired; Schulte was also arrested for having falsified his *Fragebogen*. In a final irony, however, the British could find little incriminating about the security detail that had protected Schumacher over the night of 15/16 May. Some of the men had been *Parteigenossen*, but only one had enjoyed 'honourary' SS membership (SS rank had been a 'privilege' awarded to many members of the Criminal Police under the age of forty-five). Schumacher was informed of the results of this investigation and pronounced himself as satisfied.[31]

Aside from the denazification of local government and police, the purging of the primary institutions of German national life also tended to lag. The British, as noted, gave considerable priority to the educational system, but considering their approach to the issue – that of providing guidance rather than control – their attitude toward the denazification of teachers was lackadaisical. British officers accepted the need for a purge in the abstract sense, but in practice it was regarded as a hindrance to the reorganisation of German schools. Officers in one military government detachment complained that cutting all Nazi Party members from the teaching profession would have 'catastrophic implications'. 'In country districts,' they reported, 'between eighty and ninety per cent of all teachers will have to go, in towns between sixty and eighty per cent... The German reaction to this method of dismissing teachers is sure to be unfavourable, NOT less on the anti-Nazi than on the Nazi side.' As matters turned out, 16,000 primary and secondary school teachers were dismissed and teacher training colleges were particularly devastated – the Nazis had recognized the importance of education by heavily Nazifying these institutions – but the real state of affairs is revealed by the fact that teachers in the Bremen Enclave, which was run by the United States, fled to the surrounding British-controlled hinterland, where denazification standards were widely regarded as more lax.[32] Before 1948, young teachers were in a strong position, particularly because many of them benefitted from a youth amnesty, but older 'denazified' teachers later came surging back, which caused a degree of generational tension.[33]

In higher education as well, there was no lasting purge of the professorate. As with the purging of teachers, the process tended to be qualitative rather than quantitative, and although it eventually resulted in the dismissal of approximately one-third of all professors, their colleagues kept open their chairs so that as the severity of denazification diminished, the castaways could resume their posts.[34] The potential for scandal festered particularly at Göttingen, the most important university in the British zone. The University Control Officer at Göttingen, Geoffrey Bird, considered his main mission as getting acquainted with faculty and students, to whom he would proffer friendly advice. Bird and his colleagues hesitated to interfere with the renowned scholars teaching at Göttingen, particularly in the physics department, and most professors who were denazified received a practical exoneration by being situated in the 'Follower' category. As the British realised, the university was also full of collaborators who had accepted the Nazi regime, despite its farcical intellectual foundation, but such individuals fell outside the formal bounds of denazification. In addition, the British allowed Göttingen's admissions policy to give preference to discharged *Wehrmacht* veterans and disabled servicemen. In the summer of 1946, nearly twenty-eight per cent of the university's students were former career or reserve officers, a statistic defended on grounds that the *Wehrmacht* had commissioned well-educated young men otherwise likely to attend university, although it also meant that many strident nationalists and militarists had been let through the door. As a direct result of such admissions, professors regularly avoided criticising Hitler or the Third Reich, and one educator who transgressed this norm faced a mass walk-out of 400 students.[35] When Martin Niemöller was snubbed at Erlangen, leaflets celebrating the exploit circulated amongst students, although 3,000 attendees remained quiet when Niemöller lectured at Göttingen.[36] By early 1946, reports suggested that nationalist students at Göttingen were using the fascist salute and greeting each other with the salutation '*acht und acht*', the 'double eight' that referred to the eighth letters of the alphabet. 'HH' was said to stand for '*Heil* Hitler!' The British publically claimed that use of the '*acht und acht*' phrase was a 'joke', although Field Security and the Foreign Office both privately reported that Göttingen was a hotbed of Nazi and neo-nationalist sentiment.[37] As late as 1947, Göttingen's rector, F.H. Rein, was still denying pervasive rumours of Nazi underground activity.[38]

There were also troubles elsewhere. The British Control Officer at the Aachen Technical *Hochschule* eventually admitted that the local denazification process 'removed no one but one or two opportunists', while the Control Officer at Cologne University later emphasized, 'what a most unpleasant and unpleasing task it was for the British ... to have to probe into all the details of every academic's background'. At Kiel University, a bulwark of reactionary thinking, the British removed the *Rektor* because he was caught manipulating a review of his professors' *Fragebogen*. Not incidentally, the Control Officer at Kiel was Caroline Cunningham, who showed more perseverance than some of her colleagues in tracking down Nazis. In the port city of Hamburg, the local chairman of the SPD complained that Hamburg University was staffed by a faculty that had been comfortably in place during the NS-*Zeit* and that 'the professors actively co-operating in the revival of democracy can be counted on ten fingers'. He called the school 'the birthplace of future German nationalism'. By early 1946, the British authorities were scrambling to react. In February, they introduced a new 'control instruction' for the admission of university students. All students in the 'mandatory removal' categories specified by CC Directive 24 were henceforth banned from admission. Preference was given to applicants who were never members of the Hitler Youth or the party – a small number since Hitler Youth membership was obligatory after 1939 – followed by young people who had been part of the Hitler Youth but *not* the party, followed by applicants who had been 'nominal members' of both the Hitler Youth and the party. The aim was to reduce, by indirect means, the number of ex-officers attending universities in the British zone. Regulations were again shifted for the winter semester of 1946/47, since the British issued a sweeping youth amnesty that matched that of their counterparts in the U.S. zone. In order to limit Nazi and nationalist influences, 'active' officers were directly banned from admission between November 1946 and February 1947, something of an embarrassment since the British were concurrently arguing at the Control Council that there should be no prohibition on the university attendance of former *Wehrmacht* officers. Military Government officers also encouraged German rectors to admit more working class students, although changes in this regard were connected to larger structural barriers within society and came about only slowly.[39]

The denazification of the legal profession ran unto similar difficulties. Like the civil service, the German judiciary had constituted a right-wing bastion during the Weimar Republic, and many magistrates and lawyers quickly acclimatised to Hitler's New Order. When the Association of Prussian Judges dissolved in 1933, it advised all its members to join the NSDAP. Upon the arrival of the British, the occupiers were faced with the crippling fact that ninety per cent of German jurists had been members of the *Rechtswahrerbund*, the Nazi-affiliated organisation for the legal profession. Such men claimed, of course, that they had been forced to join the *Rechtswahrerbund* and even the party, if only for professional purposes, although the Nazis had not punished the few lawyers who had refused to join, and certainly they had not denied pensions to judges who had chosen to sit out the Nazi period. Despite the practical collapse of legality during the Third Reich, the British wanted to maintain the legal system, at least to save themselves the bother of directly attending to the thousands of minor felonies, misdemeanors and civil matters that took up the bulk of court time. In fact, there was a huge backlog of such cases. As a result, one of military government's legal experts, Jack Rathbone, suggested that fifty per cent of functioning lawyers and judges could be 'nominal members' of the party, a proposal that aroused dogged opposition from the Public Safety Branch but was eventually approved. In November 1945 Rathbone admitted to military government's Standing Committee on Denazification that thirty per cent of prosecutors and judges were currently *Parteigenossen*. Some had even been officers in the SA. British military government also allowed German lawyers to oversee the vetting of their own colleagues, with predictable consequences. In 1946, Rathbone recommended ending the fifty per cent limitation, calling denazification a 'ghastly witchhunt', and in the following year he admitted to an American colleague – somewhat shamefacedly – that thirty-eight of the top 121 legal officials in the British zone were former Nazis or members of the SA, many of whom had still not been denazified.[40] By 1948, seventy-one per cent of the judges and states attorneys in *Land* Lower Saxony were ex-Nazis.[41]

Lax measures also characterised the British denazification of the economy, at least initially. The British approach to such matters was of crucial importance because the Ruhr district, which was under British control, constituted the industrial heart of Germany and Hamburg, which was also part of the British zone, was one of the country's major financial centres. In the Ruhrgebiet, even the Americans, who were relatively more strident denazifiers, set a pragmatic tone during their brief occupation. Fundamental Allied decisions on 'industrially disarming' Germany or internationalising the Ruhr were still pending, so the doctrine of 'military necessity' became determinant. Although Alfried Krupp was on a list of war criminals and was put under house arrest, AMG officers dealt with Krupp's chief deputy, Edouard Houdremont, despite the fact that Houdremont was a party member and had obviously worked closely with the Armaments Ministry in organising weapons production. Considering practicalities, the conquerors sought the 'exercise of influence' by such men in restoring utilities, while the industrialists hoped that by clearing rubble and repairing essential services, they could establish a wedge that would eventually allow them to restore production. They also sought to win the trust of the occupiers by demonstrating functional efficiency. Thus, it was 'business as usual', at least until the summer of 1945, with steel and coal managers supporting conservative local *Bürgermeister* in the establishment of a supposedly apolitical regime of experts. The seigneurs of Ruhr industry argued that a small clique around Hitler had conducted the war, and that denazification should therefore fall upon the heads of a few activists in senior positions within the NSDAP. According to Walter Rohland, the chairman of *Vereinigten Stahlwerke* and a close confederate of Albert Speer, most pre-1933 members of the party had joined under pressure of the emergency conditions in the Weimar period, while many post-1933 members had signed up with the conscious intent of moderating party policy 'and thereby serving the Fatherland'. Another industrialist, Günter Henle, warned that the cohort of business leaders in the age range of forty-five to sixty-five was already sparse because of losses of manpower during the First World War, and he argued that any extensive purge of the survivors would decapitate the German management elite.[42] In fact, a few of the industrialists even dared to portray themselves as victims of the Hitlerite command economy. According to Chambers of Commerce in the British zone, economic denazification should be organised by German panels of two businessmen, with a lawyer serving as chair. Such a method, they advised, would eliminate the possibility of interference by 'political' elements.[43] Houdremont and others felt sure that the Allies would leave the old managerial structures in place, and that they would be allowed to dominate reconstruction.

And indeed, when British military government set up shop, they seemed comfortable with leaving men such as Houdremont, Rohland and Henle in positions of tremendous power. The head of the Economics Section of British military government was a temporarily commissioned industrialist named Percy Mills, who felt that his new wards 'were not Nazis, they were businessmen'. Mills and his colleagues also feared that German workers would exploit economic denazification for political ends, seeking to revolutionise the nature of property relations. As a result of his relative inaction, Mills faced a chorus of complaints from the SPD, the KPD and the CDU, as well as from the Russians and the 'Morgenthau Boys' in U.S. military government. The political officers with military government noted that the failure to denazify private enterprise 'was giving rise to adverse comment, not only by the Germans themselves, but also in the US press'. Officers in the Economics Section excused their passivity by citing the lack of a specific denazification directive for industry. Although the absence of such a directive was actually Mills' preference, the question was referred back to the main headquarters of military government, which replied that its forthcoming *Directive on Arrest and Removal* was still under preparation. Meanwhile, it was advised that the British counter-proposal to JCS 1067 was the closest thing to a determinant policy, and this document specified that *Parteigenossen* who were 'more than nominal participants' were to be purged, even 'from positions of major responsibility in important private undertakings'. One senior officer warned Mills that failure to pursue a more proactive approach was allowing 'many prominent Nazis' to hold 'positions of unofficial influence', although this practice was 'not consonant with our general policy'. As F.S.V. Donnison notes, the response to Mills' enquiry widened the practical scope of denazification, although British officers still had room for exercising broad discretion, including the exemption of economic 'experts'.[44] Certainly, the British were horrified by Clay's Law Number 8, which Con O'Neill called 'an example of systematic and meticulous imbecility', and they had no intention of applying such a sweeping standard in their own zone.[45] On the other hand, the complete *laissez faire* of the early occupation period was abandoned. In August, the Potsdam decisions created an extra incentive by calling for an end to the 'excessive concentration of economic power as exemplified by cartels, syndicates [and] trusts', a formula that was later codified in CC Law Number 27, which prohibited ownership or control of industrial assets by anyone who had 'furthered the aggressive designs of the National Socialist Party'. Certainly, such wording seemed to imply the need for a harsh denazification of the business elite.

The British raised the stakes on the morning of 10 September, when they arrested the members of the Krupp *Direktorium*. Major Airey Neave, an officer in the British war crimes prosecution unit, led a convoy of Field Security jeeps and armoured cars on a major raid through Essen. Most of the leading Krupp personalities were arrested in their offices in *Bürogebäude* 5, whence they were hauled away and locked up in a large cellar used as a holding pen. Houdremont, who later stood trial as a war criminal, was forced to hand over control of Krupp to the few of his colleagues who had never joined the party or the SS, notably Paul Hansen and Hermann Hobrecker. There was little protest outside Krupp, although the optimism of the steel barons still at liberty began to evaporate. Walter Rohland was arrested in early October, while visiting his family in the French zone, and he was thereafter sent to Special Camp 'Dustbin', near Frankfurt, where he faced tough questioning over his services for the Speer Ministry. On the night of 1 December, another Field Security raid netted seventy-six further executives, namely the leading lights of the August Thyssen *Hütte*, Hoesch AG, Dortmund-Hoerder-*Hüttenverein* and *Vereinigten Stahlwerke*. These men were kept for several days in local jails and were then shipped eastwards – they feared to the Russian zone – although they traveled only as far as the Bad Nenndorf Camp near Hanover. Suddenly, the high and mighty of German industry found themselves sleeping on cots with no mattresses and working in street sweeping *Kommandos*, where they rummaged through garbage cans for leftover food and cigarette butts. *The Times* thundered that there was 'no place in the new Germany' for such men, while the businessmen themselves nourished a newfound resentment of the British. In their experience, they noted, '*die Engländer*' were much more draconian than the Americans. Some speculated about a supposed British attempt to placate public opinion and thereby deflect a French request to internationalise the Ruhr region. Most of the detainees were held into 1946 or 1947.

Beyond the arrests there was a wave of denazification dismissals (although as late as 29 September, a 30th Corps directive on the economic purge suggested that any action 'against firms or individuals must NOT be such as might hold up the production or distribution of food or impair the housing or health situation during the winter'.) In the summer of 1945, 600 *Parteigenossen* had already been dropped from the middle and senior echelons of Krupp. Near the end of the year, Thyssen *Hütte* was forced to release nearly fifty executives, who were prohibited from performing anything more than manual labour. The board of the company darkly referred to this episode as 'a matter of far-reaching importance'. Soon after, *Deutsche Röhrenwerke* AG lost fourteen senior personnel, and the Duisberg Works of Demag was forced to dismiss more than a third of thirty whose cases were reviewed.[46] In Düsseldorf, the British caught the widow of NSDAP stalwart and 'Economic Defense Leader' Paul Schweitzke, who had been killed during the war, attempting to use less incriminated Nazis as dummy directors for her husband's metal works, while she retained a hidden financial and managerial interest.[47] One of the coincidental consequences of British sanctions was to strengthen the position of Workers' Factory Committees (*Betreibsräte*), which generally benefitted during this period from the fact that German proprietors and bosses were compromised. Workers' ability to provide *Persilscheine* for implicated supervisors naturally produced a sense of indebtedness that increased proletarian bargaining power.[48] Although the British usually avoided the direct socialisation of heavy industry,[49] the reduction of power differentials encouraged by denazification paved the way for the famous co-determination agreements of the 1950s.

The situation in German coal mines merits special consideration, since lack of coal lay at the centre of the notorious 'vicious circle' that prevented western German economic recovery during the 'Potsdam era'. The inadequacy of coal production initially owed to lack of wagons and manpower (the latter of which was in the *Wehrmacht* or dispersed throughout a number of evacuation centres). However, as the problem took shape over the course of 1945/46, the on-going shortage of food supplies contributed to raging absenteeism and poor production rates by underfed miners, which in turn crippled German transport and industry and prevented the manufacture of exports needed to pay for food imports – and so the cyclical nature of the problem. Aside from being underfed, miners were also demoralised by the widespread knowledge that coal was being provided as reparations to France rather than being prioritised for the support of German economic recovery. More than any other zone, this issue effected north-western Germany because the region produced seventy per cent of Germany's coal and seventy-eight per cent of its iron and steel, although it suffered from a severe deficiency in food production.[50]

As early as May/June 1945, a joint Anglo-American team, the Potter-Hyndley mission, toured Germany and warned that inadequate supplies from German mines, continental Europe's largest source of coal, would threaten the future economic health of all north-western and Mediterranean Europe. Potter and Hyndley also advised the Allies to cooperate with 'experienced German management', and indeed SHAEF, and later 21st Army Group, initially worked closely with mine owners and technical management in trying to revive production, even continuing to use the administrative machinery of the Rhenish-Westphalian Coal Syndicate (RWCS), a combine of collieries that controlled coal production and transport. As part of this policy, military government's deputy controller for coal production, Henry Collins, kept in place a large cadre of Nazi overseers and pit bosses, some of whom had been guilty of abusing foreign labour, and even German miners, during the war. Such policies quickly gave rise to complaints from the Political and Intelligence divisions of military government, which argued that toleration of the RWCS was alienating Ruhr miners, who had expected a tougher line, and that it was also leading to adverse commentary in the U.S. and British press. A critical story by Robert Kuh, published in *The New York Times*, was a particular source of embarrassment. As a result, Robertson decided to incarcerate the leading figures of the RWCS, if not to dissolve the entire organisation. On the night of 5/6 September, three days before the operation against Krupp, Field Security units swarmed through the principal towns of the Ruhr and arrested forty-four leaders of the RWCS. Famous names such as Hugo Stinnes Junior, Gustav Knepper and Georg Lübsen were literally roused from their beds and escorted to an internment camp. A month later, the British authorities also launched a large scale drive to denazify the mines, distributing *Fragebogen* to officials in every pit. By 1946, 14,000 individuals had been investigated and 958 removed from the industry, including most of the overseers and mining engineers who fell into mandatory removal categories.

Such disruptions were not without consequence. On 2 January 1946, Collins' staff, the North German Coal Control (NGCC), complained that the new denazification regime had denied it the services of the most experienced pit bosses and supervisors, which in turn had hindered the absorption of untrained labour, the only available supply, and was exposing the remaining overseers to the threat of denunciation. The direct consequence of the latter was a loss of labour

discipline. The overall result was that production was falling and there was relatively less professional attention being paid toward the dangers of coal extraction,
particularly the possibility of cave-ins and explosions of volatile gases or coal dust.
NGCC thus claimed that it desperately needed the retention of the remaining
five per cent of bosses who were in the mandatory removal categories, as well as
complete sufferance for management figures in the discretionary removal categories – in other words, it wanted a practical exclusion of coal mining from further
levels of denazification.[51]

Collins got an especially good opportunity to make his case because of several
mine disasters that claimed the lives of 464 men. At Peine, a cage carrying German
miners to the surface slipped to the bottom of the shaft, partly because personnel
at the pithead had failed to heed regulations for securing the hoisting cable. This
disaster on 22 January 1946 killed forty-six of forty-seven miners riding in the
elevator. A month later, a catastrophe of even greater proportions occurred at the
Mine Monopol Grimberg, near Unna. In this case, a violent explosion of coal
dust buried or cut off nearly 500 miners; the blast was so powerful that its force
reached the surface, destroying the elevator winches and killing two men at the
pithead. In his report on the disaster, Collins hinted that the firing of twenty-one
Nazi mining engineers had hindered safety arrangements, particularly because
the Nazis had been replaced partly by geriatric pensioners who could not properly attend to their duties, but it was during the rescue effort that German crews
proved especially disorganised. The chief mine inspector had been killed in the
explosion and the highest ranking survivor was a *Parteigenosse* who had recently
been denounced by his subordinates and then interrogated by Field Security, an
experienced that had thoroughly discomposed him – or so Collins claimed. After
twelve hours of fumbling, during which only fifty-seven men were rescued and
no contact was made with a remaining 427 men underground, NGCC assumed a
more direct role in the rescue effort. With fires blasing out of control, management
and the workers soon decided to seal the pit, along with the fate of any survivors
still within it, although the British then allowed the emergency re-employment
of Dr Stodt, a Nazi who had recently been dismissed. Stodt wisely postponed the
sealing and on the fourth day after the blast, he managed to extract eight more
miners. Yet another man also emerged from an escape shaft. Overall, however, the
disaster cost the lives of 418 men, including three British mine inspectors, which
made it the worst mining disaster in German history.

Collins knew exactly where to lay the blame and precisely what conclusions
to draw. Denazification, he fumed, was the cause 'of the dry-rot which pervades
the [mine] inspectorate', and to persist in such folly would not only endanger the
lives of additional NGCC personnel, but would further imperil German miners,
who were supposedly fed up with the consequences of the purge. 'The clamour
for so-called denazification,' Collins snorted, came only from 'a noisy minority
with decidedly left-wing tendencies. Pandering to this element is fast leading the

German miners to Communism and the last stage will be worse than the first.'[52] German trade union chief Hans Böckler disagreed, arguing that the Grimberg pit had hardly been denazified at all, and that discipline was bound to remain poor 'if the miners had to go on working under men they regarded as enemies'.[53] In evaluating both the Peine and Grimberg disasters, Sir Arthur Street, Permanent Secretary of the Control Office, made a rather more measured assessment, 'The cause of the first seems to be obscure; the causes of the second were bad safety discipline and bad workmanship. There is no real evidence that either was due directly to the removal of skilled Nazis. There is, however, ample evidence that the rescue efforts at Grimberg were hampered almost to the point of frustration because nearly all the skilled people connected with the mine had been removed.'[54] Montgomery's intelligence chief, Edgar Williams, later remembered the Ruhr accidents as a turning point for denazification overall, since the policy had increasingly seemed to assume a vindictive (and dangerous) edge.[55]

Varying interpretations aside, NGCC in March 1946 was able to secure a 'suspension' of the active denazification of the German coal industry. In truth, the vetting of *Fragebogen* and the categorisation of individuals continued unabated,[56] but the number of mandatory removal cases employed in the mines actually increased from seventy-seven on 23 March to 131 by 4 June. Meanwhile, German trade unions and leftist political parties continued to scream about flagrant abuses of Allied directives, claiming that even violent Nazi enthusiasts and former *Wehrmacht* officers were still supervising the work of stolid German proletarians, while at the same time a number of relatively inoffensive Nazis had been removed from the pits. Worse than the mining engineers, they alleged, were the Nazis in the front offices and board rooms of the mining concerns, although they were willing to admit that many of these figures were spiritual Nazis rather than outright *Parteigenossen*. The answer to such outrages, said organised labour, was to start a new phase of denazification based upon miners' committees. These bodies would judge foremen and inspectors *not* upon the basis of *Fragebogen*, but through a case-by-case assessment of a person's overall character and political sympathies. Several officials in military government, particularly the famous public intellectual Noel Annan, then a young officer in the Political Division, suggested that only a commitment to nationalize the mines would probably be sufficient to mollify German labour.

In April 1946, the Control Office encouraged Robertson to solicit advice from the trade unions, and after due consideration, Roberston created a 'Special German Coal Advisory Denazification Commission', which was an attempt to find a compromise between organised labour and the NGCC, while at the same time avoiding any promises about future nationalisation. The 'special commission' was comprised of five representatives nominated by the labour movement, plus three technical experts chosen by NGCC, and it was chaired by Dr Josef Wiefels, a judge from Bielefeld. The broad span of German opinion, from technocratic-conservative to communist, was included in the composition of the body. Its mandate was to review any cases forwarded by the trade unions and works councils, especially pertaining to suspicious personnel still employed in the pits, and to make determinations regarding possible reinstatement of persons already dismissed by British military government. The names of candidates in the latter category could be forwarded either by the labour unions or by NGCC. Collins was bound by the process but had certain rights of appeal. The Wiefels commission met from 13 August to 10 October 1946 and eventually decided 337 cases, ruling for retention or reinstatement in all but sixteen instances, although twenty-five of the men retained or rehired were downgraded in status. In keeping so many men on the job, members of the commission were deeply affected by considerations of mine safety, although they found weaknesses in the positions advanced by both the trade unions and NGCC. Much of the information provided by the labour unions was amorphous and therefore not actionable, while the NGCC could find only eighteen men that it could justifiably nominate for reinstatement. In the final analysis, most ex-Nazis with truly bad records refused to face the panel. The final decisions were not always pleasing to either side, but most of the commission's findings were unanimous, which left little to quibble about. Despite the fact that relatively few Nazis were sacked, the overall position of labour within the coal industry was actually legitimated and reinforced.[57] Having achieved much, on 6 November 1946 the British declared that denazification in the coal industry had come to an end.[58]

While a degree of venom was eventually injected into British policy toward heavy industry and mining, at least momentarily, the treatment of German banks was moderated by the influence of the British Treasury, which advanced a position diametrically opposite to its American counterpart and was deeply concerned with the revival of the German financial system. The Americans had long been troubled by what they saw as a British tendency to 'ignore' the denazification of German financial institutions, and during interdepartmental meetings in Whitehall, Edward Playfair argued against American proposals to purge the *Reichsbank*, contending that in the absence of party members, no one would be left capable of running German financial affairs. 'Only those who are really bad should be removed,' contended Playfair. 'The rest should be kept on.'

Influenced by such arguments, the Financial Section of British military government subsequently attempted to secure the help of leading German bankers and financiers. Although SHAEF's technical manual on banking specified that Allied financial officers should seek out and dismiss German bankers sympathetic to the Nazis, as well as those who were actual members of the party, the head of the British financial section, Paul Chambers, later noted that 'the manuals were thrown away', and that he allowed his staff, mostly British civilian bankers in uniform, a great deal of discretion in dealing with their German opposite numbers. In Hamburg, one of the three main German financial centres, less than fourteen per cent of German bank employees were removed or suspended from their jobs – 637 of 4689 personnel. And of this number, only nine had been arrested by Field Security by the fall of 1945. Chambers later contended that he regarded denazification as 'fundamental', but that his chief task was to kick-start the German economy, 'despite French, American and Russian opposition and criticism'.

Since banking was an international business, many of the personnel in the financial section of British military government had a prewar acquaintanceship with German banking executives. A particular controversy developed when Chambers' banking expert, Charles Gunston, located and then recruited his old friend Hermann Abs, despite the fact that Abs had been in charge of Deutsche Bank's operations in conquered territories – that is, the organised commercial plundering of non-German assets – and that he was on an automatic arrest list. Gunston hired Abs as a consultant, although Abs also used his position as chief of Deutsche Bank's provisional headquarters to re-establish secret links between bank branches and reorganise the firm's operations. When Chambers' American counterpart, Bernard Bernstein, learned of Abs' employment, he could barely contain his anger. In a prolonged tug of war, Bernstein managed to secure permission to interrogate Abs, although in Hamburg, not Frankfurt. One member of British military government later recalled that since Abs had not been a member of the party, 'we gave him protection'. By late 1945, however, Bernstein was getting the upper hand, particularly since he had the aid of a sympathetic British officer, who was threatening to expose the affair in the *Daily Mirror*. Thus, Gunston reluctantly confided to Abs that 'there is political pressure to get you and I can't stop it'. Shortly after Gunston's recall to England in January 1946, Abs and thirty other senior bankers were arrested in a Field Security sweep analogous to the earlier blows against the steel and coal magnates. Abs was also stripped of his corporate directorships – some forty-five in total – and he soon found himself in Hamburg's Altona jail, where he shared a cell with the chairman of Dresdner Bank, Carl Leur.[59]

Although many of the industrial and financial grandees were psychologically and physically humbled – some thought that they would never again hear the hum of a functioning economy – the fact is that most of them eventually returned to their firms, and that the firms themselves, some of which had been placed under trusteeship by the Allies, were eventually restored to the control of former managers and owners. In interdepartmental fighting, the Economic and Financial Sections of military government launched bitter counterattacks against the denazifiers, noting that denazification was 'seriously hampering' the cause of economic reconstruction. Such complaints occasionally achieved reversals of policy or exemptions for favoured elements in the economy. As early as the spring of 1946, one coal mining company, *Bergbau* AG Lothringen in Bochum, was already promising an arrested colleague that he would be welcomed back upon release. Hermann Abs was freed in April 1946, if only after a mighty push by the Financial

Section of British military government, to whom Abs refused counsel while he was incarcerated. After narrowly evading trial as a war criminal, he was eventually hired to disperse Marshall Plan aid, albeit with the misgivings of General Clay, and he resumed the chairmanship of Deutsche Bank. On 12 July 1946, even the Intelligence Division – relatively strident denazifiers – recommended the release of 130 prominent businessmen still being held in confinement, offering as a rationale the fact that other Nazis just as bad, if not worse, had been allowed to remain at liberty. Hugo Stinnes Junior, who held champagne parties in prison, was released in August 1946, and despite his bad record for treatment of slave labour during the Second World War, he managed to convince a Düsseldorf denazification panel that he had supported anti-Nazi resistance circles in the *Abwehr*, a finding that resulted in his full exoneration. His property was returned in the 1950s. Many of the coal company directors dismissed in 1945 were reinstated in 1948, when the *Deutsche Kohlenbergbau-Leitung* applied on their behalf and the bizonal authorities compliantly set up a committee of the U.K./U.S. Coal Control in order to process such cases.

One case that particularly illustrates the importance of international business relationships is that of Werner Carp, a Ruhr coal and steel magnate who also held directorships in the Deutsche Bank and the German subsidiary of ITT. A party member from 1933 to 1945, Carp was swept up in the autumn 1945 raids and remained interned until May 1947, when he was released 'for health reasons' and was slotted into denazification category three. Despite complaints from the communists, a German denazification panel re-categorized him as a 'Follower', although there was a technical glitch during his hearing and his case was thrown back into a pile of 35,000 files awaiting full processing. Meanwhile, United Kingdom Chemicals (UKC) Limited had negotiated with one of Carp's companies, *Gewerkschaft des Steinkohlenbergwerke, Rheinpreussen*, in order to launch German production of carbon black, which was to be processed from oil along the lines of a secret method developed by UKC. This enterprise was supposed to be crucial to British well-being because it would break the United States' monopoly on the production of carbon black and thus help conserve Britain's valuable exchange reserve of U.S. dollars. Because UKC would share its trade secrets only with Carp, 'in whose integrity they trust', the company tried to intercede in Carp's denazification, only to be told by the German prosecutor that 'special representations' might expedite another hearing of the case. Subsequently the Board of Trade asked the Foreign Office to help move along the process, and within three months Carp had been fully reinstated and his business privileges restored.

By 1947, the British – with the exception of Attorney-General Hartley Shawcross – had lost any appetite for trying industrialists as war criminals, although they did agree to transfer Alfried Krupp and his directors to the Americans, who promptly placed these men before a military tribunal. Krupp and his associates were found guilty of abusing slave labour and given sentences of various duration, which they served at Landsberg Prison, Hitler's onetime place of confinement, although by early 1951 they had all been released. Krupp was also mortified by the confiscation of his iron and steel empire, which even after dismantling, reparations and decartelisation was worth over half a billion dollars, but this prize was also returned during the Korean War, by which time the Western Powers were seeking to boost German industrial production.[60]

While there is no doubt that the German business class bore a considerable shock from denazification, leftist and liberal historians make a legitimate point in claiming that the program was severely moderated by functional considerations and that it produced few lasting effects upon basic matters of ownership and control.[61] As early as 1946, the Intelligence Division warned that many senior businessmen were already 'escaping the net. Among them are some who materially assisted the Nazi Party in its struggle for power and/or were intimately connected with the building up of the war machine, and it is submitted that the whole object of the Denazification Policy will be set at nought if the German public has the impression that while dealing ruthlessly with the "small fry", the British Authorities are letting the big men escape'.[62]

In several other respects as well, an initially severe approach to denazification was followed by rapid backpedaling. Throughout 1944 and the first half of 1945, the Political Warfare Executive, the responsible authority for wartime propaganda, increasingly insisted on ramming home the theme of collective culpability, and as Michael Balfour notes, the wartime BBC became steadily less willing to draw distinctions between 'Nazis' and 'Germans'. This tactic was called 'guilt mobilisation'. Thus, the PWE directive for 18 April 1945 ordered subsidiary agencies to 'revert to "war guilt"', of which Germans in the occupied territory have almost no sense', and a week later radio broadcasters were told, 'to support the long-term themes of German war-guilt, German responsibility for brutality and crimes … Germany dishonesty, etc., without any regard for the feelings or sensibilities of the listener'. PWE continued to issue such directives well into the post-war period, supported by the Public Relations and Information Section of British military government. However, a few individuals were already growing skeptical. In the Foreign Office, Con O'Neill, who was a propaganda specialist, noted on 10 May that 'I am by no means averse to their being a moderation of forthcomingness in what we ourselves say, over the radio, to the Germans. I think it would be a mistake to refuse to admit any possibility of repentance or re-education.' Richard Crossman, the guiding spirit in the SHAEF PW unit, became frankly obstructive, issuing unauthorised propaganda that boosted the idea of an alternate – or 'good' – Germany.[63] By the mid-summer of 1945, 'collective guilt' propaganda was being denounced by Germans and British officers alike, particularly after Bishop von Galen issued a rhetorical blast against such claims. 'It is said,' he noted, 'that the whole German people – everyone of us – participated in the guilt for all the

crimes committed abroad and in Germany, above all in the conc(
This accusation, he declared, was 'unjust and untruthful', partic
Germans had themselves ended up in concentration camps.[64] Ac(
Welch, once British troops became immersed in the messy business o(b
Germany, 'memos pontificating on the moral dimension of the occupier's (
tended to disappear in a bureaucratic maze'.[65]

The same pattern of diminishing toughness characterised the British internment programme. Initial planning by 21st Army Group suggested that as many
as 300,000 people might have to be interned throughout Germany, 70,000 of
that number in the British zone. By May 1945, three camps, each capable of
holding 10,000 internees, had already been organised, and within several months
66,000 Nazis had been arrested and detained. In September, the *Directive on Arrest
and Removal* introduced the idea of 'mandatory investigation', a substitute for
pursuing certain categories of Nazis previously listed in the automatic arrest classifications, but by that time there were few senior party members left to arrest.
Nonetheless, several thousand further Nazis were captured by the end of 1945, so
the total number of internees eventually stood at 68,500. By this time, the question of what to do with these detainees had become one of the burning problems
of the British occupation, particularly since they were often housed in crowded
and unsanitary conditions. Food rations dropped to a level of 900 calories a day,
which internees – unlike other Germans – could not supplement by foraging.
Of course, the inmates were ultimately responsible for the string of events that
had led to this incarceration, and it was only natural that in a country – and a
world – short of food, they should stand at the back of the queue. In addition, the
number of internees was only a fraction of the sum whom the Nazis themselves
had held in concentration camps. Nonetheless, public scandal loomed. A House
of Commons committee noted that the situation hardly enhanced the prestige of
the occupying power, nor was it 'attract[ing] Germans to the British way of life'.
Even a military government officer admitted that prolonged detentions without
trial were 'not compatible with the professed restoration of the rule of law and
the professed abolition of Gestapo methods', and he admitted that such tactics
reinforced German cynicism because they suggested Allied moral ideals were
merely a cloak for the continuing exercise of arbitrary power.

By early 1946, British military government had set up a network of Review
Boards, which was similar to a system already in use in the American zone, and
which had the same aim – namely, to reduce the number of internees. The Foreign
Office reported in February 1946 that it hoped to see the release of most 'militarists' before 31 March and most Nazis before 31 August. Although matters did not
proceed at such a rapid pace, 24,000 prisoners had been reevaluated and released
by July 1946. Unfortunately, the system moved too quickly to be reliably fair or
uniform in its judgements, and there was little room for correcting mistakes. For
instance, many of those released in 1946 were members of organisations later

eclared criminal conspiracies by the Nuremberg Judgement, although it was too late to retrieve them for trial before a newly evolving system of denazification courts called the *Spruchgerichte*. These courts were located around the major internment camps at Sandbostel, Recklinghausen, Neuengamme, Fallingbostel and Paderborn, and there was also an appeals court at Hamm. The *Spruchgerichte* consisted of two levels of tribunals, the *Spruchsenaten* and the *Spruchkammern*, although the later shared only a name with its U.S. zone counterpart. Both levels of the *Spruchgerichte* were purely criminal courts and had the power to levy major punishments only, such as incarceration or hefty monetary penalties, although in practice most of the defendants were released on the basis of 'time served'. Some were also fined. In 1947, Operation 'Old Lace' oversaw the release of most junior officers in the criminal organisations, although these trials frequently were 'reduced to [being] an elaborate release procedure'. Nonetheless, operations of the *Spruchgerichte* quickly reduced the number of internees to 19,000, most of whom were still awaiting denazification, and in November 1947, the British released on parole SS NCOs and junior officers, cutting the remaining total in half. Even at the end of the process, there were still more than 500 prisoners who were felt to be so dangerous that release was not an option.[66] Remembering the banishment of Napoleon on St. Helena, the British considered sending such hard-core Nazis to the North Sea island of Adelheide, where they would have lived in isolation with their families, although their right to leave the island would have been severely restricted. After some rumination, however, this bizarre proposal was rejected.[67]

By the winter and spring of 1945/46, the British faced many of the same denazification problems as the Americans. There were imposing backlogs of unprocessed *Fragebogen*, which were steadily growing more huge, plus large numbers of demoralised 'minor' Nazis who were awaiting denazification decisions but meanwhile were excluded from practicing the means through which they had made a living. Noel Annan later recalled that British political intelligence was 'rather good', but that nothing was done in depth, 'What of course we never had was the follow-up and the business of ... finding out the truth about "X": is he/was he a Nazi, what kind of person was he, either to say this is a good chap and we ought to use him for the administration of Germany, or alternately, that he is a swine and we must get him.'

Montgomery's strategy was to promise a definite end to denazification in the not-too-distant future, which he felt would buoy German spirits, and in March 1946, military government's 'Standing Committee on Denazification Policy' appointed Brigadier Heyman in order to find a means of bringing denazification 'to a final conclusion'.[68] The problem was how to reach this goal. Although some British responses were similar to the palliatives devised by the Americans, the British demurred in following the American model of fully devolving denazification. In fact, by early 1946 they believed that both the Americans and

the Soviets were assigning more responsibility fo...
The Intelligence and Political Sections of British...
pushing for implementation of the same approach,
although many elements within military governm...
Nonetheless, Zonal Policy Instruction 3, of 3 January 194...
work of 'Denazification Panels', one per *Kreis*, and these
empowered to nominate members for hundreds of 'Denazific...
which the British hoped would be manned by staunch anti-...
trade unionists. All members were vetted by the Special Branch ...andate
of these bodies was to sift through *Fragebogen* and other forms ...r evidence,
although in the final analysis their advice on job dismissals was treated by the
Public Safety Branch essentially as advice, *not* as final determinations. In addition,
their work was supervised by Special Branch officers. As in the U.S. zone, there
was an appellate mechanism comprised of five 'appeal committees'. By February,
denazification panels and committees were forming throughout the British zone,
although the process in *Hansestadt* Hamburg was awaiting convention of the
municipal assembly, the *Bürgerschaft*, rather than having have the mayor nominate
all members of the bodies himself. In the following month, Brigadier Heyman,
like his American counterpart, Charles Fahy, recommended handing extensive
powers to this newly established system, a proposal developed by Annan, although
it was opposed by the Internal Affairs and Public Safety Branches. In addition,
the 'Regional Commissioners', who arrived in the British zone in April 1946
in order to oversee local German administrations, advised unanimously *against*
assigning the Germans too much responsibility. In Schleswig-Holstein, the
'Regional Commissioner', H.V. Champion de Crespigny, warned that German
advisory panels and committees were, 'not entirely objective in their findings.
They are apt either to "whitewash" cases which would not pass or, even worse,
to allow personal feelings to influence their decisions, and to raise the very grave
suspicion of victimisation.' Although Heyman's proposal was officially approved
by the British Cabinet's 'Overseas Reconstruction Committee', in practice the
British retained a large degree of executive control over the denazification system, and they remained the final authority for appeals.

Once the Control Council adopted Directive 38, a new British policy brief,
Zone Executive Instruction 54, subdivided the four categories of guilt in Directive
38 into twenty-three groups. Military government retained direct control over the
disposition of 'Major Offenders' and most of the subgroups within the 'Offender'
category, which were handled by the Review Boards that had worked on the
cases of internees. German denazifiers were left to assign the financial penalties and work restrictions imposed upon defendants in the two lesser categories
of guilt. The British also followed the American expedient of releasing 'young
people' – that is, those born in 1919 and after – from inclusion in the programme,
although to please the Germans this measure was called 'exoneration' rather than

first term implied forgiveness of guilt, but Germans contended
was no guilt, since people not old enough to vote in the 1930s had not
mature enough to stand responsible for the rise of National Socialism. SS
personnel were exluded from the amnesty. The Deputy Chief of Staff in British
military government, General Bishop, argued that Instruction 54 marked the
beginning of 'the constructive side of De-Nazification'. Categorising would supposedly allow Germans to get on with their lives 'and gradually construct a sound
democratic society'.

The limited devolution of denazification brings us to the rather uncomfortable
matter of the British relationship with German anti-Nazis. While some British officers sang the praises of the SPD, and there was even a suspicion that the British
favoured social democrats in job appointments and in the allocation of paper for
the party press, even the most moderate of officers found it impossible to cooperate with German communists.[69] By mid-1946, senior figures in British military
government and the Foreign Office felt that their principle security responsibility was to foil 'communisation' of the zone. In addition, there were many military
government officers who shared a general dislike of left-wing Germans, no matter
what their permutation. For instance, the commander of the British garrison force,
General Richard McCreery, warned in 1947 that German communists were threatening to exploit the entire trade union movement as a vehicle for their purposes,
a point that he tactlessly hammered home by comparing the German situation
to communist influence in the British labour movement. Convenient cover for
such attitudes was provided by the 'collective guilt' doctrine. Such British elements feared that German socialists and communists would use domination of the
denazification process for partisan purposes – an irony since the original fathers of
denazification, Marcuse and Neumann, had intended precisely such a course – and
Robertson claimed that it was hardly Britain's responsibility to aid such efforts,
particularly after denazification was eventually transferred to the purview of the
Land governments.[70] When challenged with the idea of 'let[ting] the Left have a go'
and 'blowing off the lid', one military government officer explained that the British
intention was quite the opposite, 'Our job was indeed to put the lid on, and secure
it there with thumbscrews.'[71] German conservatives reciprocated the feeling; they
preferred to see the most important aspects of denazification remain with the occupying power. The NLP premier of Oldenburg, Theodore Tantzen, argued that if too
much responsibility was placed in German hands, *Schweinerei* (dirty dealing) would
result.[72] In the meantime, many Germans who had hoped for a genuine restoration of democratic values – and for the accompanying purge of the administrative
and economic structure – became bitterly disillusioned, and leftists began to argue
that denazification was wholly negative and did not ensure the creation of 'a new
progressive social order'.[73]

It should also be noted that the limited devolution of denazification was part
of a larger British hesitancy to delegate political power to the Germans. At the

beginning of the occupation, this autocratic tendency was no more evident than in the American zone – indeed, it was less tangible – but as early as the summer of 1945 there were signs of its growth. By 1947, the British had in place a 'dyarchy', somewhat similar to the power-sharing system in interwar India, in which *Land* legislatures enjoyed a relatively restricted range of prerogatives moderated by the powers of the 'Regional Commissioners'. This was quite unlike the U.S. experience because the British had never allowed demobilisation pressures to shrink the military government component of the British presence in Germany, at least to a degree comparable with that of their principle ally. By the end of 1945, the number of American troops subordinated directly to AMG had diminished to 12,000, while in the British zone, the number of personnel in military government had actually increased to nearly 26,000 (although British military government included administrative and intelligence elements that were subordinated to the regular army in the U.S. zone). In fact, there was grumbling in the home counties, *c.*1946/47, that British military government was unnecessarily swollen and was plagued with carpetbaggers whose main interest was cultivating personal profit at the expense of both the public purse and the defeated Germans.[74] On the other hand, there is no doubt that the presence of such elements allowed the British considerable discretion about when or where to hand over power to German officials. Ironically, it was precisely because of the limited scale of the British denazification programme, especially when compared to its American equivalent, that the occupation authorities were able to keep it under a tighter degree of control for a longer period.

Despite the fact that the British denazification programme never functioned at the grandiose scale of its American counterpart, and despite the fact that it was not devolved as rapidly as the U.S. zone programme, it suffered from many of the same difficulties. Punishments by German panels and committees were often lenient, particularly since the programme was only delegated when a degree of original enthusiasm by German leftists had faded, only to be replaced by cynicism. It was difficult to recruit adequate personnel, and the actual operation of bureaucratic machinery was ponderous. Indeed, panels reopened many cases that the British had already heard a year before (although this was sometimes necessary). The investigations of denazification committees were limited mainly to examining *Fragebogen*, and the individuals who were screened were frequently not called before the committees in person, thus ensuring that there was a subsequent flood of appeals. In fact, the absence of any degree of openness in committee deliberations left the bodies vulnerable to the charge that they were 'star chambers' (*Femegerichte*). The process was also subject to corruption, especially through the paid provision of *Persilscheine*, and it was not unknown for well-connected individuals to go over the heads of panel members and appeal directly to the British, often successfully.[75] As a result, there were discrepancies in the severity of punishments meted out to 'minor' and 'major' Nazis. Since only those

seeking employment were required to come before denazification panels, important Nazis could avoid appearing entirely if they could find a means of subsistence,
or if they could delay their appearance until the system was no longer functioning
with much sense of purpose. Wolfgang Krüger claims that the lack of a general
registration of the population actually facilitated the pursuit of such strategies, and
he points out that many nefarious Nazis, including Goebbels' right-hand man,
Werner Naumann, were able to submerge themselves amongst the population.
In the heavily-populated *Land* of North Rhine-Westphalia, only ninety persons
wound up categorized as 'Major Offenders' or 'Offenders'.[76] Thus, as one British
military government officer realised, 'we waste time, energy and money catching … little fish in our net, [b]ut the big sharks bide their time and swim around
it.'[77] As one might expect, the quantitative results of British denazification were
modest compared to numbers from the U.S. zone, although they were not insig-
nificant. By June 1946, 870,000 *Fragebogen* had been scrutinized, of which 1400

were being challenged for the provision of incorrect information. Nearly 111,000
people had been dismissed from employment and another 61,615 were refused a
job. In early 1947, the British reported to the Council of Foreign Ministers that
200,000 ex-Nazis had been had been subjected to purge and control measures.[78]

By 1947, even the Control Office was publically portraying denazification as
a necessary evil – 'a horrid tiresome business' was how it was described in parliament by the new minister responsible, Lord Pakenham[79] – and the British were
only too happy to end their participation. As early as January 1947, the Control
Office was encouraging British military government to consider rapid termination of the programme. Pakenham suggested concentrating on the cases of greatest
importance, extending the youth amnesty and telling the trade unions and anti-
Nazi parties to restrict the number of denunciations, many of which were now
regarded as frivolous. The Control Office also encouraged military government to
turn executive responsibility over to the German *Land* governments, at least once
these were elected. This procedure had been adopted experimentally in *Hansestadt*
Hamburg, which had elected a government in October 1946, and as Pakenham
noted, 'the experience gained in the case of Hamburg will be used in planning
the transfer of denazification to the Laender'. The 'Hamburg model' suggested the
appointment of a *Staatskommissar* for Denazification, and the further empowering
of existing eight-man committees to make near-final decisions, with the British
retaining the right of intervention only in exceptional cases. Robertson quibbled
with some of Pakenham's suggestions, but he agreed with his basic demand that
denazification now be handed off to the Germans as quickly as possible. Final
efforts to coordinate denazification with the Americans – who were now linked
to the British through the Bizone – and with the Russians proved abortive, but
when the Soviets signaled that they were winding up involvement in their own
programme, the British found a convenient precedent for limiting their own
intervention. As was the case with U.S. military government, the increasing rivalry

with the Russians, and the concurrent desire to strengthen western G
proved decisive in encouraging a change of policy, although the rapid sh
American policy caught the British off-guard. Meanwhile, Germans in the L
governments huffed and puffed about their refusal to take over a failed Britisн
instrument in its existing form – they wanted a wholly restructured denazification process with public hearings by *Spruchkammern* and absent the form of
categorisation promoted by the Allies – but their demands were largely ignored
by the occupying power.

On 31 October 1947, Ordnance 110 officially handed over denazification to
the zonal *Land* governments, and the latter, as in the U.S. zone, were asked to
adopt denazification laws based on CC Directives 24 and 38. As a face-saving
measure, ultimate control remained vested with the 'Regional Commissioners',
who were still opposed to any transfer of the programme, feeling that it would
lead to political chicanery and witch-hunts. Whatever the truth of this claim,
the commissioners retained the right to involve themselves in the categorisation
of individuals in the two highest classes of guilt. The British also continued to
administer Civil Internment Camps and they reserved the power to categorize
and punish former members of the *Wehrmacht*.

By this time, 2.144 million cases had been examined, which had produced
over 347,000 job dismissals and 2320 prosecutions for providing false answers
to *Fragebogen*. Since the population of the British zone was larger than that of
the U.S. zone, these numbers reflected a substantially lower per capita rate of
denazification punishments. In response to Foreign Office pressure, there were
no further firings after 1 January 1948, which was also the termination date for
the reopening of cases already heard (unless there was clear evidence of deceit
in responses to *Fragebogen*).[80] Meanwhile Pakenham, who was the smiling face
of British goodwill, claimed that re-education and other positive features of the
British presence had assumed 'the utmost importance'.[81]

The British zone *Länder* were disappointed by the terms of Ordnance 110, which
they had heartily opposed. They disliked the idea of rigid categorisation and they
were offended by British hesitancy in reopening files. As a result, the *Länder* pursued their responsibilities in lukewarm fashion. Only *Land* Schleswig-Holstein
passed the kind of law desired by the British and then only after military government pressured the *Landtag* to give up on the idea of extending the youth amnesty
to include people born between 1913 and 1918. The legislatures in Lower Saxony
and North Rhine-Westphalia authorised the programme through decree because
their denazification bills were regarded as unsatisfactory by the British and were
therefore vetoed. The North Rhine-Westphalian bill had pushed a maximalist
version of the German programme: no categorisation, a review mechanism for
past judgements and a youth amnesty including the 1913-18 cohort. The British
had found the Lower Saxon bill only marginally less objectionable. It had not
made provision for a review process, but the radical changes that it suggested for

the categorisation system would have meant the practical abandonment of that process.

By late 1949 there was evidence that unregenerate Nazis were flying through denazification hearings, and that some were being reinstated in their former jobs after a perfunctory period of exclusion, which Whitehall naturally saw as a threat to the achievement of Allied goals in Germany. In Hanover, for instance, a denazification panel classified Wilhelm Stuckart as a *Mitläufer*, even though Stuckart had been a former state secretary in the Reich Ministry of Interior, where he had implemented the Nuremberg Laws, and even though he had attended the Wannsee Conference, where SS officers and state bureaucrats had made technical arrangements for the Final Solution. In Düsseldorf, former Reich Finance Minister Lutz *Graf* Schwerin von Krosigk was slotted into category III and banned from future public service. In Bielefeld, Baron Kurt von Schröder, the man who had arranged the alliance between Hitler and Franz von Papen, received three months jail time and a small fine, a judgement so outrageous that it was greeted with protest strike by Bielefelder workers. The Foreign Office blamed British military government for such 'lackadaisical' results, while the latter shot back a reminder that it was the Foreign Office that had pressed for devolution in 1946/47. As in the U.S. zone, the Federal Republic finally coordinated a series of actions by the *Länder* in wrapping up the programme, although even then the British doggedly retained control over the two most serious categories of Nazis until 1953.[82] Wolfgang Krüger, in applying the Niethammer formula to the British zone, argues that the rehabilitative aspect of late British policy was actually a positive development, since it allowed for the reintegration of a potentially sullen and disruptive element.[83]

In assessing the impact of denazification in the British zone, voices on the Left have sometimes charged that it was even less successful than its U.S. equivalent. There is no doubt that the failure to permanently weaken the economic supporters of Nazi aggression was a scandal. In fact, one of the 'Regional Commissioners', George Macready, was warning as early as 1946 that reinstated Nazis in business were only paying lip service to the new tenets of democracy. Even in this regard, however, there was no guarantee that the removal of such people would have brought about the rise of new elements who were any more enlightened.[84] We might otherwise argue, however, that the British version of denazification was actually more successful than its American counterpart because it created fewer expectations and avoided at least the worst kind of policy oscillations that did so much to discredit AMG. Perhaps more than any other occupation policy, American-style denazification emphasized the discrepancy between Allied ideals, which were so loudly proclaimed, and actual practice, particularly since the arbitrary nature of the programme did nothing to suggest the rule of law.[85] As a result, any limitation of the sweeping and schematic nature of denazification was bound to win plaudits for the British and for the more positive policy goals that they supported. Ian Turner and Constantine FitzGibbon give credit to British military government for screening only 'persons in positions of authority', rather than the entire population, although Wolfgang Krüger rates this practice as one of the programme's weaknesses, since its effect was to focus attention upon civil servants at the expense of identifying and punishing Nazis in wider circles. Some historians have suggested that even British authorities created an overly broad and bureaucratic process, which often missed senior Nazis in the mania for removing large masses of people. Nonetheless, the popular mood of 1945, combined with the influence of the American model, meant that a more pragmatic approach was impossible to fully sustain.[86] Even in the limited scale of its application, the British version of denazification generated considerable bitterness among Germans and it encouraged the *ohne mich* (opting out) attitude toward politics, a traditional German tendency that had caused trouble in the past and was unfortunately carried into the post-war period.[87]

4

THE RED BROOM

It used to be commonly assumed that the Russian version of denazification was far different from its Western counterparts. When Western observers made passing mention of the Soviet purge, they often tended to portray it as part of a preconceived Stalinist communisation scheme – a 'master plot' – upon which all elements of the Soviet state and military were agreed. Thus, they concluded that the Soviet denazification programme had little independent importance, but was merely an intial means to achieve a more nefarious end.[1] Signs of contrasting trends within Soviet policy development were usually regarded as tactical manoeuvering, and as William McCagg notes, rampant evidence of Soviet policy confusion in occupied Germany discombobulated Western historians and political scientists.[2] How could there have been genuine differences among autonomous centres of power within the Stalinist state? Although much remains obscure, evidence from newly opened archives indicates a pattern of policy formation quite different from that suggested by Western models of totalitarianism or autocratic dictatorship. Although the Soviets might have wished to have been so clever, in practice they were hardly the superbly prepared Leninist intriguers portrayed in the West. Rather, like the Americans and the British, they were poorly organised, confused and indecisive. In the early phase of the occupation, Soviet commanders often replicated the tendency of the Western Allies to leave Nazis in place; like the Western Powers, they botched implementation of 'top-down' directives and were left reacting to local conditions; and as was the case with the Americans, Soviet policy was muddled and self-contradictory.[3]

In theory, the Soviets had an ideological conception of Nazism – a point in common with the Americans – but the set of goals that sprang from this understanding were hardly revolutionary. In 1935, the Comintern developed a new theory of fascism that was an obvious response to the rise of Hitler in Germany and Dollfuss in Austria, plus the near collapse of the French Third Republic in 1934. In the Comintern reckoning, fascism had always been a manifestation of the 'crisis of capitalism', but by the mid-1930s it had begun to dawn on Soviet and Comintern leaders that the supposed final collapse of capitalism – in the form of the Great Depression – was not furthering the advent of communism. Rather, fascists of various stripes were profiting as communist parties squabbled with social democrats, their fellow Marxists, in a bitter fight to dominate the working class movement and lead it to its supposed inheritance. By 1935, communist parties everywhere were in a weaker position than they had been in 1929/30, at the start of the international economic crisis, and the KPD and Austrian Communist Party had been smashed almost beyond repair – their members 'outlawed and hunted and beaten to death', as Arthur Koestler later noted. Thus, Comintern boss Georgi Dimitrov introduced a revised understanding of fascism: no longer was it just a standard form of bourgeois-capitalist reaction, it was now 'bestial chauvinism' and a model of 'medieval barbarity and bestiality'. Having thus identified fascism as an anomaly, special measures were appropriate in combating its profusion. From 1935 onward, the Comintern authorised communist parties to form 'Popular Fronts' with social democrats and even bourgeois liberals in an effort to fight the spread of fascism. Soviet foreign policy was oriented in the same direction, as the Kremlin showed a new openness to prospective Western allies and to the 'collective security' doctrine embodied in the League of Nations. Although this course underwent substantial alteration during the phase of Nazi-Soviet quasi-friendship from 1939 to 1941, Moscow went back to the 1935 policy after the German invasion of Russia, particularly through encouraging the formation of broad anti-Nazi resistance movements.[4]

For the Soviets, German nationals living within the USSR formed a special focus of interest. These elements were divided into two groups: first, German communist émigrés, most of whom had arrived in the 1930s, and second, the increasingly large pool of German prisoners-of-war, a congregation that swelled into the hundreds of thousands after the key turning point battles at Moscow, Stalingrad and Kursk. After several years of preparatory work, the Soviets merged KPD activists with willing PoWs in an anti-Nazi creation called the National Committee for a Free Germany (NKFD), although this innovation pushed the bounds of the 'Popular Front' doctrine by including conservative German military officers and even reform-oriented Nazis within the anti-fascist alliance. In fact, the Soviets pandered to the proclivities of such men by adopting the tricolor of the old Bismarckian-Wilhelmine Reich as the NKFD's flag, and by encouraging the KPD-in-exile to drop its demand for the 'elimination of the Hitler party's power apparatus and the Nazi system'. Thus, the essential job of the Free Germany movement was defined in relatively limited terms: it was to encourage the German Army to overthrow Hitler and thus bring the war to an end without a direct Soviet invasion of Germany. In late August 1943, the Soviets came within a whisker of describing the NKFD as 'the nucleus of a new German régime', although this concession was withheld because of secret peace feelers with the Nazis, which were preceding through Sweden and suggested that the Soviets might have to provide recognition to the existing German government. In any case, the NKFD failed to achieve the overthrow of Hitler. It had few contacts with the July 1944 conspirators who nearly succeeded in bringing about the dictator's ruin, and it was ineffectual even in encouraging *Wehrmacht* mutinies or mass desertions at the front.[5]

As both the NKFD and the covert Stockholm negotiations demonstrate, the Soviets throughout most of 1943 were still willing to sign a separate peace that involved no large-scale movement of the Red Army into Germany and that implicitly regarded denazification as a matter for Germans to work out. However, by the end of 1943, it was starting to look as if Soviet armies would have to complete the liberation of the homeland by force and then fight their way into Germany, just as the Western Allies were also preparing to do.[6] Stalin, it will be recalled, issued fearsome declarations at Teheran about the nature of a future occupation, although there was no consensus within the Kremlin about the essential character and goals of such an operation. As in the United States, various figures in the State Defense Committee, the *Politburo*, the Soviet bureaucracy and the KPD-in-exile tended to support different plans.

Essentially, there were three schools of thought. The 'hard peace' approach paralleled many of the notions put forward in the West by Morgenthau and Vansittart. This tack was first adopted by two special committees created by the *Politburo* in late 1943, when the success of military operations, as well as the goodwill at the Moscow and Teheran conferences, convinced the Soviets that it might be possible to get a foothold in Germany. The committee on post-war conditions and peace treaties was headed by one of the deputy ministers of foreign affairs, Maxim Litvinov. A second committee on reparations was chaired by the former Soviet envoy in London, Ivan Maiskii. Both committees recommended the dismemberment of Germany, and Maiskii suggested that the partitioned German states should be forced to recruit five million workers a year in order to perform forced labour in the USSR. Maiskii and one of the chief members of the Litvinov panel, Deputy Foreign Affairs Commissar Lozovskii, also pushed for the deindustrialisation of the prospective German successor states, particularly Prussia and the Rhineland. In 1944, the Maiskii-Lozovskii position was supported – in a fashion – by Georgi Malenkov, the chair of a cabinet-level 'Special Committee' that was closely connected with the heavy industry commissariats. For a period in 1944/45, Malenkov convinced some of his colleagues that the Western Powers would never permit the Sovietisation of Germany and that the USSR's best bet was simply to dismantle and extract massive quantities of industrial booty as quickly as possible, treating the occupation like a glorified pillaging expedition. Not coincidentally, such a course would strengthen Malenkov's own hand by securing massive 'direct reparations' controlled by the 'Special Committee'. Thus, it was Malenkov who was responsible for eventually dispatching the infamous dismantling teams

– 70,000 strong – which rummaged throughout eastern Germany, clothed with military uniforms and rank but answerable only to Moscow, and whose presence infuriated Red Army commanders trying to stabilise the condition of German civil society. Malenkov's representative in Germany was Maxim Saburov, whose dictum was, as expressed in June 1945, 'if we can't ship it out, it's better to destroy it, so that the Germans won't have it'.

Finally, we should also note that the influence of the 'collective guilt' doctrine increased dramatically during the last six months of the war, particularly after the failure of the NKFD's strategy of rousing an anti-Hitler revolt in Germany. In the official Soviet/KPD view, Germans had made themselves accomplices in Hitlerite crimes by failing to rise up or form active resistance movements. In particular, Ilya Ehrenburg, a prominent writer and member of the Jewish Anti-Fascist Committee, published some extremely caustic observations about German 'national character' and the type of treatment that Germans could expect from a vengeful Soviet host. Ehrenburg was a favourite contributor to *Krasnaya Zvezda* and earned a large following among Red Army combat troops, or *frontoviki*. His comments, along with some of Stalin's less flattering remarks, were the tinder used by Red Army political officers to fire Soviet soldiery into a vindictive mood as they descended upon Germany's eastern provinces, at which time the disciplinary code controlling military-civil relations was effectively suspended. The resulting mayhem of looting, rape and murder exceeded the bounds of anything that could have been imagined and was difficult to contain once it had exploded. The unintended effect was disastrous. Nothing so prejudiced the long term goals of Soviet forces, and of the KPD, as much as German popular knowledge of these abuses. Resentment lasted literally for generations.

A second school of thought suggested keeping Germany intact but Bolshevising it, or at least Bolshevising the zone directly under Soviet control and hoping that revolutionary currents would spread from there. This view was backed by the powerful Andrei Zhdanov, the Leningrad party boss and soon-to-be organiser of a nationwide reassertion of communist party authority, and by a group of Zhdanovite ideologues who published in the journal *Bolshevik*. These elements were determined to insert the idea of 'class struggle' back into Soviet foreign policy. In addition, Zhdanov had influence in the Red Army's Political Department, where one of his chief acolytes was Colonel (later General) Sergei Tiul'panov, a Leningrad university professor and eventual head of the propaganda service attached to Soviet military government. Although officially part of the army, the Political Department reported to the International Department of the Soviet communist party Central Committee, which was led first by Dimitrov, and later by Zhdanov. Certain figures of the KPD-in-exile also followed Zhdanov's lead. Like some Western intellectuals, members of the 'Bolshevising' faction saw the roots of the 'German problem' in the consistent success of reaction at various turning points in German history, notably the Reformation, the Peasant Wars, and the abortive revolutions of 1848 and 1918, and they emphasized how an archaic, militarist elite – the Junkers – had survived into the modern period. Thus, as in Russia in 1917, Germany was not ready for socialism in a classic Marxist reckoning (although unlike Russia at the time of the October Revolution, it had a working class majority). Nonetheless, the path to the future could still be cleared by Leninist shortcuts: that is, a rapid transition through a period of bourgeois democracy, seizure of the administrative apparatus, the nationalisation of industry – *not* its dismantling – and a rapid land reform campaign designed to break the power of the Junkers and supposedly deprive Nazis of a key base of support. Such maneuvres would implicitly follow the Russian model and would be concluded by a quick monopolisation of power by the KPD. Talk of democracy aside, some communists were also aware of the popular support that Hitler had enjoyed, and this factor alone seemed to justify the implicit creation of a custodial dictatorship.[7]

It was a disadvantage, of course, that the overtaxed Soviet and Red Army administrative systems lacked much of a revolutionary instrument for Germany. These elements had found little time to prepare for the occupation and the army was bereft of a distinct military government organisation, except at its most senior levels. Among the men who would serve in the Soviet Military Administration (SMA), few were familiar with Germany and scarcely any had received special training. Although the SMA's internal pattern of organisation was based heavily on the American model, there was precious little evidence of the handbooks or directives that were so important amongst the Western Allies. The result, as even the Soviets themselves admitted in 1944, was that they intended to control the German administration, *not* have Red Army soldiers directly govern Germans.[8] Such factors put a premium upon the potential of special KPD teams, or 'Initiative Groups', which were assembled under the leadership of Walter Ulbricht, Anton Ackermann and Gustav Sobottka, and were trained to accompany Soviet combat forces into Germany. The leaders of these teams were influenced by a more moderate conception of Germany's future that came to dominate Soviet thinking in 1944/45, but it is notable that the KPD's instructions for functionaries in Soviet-occupied territory, issued on 5 April 1945, recommended that appointments to key positions in regional and local administrations should go *not only* to German communists, but to KPD members who had gone into exile, a position that makes the broader concern for 'democracy' look rather disingenuous. Damian van Melis claims that the Initiative Groups 'served the establishment of communist hegemony in the Soviet occupation zone', and he cites one communist functionary explaining that the only purpose for more liberal Soviet policy directives was to provide cover to KPD operatives and prevent them from being popularly identified as 'agents of Moscow'.[9]

Incidentally, the aggressive and highly organised use of German refugees and re-educated PoWs was one of the methods that most distinguished Soviet policy from that of their American and British counterparts. The Anglo-American reluctance to employ sympathetic German émigrés, at least in anything more than incidental fashion, caused the Westerners problems in the early phases of the occupation,[10] although they also escaped the charge that they had foisted 'their' Germans upon the prostrate Reich. The use of former PoWs, however, was not always pleasing to the KPD, which was aware that thousands of Russian-trained ex-Nazis and *Wehrmacht* officers in the NKFD were being brought to Germany and installed in various administrative positions, some in the senior echelon.[11]

A third school of thought worked to preserve the 'Popular Front' strategy, which advocated the establishment of an anti-fascist German bourgeois order and the 'completion' of the 1848 Revolution, although it has been argued that this line of thought also descends from an old tradition of pragmatic fraternity between German and Russian ruling elites. In this concept, a phase of bourgeois democracy in Germany would still serve as a way station on the ultimate path to socialism, but it might be an extended period during which the Soviet Union would encourage a wide range of anti-fascist German forces and would work closely with the Western Allies. Such a course required re-education, land reform and decartelisation, but it otherwise implied less immediate interference in German affairs than schemes advanced by either the 'hard peace' faction or the 'Bolshivisers'. Germany would remain unified and its economy would not be weakened in any radical fashion. Politics would be revived under the banner of a widely-based 'Bloc for Militant Democracy', which comprised an attempt to learn the lessons of the early 1930s and create a broadly anti-fascist 'Unity Front'. This policy was championed by a third post-war planning committee, this one chaired by Klement Voroshilov, the minister of defense and a member of the State Defense Committee, and also by the Foreign Affairs Commissariat, whose two chief occupation planners, Andrei Smirnov and Vladimir Semenov, prepared many of the directives for Soviet forces in Germany. Semenov later went on to serve as the SMA's political advisor, a capacity in which he became an outspoken enemy of the radical Tiul'panov. One can find similarly moderate currents of thought promoted by the early leaders of the SMA, particularly the military governor, Marshal Georgii Zhukov, and by certain figures in the KPD-in-exile, especially the communist poet, Johannes Becher. Like the British, both Zhukov and Becher had a special interest in re-education, and Becher foresaw a prolonged gestation period of liberal democracy during which the German people would be philosophically remolded. Becher's position, not surprisingly, drew eventual scorn from Tiul'panov. Anton Ackermann, the chief KPD advocate of a 'separate German path to socialism', fell into the same liberal category. At the top of the administrative pyramid, Stalin originally backed the 'hard peace' school of thought, but during the spring of 1945 he opted for the 'gradualist' policy, perhaps because he feared that the Western Allies would bid for German affections and increasingly attempt to undercut the Soviet position. He expressed such concerns to a Czechoslovak delegation in March 1945. Two months later, he told German communist leaders that the need of the hour was an anti-fascist parliamentary regime and that the time for the 'Sovietisation' of Germany was not yet ripe.[12]

There is certainly no doubt that this more liberal approach shaped Soviet public rhetoric as the Red Army completed the last phase of the invasion of Germany. On 14 April 1945, Ehrenburg's Germanophobic invective was officially denounced in *Pravda* – significantly, by one of Zhdanov's colleagues – and within days the tone of Soviet propaganda had shifted from one of anti-German hatred to an attitude of tolerance and respect. Red Army troops subsequently plastered Berlin with banners and placards quoting Stalin's famous 23 February 1942 order-of-the-day, 'Hitlers come and go, but the German people and the German state remain'. The British, who had expected unrelenting Soviet harshness, were shocked by such an approach, as were the Americans. One U.S. officer ruefully noted that there were no 'collective guilt' posters in the Soviet zone; rather, the Red Army proclaimed that it 'does not make war on the German people' and that it had 'saved Berlin'. On 20 April, Stalin ordered Red Army troops 'to change their attitudes toward the Germans … and treat them better'. In his victory speech on 9 May, he abruptly announced that the Soviets did not wish to dismember Germany, although he had vigorously pushed such an objective at both Teheran and Yalta. In addition, the Soviets bragged that their troops were actively engaged in clean-up and reconstruction, and they were subsequently the first occupier to sanction German political activity.[13]

Despite the late dominance of the 'Popular Front' approach, 'hard peace' and 'Bolshevik' undercurrents remained tangible, and as Soviet forces arrived in Germany, various factions within the SMA, the occupation garrison, the dismantling teams and the Soviet secret police were driven by different sets of priorities. It was in this confusing atmosphere, further complicated by the inherent chaos of the situation, that Soviet denazification policy crystallised.

In the view of the Maiskii-Malenkov-Ehrenburg school of thought, the denazification programme should naturally be tough. The Maiskii committee suggested, for instance, that not only war criminals should be severely punished, 'but also the members of the SS, the SA, the Nazi Party apparatus and wide circles of the military, naval and air-force leaderships.' In January 1945, Maiskii told the U.S. ambassador that millions of Germans brought to Russia for forced labour would come from the ranks of lesser war criminals and Nazi Party activists.[14] Maiskii also talked about re-education, but it was obvious that for the hardliners, the desire to punish past behaviour outweighed the need to rehabilitate or reintegrate 'small fry' Nazis. Nonetheless, denazification enjoyed only secondary consideration amongst such elements because it was assumed that German power would be broken by large-scale industrial confiscations and that the entire population would be terrorised into submission.

The 'Bolshevik' policy put a premium on changing the nature of German society and thus achieving denazification in the most holistic sense. Walter

Ulbricht, for instance, advocated the 'liquidation of the foundations of German fascism'. German communist leaders also talked about a wide scale purge of the Nazi administrative apparatus, although it was clear that such measures were really meant to supplement the broader strategy, particularly by facilitating the installation of their own cadres in the administration, justice system, schools and police.

The logic of the 'gradualist' course suggested a denazification drive closely coordinated with the Western Powers, including the use of *Fragebogen* and a dependence on job dismissals as the main form of punishment. However, one of the most distinctive features of Soviet denazification policy was also rooted in the 1935 Comintern definition of fascism (and all that flowed from it). Because fascism was supposedly a unique form of dictatorial barbarism, many rank-and-file *Parteigenossen* had presumably been dragooned into the NSDAP and were therefore not fully responsible for their actions. This exculpation of 'nominal' Nazis came to dominate Soviet denazification rhetoric and eventually became the source of considerable conflict with the Americans, particularly since it was a view shared by the 'Bolshevisers', who argued that 'nominal' Nazis were dangerous only so long as they served as the tools of Junkers and business magnates. Once the latter elements had been dispossessed, 'ordinary' Nazis were presumably no longer a major problem.[15] 'From the very beginning,' the SMA boasted, 'principal attention was mainly directed to [the] tracing and bringing to trial of leading officials of the Nazi party', an approach that supposedly avoided the trap of chasing large numbers of 'nominal' Nazis while 'real criminals' escaped justice.[16] The Americans simply saw the Soviets employing whoever seemed amenable to their purposes, a source of worry because it suggested that the Soviets might be able to revive their zone more quickly than its western counterparts.[17]

Aside from a set of contradictory goals and the initially poor codification of standards, early Soviet denazification practice was characterised by the near independence of Red Army combat commanders, who typically served as the first generation of town commandants. This practice marked the continuation of an old Russian military custom. The headquarters of town commandants, called *Kommandaturas*, ran German cities and rural counties like mediaeval fiefs, particularly before the official creation of the SMA on 6 June 1945, but for several months afterward as well. They rarely consulted senior echelons in the Red Army, much less accepting advice from German anti-fascists, although the truth was that such local headquarters rarely employed anybody with specialised knowledge of Germany and they were frequently out of depth. In each *Kommandatura*, the deputy commandant ran the local Operations Group (*Opergruppa*) of the Soviet security ministry, the NKGB, and he concerned himself with 'terrorists, diversionaries and other fascist elements', although this task obviously overlapped with denazification.

The autonomy of Red Army commanders was facilitated by administrative directives that were exceedingly broad. First Ukrainian Front and Second

Byelorussian Front merely instructed town commandants to choose mayors, *Landräte* and police chiefs who were 'anti-fascists'.[18] One officer admitted,
'There are no good Germans, only Germans. For Buergermeisters we select
any non-Nazis, democrats, Socialists, even Catholics.'[19] In Mecklenburg, the
Russians explained merely that they wanted members of the local elite who were
familiar to the population but were not part of the NSDAP.[20] However, apart from
the positive act of appointing non-Nazis to various posts, the development of a
thorough screening process was originally a secondary concern, and it was only a
matter of luck that the programme was facilitated by a mass flight to the west of
many Nazi mayors, administrative personnel and economic elites.[21]

Unfortunately, the decentralized nature of denazification meant that many
Nazis and extreme nationalists were able to slip through the initial appointment
processes. For instance, in many small towns in Saxony, Thuringia and Prussian
Saxony, which were briefly occupied by U.S. troops, American town-majors had
retained Nazi holdovers and the Russian commandants replacing them did the
same. Moreover, as an NKGB officer reported in July 1945, many Nazis, state
bureaucrats and 'Gestapo men' were flooding back into these areas, after having initially fled across the Mulde River.[22] Thus, in Lünzenau, Eisleben and
Beckendorf, Nazi *Bürgermeister* remained in place throughout the summer of
1945 (although in the last case, the incumbent claimed that he had once been
a social democrat). In such instances, local KPD members launched repeated
protests to Russian officers. In Liebertwolkwitz, for instance, members of a local
anti-fascist group complained that the *Bürgermeister* 'consciously sabotaged Antifa
[anti-fascist] measures', denying group members the jobs of Nazi placeholders
and allowing *Parteigenossen* to stay in their homes. Nonetheless, the local Russian
commandant allowed the mayor to remain in office, albeit advising him to undertake measures demanded by the town's anti-fascists. In Ballenstedt, the police
chief was a *Parteigenosse* and a fanatic opponent of the occupying power. In the
Harz Mountain town of Quedlinburg, the mayor, Dr Falz, was a former member
of the Nationalist Peoples' Party and was hated by local leftists, particularly communists, who whispered that through Falz's retention, 'the [town] commandant
is doing the same thing as the English and Americans have done.' By all accounts,
relations between the Soviet commandant and the Quedlinburg chapter of the
KPD were poor, and the latter was hindered in its attempts to organise. In the
Saxon city of Grimma, the KPD charged that the mayor's agricultural administrator was actively spreading 'fascist' propaganda, and in the county around
the city, nineteen of sixty-nine village mayors were still Nazis (versus eleven
communists, nine social democrats and three liberal democrats).[23] In Thuringia,
the initial *Land* denazification decree of 23 July ordered a blanket removal simply of
Nazis who had joined the NSDAP before 1 April 1933, with 'mandatory removal'
categories covering only leaders and security personnel amongst post-1933 members. Such haphazard denazification measures left a third of NSDAP bureaucrats

still in place at the end of 1945, although the *Land* premier still complained that removals were crippling his administration. Thuringia, he claimed, had been such a heavily Nazified *Land* that it was nearly impossible to find replacements.[24]

Lest we accept that such episodes owed to the bad example set by American combat commanders, a claim that East German historians were wont to make,[25] it is worth noting that a similar lack of denazification initiative occurred in areas overrun directly by Red Army forces. Although many of these districts had experienced spontaneous forms of denazification launched by anti-fascist committees, the Soviets were suspicious of such bodies because they lacked central control and were the source of undirected revolutionary impulses. Thus, as in the western zones, most anti-fascist committees were dissolved by fiat.[26] The most important anomaly was in the Schwarzenberg district, along the northern slopes of the Ore Mountains. This remote and sparsely populated sector remained unoccupied until late June, so it was local anti-fascists who liberated the region's principal towns and fought Nazi bandits who fled to the hills. On 9 May, an anti-fascist committee overran the town hall of Meinersdorf, arresting the NSDAP mayor and functionaries, and a similar sequence of events unfolded three days later in the town of Schwarzenberg, where an armed anti-fascist detachment chased off the Nazi *Bürgermeister*. Such groups enjoyed total executive power until the Red Army arrived.[27]

In many regions, however, the Soviets kept Nazis in place because the latter possessed vital technical or administrative expertise, and even SA and SS members sometimes managed to find their way into municipal police forces. One Russian rationalized such practices by arguing that the SMA was unlikely to be influenced by the Nazis ideologically, so 'we [feel free to] use the brains of the Nazis as much as possible'. In Kyritz, a German communist functionary reported in July 1945 that Nazis filled the local administration, 'while old KPD comrades are occupied with other physical tasks'. During the same period, another KPD cadre made a similar claim about the town of Plau, near Parchim, admitting that while the mayor, deputy mayor and police chief were either communists or social democrats, all second-tier officials were Nazis, and that *Parteigenossen* still had practical control of the town. In Niederbarnim, the local Soviet commander actually told district mayors that 'Nazis should not be treated in a different manner from the remaining population', and he prohibited the assignment of 'discriminatory special work' as a punishment. In Neuruppin, the Soviet commandant backed the local *Landrat*, Jerx, himself a former Hitler Youth leader and NSDAP member, in his defiance of a severe denazification order circulated by the new Brandenburg *Land* government. Jerx argued that the worst Nazis had already been dropped from office, and that a local investigatory committee, aided by the propaganda department of the Red Army, would deal with the remainder, cognisant of the need to gather the harvest. In early September, Jerx's committee produced a list of fifty-seven incriminated Nazis, although this was reviewed by the Soviet commandant and

cut to a mere fifteen persons. In addition, mayoralties in the country villages surrounding Neuruppin were occupied almost entirely by Nazis, whose political fate
was awaiting collection of the harvest. In yet another town in *Land* Brandenburg,
the mayor was a Nazi Party member who had destroyed local party records in an
attempt to foil Soviet denazifiers. This same individual also held a job as a school
teacher, where he continued to permit children to address each other with the
'*Heil* Hitler!' greeting. A local scandal developed when it came to light that the
Russian town commandant had become aware of the *Bürgermeister*'s identity, but
allowed him to remain in office anyway.[28] In the brown coal mine 'Bergwitzer',
near Wittenberg, the occupying power initially fired and even arrested a few personnel, but it took a bruising struggle by communist and socialist trade unionists in
order to sack their employer, Director Danert, although the latter was a Nazi and
had allegedly lied to the authorities about the pace of denazification. Even when
finally toppled, Danert was promptly reinstated by the local SMA headquarters
in Halle.[29] In the Hanseatic port town of Greifswald, none of 236 Nazis in the
municipal government was fired, and in *Land* Mecklenburg-Vorpommern, 239 of
371 senior officials were NSDAP members. In August 1945, the Soviets ordered
the *Land* government to fire twenty-seven key Nazis, although as late as October,
nearly thirty per cent of the *Land*'s 3,800 employees were still *Parteigenossen*.[30]

On the other hand, some zealous Red Army commanders organised sweeping dismissals, occasionally even executing Nazi officials.[31] Certain Soviet officers
allowed local anti-Nazis to continue playing a role in overthrowing the Hitlerite
order, or they allotted special powers to the KPD, quite in opposition to official SMA policy. In Leipzig, for instance, the Soviet *Stadt* commandant, Trufanov,
appointed a joint SPD/KPD committee to purge the municipal administration.
In Meissen, the Soviet commander allowed a band of revolutionary Marxists
to run the town and clear out local Nazis, even sequestering factories that had
belonged to Nazis and 'Nazi collaborators'. Overall, 6,842 Nazis had been fired in
Land Saxony by mid-November 1945, a number that included nearly all mayors,
Landräte and town council members in the state. In Belzig, the ardent Soviet garrison commander, Kovalov, talked about maintaining the occupation 'until the
last fascist lies in the earth', and he refused to distinguish between 'small' and
'big' Nazis. Kovalov appointed a KPD *Landrat* and allowed the functioning of an
anti-fascist committee, particularly since he saw such elements as essential allies
in an on-going war with the 'fascists', '[who] are continuously disrupting work
in the cities and the villages'. 'The Nazis,' explained the *Landrat*, 'will be handled
the same way they handled us, that is: hard.' Local communists reopened the
Niemegker concentration camp and filled it with incarcerated Nazis, even refusing such people the ministrations of a local pastor – 'we cannot allow a feeling of
sympathy to develop'. In Angermünde, the Soviets permitted German anti-fascists
to assemble a list of Nazi Party members, mainly by using residential registration
records, and then to force these people to perform 'dirty work', including the

exhumation of dead bodies. In Stralsund, the Soviet military intendant, Colonel Fomenko, swept the decks of Nazi administrative officials and teachers and his choice as police chief, the communist labourer Schmitz, threatened to 'rub out' all fascists. Fomenko also seized property individually owned by Nazis or by anybody else who had fled the town or committed suicide. Fomenko had an interesting relationship with the leader of the Stralsund SPD, Otto Kortüm. Although he appointed Kortüm to the mayoralty, he also frequently threatened to shoot him. In August 1945, when reports came to light suggesting that Kortüm had hidden onetime membership in the NSDAP, the unhappy mayor – his health already broken by tension – was unceremoniously fired. And in Breddin, the Soviet-appointed mayor ejected eleven families from their homes and ordered them not just to leave the village, but to vacate the entire district of Ostprignitz. Several of these expellees were 'nominal' Nazis and one was merely the wife of a party member. After a review, these actions were eventually overturned by the Justice Ministry of *Land* Brandenberg, which ordered the expropriated property returned to its owners. In such cases, German leftists often exploited the situation to settle private scores and vendettas, but as Michael Balfour notes, this proved of little interest to the Russians, who 'were not much concerned about doing justice to the Germans'.[32]

Much depended on the individual personality and preferences of Soviet commanders. In the city of Görlitz, situated on the new border with Poland, the first Russian commandant, Nesterov, denounced the NSDAP but otherwise made it clear that he would not persecute 'fascists' who had been 'forced' into the Nazi Party, at least as long as such elements were willing to help in reconstruction, nor would he interfere with most forms of private property. Only teachers, Nesterov insisted, had to be beyond reproach, and his city school superintendent, Paul Gatter, a former concentration camp inmate and SPD member, was able to cleanse the school system because of the flood of refugees from Polish-occupied territories. This surge had created a local surplus of teachers, some of whom were untainted. In the fall of 1945, however, Nesterov was replaced by his less liberal successor, Saizev, who immediately demanded the release of all National Socialists from the Görlitz civic administration. Saizev cooperated with the new *Bürgermeister, Herr* Oehme, and the latter proved exceedingly eager to please the SMA, although he put himself in an awkward position by arguing for the retention of five municipal employees – three nurses and two cashiers – who he argued it would be difficult to replace. In November 1945, Oehme was arrested by the Soviet secret police, who had discovered that he – or a man with the same name – had joined the Anti-Bolshevik League in 1919.[33]

There was a somewhat more consistent course in areas where the three 'Initiative Groups' exercised direct influence, especially since they worked with extensive 'white lists' that had been compiled before the advance into Germany, and they also had the contacts necessary to bring NKFD-trained mayors and police chiefs into the defeated Reich. The 5 April instructions for KPD functionaries ordered the cleansing of both the private economy and public administration, although in the latter field it was allowable to employ carefully screened 'nominal' Nazis, particularly engineers, teachers and doctors, and to retain the wives of Nazi Party members.[34]

In Berlin, the situation initially encountered by Ulbricht's 'Initiative Group' resembled a scene from Dante's Inferno: the Reich capital had been transformed into an ugly landscape of shelled and bomb-demolished rubble studded with hungry and demoralised civilians, drunken Soviet victors and dazed *Wehrmacht* defenders. The bodies of dead soldiers littered the ruins. Soviet artillery pieces were still blasting at buildings containing SS hold-outs and the sky was obscured by smoke billowing from the ruins. The civilian inhabitants of the city numbered less than half the prewar total of four million. Raging Soviet troops terrorised the population – at least 100,000 women were raped – but Red Army officers had also begun the distribution of food from captured German stocks.[35]

Russian officers, led by the new Berlin *Stadt* commandant, General Nikolai Berzarin, found it difficult to find anyone brave enough to serve as civic officials, particularly since they did little to protect German civilians in their service and when such people were killed, they took no retaliatory measures. As a result, the officials chosen by the Soviets included a large number of incompetents, opportunists or active Nazis, some of whom had been taken away for questioning, but were then returned to their posts if they showed signs of a hasty 'conversion'. Starting on 2 May, however, Ulbricht's personnel circulated throughout the shattered city, purging Nazis and 'reactionaries'. In Köpenick, Ulbricht's men listened attentively as local communists complained 'that the fascist movement is not dead, that the Nazis organise illegally and make demands … [and] that more must be done against fascism'. In the borough of Friedenau, where a local Soviet commandant proved negligent in retaining Nazi holdovers, Ulbricht went above his head, remonstrating directly to Zhukov and even using his connections with the NKGB to secure an *Opergruppa* willing to 'clean up' the precinct. As new mayoral appointees, Ulbricht typically favoured social democrats in working class boroughs and Catholics or liberals in bourgeois districts. True power, however, was reserved for deputy mayors, who were always German communists (and at a key points, Moscow émigrés). Ulbricht paid lip service to the 'Popular Front' doctrine, but actually did his best to lay the groundwork for a future 'Bolshevik' course, treating the 'gradualist' elements of his orders with a wink and a nod. 'It's got to look democratic,' he confided to members of his 'Initiative Group', 'but we must have everything in our control.' In late May, he chose the frail and unenergetic Arthur Werner as *Oberbürgermeister* of Berlin, although in keeping with established practice, real power lay in the hands of Ulbricht's lieutenant, Karl Moran, who was appointed deputy lord mayor.[36]

Despite whatever qualms we might have about Ulbricht's methods, there is no doubt that public administration in the German capital was effectively denazified. In the first three months of the occupation, 16,000 Nazi placeholders were dropped from municipal service and then further punished by being assigned to clear rubble, particularly 'Nazi-connected women'. Nazis were also penalised with restricted access to rations.[37] When U.S. forces arrived in their occupation sector in July 1945, they found that local officials were 'pure', although there was a resulting problem with incompetence. 'This was the price,' one American officer noted, 'that had to be paid for cleaning out Nazi officialdom.'[38] Of 12,000 former members of the Berlin municipal police, only 160 were still in uniform.[39] Somewhat less impressive was the fact that NKGB secret agents continued to swoop into the western sectors of the city in illegal searches for surviving Nazi placeholders, a practice that eventually resulted in an ugly confrontation between Western Allied and Soviet representatives in the four-power *Kommandatura* controlling the city.[40]

If one overarching theme characterised the early Soviet occupation effort, it was a wide scale pattern of arrests. Among Soviet commandants and members of the 'Initiative Groups', almost everyone agreed that large numbers of enemy civilians merited confinement. As a result, the NKGB *Opergruppy* had free run of the Russian zone from the first days of the occupation, although their efforts in the early phase focused mainly on confining security suspects and levying workers for forced labour in the USSR. Captive Nazis often tripped over themselves in a rush to provide denunciations before they themselves were denounced, and the Soviets also extorted such prisoners into helping the NKGB track down fugitive German officers and NSDAP members. Squads with sniffer dogs diligently searched apartments, cellars and allotment sheds throughout the captured German territories. In total, 138,000 Germans had been arrested by mid-April 1945. On 18 April, however, secret police boss Lavrenti Beria ordered the *Opergruppy* to worry less about deporting large numbers of Germans to Russia – if fact, he specified that non-Nazis should now be released – but he also supplemented NKGB arrest lists with 'automatic arrest' categories, which were loosely based on American models. Because the Americans had already given the Soviets extensive information about their own denazification plans, including copies of the SHAEF *Handbook*, the Soviets apparently realised that there was no room in Allied planning for the implementation of the Maiskii scheme, that is, the deportation of millions of Germans as slave labour. Subsequently, all they could do to circumvent this restriction was to continue treating captured SS and SA officers as if they were members of the German armed forces, thereby rendering them subject to evacuation to Soviet PoW camps and thus exploitable as forced labour. In the western zones, most SS and SA internees were kept in the domestic internment camp system.

Meanwhile, tens of thousands of civilian detainees quickly came to populate a series of eleven Soviet zone detainment camps, including some facilities that had formerly been run by the Nazis. At *Speziallager* Bautzen, for instance, a three-week period in June 1945 saw the number of prisoners climb from 1,000 to over 4,000, mostly 'active' Nazis, although at this stage mere possession of a NSDAP party book was considered sufficient evidence of 'activism'. Some estimates suggest that as many as 240,000 people eventually found themselves deposited in these camps. In general, conditions were even worse than in the similar facilities in the western zones and detainees were typically held for a longer period. Lack of food and medical care meant that a large proportion of the internees, perhaps a third or more, died in Soviet custody, a ratio almost as high as the rate of mortality in Nazi concentration camps. Those who perished from dysentery, tuberculosis and starvation were often buried in mass graves on the perimeter of the camp wire. The remainder waited at least three years until they were finally freed through various amnesties, mostly in 1948 and 1950.[41]

Aside from indisputable success in organising mass lock-ups, however, the initial Soviet denazification effort soon showed signs of flailing. Zhukov had twice ordered that Nazis be restricted to manual labour, but such commands had little practical effect, either because they were poorly disseminated or because they came in such flurries that they could hardly be digested.[42] It was only in the fall of 1945, a year after the Soviets had grabbed an initial foothold in East Prussia and six months after the final conquest of eastern Germany, that a set of coherent denazification orders were issued. On 13/14 November, Zhukov told a gathering of *Land* premiers that unreconstructed Nazis were disguising themselves as anti-fascists and thereby hindering administrative work and spreading rumours. As a result, a radical acceleration of denazification measures was necessary.[43] One fundamental instruction, reflecting the spirit of the Potsdam declaration and the forthcoming CC Directive 24, required that Nazi Party members be dropped from public office within two months. On 29 November, this directive was supplemented by SMA Order Number 153, which made adult *Parteigenossen* eligible for participation in labour gangs, and indicated that the job of such groups was to perform 'especially dirty and unpleasant work', mainly agricultural labour, rubble clearance and foraging for firewood. On 30 October, Order Number 124 confiscated the property of National Socialists and militarists, resulting in the sequestering of 7,890 private firms. And finally, on 23 December, the SMA issued Order Number 128, which instructed *Land* officials to aid in the operations of Allied military tribunals and to prosecute war crimes cases in which the victims had been German nationals or stateless persons.

The issuance of these instructions marked the launch of a lumbering denazification drive over the winter of 1945/46. Officially, Soviet officers would brook no deviation from these commands and by early 1946, over 300,000 Nazis had been released from municipal and *Land* governments. In some places, the programme scored notable successes. In *Land* Mecklenburg-Vorpommern, a powerful member of the maximalist wing of the KPD, Interior Minister Johannes Warnke, had already ordered the dismissal of *all* Nazis, including 'nominals', and he made only limited concessions for 'urgently needed' specialists. As a result, Mecklenburg-Vorpommern released Nazis more quickly and more completely than any other state in the Soviet zone, and the *Land* was largely swept clean by the beginning of 1946. On the other hand, there was a wide range of Nazi-friendly subterfuges that the occupation authorities tolerated (if not endorsed). For instance, the SMA indicated in January 1946 that if ex-Nazis had joined 'a socialist party', meaning the KPD or SPD, they could be retained in office without special permission from the SMA. This loophole was successfully exploited in Calau, where the local commandant, Lieutenant Colonel Kolessov, was thwarted in his attempt to impose a strict interpretation of the November decree. In *Land* Brandenburg, the authorities lightened their burden by amnestying all Nazis born after 1920, a measure that was later reinforced with legislation by the state assembly. Local administrations also took advantage of a tactic that had been used in the western zones: technical experts who were released as employees were rehired on contract, being paid by the hour. Similarly, tenured civil servants (*Beamte*) could be rehired as salaried employees (*Angestellte*) or – somewhat more humiliatingly – as manual workers (*Arbeiter*). German authorities skirted SMA Order 153 by excusing Nazi forced labourers from their assigned tasks or by providing them with a validation of labour even if they had failed to show up for work.

According to Soviet instructions, all Nazis should have been dropped from public offices and jobs by the end of 1945, but it quickly became clear that this was not the case. In an especially serious charge, the SMA's transport administrator, P.A. Kvashin, claimed that not only was the *Reichsbahn* keeping fascists in positions of responsibility – a longstanding accusation – but that it was actually harbouring Nazi saboteurs. Even in Mecklenburg-Vorpommern, the *Reichsbahn* was still full of Nazis. Despite such concerns, however, the SMA soon had to concede defeat, admitting that it had allowed so many exemptions to denazification that the exception had become the rule. SMA officers, understaffed and flummoxed by the magnitude of their responsibilities, were in no position to run a programme undertaken at such a grand scale. Saxon anti-fascist administrators trying to get permission to fire Nazi mayors, *Landräte* and school administrators found that their requests sometimes sat in SMA offices for six to eight months before being acted upon. It was also obvious that a year's worth of inconsistent instructions and unattainable deadlines was already hindering reconstruction. In consideration of such circumstances, SMA told the Germans that 'all remaining former National Socialists may be further employed for the present,' although none should be retained in 'leading positions' and technical experts should be hired as paid-by-the-hour contractors. Nazis who had already been dropped were still banned from reapplying for their old jobs. Even these limited concessions proved inadequate, and it soon became clear that many Nazis were still in supervisory positions, whether or not they were officially employed at such a pay grade. By the summer of 1946, the *Land* government of Brandenburg was swamped with requests to rehire dismissed Nazis, and a *Landrat* in Saxony complained that 'public employees give former Nazis certificates, which state that these Nazis are to be treated as though they were Antifas [anti-fascists]'. In Prussian Saxony, the state premier, Dr Erhard Hübner, fought for the jobs of a number of placeholders and rejected the conduct of a wholesale purge, telling the SMA, 'Fire only the less productive, instead of [having] "a political cleaning".'[44]

Considering the Soviet attitude toward private property, Order Number 124 seemed an especially important initiative, although – typically – it was mishandled. 'Sequestering' of German material and assets had been occurring since the start of the occupation, although as Vladimir Semenov admitted, such actions had frequently amounted to nothing more than looting. Order 124 did little to improve the situation. Soviet officers continued to grab cars, apartments and houses, which often belonged to 'nominal' Nazis or even to non-Nazis. In the spring of 1946, when SMA officers calculated that several hundred Russians would probably visit the Leipzig Trade Fair, which they were about to revive, they casually commandeered 300 residences, along with furniture and radios (although there was some doubt about whether the latter objects were even included under Order 124). The SMA's German communist allies also ran amuck, seising houses, factories, warehouses and workshops, often for their own personal enrichment. In *Land* Saxony, for instance, a communist *Landrat*, Kurt Böhme, comported himself like a medieval prince, seising everything from chickens and rabbits to whole houses. It was also alleged that he had stolen two precious postage stamps, valued at 100,000 *Mark*, during the confiscation of a Junker estate. Another communist official, *Bürgermeister* Neuber of Bennewitz, boldly proclaimed that 'property rights of Nazis do not exist in the new Germany'. Rather than worry about such excesses, Ulbricht convinced the 'German Committee on Expropriations and Sequestering', which was set up in the spring of 1946, to expand its targeting to any factory-owner who had benefitted from the war – that is, almost all factory owners – although such elements often put up tough legal fights, which left sequestration cases clogging court dockets. Some Nazis tried to bribe the new authorities and thus avoid arbitrary seizures, sometimes with a degree of success. In Zwickau, the public complained that 'minor' Nazis suffered the loss of their radios and furniture, but that the villas of major Nazis were declared off-limits, and the same type of complaint came from Eisenach, where refugees were jammed nine or ten to a room, but senior Nazis 'were still living happily in wonderful homes'. The infamous Kurt Böhme helped Nazis keep refugees out of their houses or he aided them in flights to the western zones, at least if they were able to pay for such services.

In Saxony, which had the most industry of the five Soviet zone *Länder*, Fritz Selbmann, the communist labour and economics minister, saw problems with Order 124 and tried to apply the breaks, 'Command 124,' he averred, 'has been properly implemented almost nowhere... One needs sensitivity. It is important not to go after the little NS party members.' He also noted that 'nominal' Nazis were supposed to be retained as trustees in sequestered firms, but that such elements were frequently being purged and replaced by unqualified trustees. The result was lagging production, not only in the sequestered companies but in a wider circle of firms that were connected through supply chains. As a result of such realisations, there was soon rapid backpedaling, particularly in Saxony-Anhalt and Thuringia, where there were extensive delays in sequestration and an increasing appetite for entertaining appeals. In some areas, the Soviets approved a limited return of firms to their previous owners or the retention or rehiring of Nazis. German communists and trade unionists were shocked to find that in sequestered companies to which the Soviets established direct title – so-called *Sowjetische Aktiengesellschaften* – Russian managers frequently privileged technical competence over ideological goals and were thus comfortable with employing Nazi directors and engineers. In Schwarzheide, for instance, a Soviet commandant running the local synthetics works countermanded a German communist resolution to fire 175 'active' Nazis from the factory's staff, admitting – amasingly – that the USSR's purge of its own economic management class had proven a costly mistake! In Berlin, the Russians brazenly recruited *Herr* Benkert, an 'active' Nazi whose presence on the Siemens' company directorate had been scored by the communists and who was eventually dismissed by the British and then condemned by a denazification panel in Spandau, which held him directly responsible for the death of a Jewish forced labourer. Nonetheless, the Soviet Technical Governmental Commission hired Benkert and then sent him to the KTB concern in Niedersedlitz, where he worked on the mass production of electric motors. Meanwhile, in *Land* Saxony-Anhalt, a government official conceded that there were twenty-four Nazis employed in the authority controlling sequestered companies.

In an effort to show that there was popular support behind Order 124, the Soviets scheduled a referendum on the measure in Saxony, the most Left-leaning *Land*, and Tiul'panov got busy in bullying the zonal chapter of the CDU into backing the motion. The referendum passed in July 1946 and allowed the Saxon Government to become the first German state authority to convert expropriated assets into 'people's property', The same model, *sans* referenda, was then followed in the remaining Soviet zone *Länder*.[45]

Another troublesome field was education. Since Soviet leaders had themselves created a totalitarian society, they were acutely aware of the ideological role played by teachers and university professors. Thus, they distrusted the surviving remnants of the past system, which had once been as thorough as their own in indoctrinating young minds. As a result, Moscow tormented the SMA's Education Department with demands to replace Nazi educators, even though the sad truth was that over seventy per cent of teachers in the Soviet zone had been *Parteigenossen*, a much higher number than the Germany-wide average of fifty-five per cent. In *Länder* Mecklenburg-Vorpommern and Thuringia, the ratios exceeded eighty-five per cent, and such high proportions meant that tainted teachers were difficult to replace. In May and June 1945, the Soviets fired a quarter of all the teachers in Berlin and then reopened the capital's schools on 11 June, although they were already short of anti-Nazi replacements. In August and September 1945, the occupiers organised a series of three week training courses for 'new teachers', mostly KPD and SPD members drawn from the working class, but they had time to train only a trickle of personnel – 15,000 – by the time that the new school year started on 1 October. As a result, there were still numerous NSDAP members active in the zone's schools. In March 1946, there were 2,336 *Parteigenossen* teaching in *Land* Brandenburg, and the educational system in Saxony-Anhalt remained full of 'active' Nazis, even as late as the summer of 1947. Moscow harshly criticized the SMA's Education Department for these failures, despite the fact this section's cadres were overwhelmed with the enormous magnitude of their task. In fact, there was no other field where the purge was so carefully monitored or where such narrowly fixed criteria were set to define success. Teachers were the only occupation group upon which the Soviets imposed a quota for the employment of non-Nazis: at least ninety per cent of teachers, they stipulated, had to be free of the taint of NSDAP membership, although in 1947 they were forced to re-certify many 'nominal' Nazis, arguing that these people had been effectively rehabilitated.[46]

Similarly radical measures were undertaken in institutions of higher learning. SMA's Education Department carefully tracked the number of Nazi professors at universities in the zone, and in August 1945, Zhukov ordered all professors to fill out a form explaining not only their relationship to the NSDAP, but outlining their general views on pedagogy and higher education. Subsequently, 'active' Nazis were dismissed and then the 'nominal' variety as well. Unlike the case in the British zone, professors in eastern Germany showed a distinct lack of success in defending themselves against the purge or defying schematic denazification. Denazification, combined with a mass flight to western Germany by both Nazis and non-Nazis, left only a quarter of the professors in the zone's six major universities – 329 of 1,260 scholars – still in the classroom by the beginning of 1946. Of this number, only a dozen were Nazis, and this few survived only because they had wrangled qualifications as 'exceptional personnel'. Naturally, the lack of adequate replacements meant a deterioration in the quality of teaching. The universities were also ordered to increase the admission of working class students to at least thirty per cent, although as in the western zones, structural problems – and the resistance of surviving faculty and students – made this a difficult proposition. The Soviets also opposed the admission of former *Wehrmacht* officers as students. Even despite such strident measures, the Soviets soon began to worry about the survival of 'reaction' at German universities. In Moscow, members of the Central Committee excoriated P.V. Zolotukhin, the head of SMA's Education

Department, and they noted that even non-Nazi professors remained advocates of German idealism and were unwilling to entertain the philosophical worth of materialism and political economy, by which they meant Marxist Leninism. In Halle and Leipzig, anti-communist student groups were caught doling out propaganda, and a few communist students admitted that were sometimes subjected to violent assaults. Matters only improved when Soviet liaison officers were attached to each university administration and told to direct the 'ideological-political life' of the institutions.[47]

As in the U.S. and British zones, the answer to mounting denazification problems was to devolve the programme, particularly since the Red Army, like its American counterpart, was rapidly shrinking as men were demobilized and sent home.[48] On the other hand, the Soviets, like the British, were relatively cautious in exploring this option. The all-party coalition in the Soviet zone, the 'Anti-Fascist Bloc', had suggested creating German-staffed denazification committees as early as August 1945, but the most the Soviets would allow was the formation of 'Anti-Fascist Committees', which were manned by representatives of the 'anti-fascist' parties and functioned as informal denazification commissions. Since these groups lacked a consistent structure, their work and decisions were not tabulated statistically. Meanwhile, the bulk of the SMA's efforts went into its own ham-fisted denazification drive over the winter of 1945/46. In January, the proclamation of CC Directive 24 created a potential burden of such magnitude that the establishment of more formal denazification bodies seemed vital. However, except in Berlin, where the Soviet sector of the city was under a measure of four-power control,[49] the Soviets deferred action, rather sitting back to see how devolution would proceed in the U.S. zone. For much of 1946, the Russian and German communist media heaped scorn upon the 'time-robbing work' of the U.S.-zone *Spruchkammern*, although they also faced embarrassing questions about why Directive 24 was not being applied within the Russian zone. The Americans claimed, for instance, that they were being held to standards of denazification propriety that the Soviets failed to apply in their own zone.

Obviously, the Soviets were, in the colloquial phrase, in a holding pattern. After the failure of direct purges by the SMA, the Russians decided to postpone denazification, at least temporarily, in order to influence the votes of the large cohort of 'nominal' Nazis. In the spring of 1946, the Saxon Government decided to distinguish between 'small' and 'active' Nazis by allowing the former to vote, an initiative soon replicated elsewhere in the zone. Meanwhile, the Soviets had also fostered the creation of the 'Socialist Unity Party' (SED), a zonal fusion of the KPD and SPD that they hoped would dominate the *Land*, county and communal elections scheduled for the fall of 1946. However, the new SED feared repeating the alleged errors of the communist party in Austria, where an aggressive brand of anti-Nazism had alienated much of the population and had cost the party dearly in the elections of autumn 1945. As early as January 1946, KPD chief

Wilhelm Pieck argued that only 'major' Nazis should be barred from political life, and when the Liberals subsequently charged that the SED was even more permeated by 'small' Nazis than the middle class parties, the SMA admitted as much, but contended that the Marxist party was exercising rigid control of such elements and re-educating them at maximum speed. The SED claimed to spearhead initiatives favouring 'the integration of masses of former nominal Nazis and fellow travelers in the democratic reconstruction of Germany', and in June the party's central committee lauded the Saxon legislation enfranchising 'small' Nazis. Throughout the summer of 1946, the SED also ran a series of meetings between SED cadres and 'nominal' Nazis, hoping that they could inspire the latter's passive connivance, if not their allegiance. Only after the 1946 elections resulted in modest SED victories did the Soviets feel free to revive denazification, albeit this time under a greater degree of German oversight.[50] The creation of relatively reliable *Land* governments, usually three-party coalitions dominated by the SED, also allowed the Soviets to undertake a more general devolution of political power to German civilian authorities.[51] In addition, promulgation of CC Directive 38 in October 1946 created a further incentive to denazify.

In a meeting of *Land* personnel directors on 12 December 1946, the Soviets announced the need for a 'complete screening of workers in public and semi-public offices'. In a classic piece of Stalinist buck-passing, German *Land* governments were now blamed for 'laxity' in executing CC Directive 24, although they had never been ordered to implement the decree in the first place, and only Mecklenburg-Vorpommern had taken any action to do so. In order to deal with the supposed indolence of their German friends, the Soviets were allegedly 'forced' to deal with matters themselves by ordering the formation of county-level denazification commissions, which were officially called '*Ausschüsse zur Durchführung der Direktive 24*' (Commissions for the Implementation of Directive 24). These bodies were secretly called into being in December 1946, with a *Land* commission in each state overseeing networks of smaller commissions, one for each city and each rural *Kreis*. The *Land*-level commissions dealt with NSDAP members employed in state justice and police ministries, banks, chambers of commerce and the insurance business. All other Nazis holding public or private posts were forced to fill out *Fragebogen* and appear before the lower-level commissions, although in *Land* Thuringia juveniles, the disabled and manual labourers in the public service were all amnestied. Cases handled in the initial round of denazification were now reopened and little was said about the possibility of rehabilitation, at least initially. People fitting into the 'compulsory dismissal' categories outlined in Directive 24 were supposed to be sacked by 1 January 1947, although in practice most were retained pending a hearing by a denazification commission. Those in 'discretionary dismissal' categories were put on notice that they too had to appear before a commission. Although most members of this group survived the process, their jobs seemed to hang by a thread.

As in the western zones, the Germanized version of denazification also dealt with the private sector of the economy. It will be recalled that many firms had already been sequestered under the authority of Order Number 124, and it is also true that other large-scale businesses had been either nationalized or brought under direct Soviet control and ownership (although this was hardly a guarantee of adequate denazification). Despite such measures, a mass of small and medium-size concerns were still in private hands. Since the Soviets reasoned that business enterprises, unlike *Land* and municipal governments, could not be *ordered* to release Nazi personnel, they proposed to revoke the business licenses of anybody belonging to the 'compulsory dismissal' categories in Directive 24. Local administrators were supposed to expropriate the property of suspect license holders, indemnifying the latter either by reselling or renting the concern. A few occupational groups were singled out for special treatment. Indeed, *Gastwirter* – publicans, inn owners, restauranteurs – faced a relatively severe degree of punishment because it was assumed that they had often provided public spaces for Nazi meetings and it was difficult for *Gastwirter* to argue that they had a crucial role to play in reconstruction. In Mecklenburg-Vorpommern, the ranks of chimney-sweeps – a heavily Nazified occupation – were cleansed to such a degree that there were complaints about shortages of such maintenance personnel. The Soviets also reserved a special role for Works Councils, which were likely to favour a tough approach to denazification, and *Land* Saxony-Anhalt distinguished itself by placing the entire process of economic denazification in the hands of the trade unions (despite protests from the Liberals, who claimed that denazification was rightly the preserve of all the 'anti-fascist' parties).

In most instances of economic denazification, however, it was the indulgences that were more notable than the stringencies. *Land* Brandenburg, for instance, ordered an exclusion for all manual labourers, although it was the only one of the five Soviet zone *Länder* to do so. In *Land* Saxony, only small businesses specially designated by *Oberbürgermeister* or *Landräte* were subjected to denazification, with the result that by April 1947, only 3,500 persons – of a workforce of over 500,000 – had been dismissed. Also, businesses judged crucial to the process of economic recovery, particularly food producers and repair shops for agricultural vehicles and equipment, were treated leniently. In general, the fact that shopkeepers and tradespeople usually sailed through denazification gives the lie to the claim that Soviet zone denazification began as means of displacing one social class with another. On the other hand, such concessions were acceptable even to the 'Bolshevisers', who were intent upon a Leninist seizure of the instruments of state administration and were initially less concerned with 'cleansing' the private economy.

After the introduction of the 'Directive 24' reforms, new local commissions were comprised of nominees put forward by the 'anti-fascist' political parties and by organised labour. Each was chaired by the local *Landrat* or *Oberbürgermeister*, and consisted of one representative each from the SED, the CDU and the Liberals, plus a trade unionist. Since *Landräte* and mayors were usually SED members, as were most trade unionists, the arrangement was designed to give the SED a functioning majority on the commissions, although the frequent absence of commission members during hearings meant that decisions were often left in the hands of non-socialist commissioners. Most commission members were skilled labourers, white collar workers or party officials. Identification of Nazis was facilitated by an August 1945 directive, in which the SMA had ordered all German military officers, SS men, Brownshirts and NSDAP members to register with local Soviet commandants, although commission staffs and the 'Fifth Department' of the Criminal Police, ancestor of the notorious Stasi, also carried out supplementary investigations through interviews or the use of captured records. Typically, little came of these secondary investigations, and the Americans – angry that the Russians rejected their example of screening the entire adult population – complained that the Soviet system was ineffective in identifying all Nazis.

As in the French occupation zone, commission hearings were considered a political rather than a legal process: there were no lawyers to provide defense counsel and there were no prosecutors, although commission members sometimes assumed a prosecutorial stance. The chief duty of the commissions was to categorize Nazis along the lines prescribed in CC Directive 38. Nazis who appeared in categorisation hearings often provided the eastern version of *Persilscheine*, or even oral statements from witnesses, in order to sway decisions in their favour. The testimony of mayors and other local 'anti-fascist' personalities often proved most valuable, as did a clumsily named class of documents called 'certificates of harmlessness', which 'nominal' Nazis had obtained from the Anti-Fascist Committees in 1945/46. When denazification commissions judged an indicted Nazi – a so-called 'petitioner' – to have been a 'nominal' member of the party, they could either 'approve' or 'conditionally approve' continued employment; a finding of anything greater than 'nominal' status resulted in immediate job dismissal. Such 'active' Nazis were stripped of the means to earn a living and forced to struggle at the margins of society. In *Land* Brandenburg most 'petitioners' – between seventy and eighty per cent – were awarded with 'nominal' status. The SMA retained the final prerogative to review committee decisions, but there is little evidence that they exercised this right in any systematic fashion. In 1947, the SMA did review 568 appeals of decisions by the *Land*-level commission in Brandenburg, but it only overturned ninety-three verdicts, in each case ordering the immediate dismissal of personnel who had been vetted by the Germans. Despite the fact that the authorities had structured a process that was necessarily time-consuming, commissions were under intense pressure to produce speedy results: the Soviets originally set their mandate to expire in June 1947, but they soon reset the target to 28 February. Apparently, the occupiers had learned nothing from their earlier tendency to set unrealistic deadlines, and there was clearly a political imperative to produce dramatic outcomes in time for the Moscow Conference.[52]

Finally, it should be noted that three key economic and communications systems – coal mining, the *Reichsbahn*, and the post office – were exempted from having employees appear before the district commissions, instead being allowed to develop their own 'extraordinary denazification commissions', which oversaw in-house purges. All three systems were regarded as so important to the maintenance and recovery of the economy that the Russians were initially reluctant to interfere with their autonomy. Senior officials of the *Reichsbahn* and the post office could also be called before the *Land*-level commissions.[53]

As with many things in the Soviet zone, renewed action on denazification produced chaos. The Brandenburg minister of interior, Bernhard Bechler, complained about 'indifference' among local administrators and he ordered that 'no allowance [be made] for those individuals who one may believe are "irreplaceable", but who will then be able to fish in troubled waters'. Many officeholders who were supposed to be dropped were still working long after their firings had been ordered. A February 1947 study of the Saxon *Land* Government showed that thirty Nazis were still occupying senior posts in the administration, and that half of these men had either received or applied for membership in the SED. In Saxony-Anhalt, nearly nineteen per cent of post office personnel were still Nazis, and in Dresden and Cottbus, a third of all *Reichsbahn* officials were still *Parteigenossen*. Harried German officials also reverted to the familiar practice of reclassifying Nazis as contractors paid by the hour, and after several months, many such people were boosted back into salaried positions, often of a supervisory nature. Even with such expedients, German authorities complained that the renewed denazication programme was depriving them of necessary technical experts and thereby stalling reconstruction. The mayor of Beeskow, for instance, howled about the work of the local denazification commission, which he said had crippled his ability to run the town. Complaints from rural *Kreise* were particularly loud. In such small administrations, changing a few key appointees was vital to shifting the atmosphere of local governance, but the administrative or technical skills of Nazi placeholders were at a special premium and such people were difficult to replace. In *Land* Thuringia, the head of the Chamber of Industry and Commerce, *Herr* Bock, begged the government to leave remaining Nazis in place, lest the economy suffer potentially catastrophic results, and in Saxony-Anhalt, the premier asked SMA to retain 100 'nominal' Nazis in the Ministry of Justice, where they were needed to deal with the crime wave that effected the state. Elsewhere, dismissed public employees simply moved from one district to another and then lied on their application forms for new jobs. There were reports of such people being hired. Worst of all, some SED cadres used the denazification programme as a thin cover for stealing the property of their Nazi opponents, a venal practice that one SED leader admitted could 'destroy all the sympathy in the entire village'.

Meanwhile, members of denazification commissions found themselves swamped with work, and their operations proved difficult for the Soviets to vet and control. A new bureaucratic monster threatened to spiral out of control. By March 1947, over 390,000 people had reportedly been dismissed and/or barred from employment, a figure higher than in any other zone, but eastern Germans had developed such a range of subterfuges – reclassification of workers, re-employment of labourers in mufti, sheer refusal to obey dismissal orders – that the real number was probably less impressive than the formal enumeration. Internal Soviet zone assessments admitted that a statistical accounting of people affected by denazification was actually unavailable.

As happened over the winter of 1945/46, the Soviets had again overshot their objective and had to rein in their efforts. Stalin, for one, was fed up, particularly since he began to fear that Soviet zone denazification was stampeding 'nominal' Nazis straight into the arms of the Anglo-Americans. When the dictator met with SED leaders in late January, he told them that pressure against 'small' Nazis should be 'alleviated' – there were, he averred, many good patriots and well-meaning workers among such elements – and he even suggested allowing such people to re-emerge as a quasi-independent political force, which he ventured calling the '*National-Demokratische Partei* (NDP).' This proposal met with a glum reception, especially since members of the SED delegation realised it would make a mockery of their own strident position on the lack of denazification in the Western zones, and Stalin eventually withdrew it, admitting that the time might not yet be ripe. Nonetheless, Stalin would eventually come back to this idea in June 1948, when conditions had apparently matured to the point where formation of the NDP was feasible.

While the NDP proposal was pushed off into the future, there was an immediate slackening of tension in the denazification process. On 13 February, Tiul'panov's chief press organ, *Tägliche Rundschau*, published an influential editorial in which U.S. methods of mass denazification were once again vilified, but it was maintained that in the Soviet zone, 'former nominal PGs, above all from the working class', were supposedly recognized as a potentially valuable asset in organising reconstruction. In addition, the relatively high rate of dismissals and arrests in the Soviet zone allowed officials to argue that they had already done enough. Thus, the *Tägliche Rundschau* article signaled a shift in strategy, and within weeks German officials were citing the editorial in an effort to rehire dismissed personnel. One mayor noted that 'we want to make it as easy as possible for these normal [sic] PGs to find a way into the newly constructed society ... whoever reads the article in the *Tägliche Rundschau* regarding the question of the rank-and-file PGs will be of the same opinion.' In Eberswalde, a hospital applied for the reinstatement of nine dismissed personnel, although the Brandenburg Interior Ministry refused, noting that the hospital already had a bad record in releasing employees classified under Directive 24 and that the *Land* Denazification Commission was, 'not about to allow hospitals to become a safe haven for fascist reaction'.[54] In Saxony-Anhalt, the regional authorities managed to wrangle SMA permission to retain three Nazi technical experts in the Merseburg waterworks, which in turn led the boss of the zonal waterworks authority, Dr Herbst, to call for a more general reinstatement of Nazi technical personnel. Although Herbst was an SED member, his intra-party enemies quickly denounced him as a 'reactionary' and a friend of the illegal remnant of the SPD, which was functioning underground.[55]

The February turn marks the beginning of a fundamental transformation of denazification, particularly because it was part of a larger shift in Soviet politics favouring the promotion of more overtly ideological goals. In order to understand this process, it is necessary to take brief notice of several broad developments.

First, despite the dominance of the 'gradualist' school of thought, many German communist and Soviet 'Bolshivisers' had never stopped advancing their agenda, albeit under cover of the 'Popular Front' strategy. As early as June 1945, they had pushed an accelerated schedule for land reform, even prompting the intervention of Dimitrov in order to moderate the tone of the programme, and they also suggested a rushed relaunch of the KPD, although they mistakenly thought that the party would flourish at the same level as its French and Italian counterparts.[56] In truth, the KPD failed to gain much popular support, partly because it never bothered with the niceties of functioning in a democratic environment and thus felt free to act in a heavy-handed manner, exploiting its privileged access to Soviet resources and police help.[57] As a realisation of the KPD's failure dawned on Soviet officers, they began working to fuse the zonal KPD and SPD, a 'shotgun marriage' that assembled a potentially more effective instrument for the exercise of power, although it also created an open breach with the Western Powers, which respected the western SPD's reluctance to sanction the merger or to entertain similar fusions in the other three zones. This divergence marked the first fork on the path to Germany's eventual division into mutually antagonistic halves. Certain Soviet officials, such as Vladimir Semenov and Zhukov's civil affairs lieutenant, General F.E. Bokov, saw the SED as a specifically German creation that might yet forge an independent course and would continue to collaborate with the bourgeois parties, but the real forces behind the merger, Tiul'panov and Ulbricht, regarded the new party as a Leninist creation, while conceding that it might not yet be opportune to advertise the party as such.[58] It is certainly worth noting that some German communist cadres began developing an exploitative approach toward denazification, since they regarded the programme as part of a massive sociopolitical displacement that would ultimately put their own cadres into power. At the height of denazification's 'second wave', for instance, officials of the Cottbus SED were already instructing party members that 'we must utilize this opportunity... [A]n opportune means has been provided to eliminate the PGs and to install our comrades.'[59]

Second, as the KPD/SED increasingly pushed goals favoured by the 'Bolshevizers', the rival schools of thought became discredited. Ehrenburg was already in disfavour, and the deindustrialisers made such a mess of dismantling – with great quantities of equipment stolen, irreparably damaged or left on railway sidings and exposed to the elements – that Malenkov was in eclipse by late 1945. During the following year, the dismantling teams were brought under SMA oversight, and a special investigation eventually recommended terminating the entire programme, much to the joy of Zhdanov and Tiul'panov.[60] As for the 'gradualist' strategy, it experienced reversals as well. May 1946 saw the suspension of reparation deliveries from the American zone and the concurrent refusal of the British to internationalize the Ruhr, events that crystallised Soviet resentment over quadripartite economic policy. Meanwhile, the main patron of the 'Bolshevizers', Andreii Zhdanov, reached the peak of his power and influence in Moscow, and the recall of Zhukov, who was accused of Napoleonic grandstanding, removed an important advocate of the 'Popular Front' course. Zhukov's replacement as military governor, General Vassily Sokolovskii, was a desk officer and communist party functionary. Although Sokolovskii favoured a degree of German political and administrative autonomy, he also promptly announced that there was no middle ground between socialism and the supposedly receding ideology of capitalism. The positions of Tiul'panov and of Soviet communist party cells in the SMA, directly answerable to the Central Committee, were also reinforced (although Tiul'panov's allies in Moscow began to wonder about his tactical competence). In November 1946, General Bokov was removed from the SMA, where he had been a leading element trying to promote 'gradualism' and restrict Tiul'panov's influence.[61] In 1947, the formation of Bizonia, the failure of the Moscow Conference and the announcement of the Marshall Plan – so-called 'dollar imperialism' – signaled the start of Cold War in Germany, although Stalin stuck with the 'all-Germany' concept until the failure of another four-power conference in London during November-December 1947. In March 1948, the Western Powers signaled their readiness to entertain the idea of a West German state and the Control Council collapsed. A month later Tiul'panov proclaimed the death of the 'German path to socialism', which to him had always smacked of bourgeois chauvinism, and one of his colleagues complained that he (Tiul'panov) was having great success – despite all orders to the contrary – in promoting the idea that the Soviets were building a socialist German republic rather than a liberal democracy. In August, Ulbricht began openly preaching the merits of the Soviet model of development, and a month later he called for 'a sharpening of class warfare', claiming that the task at hand was 'the building of Socialism'. Meanwhile, the electoral strength of the Soviet zone chapters of the CDU and the Liberal Democrats had already been whittled away by a Russian campaign of arrests and intimidation, all of which had been encouraged by Tiul'panov.[62] Finally, the depth of East-West animosity was fully revealed by the Berlin Blockade, which began in

June 1948 and continued for nearly a year. Thus, the general course of develop-ments gave the 'Bolshevizers' the means, the rationale and the opportunity for separating the eastern zone and totally 'Sovietising' its social and political system, a process that culminated with the creation of the German Democratic Republic (DDR) and the subsequent socialisation of that country's economy.

The 'Bolshevisers' eventually got their way both because of their determina-tion and because senior advocates of the gradualist course, such as Semenov and Bokov, refused to make key decisions. Perhaps the latter actually understood no other way to organise society than through the model presented by Tiul'panov. Moreover, the collapse of relations with the West worked in favour of the 'Bolshevisers'. Wilfried Loth describes a 'creeping Stalinisation' and East German separatism that undercut 'gradualist' aims, and Vojtech Mastny likewise suggests that at the pinnacle of the Soviet system, Stalin 'was not implementing a design but reluctantly discarding the one that had not been working'.[63]

How did this course of events effect denazification? First, the hand of the SED was strengthened, even as the party itself was becoming more openly Stalinist, eschewing talk of 'a separate German path to socialism'.[64] In August 1947, SMA Order 201 and its various implementation decrees reconfigured the denazifica-tion commissions and brought them more fully under SED control. Since it was still unseemly to appoint outright more SED representatives than those from the CDU or the Liberals, the Soviets slid around this problem by swelling the commissions with appointees from the 'mass' organisations, such as the German Women's Union and the Free German Youth, most of whom were SED mem-bers. This subterfuge provided for solid SED domination of the denazification commissions, usually majorities consisting of five or six SED members, versus two or three non-party figures or representatives of the bourgeois parties. The commissions were also supposed to work more closely with the court system, which was itself being brought under SED influence. Erich Mielke, boss of the Soviet zone interior administration, described Order 201 as 'part of the further securing of our power', and Paul Hentschel, the chair of the Brandenburg *Land* Denazification Commission, emphasized the 'class character of Order 201', argu-ing that its successful implementation meant using it as, 'a political weapon in the struggle for the vanquishing of political opponents'. Walter Ulbricht also began talking about the 'class' aspect of denazification, in which Nazi 'activists' would be not only 'driven out', but fully expropriated, and he and his colleagues began encouraging radical trade unionists to seek out 'active fascists and militarists [still] in management of their firms'.

Second, the central authorities in Berlin, such as the interior administration, now proposed to supervise closely the work of the denazification commissions, setting up *Land* control committees and collecting denazification data in a central registry. The idea behind these innovations was to ram home 'the urgency and political meaning of Order 201', and to increase the 'antifascist consciousness' of commission members, although as Damian van Melis notes, such innovations were also a symptom of declining *Land* autonomy in the face of the central zonal agencies that would eventually metastasize into the government of the DDR. As well, the 'extraordinary commissions' earlier set up to denazify the coal mining, rail and postal systems were dissolved and their functions shifted to the district denazification commissions. It was well known that the rail system, in particular, had not released many personnel categorized under Directive 24, and an SED estimate suggested that the Soviet zone-*Reichsbahn* still employed nearly 47,000 Nazis, over nineteen per cent of the service's total workforce.

Third, Order 201 strengthened the hand of the Fifth Department of the Political Police, the most thoroughly communized of all the Soviet zone's police forces. Ulbricht encouraged officers of the Fifth Department to pay limited attention to 'small fry' Nazis, but to seek out the *real* thing, by which he meant Nazis – and facilitators of Nazism – who were economically and financially powerful. In order to execute its mandate, the Fifth Department was allowed to penetrate zonal and *Land* administrative agencies with spies and to recruit large numbers of working class cadres, who were trained at special schools and were supposed to be intimately acquainted with the subtleties of Order 201.

Fourth, the Russians used the SED to launch a large-scale agitprop campaign in favour of denazification, the first of its kind in Soviet-occupied Germany. The public was invited to identify all 'active' Nazis and to attend denazification hearings and mass meetings. *Land* interior ministers were also instructed to maintain 'the closest personal relationship to the editors of the daily newspapers' and to keep the press flooded with material on Order 201.

And fifth, the denazification campaign was increasingly reoriented toward the 'rehabilitation' of Nazis, which centered particularly on the ritual of public chastisement. Sokolovskii and Semenov had long been encouraging an application of CC Directive 38 to inmates of the overcrowded detainment camp system, a process that would lead to the internees' categorisation and release. The SED also admitted that 'we must try to win over former nominal members of the Nazi Party and educate them for active cooperation in democratic construction'. Of course, such 'rehabilitation' was also an emergent aim of the U.S. programme, but in the Soviet zone, the reconstruction meant to profit from 'rehabilitation' was increasingly interpreted as the socialisation of the zone's agriculture and industry.[65] By 1947/48, for instance, the Soviets were imposing a form of central economic planning, they were insisting on 'innovations' based on their own economic practices, and they were already launching the early precursors of agricultural collectivisation.[66]

As with the first two waves of Soviet zone denazification, this final campaign also failed. The SED helped launch a massive propaganda offensive in early October 1947, but the press campaign died out quickly and the general public remained uninspired, refusing to inform on fellow Germans or to attend mass meetings. In Spremburg, for instance, the *Landrat* refused to participate, arguing that the harvest and winter planting were 'much more important' than meetings to support Order 201. In Neustrelitz, the Soviet *Kommandant* showed a similar hostility and employed a similar rationale; he would allow denazification commissions to convene only after 9p.m., fearing that they would otherwise interfere with the harvest. In late October, an SED report claimed that many authorities treated Order 201 as 'a secret operation' suitable for handling by the police or the 'mass' organisations, rather than as 'a matter for the entire population'. Party leaders frequently failed to rouse SED-affiliated 'mass' organisations into action, and a meeting of *Land* interior ministers on 22 December 1947 concluded that 'the cooperation of the democratic parties and mass organisations is today still wholly insufficient'. Only in *Land* Mecklenburg-Vorpommern was there any indication of a greater popular readiness to supply the data and materials needed to prosecute denazification cases. *Land* Thuringia reported that 'the population remains passively disposed toward the execution of Order 201. Despite appeals and informational lectures, scarcely any information comes in from the public.' The SED candidly admitted that programmes in all the *Länder* suffered from 'lesser or greater degrees of weakness', although the *Land* authorities claimed that a high percentage of Nazis in their administrative apparatus were being successfully purged. SED cadres were themselves deeply divided. Some party members expressed sympathy for Nazis and individually offered aid, but many more worried about the 'rehabilitation' aspect of Order 201. These critics argued that the denazification process would henceforth absolve Nazis of past sins, thus diminishing the advantage for SED members in competing for plum administrative positions. Worse yet, there might even be a rollback of earlier appointments made at the expense of discredited Nazi placeholders. In *Land* Mecklenburg-Vorpommern, Johannes Warnke was forced to deny that Order 201 meant the automatic absolution of Nazis or that *Parteigenossen* would come flooding back into the administration.

On the other side of the political fence, there is no doubt that some Nazis were pleased about Order 201, sensing that the directive would allow them to resume a normal existence as long as they pledged fealty to the new order and adopted its goals. During the Order 201-phase of denazification, most 'petitioners' were only too happy to sanction the new economic system or praise the Soviet Union, at least when prompted to do so by denazification commissioners. An especially attractive aspect of the new policy was the promise of a rapid resolution of denazification, since the programme was now supposed to be wrapped up by mid-December 1947. For a while, an increasing number of ex-Nazis began applying for government jobs. On the other hand, a slough of newspaper stories about tough denazification verdicts eventually produced a sense of pessimism among *Parteigenossen*, which the authorities blamed on the inability of the press to balance news about the negative and positive aspects of the programme. Party members also loathed making the admissions of guilt demanded by the new order – most felt little or no sense of culpability for Nazi crimes – and many were unable to fathom how conformist behavior in 1935 or 1942 had now been re-conceptualised as improper conduct.[67]

By the first months of 1948, termination of denazification was overdue and it was also increasingly clear that Order 201 notwithstanding, the Russians and the SED had failed to exploit the programme as an effective means of revolutionising German society. Ideological preconceptions had proven a poor basis for a workable programme. The attempt to exert central control of the process faltered because of the reluctance or inability of local officials to provide adequate information to ulterior authorities or to the SMA. The *Land* governments resented interference from Berlin. In addition, the coal extraction, postal and rail systems provided particular centres of resistance, since they resented losing control of autonomous denazification programmes and were in a special position to claim the importance of technical abilities by effected personnel. For instance, the czar of the coal mines, Gustav Sobottka, bristled at the dissolution of the 'extraordinary commissions' in his bailiwick, and he demanded the right to clear all future dismissals and to re-employ incriminated personnel at alternate positions. The post office and *Reichsbahn* also claimed the right to have their personnel chiefs present during procedures against postal or rail service officials, and to have such cases handled only by the *Land*-level commissions, although the *Landeskommissionen* objected to any such concessions.

Most importantly, the SED admitted that many of its cadres had not grasped the political potential of Order 201 and that they had failed to establish 'real control' of the directive's implementation, rather turning the process over to disinterested elements of the state administration. In fact, the restructured denazification commissions rarely acted differently from their less SED-dominated predecessors, apparently because SED members failed to vote as a bloc or to out-maneuvre surviving CDU and Liberal committee members. Often they deferred to the opinions of local authorities, such as mayors, who were presumed to have greater insight into local affairs than district commissioners, although they often lacked much revolutionary zeal. As a result, denazification commissions continued to act much like the '*Mitläuferfabrik*' in the U.S. zone, turning out scads of 'nominal' Nazis. In *Land* Brandenburg, the percentage of public employees cleared for continued service actually increased after the promulgation of Order 201. In Wittenberg, senior officials discovered that the local denazification commission was routinely awarding 'positive decisions' to 'active fascists'. In Stralsund, 16 longtime SS members were vetted for continued employment, mainly because they were able to produce *Persilscheine* from the *Bürgermeister*, the Police Commissar and a Justice Ministry Inspector, and in Nordhausen a similarly innocuous finding was awarded to several veterans of the 'Condor Legion', one of whom had the gall to declare that 'if any changes ever come, the communists will be the first to hang'. In Erfurt, the local commission imposed *Zwangsmassnahmen* (compulsory measures) upon only 205 of 904 'petitioners' heard by the end of 1947; in Hildburghausen it was only nine of 391 cases; in Wörbis, it was eleven of 132. Interior Ministry officials in *Land* Saxony-Anhalt complained 'that some commissions work as if they want to reinsure themselves against any contingencies', and a *Landrat* in Saxony suggested that Order 201 had been implemented 'in extremely lax fashion'.

Of course, such an approach paid both negative and positive dividends: it failed to orchestrate immediate changes in the nature of eastern German society, but it also allowed for the reintegration of ex-Nazi elements that the Soviets required for an eventual process of socialist reconstruction. Most of these people were so happy to keep their jobs that they hardly dreamed of sabotaging further changes in eastern Germany's sociopolitical order. However, even the Soviets worried about the predominance of Nazis in the principal bureaucratic instruments intended to create the new order. In the main mechanism of central economic planning, the German Economic Commission, twenty-eight of the body's 101 commissioners were either *Parteigenossen* or ex-*Wehrmacht* officers, and forty per cent of its functionaries had once loyally served in the bureaucracy of the Third Reich.[68]

As for those 'active Nazis' who received no absolution, the worst were transferred to the courts and were then interned, despite SED concerns about the maintenance – and even expansion – of a labour camp system that was already overcrowded and was attracting derogatory comments from the Western Powers. All arrests were subject to confirmation by the Internal Affairs Department of the SMA. Since the Soviets believed that German courts retained an unwarranted regard for legal niceties, they pushed such bodies to be aggressive in prosecuting major Nazis; occasionally exasperation triumphed and the Soviets simply took over trials and punished the accused directly. 'Active' Nazis who had not been party leaders, war criminals or secret policemen were typically put to work as day labourers, although the Soviets – like the other occupying powers – found it difficult to redeploy masses of unskilled workers in a modern economy, particularly since incriminated Nazis had little interest in physical labour and could often produce doctor's notes showing that they were unfit for corporeally demanding work. In Saxony they were assigned tasks that amounted to odd jobs. In Aue, they worked at making toys, baskets and other crafts; in Schwarzenberg, they were used as painters in reconstruction projects; in Plauen, they laboured in a polish-making works. Some faced such bleak prospects that they fled to the western zones, which the authorities regarded as an acceptable outcome because it further cleared the decks for a future socialist transformation. On the other hand, the authorities were also aware that many penalties levied by the denazification committees simply went unenforced. Thus, even though some Soviet-zone *Länder* set up special bureaux to impose *Zwangsmassnahmen*, an SED study in January 1948 claimed that execution of such measures was 'partly very poor'. In August 1949, most Nazis subjected to manual labour were pardoned by an amnesty (despite an accompanying raft of complaints by the security police and by elements in the SED).

In early February 1948, as relations with the West plummeted to new depths, Ulbricht admitted to the *Land* interior ministers that denazification had been unsuccessful and that it was causing adverse effects, particularly 'nervousness' in the economy. Since the SED leadership had now taken to blaming most of its problems on agitation propaganda from the West, rather than on last year's excuse, 'the political poisoning of the masses by Nazi ideology', Ulbricht began to warn of new threats, particularly pro-Western 'saboteurs'. In contending with such fresh menaces, he claimed, 'we cannot allow ourselves to be set back by ancient history'. As a result, he 'recommended' that the work of the denazification commissions be terminated as soon as possible – they were, in fact, dissolved within a month by SMA Order 35 – and the end of bureaucratic denazification was also supplemented by a mass amnesty for the 'nominal' Nazis and young 'Werewolves' held in the zone's system of detention camps. By the summer of 1948, 46,000 internees had been released. Despite such measures, however, Ulbricht also promised that 'investigative organs' would continue to pursue and prosecute Nazis. Talk of such an unpublicised but continuing purge actually dated to 1947, and Damian van Melis identifies such threats as the real start of the political degeneration of denazification, in which it came to resemble a more standard type of communist purging and 'fascists' were increasingly reinterpreted as any sort of non-communist opponent. 'Administrative' denazification did subsequently take place. In the summer of 1948, for instance, there was a wide-scale purge of the zonal police aimed at *all* former members of the NSDAP, ex-HJ and certain highly desirable technical experts excepted. One other exception to the end of denazification involves Berlin. Although denazification commissions in the Soviet zone were dissolved, their counterparts in the Soviet sector of the German capital continued to operate under a semblance of four-power control and thus kept functioning for almost another year, until the East Berlin magistrate finally called for their cessation by the end of March 1949.

As a result of the February 1948 decisions, the denazification commissions spent the last months of their existence working furiously through remaining cases, and they also began transferring records to the police and to *Land* interior ministries. In Görlitz, the local commission had been hearing a case every half hour, but on 9 March they began processing an average of over twenty cases every ninety minutes. Ironically, the late winter of 1948 was the only period in which the commissions began acting like the revolutionary tribunals envisioned by the authors of Order 201, and in January 1948 findings of 'nominal' status fell to sixty per cent of the cases evaluated in the Soviet Zone. Nonetheless, the SED Central Committee regarded even this percentage as too high and it pilloried the commissions in Saxony-Anhalt for continuing to pardon over seventy-three per cent of 'petitioners' and for allowing a backlog of cases to accrue. Over the next several months, denazification commissions in *Länder* Brandenburg and Saxony, the two toughest and most summary jurisdictions, brought the award of 'nominal' status to below fifty per cent of all decisions and proceedings in these states finally evolved into the catechistic formalities typical of trials in totalitarian systems. Apparently, this shift resulted from a desperate effort to concentrate on files of outstanding Nazi 'activists' who had so far escaped prosecution. In Mecklenburg-Vorpommern, for instance, the SMA ordered the authorities to focus on 186 of the 1,152 cases still on the docket, presumably the worst of the worst. In *Land* Brandenburg, the change in course also meant a last minute focus on manual labourers, whose exclusion from denazification had been sharply criticised by Mielke and was lifted in January 1948.[69]

Historians estimate that over 500,000 Nazis were effected by Soviet denazification measures from 1945 to 1948, a number equaling almost three per cent of the population of eastern Germany, and most historians admit that it was the most thorough of the four zonal programmes.[70] In many ways, however, the Soviet effort was similar to that of its western counterparts. Despite the Russians' vaunted concern for 'nominal' Nazis, they were just as severe with this group as the occupiers in the western zones, particularly in *Land* Mecklenburg-Vorpommern. Indeed, while the Soviets were often forced to keep skilled *Parteigenossen* in place, many 'small' Nazis were frequently dropped from their jobs, and in Saxony-Anhalt, Erhard Hübener complained in 1948 that the rehabilitation of 'nominal' Nazis never actually occurred. 'This divergence between the clear command and the actual practice,' Hübener claimed, 'has created a great unrest.'[71] Helga Welsh claims that the key criteria for retention of one's post was for the officeholder to adopt the worldview and political leadership of the SED, and that this stipulation applied to 'active' and 'passive' Nazis alike.[72]

Even the Soviet broom failed to find and sweep up most Nazis; in *Land* Brandenburg, less than one-ninth of all Nazi party members were handled by the denazification commissions of 1947/48 – only 30,000 of 273,000 possible cases – and of those who did appear, nearly two-thirds were 'nominal small fry'. After the purge was completed, three quarters of incriminated public employees remained in government service. In *Land* Thuringia, 1563 'rehabilitated' Nazis returned to their old jobs between May 1948 and December 1949. Thus, even the contemporary intellectual heirs of the DDR, such as Gregor Gysi, admit that East Germany's image as an 'anti-fascist state' was a lie from the beginning, and it has also been observed that the quick abandonment of the 'collective guilt' thesis by the Soviets and the KPD/SED eroded any sense of responsibility for Nazism in the East German republic. Indeed, the proliferation of post-unification neo-Nazis in the eastern *Länder* suggests that Soviet zone denazification hardly had a lasting intellectual or moral effect.[73]

The Soviet denazification programme was also characterised by the same type of dramatic shifts as its American counterpart, with four major purges alternating with months of relative inactivity or liberality. *Unlike* the situation in the West, however, these violent surges owed not to military government's reaction to public or media indignation, but to bureaucratic rivalries and gamesmanship within the SMA.[74] The lack of democratic accountability in eastern Germany did *not* ensure a policy course any more consistent than that pursued in the western zones, but it did mean that the fight to determine policy was carried out in far more inaccessible corridors of power and that it involved the engagement of strategically placed elites rather than broader masses of opinion.

Finally, it must be noted that the Soviets initially pursued a 'gradualist' approach to policy for Germany, which meant that while Nazi placeholders came under hostile scrutiny, the bourgeois environment around them was less exposed. Even Order Number 124 and the splitting up of landed estates – both carried out in 1945/46 and both seen by the Soviets and the KPD as integral aspects of denazification – could justifiably be seen as part of the 'gradualist' strategy rather than as 'first steps' in the 'Sovietisation' of eastern Germany.[75] On the other hand, there is also no doubt that Red Army officers and SMA officials bore little appreciation for private property rights, at least compared to their western colleagues, and that the seizure of property played a larger role in the Soviet zone process than it did it western Germany.[76]

TOUGH BUT SENSITIVE

As an occupying power, France was in a peculiar situation. It was the only country running an occupation zone that had itself been totally occupied. Although the Gallic cock had turned the tables on the German eagle, Free French planning for the occupation had begun in the chaos of exile and after France's liberation in the summer of 1944, there was not much further time in which to prepare. In fact, while cabinet-level, interdepartmental planning committees were already functioning in Washington, London and Moscow by 1943/44, the equivalent in Paris was only formed in July 1945 (as the *Comité interministériel des Affairs allemandes et autrichiennes*). By this time, of course, the war was over and the occupation of Germany had already begun. As a result, the French, even more than the Soviets, had a military government apparatus that was unprepared and whose personnel were only hurriedly assembled over the winter of 1944/45, when they were run through four-week training courses at the Sorbonne.[1] General Louis-Marie Koeltz, who ran the programme, was desperately short of personnel, especially those with any sort of administrative experience. In fact, although the Free French had long assumed that Germany would be occupied, and Free French leader Charles de Gaulle had requested autonomous French participation in this enterprise, Roosevelt and Stalin only consented at Yalta, and even this concession came largely at the behest of Winston Churchill, De Gaulle's sole champion among the Big Three.[2] Consequently, the French only belatedly secured the right to sit a representative on the Control Council and the country's occupation zone was demarcated at the last minute, carved out of lands in south-western Germany that Allied planning had already allocated to U.S. and British forces. The resulting territory had an odd, hourglass shape and was the smallest zone of occupation, both in geographic size and in population. A British assessment also pointed out that the French, alone of the occupying powers, lacked the respect that the Germans accorded to legitimate conquerors.

On the other hand, the French could count themselves lucky in several ways. French military government detachments had narrowly escaped direct subordination to British and American officers, which was the original intent of JCS and the British Chiefs of Staff, and was avoided only because Eisenhower bucked, realising how deeply such an arrangement would embarrass the French. In addition, the French zone of occupation covered much of Baden and the Rhenish territory adjacent to France, a region of great security concern, and France emerged as the only neighbour of Germany to receive an occupation zone. The relatively small size and proximity of France's zone, as well as its absence of large cities, also meant that the occupying power could attempt methods of governance that might not have worked at the scale of control necessary in the larger zones. And finally, France had the good fortune of governing a region that had relatively little bomb damage and was a traditional heartland of German liberalism. South-west Germany was relatively the least Nazified portion of the Reich and many local Nazi nabobs were absent because they had fled eastward at the outset of the French invasion, although a *Gouvernement Militaire* (GM) study in September 1945 estimated that there were still as many as 500, 000 party members in the French zone, 30, 000 of whom were 'virulent Nazis'.[3]

Two principal impulses motivated French behavior in Germany, although these derived from different sources of inspiration and sometimes tended to work at cross purposes. First, French enmity toward Germany was more ingrained than that of the other Allied Powers. Rather than dating back one or two generations, anti-German sentiment was part of a centuries-old tradition, although there is no doubt that such feelings had crystallised with the unification of the Reich in the 1860s and 1870s. France had since faced Germany in three wars (plus a quasi-war in the Ruhr), so the Reich had assumed a status as the *Erbfeind*, or archenemy. Edmond Vermeil, a professor at the Sorbonne and the French equivalent of Robert Vansittart, argued that Germany had experienced a 'special path' through history, a '*Sonderweg*' that had made most Germans incorrigible opponents of rationalism and human-ism. As a result of such perceptions, French nationalists determined – as they had in 1918/19 – to ensure their country's future security through tough geopolitical means. Free French mandarins like Vermeil, Laurent Blum-Picart and René Massigli sat in on a series of study groups in London and Algiers, all of which explored possible means of neutralising the 'German problem', and Vermail also later helped train French cadres bound for occupation duties in Germany. However, nearly all the papers produced by these groups called for a radical decentralisation of Germany and the future reorganisation of the *Länder* as a loose confederation. Gaullists further sought to detatch the Rhineland from Germany, mainly with the intention of creat-ing an autonomous state or a zone under international control. In addition, Gaullist planning slated the Saarland for direct annexation and sought the internationalisa-tion of the Ruhr and the distribution of that region's resources for the common European – that is, French – benefit. Historians have often regarded the economic dimensions of this scheme, somewhat less generously, as a form of organised plun-dering. France's powerful new Christian Democratic party, the Popular Republican Movement (MRP), committed itself to such objectives, as did French communists and socialists, since both the Marxist parties were seeking to portray themselves as good patriots, although many socialists were unsure about the wisdom of outright dismemberment or annexation.[4] Ironically, some of the strongest irredentist voices came from former Vichyite military officers, who were scattered in a fair proportion throughout *Gouvernement Militaire*.[5] This paradox has sometimes been attributed to a desire by such men to mask formerly pro-Nazi inclinations, but was probably actually rooted in a conservative 'realism' and xenophobia that had previously been moderated in order to conform with the fact of German domination, but was now again unleashed in its original form.

Scholarship in recent decades has come to suggest, however, that there was more to French occupation policy than just draconian territorial and economic objectives.[6] French leftists, particularly young officers from the French Resistance, brought with them the spirit of the Enlightenment, which in practical terms meant reintegrating Germany into a greater European tradition and signaled a deep respect for individualism, which Roy Willis calls, 'one of the profoundest contributions of the French mind'. In the French reckoning, the best way of inculcating a democratic spirit was through a '*Kulturpolitik*' based on encouraging knowledge of the French language and system of values, an idea that recalled the secular evangelism of the First Republic and First Empire, plus the imperial '*mission civilisatrice*' during the early decades of the Third Republic. The British called it 'cultural colonisation'. Such notions had more recently been applied in the recovered territory of Alsace, where it was assumed that the population would happily work to master the intricacies of French language and thought. Thus, the idea of *Kulturpolitik* revolved around the importance of re-education, which assumed a centrality in French policy even more important than in British planning and practice. Even in post-First World War Alsace, French administrators had purged nearly a thousand teachers and school administrators, replacing such people with educators brought from the interior of France.[7] A similar approach was intended for areas of south-western Germany coming under French occupation, and there was particular hope for the success of the project in Baden and the Rhenish Palatinate, which had traditionally been under a measure of French cultural influence and where French had long been used as a second language. In fact, the French had repeatedly occupied these areas, the last time in the southern Rhineland being from 1918 to 1930. Thus, the French felt justified in bringing teachers and educational administrators into the French zone, often people of extremely high calibre, and one of de Gaulle's lieutenants, Raymond Schmittlein, was sent to run the public education directorate of GM. By mid-1946, there were 166 French lecturers and professors teaching in German technical schools and universities. In addition, the French aimed to control the future training of German teachers, mainly by setting up a series of *écoles normales*, and also to bring the universities in south-western Germany under French sway. In Mainz, they went so far as to reestablish a local university, which was meant to serve as a focal point for the extension of French cultural influence, and in Speyer they founded an Institute of Administration, using as a model their own technocratic spawning ground, the *École Nationale d'Administration*. Since all such initiatives demanded a large measure of direct control, the French system of re-education differed markedly from its laissez faire British counterpart.[8]

Rather than choosing between revanchism and *Kulturpolitik*, the *Comité intermin-istériel*'s first package of instructions for Germany, the '*Directives pour notre action en Allemagne*' (20 July 1945) endorsed *both* approaches, cleverly uniting them under the rubric of 'deprussianisation'. Both this term and concept were drawn from the work of Vermeil, who considered it the crux of his analysis. After intense internal discussions, members of the *Comité* decided that 'deprussianisation' meant both decentralising Germany, and thus weakening the unification project undertaken by Prussia in the nineteenth century, as well as combating alleged Prussian traits such as worship of the state and privileging of the collective good over that of the individual. Despite such noble efforts of will, however, the existence of more than one approach to Germany remained tangible, particularly since France had the most heterogeneous occupation garrison of all the conquering powers, and the various elements within this assem-blage – Gaullists, Giraudists, ex-Vichyites, North Africans, former resisters – were rarely aligned. In addition, early GM was organised along lines that one veteran of the occupation later described as a 'a sort of limited feudal system', with *Land* governors, district officers and headquarters officials all free to veer off in various directions. At the broadest level, executive control of the French zone was split in the mid-summer of 1945 between a staunch Gaullist, General Pierre Koenig, who became military governor, and Émile Laffont, who was appointed as the zone's civil administrator and had his roots in the socialist wing of the French Resistance. Naturally, Koenig tended to represent the revanchist hard line; Laffont was an advocate of *Kulturpolitik*, although he was intimately familiar with the *épuration*, having played a role in both the purge of Vichyites in France and the planning of the same process for Germany. Koenig remained personally loyal to De Gaulle, even after the latter's withdrawal from gov-ernment service in early 1946; Laffont was more sensitive to the chain of command created by the Fourth Republic.[9]

Unfortunately for supporters of American-style denazification, neither of the dominant streams of thought in French discourse suggested a tolerance for sweep-ing categorisations or wholesale purges. The right-wing jingoists were prone to think of all Germans as bad, which made demonising members of the Nazi Party seem pointless, while the assimilationists, as products of the Enlightenment, wor-ried about issues of individual responsibility, although their bureaucratic rationalism also made them relatively more sympathetic to schematic solutions. The final result, however, was that almost all French officers – Right, Left and centre – agreed that the character of a potential German administrator or manager should count more than mere membership in the NSDAP, and they decided that only after thorough examination of such character should the authorities make relevant decisions about retention, dismissal or arrest. Or as it was phrased by Michel Bouquet, the French representative to the Berlin *Kommandatura*: 'We can't ignore our directives ... but we could interpret them with a little more attention to the individual and his circumstances.'

There were several other factors also at play. First, French officers were acutely aware of the way in which recent purges in their own country had careened out of control, at least briefly, and empathetic Vichyites tended to display an aversion to any kind of blanket charges based upon past political behavior that had sometimes been influenced more by situational determinants than by preference.[10] Second, both the revanchists and the cultural reformers had answers to the 'German problem' that involved long range changes in either the shape or the character of Germany, so neither side saw denazification as an end in itself. Vermeil regarded denazification as insufficient, at least compared to his notion of 'deprussianisation', and Laffont suggested that denazification was merely an instrument facilitating a broader 'economic and social plan'.[11] Third, the French, like the British, regarded denazification mainly as a device to facilitate internal security within their zone of occupation. As Laffont explained it, the French desire was *not* so much 'to eliminate indiscriminately all former adherents of Nazism as to prevent them from engaging in harmful acts by assigning them to positions of secondary importance or by placing them under the strict supervision of other public officials, appointed or promoted for their staunch anti-Nazi conviction'.[12] Fourth, advocates of *Kulturpolitik* were willing to limit the denazification policy in South Baden and the Palatinate, the main targets of cultural hegemony, if only to help win over local elites to a pro-French orientation. In fact, the French were only too willing to employ Nazis if they thought that the latter were willing to submit their political predilictions to the French desire to foster local forms of separatism.[13] And fifth, the French, as the occupying power most opposed to anything smacking of centralisation in Germany, generally made few contributions to the work of the Control Council and initially took little note of its directives, including those related to denazification.[14]

As in the other occupation zones the early phase of French occupation was characterised by ambiguity and confusion, particularly since ulterior forms of control were absent and important decisions were often left to town commandants. Although the French First Army was bound by SHAEF directives and by the *Handbook*, as well as by orders from the headquarters of Sixth Army Group, these documents were the product of exclusively Anglo-American concerns and French officers typically paid them little heed, although they did comprise the formal basis of early French policy. In fact, GM detachments, *unlike* their British and American counterparts, were officially subordinated to the *5ème Bureau* of the French First Army rather than to SHAEF G-5, an arrangement that Eisenhower had approved in response to French sensitivities. During April 1945, the 'Stuttgart Affair', in which French troops independently captured the Württemberg capital and then refused to evacuate it, despite American threats of retaliation, created even greater French resentment of SHAEF. In addition, the French feared that their British and American allies had designs on the northern part of the French zone and that they were encouraging hostile propaganda among

Germans in that region. On the other side of the fence, such accusations encouraged the Anglo-Americans to avoid further disputes, which left SHAEF officers literally walking on eggshells in order to respect the autonomy of French military government. The French also felt unbound by the Potsdam decisions, to which France was not a party because de Gaulle had not been invited to the meeting, although the French Government and French commanders sometimes cited the Potsdam protocol as a source of policy. Finally, French town commandants and GM officers were bereft of directives from Paris, at least until July 1945, and the first military governor, General Jean de Lattre de Tassigny, unfortunately failed to establish an efficient chain of command. The height of anarchy was reached in July 1945, especially in the few weeks after the First Army's *5ème Bureau* was dissolved but before the organisation of alternate arrangements for control of military government machinery.

In May 1945, the *5ème Bureau* issued several orders pressing subordinate detachments for the enactment of the 6th Army Group regulations on the dismissal of German personnel. In early May, GM ordered the release of all *Landräte* and *Bürgermeister*, and three weeks later, Pierre Arnal, the boss of *5ème Bureau*'s General Administration Section, ordered French units to dismiss all Germans specified in the SHAEF *Handbook*. Exceptions had to be justified on grounds of importance to French (rather than German) interests and had to be approved by the *5ème Bureau*. Such rules soon led to complaints from local GM detachments and thus to a more flexible interpretation of SHAEF stipulations, as suggested in June 1945 by Jean Robert Thomazo, the chief of *5ème Bureau*. In practice, all the uncertainty led to a glaring inconsistency of treatment by local GM units. Otto Künzel, the eventual denazification czar in Württemberg-Hohenzollern, later described 'regional actions' that had led to 'very stark differences throughout the whole South Württemberg zone'. 'In some *Kreise*,' he observed, '*alte Kämpfer* and truly guilty persons were immediately removed, while in other *Kreise*, such people were – and are – active, at least until recently.'[15]

Despite de Lattre's administrative failures, he was able to set a predominant mood, which was extremely tough and was designed to cow Germans with vigorous demonstrations of French military strength. 'Only the menace of exemplary punishments,' he later claimed, 'was capable of laying low [a German spirit] deformed by thirteen years of the Hitlerite method.' In particular, de Lattre advised French officers to seize Nazi Party members as hostages (although he piously told press correspondents that he had forbid any such practice). Hundreds of such men were held, sometimes for several months, in order to ensure the proper comportment of their NSDAP comrades, and in Reutlingen four Nazis were shot in response to the murder of a French soldier. Similar executions took place in Markdorf and Wannweil. George Orwell witnessed the French occupation of Stuttgart and described it as a fiasco. French military government was nowhere to be found; there was widespread looting; and the French arrested *all* members of the Nazi mass militia, which left them temporarily without sufficient space in which to house the enormous number of prisoners. As in smaller towns, Nazi hostages were seized as a gauge against the citizenry's

1 A German illustration (1946) parodies the new 'Germanised' version of the denazification system: black wolves are dumped into the machinery and emerge as white sheep.

DENAZIFIZIERUNGS-
DRACHEN
Vorsicht! Bissig!

(NZ-Karikatur von Helmut Beyer)

2 A political cartoon from *Die Neue Zeitung*, 16 September 1948. A Nazi 'big shot' stands complacently next to the sleeping dragon of denazification. 'He won't do anything to me,' he gloats. 'He's long since satiated with "small fry".'

Politische Fragebogen!

Die im Monat Juli 1945 mittels Fragebogen durchgeführte politische Ueberprüfung aller im Stadtkreis Koblenz wohnenden Personen muß erneuert werden, da die Fragebogen zu einem großen Teil unrichtig oder unvollständig ausgefüllt worden sind.

Jeder Fragebogen ist sorgfältig und gewissenhaft auszufüllen und

binnen 48 Stunden nach Erhalt

bei dem zuständigen Polizeirevier abzugeben. - Wissentlich falsche Angaben, lückenhafte Eintragungen oder unpünktliche Abgabe der Fragebogen werden bestraft.

KOBLENZ, den 12. Januar 1946.

Der Oberbürgermeister

3 The *Oberbürgermeister* of Koblenz alerts townspeople to the fact that new *Fragebogen* were being distributed, and that they must be filled out and returned within forty-eight hours. Most of the earlier *Fragebogen* handed out in July 1945 had supposedly been completed incorrectly or incompletely.

MILITARY GOVERNMENT OF GERMANY
PUBLIC SAFETY BRANCH – SPECIAL BRANCH SUBSECTION
DENAZIFICATION REPORT

WARNING: READ INSTRUCTIONS CAREFULLY
BEFORE FILLING OUT REPORT

Detachment No. _____ Location _____ Territorial Jurisdiction _____ Report Month of _____ Date of Report _____

A. FRAGEBOGEN HANDLED DURING CURRENT PERIOD

	Totals (1)	Key policy making or executive officials in government or business (2)	Employees of Ministry of Liberation (3)	Employees of Military Government (4)	Employees of Military Installations (5)	All Others (6)
1. Number carried over from preceding month						
2. Number received during current month						
3. Number disposed of during current month						
a. By Action Sheet or Letter						
b. Otherwise (See Instructions)						
4. Number carried over to next month						

B. COMPARISON OF FINAL DISPOSITIONS OF APPLICANTS OR EMPLOYEES OF MIL GOVT OR MILITARY INSTALLATIONS (AS SHOWN BY ACTION SHEETS OR LETTERS OF NOTIFICATION RETURNED TO SPECIAL BRANCH SINCE 1 JUNE 1946) AND OF ACTION SHEETS OR LETTERS OF NOTIFICATION OUTSTANDING, ACCORDING TO SPECIAL BRANCH FINDINGS.

Special Branch Findings on action sheets or letters of notification	Totals (1)	Employees of Military Government		Employees of Military Installations		All Others		Action Sheets or letters of notification outstanding	
		Appointed or Retained (2)	Removed or not Employed (3)	Appointed or Retained (4)	Removed or not Employed (5)	Approved Appointed or Retained (6)	Disapproved Removed or not Employed (7)	Outstanding 30 days or less (8)	Outstanding more than 30 days (9)
5. Employable									
6. Not Employable									
7. Total									

C. ANALYSIS OF FRAGEBOGEN VIOLATION CASES IN MIL GOV COURTS

	No. of Persons
8. Awaiting disposition beginning of month	
9. Prosecutions instituted during month	
10. Dismissed or acquitted	
11. Convicted	
12. Total disposed of during month	
13. Awaiting disposition at end of month	

D. PERSONNEL SITUATION IN SPECIAL BRANCH

	Military Personnel		Civilians		German Employees
	Officers (1)	EM (2)	U.S. (3)	Allied (4)	(5)
14. No. employed at end of period					

SUBMISSION AND DISTRIBUTION

a. A COPY OF THIS FORM WILL BE SUBMITTED BY EACH PUBLIC SAFETY SPECIAL BRANCH FOR EACH CALENDAR MONTH. IT WILL BE FORWARDED TO REACH THE LAND OMG (PUBLIC SAFETY SPECIAL BRANCH) BY THE 3RD OF THE FOLLOWING MONTH.

b. A COPY OF THIS FORM, CONTAINING A CONSOLIDATION FOR THE LAND OF REPORTS RECEIVED PURSUANT TO A WILL BE SUBMITTED BY THE LAND OMG AND MADE AVAILABLE FOR TRANSMISSION TO OMGUS (DIV. PUBLIC SAFETY BRANCH) APO 742 NOT LATER THAN THE 12 TH DAY   E MONTH.

4 A denazification form used by the Special Branch of U.S. military government.

Chart II
Total Findings by Trial Tribunals
by Classes and Laender Expressed as Percentages
Cumulative through 31 December 1946 (since 1 June)

U.S. Zone – 125,738 Cases

Bavaria – 55,541 Cases

Wuerttemberg-Baden – 43,663 Cases

* Includes 0.1% in Class I

Greater Hesse – 26,534 Cases

Class I Major Offenders
Class II Offenders
Class III Lesser Offenders
Class IV Followers
Class V Exonerated

5 U.S. military government graphs on denazification rates show most cases being slotted in the "Follower" category, January 1947.

SECRET

SUPREME HEADQUARTERS
ALLIED EXPEDITIONARY FORCE

OFFICE OF ASSISTANT CHIEF OF STAFF, G–2
COUNTER-INTELLIGENCE SUB-DIVISION
EVALUATION & DISSEMINATION SECTION

ARREST CATEGORIES
HANDBOOK

GERMANY

6a and b SHAEF G-2 'Arrest Categories Handbook', April 1945.

THE CATEGORIES OF AUTOMATIC ARREST AND DETENTION—GERMANY

A. THE GERMAN INTELLIGENCE SERVICES

1. All personnel of *Ämter* (Departments) I, II, III, IV, VI, *Militärisches Amt* (formerly *Abwehr*) and VII of the *Reichssicherheitshauptamt* (RSHA, or National Department of Security), together with the out stations and organisations dependent on or controlled by any of these departments.

2. All personnel of the *Geheime Feldpolizei* (*GFP*, or Secret Field Police).

3. All personnel of the *Reichssicherheitsdienst* (Reich Security Service).

B. THE SICHERHEITSPOLIZEI (Sipo, or Security Police)

1. All personnel of the *Geheime Staatspolizei* (*Gestapo*, or Secret State Police), including the *Grenzpolizei* (*Grepo*, or Frontier Police).

2. All officials down to and including the rank of *Oberst* (Colonel), in the *Kriminalpolizei* (*Kripo*, or Criminal Police).

C. HIGHER POLICE OFFICIALS

1. High Government Officials in the Police Hierarchy.
2. All *Polizeipräsidenten* and *Polizeidirektoren*.
3. All *Oberpräsidenten* in Prussia.
4. All *Regierungspräsidenten*.
5. All *Landräte*.
6. All *Höhere SS- und Polizeiführer*.
7. All *Befehlshaber der Ordnungspolizei*.
8. All *Befehlshaber der Sicherheitspolizei*.

Note : For approximate translations of the titles in Category C. *see* PART THREE.

D. THE ORDNUNGSPOLIZEI (Orpo, or Regular Uniformed Police)

All officers down to and including the rank of *Oberst* (Colonel) or equivalent in the following branches :—

1. *Schutzpolizei* (*Schupo*, or Protection Police).
2. *Feuerschutzpolizei* (*F Schupo*, or Fire Protection Police).
3. *Gendarmerie* (*Gend*, or Rural Police).
4. *Wasserschutzpolizei* (*SW*, or Waterways Protection Police).
5. *Luftschutzpolizei* (*L Schupo*, or Air Raid Protection Police).
6. *Technische Nothilfe* (*Teno*, or Technical Emergency Corps).
7. *Verwaltungspolizei* (Administrative Police).
8. *Hilfspolizei* (*Hipo* or Auxiliary Police).

Note : There are no ranks in the *Hilfspolizei* ; *see* PART THREE.

E. PARA-MILITARY ORGANISATIONS

1. *Waffen-SS* (Armed SS)—All officers and N.C.O.s down to and including the rank of *Scharführer*, all ranks of the *Totenkopfverbände* (*TV*, or Death's Head Formations) and all *SS-Helferinnen* or *SS-Kriegshelferinnen* (SS Female Auxiliaries).

2. *Allgemeine SS* (General SS)—All officers and N.C.O.s (except those who hold only nominal SS rank by reason of their being in the *Orpo* or *Kripo*, and have not taken an active part in SS work) down to and including the rank of *Unterscharführer* and all *SS-Helferinnen* or *SS-Kriegshelferinnen*.

3. *Sturmabteilung* (*SA*, or Storm Troops)—all officers down to and including the rank of *Sturmbannführer*.

4. *Hitler Jugend* (*HJ*, or Hitler Youth)—all officers down to and including the rank of *Stammführer* and equivalents in the *Bund Deutscher Mädel* (*BDM*, or League of German Girls).

5. *Nationalsozialistisches Kraftfahrkorps* (*NSKK*, or National Socialist Motor Corps)—all officers down to and including the rank of *Staffelführer*.

6. *Nationalsozialistisches Fliegerkorps* (*NSFK*, or National Socialist Aviation Corps)—all officers down to and including the rank of *Sturmbannführer*.

7. *Reichsarbeitsdienst* (*RAD*, or Compulsory National Labour Service)—all officers down to and including the rank of *Arbeitsführer*.

F. NAZI PARTY OFFICIALS

1. Administrative officials of the Party down to and including the post of *Amtsleiter* at *Ortsgruppe* level.

2. All members of the Party down to and including the rank of *Gemeinschaftsleiter*.

G. CIVIL SERVANTS (Höherer Dienst)

1. All members of the *Höherer Dienst* (Higher Grade) appointed since 1st March, 1939.

2. All Civil Servants down to and including the rank of *Ministerialrat* or equivalent, irrespective of the date of appointment.

7 American officers and reporters at Furstenhagen look at a collection of captured Nazi personnel documents, 15 November 1945. This set included the names of most *Wehrmacht* intelligence and counter-intelligence agents, all of whom ranked highly on Allied black lists.

8 Nazi Party members in Duisberg are forced to exhume the bodies of Russian and other foreign labourers murdered by the Nazi security police shortly before the Allied advance.

9 Germans in München–Gladbach read Allied proclamation No. 1, as posted by the U.S. authorities on 5 March 1945. This proclamation included the initial denazification stipulations presented to Germans.

10 *Bürgermeister* Dr Levie of Nuremberg speaks to a visiting delegation from the American Veteran's Committee. Levie, who had been held in Auschwitz, argued that Germans interpreted American goodwill as weakness and that *Spruchkammern* were dealing with Nazis much too leniently.

11 Civilians caught in a joint Franco-American swoop operation, codenamed 'Fox', on 26 August 1946. The elderly man on the right is shown holding a copy of *Mein Kampf*, possession of which had led to his arrest.

12a, b and c Three photographs showing operations of the Steglitz Denazification Board, March 1946. Steglitz is in the southern part of Berlin. Photograph 12a (*left*) shows a former Nazi Party member handing in his papers to the secretary of the board; 12b (*below, left*) shows the board in weekly session; 12c (*opposite, top*) shows the representative on the Liberal Democrats on the board, Dr Faust, listening to a witness tell about the past of a former party member.

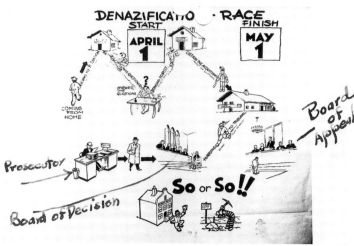

13a and b Schema explaining the denazification process in Bavaria under the 'Law for Liberation from National Socialism and Militarism'. 13a (*left*) is a pictorial representation of the denazification process; 13b (*below*) is a chart showing the denazification system.

14 A regional government is installed at Neustadt after U.S. military government officials had screened 200 prospective candidates for their Nazi affiliations. This government controlled part of Westmark and southern Hesse.

15 Major General Horace McBride, representing the U.S. Third Army, inspects the Moosberg Civilian Internment Enclosure prior to its transfer to Bavarian officials on 10 October 1946. Moosberg was the first internment camp turned over to control of a German Land government.

16 Bavarian Denazification Minister Pfeiffer (left) and Minister-President Högner (right) sign for the transfer of Moosberg Internment Camp on 10 October 1946.

17 *Above*: Civilians in München-Gladbach line up for security screening and registration at the headquarters of U.S. military government, 21 March 1945.

18 *Left*: Eduard Houdremont in Allied custody, July 1947. Houdremont, although a Nazi Party member, had received American permission to run the Krupp concern for several months after the end of the Second World War.

19 Lucius Clay in August 1947. Clay was the chief proponent and executor of U.S. zone denazification.

20 Marshal Zhukov and his staff, June 1945. Zhukov was the first military governor of the Soviet zone and believed that the Soviets should rapidly denazify (although not Bolshivise) the territory that they controlled in Germany.

21 General Clay and his senior officers at a meeting of the *Länderrat* on 5 July 1946. From left to right: Jim Pollock, Lucius Clay, Walter Muller (director of military government in Bavaria) and James Newman (director of military government in Hesse).

22 James Riddleberger, a U.S. State Department official, was one of the main figures involved in the 1944/45 debate over the direction of American occupation policy in Germany.

23 A hearing in the Denazification Tribunal at Zehlendorf, Berlin, 26 March 1946. This was the first full session of the board. Until a March 1946 law passed by the Allied *Kommandatura*, a denazification respondent had been questioned by a single interrogator and then sentenced, but the new regulations allowed for the respondent to appear before the board and provide a defence of his/her conduct.

24 The 'Big Three', Attlee, Truman and Stalin, at the Potsdam Conference. Basic decisions about the nature of denazification were made at this meeting.

25 Former members of the NSDAP are forced to tend a Jewish graveyard in Bergheim, July 1945. Their former party comrades had once desecrated the site.

26 Following the denazification debacle in Bavaria, George Patton addresses troops of the U.S. Third Army in a transfer-of-command ceremony, 7 October 1945. To Patton's right stands his successor, General Truscott.

27 Winston Churchill in military garb, 1945. In the fall of 1944, Churchill frightened British policy-makers by backing the Moregenthau Plan.

28 American troops raise the stars and stripes over the headquarters of military government in newly-occupied Aachen, November 1944. Aachen was the scene of the first public scandal involving denazification.

29 German evacuees from Aachen arrive at Homburg Barracks, 1944. In an excess of caution, American authorities evacuated and screened every German civilian who had stayed in Aachen, the first sizeable German city to fall to U.S. troops.

30 An American officer interrogated Germans who had been in charge of a prison for German civilians in Lippstadt, 26 April 1945.

31 *Top, left*: Hans Jedretzky (SPD) and Bernard Goring (KPD) shake hands to repesent the fusion of the Soviet zone SPD and KPD into the SED, 21 April 1946. The SED became the archenemy of Soviet zone *Parteigenossen*, although it also proclaimed sympathy for 'nominal' Nazis.

32 *Top, right*: German civilians at Beckum look at a display of atrocity pictures, 1945.

33a, b, c and d Scenes from the von Papen denazification trial, Nuremberg, February 1947. 33a (*left*) shows the denazification court building after being bombed, 3 February 1947; 33b (*below*) shows a crowded courtroom as von Papen's sentence is announced; 33c (*opposite, top left*) shows von Papen standing as he receives his eight year sentence; and 33d (*opposite, top right*) shows von Papen with his wife and daughters before being led away by German police, 24 February 1947.

34 General Eisenhower, the first military governor of the U.S. zone, listens sternly as a liberated slave labourer describes conditions at the Ohdruf Concentration Camp.

35 U.S. military government officials interview a city official at Ürdingen, part of a process of screening all municipal officials in order to weed out NSDAP members, 12 March 1945.

36 *Above, left*: A minor SS man caught out and arrested by British Field Security, 1945.

37 *Above, right*: Martin Niemöller, the Protestant pastor who advised his fellow Germans to accept a measure of 'collective guilt'.

Lfd. Nr.	/	Einlieferungsort	Einlieferungstag	Aktenzeichen	Buchstabe

Meldebogen
auf Grund des Gesetzes zur Befreiung von Nationalsozialismus und Militarismus vom 5. 3. 1946

Deutlich und lesbar ausfüllen (Druckbuchstaben)! Dick umrahmtes nicht ausfüllen! Jede Frage ist zu beantworten!

Zuname_____ Vornamen_____ Beruf_____
Wohnort_____ Straße_____
Geburtsdatum_____ Geburtsort_____ Familienstand ledig/verheiratet/verwitwet/geschieden
Wohnorte seit 1933:
a)_____ von_____ bis_____
b)_____ von_____ bis_____
c)_____ von_____ bis_____

1.	Waren Sie jemals Angehöriger, Anwärter, Mitglied, förderndes Mitglied der:	Ja oder Nein	Höchster Mitgliedsbeitrag monatlich RM	von	bis	Mit-glieds-Nr.	höchster Rang oder höchstes bekleidetes Amt oder Tätigkeit, auch vertretungsweise oder ehrenhalber Bezeichnung	von	bis	Klasse oder Teil B
a	NSDAP.									
b	Allg. SS									
c	Waffen-SS									
d	Gestapo									
e	SD (Sicherheitsdienst der SS)*									
f	Geheime Feldpolizei									
g	SA.									
h	NSKK. (NS-Kraftfahr-Korps)									
i	NSFK. (NS-Flieger-Korps)									
k	NSF. (NS-Frauenschaft)									
l	NSDStB. (NS-Studentenbund)									
m	NSDoB. (NS-Dozentenbund)									
n	HJ.									
o	BdM.									

*Hier ist auch nebenamtliche Mitarbeit, z. B. Vertrauensmann, aufzuführen.

2.	Gehörten Sie außer Ziffer 1 einer Naziorganisation gemäß Anhang zum Gesetz an?* Bezeichnung	von	bis	höchster Rang oder höchstes bekleidetes Amt oder Tätigkeit, auch vertretungsweise oder ehrenhalber Bezeichnung	von	bis
a						
b						
c						
d						
e						
f						

*Es ist jedem freigestellt hier auch die Zugehörigkeit zu anderen Organisationen nachzuweisen.

3. Waren Sie Träger von Parteiauszeichnungen (Parteiorden), Empfänger von Ehrensold oder sonstiger Parteibegünstigungen? _____
Welcher? _____

4. Hatten Sie irgendwann Vorteile durch ihre Mitgliedschaft bei einer Naziorganisation (z. B. durch Zuschüsse, durch Sonderzuteilungen der Wirtschaftsgruppe, Beförderungen, UK-Stellung u.ä.)? _____
Welche? _____

5. Machten Sie jemals finanzielle Zuwendungen an die NSDAP. oder eine sonstige Naziorg.? _____
an welche:_____ in welchen Jahren:_____ insgesamt RM:_____

Quittung
Vom Meldepflichtigen selbst auszufüllen und sorgfältig aufzubewahren!

Lfd. Nr._____ Bei der Lebensmittelkartenausgabe vorzuzeigen!

Herr/Frau/Frl. _____ geb. am_____
Zuname Vorname
wohnhaft in _____ Straße _____ hat heute auf unterzeichneter
Dienststelle seinen Meldebogen abgegeben.

Ort Datum Stempel und Unterschrift der Dienststelle

38 A *Meldebogen*, the questionnaire distributed under the terms of the 'Law for Liberation from National Socialism and Militarism'.

behavior, which the French First Army regarded as hostile. In Baden-Baden, Freiburg and Lindau, the occupiers held large numbers of men for 'screening', which often took such a protracted period that rumours of hostage-taking took root. In Constance, where Thomazo struggled to deal with the administrative impact of denazification dismissals and the flight of Nazi placeholders, the town had the misfortune of receiving a personal visit from de Lattre on 16 May. After a brief whirl through the city, the general ordered the arrest of the town fathers on the accusation that they had allowed damage to French posters and proclamations. One of the resultant prisoners had just been released from Dachau, but now again found himself behind bars! De Lattre later described such measures as 'the Constance method'.[16]

Like the other occupying powers, the French also launched a vigorous round of arrests and internments. Public safety officers organised eight detainment camps, the largest at Lahr, Balingen and Diez, and by the end of 1945 they had deposited over 12,500 suspect Nazis in these facilities. Another 8,000 people were placed under surveillance.[17] In order to compile the blacklists necessary for this effort, which was closely connected to the suppression of the Nazi underground, the 2ème Bureau, the Sûreté and the French Resistance waged a virtual intelligence war. Even during the occupation of France, French resisters were already buying or stealing personnel dossiers from the Germans, and the Free French gathered further such materials that were abandoned during the Wehrmacht's hasty flight from France. By late 1944, the French had lists of 20,000 target personalities, which in January 1945 they added to SHAEF's already voluminous indexes. The French also re-employed anti-Nazi politicians whom they had cultivated as informers during the post-First World War occupation of the southern Rhineland, and some of whom had taken refuge in France. One French officer admitted that 'we have contacted several of these leaders again, and sent them back to their families, and are employing them as unofficial agents who are giving us information'. Many arrests were based on denunciations of Nazis by fellow Germans, although this technique created an embarrassing parallel to the Nazi modus operandi and it sometimes produced a surplus of information.

As one can imagine, early French efforts to corral potential troublemakers were not very discriminating, and little effort was given toward protecting the rights of the accused. The 'automatic arrest categories' of the SHAEF Handbook were interpreted with varying degrees of liberality by detachments of the Sûreté, and only in January 1946 did the French issue a uniform set of rules for internments. Indeed, Henri-Paul Eydoux, the chief of the Sûreté in South Württemberg, admitted in 1947 that 'the majority of [our] internees were more or less followers with minor functions', and a concurrent screening process led to the release of nearly 1,200 internees who had been neither 'major' Nazis nor members of 'automatic arrest categories'. The French kept control of internment camps until September 1947, when they were eventually handed over to German authorities.[18]

Aside from the violence of the initial occupation, however, it must be admitted that many French officers had many of the same class affinities as their British and

American counterparts. This was especially true of the conservative elements in GM, which was full of Vichyites who were no longer trusted for combat assignments, as well as technical experts recruited from various French government ministries and private firms. This latter cadre was sent to Germany with the intention of recovering French material losses and then systematically plundering the occupation zone, although there is no doubt that such people often had old friendships with German businessmen and patricians, to whom they offered individual sympathy. French officers were frequently received in the best homes in south-western Germany, where they provided their hosts with agreeable company and with small luxuries such as cigarettes. As Pierre Cot noted, one could hardly expect an adequate denazification by men who themselves sometimes had quasi-fascist backgrounds and sympathies, and other French leftists charged that collaborationism was finding a continued means of expression. On the other hand, the influence of such men was limited and Laffon was continuing to purge them – 265 had been released by November 1945.

French Catholics were also impressed by German clerics who were ready to stand witness for members of their flocks, and the very style of French denazification meant that personal testimony counted for a great deal. There was hardly a prominent Nazi or Nazi sympathiser who, as Constantine FitzGibbon notes, did not have 'a prelate up his sleeve', and considerable wire-pulling dated from the first days of the occupation.[19] Denazification of the church's own ranks was left largely to the bishops, who were given the right to name half the members of six-man clerical denazification committees, and all such matters were handled with great discretion.[20] The French also supported Catholic elites against local Protestant minorities, the latter of which had often lurched at any early date toward National Socialism and had then usurped some of the power customarily held by their Catholic neighbours. General Pierre Billotte, the first military governor of Rhineland-Hesse-Nassau, boldly affirmed in August 1945 that 'Rhenish Catholicism had resisted [the Nazis]. Contrary to the case with Protestantism, its integrity has in no manner been damaged'. Thus 'denazification' sometimes meant reasserting the traditional weight of local Catholic majorities and the flavour was more confessional than political.[21]

Of course, ex-resistance fighters – usually socialists but also a few communists – had their own sympathies, which usually lay with their fellow spirits in the German anti-fascist movement. Partly because of such affinities, indigenous anti-fascist groups often found themselves in a stronger position than equivalent organisations in the U.S. and British zones of occupation, although their power varied widely from district to district. A few such 'irregular *Comités*' continued to operate well into the fall and winter of 1945/46, exasperating straightlaced German bureaucrats, a feat they managed because they could often claim the backing of officers in the *2ème Bureau*. Some groups thus remained a factor in public life even as a regular system of denazification panels was finally being put in place. In Friedrichshafen, for instance, the *Bürgermeister* complained to the *Landrat* about an anti-fascist committee that had 'taken it upon itself … to cleanse the administration and economy of National Socialist influences.'

The citizens of Reutlingen took a special lead in organising the '*wilde Säuberung*', or 'wild cleansing', of the early occupation period, although in this case, even the occupying power was not always helpful. Reutlingen's first post-Nazi mayor, SPD member Oskar Kalbfell, claimed that 'long before the relevant orders came out, we voluntarily and early on examined the officials and employees of *Stadt* Reutlingen, although from the start we distinguished between Nazis and PGs [*Parteigenossen*]. Whoever was known to us as a decent person and had never caused harm to others as an active Nazi was retained at his post.' The local *Landrat* supported such operations, perhaps despite himself, but the French town commandant actually withheld his sanction, warning against 'rushed actions' that might cause 'unnecessary unrest' during harvest season. Complaints about a similar French hesitancy came from Hechlingen and Tübingen, where anti-fascist groups griped about the occupiers' failure to undertake a coordinated denazification programme, particularly as they saw American officers in adjacent territories launching a more comprehensive process. In Tübingen, as in Reutlingen, the local anti-Nazi movement blamed the French for actively hindering their own efforts. In the southern Rhineland, the French observed that 'elements of the population we favour are surprised to see personalities who must be eliminated still in place', but they argued that it was difficult to find local replacements because functionaries were often Prussians who had been sent into the region from the east. Also, the impression created by the Americans was wholly different than in Württemberg. Rather than providing an inspiration for tough denazification, the Americans in the southern Rhineland had undertaken a superficial purge that their French successors regarded as sadly inadequate.

Whatever their faults, the French did show evidence of a flexibility that often eluded their U.S. counterparts. After a rough start in the contested city of Stuttgart, *Oberbürgermeister* Klett was instructed to organise a denazification committee and to purge all active Nazis, although the mayor was allowed – with 'special permission' – to retain technical experts. The conditions attached to such exceptions were that Klett had to personally guarantee that the specialists were 'technically outstanding ... [had] unblemished character ... [and would] conduct themselves as unreservedly anti-National Socialist elements'. By July 1945, the municipal government had released seven of ten section chiefs, and overall had cleansed the 9,000 strong city workforce of ten to fifteen per cent of its employees.

The occupiers in Stuttgart also allowed the re-establishment of a Württemberg *Land* government, which was purged in the distinctive French fashion. There is no doubt that the French introduced German administrators to the dismissal category lists in the SHAEF *Handbook*, and that they even sharpened the focus of these instructions by adding three categories of civil servants. In the official accounting, the Württemberg Government was thus instructed to cleanse from its ranks *all* Nazis or SA men who had been members of the party prior to 1933, as well clearing out *all* SS men and *Landräte*, *Oberbürgermeister* or senior civil servants who had served during the Hitler dictatorship. On the other hand, the French immediately devolved denazification responsibilities to the Württemberg authorities and they made it clear that there were actually no hard and fast rules, meaning that anyone in the proscribed categories could continue to serve in government, even in senior positions. Lieutenant Colonel Levy told the Württemberg justice minister, Gebhard Müller, that the French had no interest in a schematic approach, but were concerned only with individual cases, particularly, 'whether an official was spiritually and practically devoted to the party or if a certain predicament ... had brought him to the party by chance'. In late June 1945, the Württemberg interior ministry formed a fifteen-man 'Personnel Examination Committee', which by mid-July had released or suspended 175 heavily incriminated bureaucrats. According to Roy Willis, the occupiers managed to remove seventy-five per cent of Württemberg civil servants during the brief phase of denazification in which French authorities directly carried out the process.[22]

Much the same type of approach was apparent in the Koblenz-Trier-Nassau region, where General Billotte convened a meeting of local civil servants and laid down the law on denazification. Billotte ordered officials to release pre-1933 NSDAP, SA and SS cardholders, plus SS, SA, Hitler Youth and Labour Service officers, as well as all members of the military general staff, the Gestapo and the SS Security Service. To expedite this process, persons in the target groups were supposed to fill out *Fragebogen*, with the process radiating downward from the district level to municipal governments and *Landrat* offices, and then to the post office and rail service. Submissions would then be checked against captured party files or even old newspapers, in which stories on Nazi Party ceremonies often contained lists of party members, with the French retaining final power to decide on necessary dismissals. Billotte, however, admitted that denazification would cause obvious difficulties, and he went on to explain how German officials could avoid the most onerous aspects of the policy that he had just outlined. When faced with the dismissal of irreplaceable technical experts, he advised, German bureaucrats could retain such people on a month-to-month basis, although the supervisors of such personnel would be held personally responsibility for their conduct.[23]

Because of the French emphasis on education, teachers provided a particular focus for early denazification efforts, although – as noted above – the French authorities were aware that remolding German character demanded a holistic approach that went beyond the level of a mere purge. Nonetheless, the *épuration* of teachers was a starting point, and such a measure was specifically prescribed by Paris in the 20 July directives from the *Comité interministériel*. Thus, through the summer of 1945, Schmittlein, who had independent control of the project, suspended seventy-five per cent of the teachers in the zone. Obviously, these dismissals provided a huge problem with regard to reopening schools, although Schmittlein and Koenig demanded that schools restart operations in mid-September 1945, even before their counterparts in the U.S. and British zones. As a result, suspended teachers were then recalled amass, albeit without tenure, although by the end of the year many had been fully restored to service. The ultimate outcome was that by 1947, the *Volksschulen*, the vocational schools that made up the lion's share of the zone's high school system, had lost twenty-five per cent of their teachers through dismissals, although another thirty-nine per cent were retained with sanctions, and the French were not shy about controlling former party members through manipulation of promotions and pension rights. The French also responded to the shortfall in numbers by recruiting retired teachers who were politically unblemished – so-called '*Schulhelfer*' – and by opening new teacher colleges, although they were sometimes suspicious of the products of the latter, feeling that it was better to employ non-active Nazis than to trust 'those who had been brought up in the National Socialist spirit but were formally not party members'. By 1947, newly trained teachers made up nearly twelve per cent of the teaching cadre, but the overall number of high school teachers in the French zone was still 5,000 persons short of the figure in 1939.[24]

Denazification of the universities was handled in a more casual fashion. The major universities in the French zone were given a wide measure of discretion in denazifying personnel, with the result that only thirty per cent of the professorate was banned from teaching or penalized, a much lower ratio than in the elementary or high school systems. Moreover, the denazification process was monitored by only three French officers, called '*curateurs de l'université*', who were encouraged to hurry through the vetting process so that universities could open in the fall of 1945. As in other fields, the French wanted to identify *real* Nazis, a criterion that did not include all NSDAP members, but also covered ardent sympathizers outside the party.[25] When rushed, this approach led to obvious problems, although these difficulties sometimes only manifested themselves in 1946 or 1947. The University of Freiburg had a strong Catholic-conservative character that it had maintained throughout the Third Reich, and several of its professors – most notably the idealist historian Gerhard Ritter – had been involved at the periphery of the 20 July Conspiracy. As a result, there were few outright Nazis dismissed in 1945, although there were many surviving faculty members, including Ritter, who doubted the value of liberal democracy.[26] Most importantly, Freiburg was the home of Germany's foremost philosopher, Martin Heidegger, who had sealed his intellectual fate by endorsing the Nazis in 1933. The French dealt with this high-profile embarrassment by demanding Heidegger's expulsion without emeritus status, although otherwise there were fewer than twenty professors dropped from the university.[27] A similar state of affairs existed at the University of Tübingen, where the political tenor of the faculty was similar to that at Freiburg. The faculty at Tübingen 'self-cleansed' itself in the summer of 1945, although one surviving professor called the process 'most unsatisfactory', and he confided that 'I am still surrounded by former party members and my position is not safe yet by any means'.[28] Even at the much-heralded University of Mainz, which the French had re-founded and which German right-wingers derided as an open channel of French influence, the French reinstated a number of professors dropped by the institution's own denazification committee. When Laffont challenged Schmittlein on this problem, the latter claimed that as a late-comer, Mainz had to to accept and employ personnel released by universities in other zones. In addition, a minor scandal erupted when law students were heard singing Nazi march songs as they returned from a night of carousing. In 1947, the local newspaper in Mainz published an open letter from the National Socialist Students – Resistance Group Hesse-Palatinate, which claimed to have influence among both students and professors, and which openly threatened anyone serving on denazification committees. Such things occurred despite the fact that a majority of students attending the University of Mainz were from working class or lower middle class backgrounds, and despite the fact that the French rated the number of nationalist/Nazi elements at only nineteen per cent of the student body (versus twenty-two per cent at Freiburg and forty-four per cent at Tübingen).[29]

By August 1945, the arbitrary nature of de Lattre's rule, combined with his bombastic extravagance in a time of grave shortages, had prompted the general's recall to France, leaving it to Koenig and Laffont to develop a slightly more rationale form of administration.[30] At the same time, the new set of instructions from Paris – the '*Directives pour notre action en Allemagne*' – contained GM's first official guidance on denazification.[31] It is thus from the early fall of 1945 that we can begin talking about French purge policy in a more formal sense, although many of the characteristics of the ad hoc phase – the flexibility, the emphasis on individual guilt, and the readiness to allot limited responsibility to the Germans – continued to distinguish French methods.

Despite favouring a degree of continuity, Laffont realised that French denazification policy was facing a moment of potential crisis. The spotty and indecisive measures of the summer of 1945 had left pockets where little had been done to eliminate the influence of Nazism, and the French zone – much to the embarrassment of Laffont and Koenig – was winning a reputation as the 'Eldorado of Tolerance'. Eisenhower, the U.S. military governor, growled about 'French laxity', and in October 1945, an article in the *New York Times* complained that twenty-seven Germans released from posts in the American zone had already found employment with the French. Since the French were simultaneously launching a series of Control Council vetoes to block the economic unification of Germany, a policy that made them unpopular amongst their three partners in the occupation, they hardly needed anything further to emphasise their image of detachment. In particular, they sensed Eisenhower growing increasingly irate and there were frightening reports about Truman's desire to abolish veto power in the Control Council, an idea that the French saw threatening their fundamental rights in occupied Germany. Equally alarming, the Soviets too showed signs of increasing hostility. Thus, where Frances's policies still coincided with those of the other occupying powers, it was well worth emphasising such conjunctions and eliminating possible points of friction. Denazification was one such realm. In September 1945, Laffont declared that 'denazification in German public administration is at present inadequate', and he also noted that the U.S. authorities were tightening up their own regulations, with the clear implication that it was incumbent upon the French to do the same. He also argued that the shortcomings of denazification were straining French resources, as well as discouraging German anti-Nazis who would otherwise be disposed to cooperating with the occupying power. The result of this realisation was Directive CAB/C 722, which was drafted by Laffont's denazification expert, the jurist and industrialist François Amédée Curial, and was issued on 19 September 1945. This document laid down the functional basis of French denazification policy. 'Denazification,' said Laffont, '... must be carried forward with greater strictness and with the assistance of German agencies.'

Laffont was a great advocate of '*auto-épuration*', or 'self-cleansing', and the French were thus the first occupying power to devolve a degree of responsibility for denazification to the Germans. In fact, it was crucial to Laffont's objectives that the system 'appear in the eyes of the public as autonomously independent as possible from the French authorities'. CAB/C 722 thus created occupied Germany's first series of German-staffed denazification committees, which were called *Säuberungskommissionen* (or *Chambres d'Épuration*). Each *Land* had its own *Säuberungskommission*, which was based in its capital, and each of these bodies was comprised of a chair and deputy chair, two temporary 'assessors' representing management and labour in a relevant vocational group, plus permanent 'assessors' from the trade unions and – once they were licensed – the political parties. Members had to be at least thirty years of age and were chosen by German administrative officials, although French officers had the right to vet all candidates. Cases heard by a *Säuberungskommission* were sent to it by yet another kind of body called the *Untersuchungsauschuss* (*Delegation d'Instruction*), one of which was established in each *Kreis* and was similar in composition to the *Säuberungskommission*. According to a study of denazification in South Württemberg, members of the *Untersuchungsauschüsse* were usually middle aged bureaucrats, more than a third of whom had been affiliated with the Centre Party, although twenty-three per cent were ex-socialists and fourteen per cent were ex-communists. The main job of these individuals was to check the veracity of statements in the *Fragebogen*. Members of the *Untersuchungsauschüsse* also recorded the testimony of respondents and witnesses, and they then decided if a case merited consideration by a *Säuberungskommission*. If appropriate, they sent the file forward *along with* relevant recommendations, a practice to which the French were originally opposed, but for which German civil servants obtained a concession. In fact, the *Untersuchungsauschüsse* even secured the right to recommend overturning denazification dismissals made during the '*wilde Säuberung*' in the summer of 1945.

Interestingly, official criteria for operations of the *Säuberungskommissionen* and *Untersuchungsauschüsse* were still provided by the SHAEF *Handbook*, which included extremely comprehensive dismissal categories based on possession of intermediate or senior rank in the NSDAP, plus the holding of party membership before 1933. To these stipulations the French actually added 'automatic removal' qualifications for mid-level leaders in the Hitler Youth and its female equivalent. German *Land* officials insisted, however, that the *Untersuchungsauschüsse* bear the right to consider each case on its individual merits rather than mechanically applying an automatic dismissal formula, a practice that the French conceded. When Control Council Directive 24 was authorised, both Curial and Laffont realised that superimposing its provisions upon CAB/C 722, as the Americans had done with the Law for Liberation from National Socialism, would lead to mass job dismissals. Their response was simply to ignore the directive and they rejected its implications. In particular, denazification respondents in the French zone were not prohibited from performing their jobs while waiting for their cases to pass through the system. Unlike the authorities in the U.S. zone, the French also foreswore the intention of registering the entire adult population of the zone, some 3.949 million people, instead requiring only those employed in senior levels of public or semi-public administration to enroll in the denazification programme. After judging a case, the *Säuberungskommissionen* could impose four kinds of punishment: transfer, demotion, forced retirement or dismissal with loss of pension benefits. Retention of technical experts was allowed, but was governed by the same principle that had been applied by Billotte in the southern Rhineland. Personnel with technical expertise, said Laffont, were to be '... be placed under "guardianship", i.e. under the supervision of officials known for their staunch opposition to Nazism'. The French also hoped that their newly-founded public administration school at Speyer would plug the gaps left by denazification.

The *Länder* in the northern part of the French zone stuck with CAB/C 722 until the spring of 1947. The system worked relatively well, especially in Hesse-Palatinate, which was the first jurisdiction in the French zone to complete denazification of public administration. Of course, there were the usual complaints. There was an immediate flurry of objections about the diversion of time and resources into the programme – the French actually had to seize consignments of paper in order to print verdicts in the local government journal – and it became progressively harder to convince Germans to participate. *Land* bureaucrats also complained that it was impossible to replace some of their colleagues who had been fired. In October 1946, a conference of senior civil servants in Neustadt openly rebelled, declaring 'that they would not carry out dismissals provisionally approved by the ZSK [the *Säuberungskommission*] if the consequence of such work was that important tasks would go undone'. They also demanded 'that dismissals be postponed until either the job could be filled or the Political Cleansing Council had entertained appeals and made a final decision', although there were actually few provisions for an appeals process.

The nature of the denazification system raised a particular degree of bile in the Palatinate, which was an independent jurisdiction until it was united with the southern Rhineland in the summer of 1946, and which even thereafter retained a degree of autonomy. French officers offended local sensibilities by appointing a jurist and art historian, Dr Carl Felix Koch, as president of the state *Säuberungskommission*. A pacifist with a Bohemian manner and style of dress, Koch had vaguely socialist tendencies, but was *not* associated with any organised political party; indeed, he owed his appointment mainly to his reputation as a prominent Francophile. In the popular imagination, Koch was also linked with local separatists who were backed by the French and worked closely with the *Service de l'Épuration* in Neustadt, although they lacked popular support. Although Koch was a tough denazifier, there were soon whispers about his tendency to exploit the denazification mechanism for the separatist cause, particularly by using promises of lenient treatment in order to stampede Nazi respondents into the movement. Naturally the working class parties, which had a powerful base in the Palatinate, were unsympathetic, cursing Koch for the use of 'quasi-fascist methods', while the CDU charged that Palatine denazification often bore 'the character of a political *Christenverfolgung* [i.e., the Roman persecution of the Christians]'. Koch remained in office until 1947, although the French conceded that by then he had become 'public enemy No.1'.

In general, the French system of denazification got off to a rocky start. For one thing, a major distraction appeared around the turn of 1945/46 in the form of a subcommittee of inquiry, which was mandated by the Foreign Affairs Committee of the National Assembly. Of course, the fact that matters had arrived at such a pretty pass lay with French military government itself, which in the space of half a year had turned the occupation of south-western Germany from a celebrated feat of arms into the subject of almost universal scorn in Paris, mostly because of GM's extravagance, its inefficiency and its unfortunate tolerance of Vichyites. When the parliamentary subcommittee began sniffing around the dark recesses of French policy, GM responded in several ways. First, members of the subcommittee immediately found evidence that French military government had indeed allowed the hiring of Germans dismissed in other zones, even though this practice had been specifically forbidden by a Control Council paper of 5 November 1945. According to critics on the Left, this affair illustrated the supposedly underlying contempt in GM for the principle of joint Allied control of Germany. In response, Laffont organised a purge of civil service personnel hired from outside the zone, warning of an internment camp sentence for anyone caught evading the order. This instruction hit both French officers and German bureaucrats like a bolt from the blue. In *Land* Württemberg-Hohenzollern alone, forty-two bureaucrats were targeted for dismissal, although this prohibition – significantly – did not include the premier, Carlo Schmid, who himself was *persona non grata* with the Americans. In any case, the chief of GM's local '*Service de l'Épuration*', Captain Georges Vigouroux, candidly admitted that the purge was intended mainly to provide higher-ups with citation-worthy numbers, and after the subcommittee went home, most incriminated personnel were allowed to remain in office on condition that denazification committees gave their cases priority treatment. Amidst the dust stirred up by this affair, it was often forgotten that some of the released personnel hired by the French were hardly dyed-in-the-wool Nazis – Carlo Schmid and Konrad Adenauer were two noteworthy examples – nor was it mentioned that certain bureaucrats and politicians dismissed by the French had fled to the U.S. zone.

A second consequence of the parliamentary subcommittee's intervention involved the legalisation and licensing of political parties in the French zone, an issue that was loosely tied to denazification reform. After visiting Germany in February 1946, members of the subcommittee complained that wildly inconsistent results produced by the *Untershuchungsauschüsse* were the fault of French military government, which had taken little care in balancing the political sympathies of committee members. In Balingen, for instance, where the *Untersuchungsauschuss* included two former socialists and two ex-communists, and where five of eight members had suffered a sentence in Nazi jails or concentration camps, the panel recommended dropping pay levels in forty per cent of the cases it examined; in Wangen, where there were no working class 'assessors' on the *Untersuchungsauschuss* and where only one member – a dentist – had been in bad odour with the Nazis, the committee suggested dropping only one per cent of respondents from their pay grade. Obviously, the pseudo-political composition of the bodies was causing one-sided decisions, although the French authorities had no way of formally balancing such factors because alone amongst the occupying powers, they had *not* yet recognized German political parties nor officially allowed such bodies to take shape. The answer to this conundrum was to allow the *Land*-based organisation of the main political parties, which was done in the various states of the French zone from January to March 1946, and then to appoint individual representatives of each party to join *Land* advisory councils, the job of which was to advise on the composition and operation of denazification commissions. When it dawned on the French that not all of the parties had unreservedly positive attitudes toward denazification, they cajoled all of them – Soviet style – into adopting an enthusiastically-worded 'Denazification Resolution'. One of the parties involved was the KPD, but the French worried little about communists hijacking the process because the KPD was weak in the rural and heavily Catholic territories that comprised most of the French zone. Moreover, the French calculated that CDU and SPD members would always outvote KPD representatives on denazification bodies, and there was no veto power in the constitution of such panels.[32]

One final result of the subcommittee's visit was that it panicked French military government into accelerating denazification in an effort to demonstrate quantifiable results. In a flash, GM abandoned its casual attitude and instead set the end of January 1946 as a target date for cleansing public administration, thus mimicking the unfortunate Soviet penchant for setting unrealistic goals. Given difficulties in recruiting personnel and a host of other practical problems, many *Untersuchungsauschüsse* had not even begun operating by late January, and even when the system did begun to function, it often produced results disagreeable to French military government officers, who felt that they were increasingly operating under a microscope. Indeed, the leniency of the *Untersuchungsauschüsse* and *Säuberungskommissionen* worried many French observers, although this was not the only problem.

Partly in reaction to complaints by the subcommittee of inquiry, a major reform effort was launched by the premier of Württemberg-Hohenzollern, Carlo Schmid, who was given a free hand by the French. Schmidt and his bureaucrats – mostly socialists – undertook this project with such success that similar reforms were adopted in the neighbouring *Länder* of Baden and the southern Rhineland (in fact, a reform similar to Schmid's proposal was actually carried out first in Rhineland-Hesse-Nassau).

According to the parliamentary subcommittee's critique, with which Schmid and his officials agreed, one of the main problems with the French model of denazification was its extreme decentralisation. The *Untersuchungsauschüsse* in each *Kreis* had adopted their own highly divergent standards in compiling files, which meant that there was no equity of treatment throughout the *Land* (much less between different *Länder*). For instance, initial data suggested that the scale of recommendations for punishment from the *Untersuchungsauschüsse* ranged from a high of fifty-seven per cent of cases in one *Kreis* to a low of eight per cent in another. The realisation of such inconsistencies provided the chief rationale for *Land* Württemberg-Hohenzollern's 'Ordinance for Political Cleansing', which was issued on 28 May 1946. This instruction reiterated the basic principals of French zone denazification – especially the importance of individual consideration and the idea that membership in the NSDAP did not serve as *prima facie* evidence of guilt, nor did lack of membership equate with a presumption of innocence – but it also created a *Land* administration to oversee the process and thus ensure a degree of uniformity. The official charged with this function was dubbed the *Staatskommissar für die politische Säuberung* (*Commissaire d'État pour l'Épuration*). Historians are divided over the powers actually borne by the *Staatskommissar*. Roy Willis and Justus Fürstenau describe their functions as essentially supervisory, but Klaus-Dietmar Henke attributes the commissioners with much more executive power, noting that they not only had the right to appoint members of the denazification committees, but that they also dominated the final decision-making process. Even Henke admits, however, that the *Staatskommissar* in Württemberg-Hohenzollern – the dynamic SPD official Otto Künzel – exercised more authority than his counterparts in the other *Länder*. Henke also suggests that the creation of the *Staatskommissar* represented an essentially statist and political method of handling denazification – the only such system generated by Germans themselves in the western occupation zones – and that it reflected early socialist influences in the *Land* Württemberg-Hohenzollern government. The system was so streamlined that most cases were handled administratively, without so much as benefit of hearings for affected persons.

The 'Württemberg model' of denazification worked relatively well, and the French seemed happy to have found a way to revive the purge process without starting from scratch. Despite the relative expansion of the system's scope, at least in the southern part of the zone, French authorities had collected a total of only 499,985 *Fragebogen* by the spring of 1947, a number which their German bureaucrats were adequately equipped to process, particularly since they made full use of the Berlin Document Centre.[33] While this revised system of denazification was more finely tuned than the American model, it was actually not actually much more indulgent. As Constantine FitzGibbon notes, the *Säuberungsauschüsse* occasionally handed out punishments more lenient than sentences in the U.S. and British zones, but they could also be far more severe.[34] In Württemberg-Hohenzollern, Otto Künzel's no-nonsense regime ensured that the number of civil servants dismissed from their jobs rose from ten to twenty-three per cent, which left the system producing tougher sanctions than the *Spruchkammern* in

American-occupied North Württemberg.[35] Moreover, the re-appointment of fired officials was strictly prohibited, although the Germans had some success, as in the other zones, in evading the implementation of such sanctions. Until October 1946, when the French loosened standards for re-hirings, many such people were assigned to reconstruction work or placed at the disposal of *Land* labour offices. In addition, the standard of evidence for appeals in the French zone was very demanding. Only proof of work for an Allied intelligence agency or evidence of time spent in a Nazi prison were considered adequate grounds for an appeal, and as Klaus-Dietmar Henke notes, the French, throughout the occupation period, 'denied German authorities practical exercise of the right of pardon', although French officers could always make their own exceptions. By the spring of 1947, the *Säuberungsauschüsse* had imposed penalties in 195,203 cases, a number smaller than that handled by the Americans, the British or the Soviets, although if this toll is considered as a proportion of the population, it suggests that denazification affected a larger percentage of people in the French zone than in any other. On the other hand, the Württemberg-Hohenzollern ordinance, at least, allowed 'nominal' Nazis to keep their jobs, a practice that opened up the authorities to the charge that they knowingly permitted Nazis to remain in office, although it also spared the French from having to introduce the sort of 'rehabilitative' devices that gradually became such an important part of U.S. zone denazification.

Despite the fact that the French were content to stand in the background, they remained quietly involved in the denazification process. French military government lacked a uniform means to screen decisions of the *Säuberungsauschüsse*, such as the process performed by Special Branch in the U.S. zone, but it did have a *Service de l'Épuration* that approved all personnel in the German tribunals and supervised the work of the *Staatskommissar*. Plans for the *Service de l'Épuration* had originally been drafted in the summer of 1945 by two French academics with extensive experience in Franco-German affairs, Maurice Baumont and Pierre Arnal. It was led until April 1946 by Curial, then by Arnal, although much of the day-to-day work was done by thirty-one year-old jurist Alain Radenac, who was chief of the Planning and Coordination Section. The *Service de l'Épuration* had a small staff of four at its headquarters in Baden-Baden, plus five to ten personnel in each *Land* capital. The section also supervised a French military delegate in each *Kreis*, who had the power to fix the membership of *Untersuchungsauschüsse* and *Säuberungsauschüsse* and to review decisions made by these bodies. Despite the limited size of this cadre, particularly when compared against the fact that there were an estimated 11,000 French military government personnel in Germany during 1946, an AMG observer noted that French control of German denazification machinery 'has been most effective in dealing with the reluctance on the part of Germans and German political parties in the assumption of denazification responsibilities'. Indeed, the French were careful to impress upon the Germans that the final resolution of denazification matters was the province of military government. All decisions rendered by German tribunals were forwarded to the *Staatskommissar* and then sent to the *Service de l'Épuration* for endorsement. If a verdict was considered unsatisfactory, the occupiers thought nothing of returning it for reprocessing, with the acceptable decision dictated in no uncertain terms, although the French admittedly had a difficult time dealing with the flood of documents that arrived at the *Land*-level offices of the *Service de l'Épuration*.[36] The French also had no qualms about providing direction to the *Land* advisory councils. Still reeling from the parliamentary subcommittee's criticisms, Guillaume Widmer, the military governor in Württemberg-Hohenzollern, ordered the state denazification advisory council to approve the purging of at least fifty per cent of NSDAP placeholders in the *Land* bureaucracy, plus seventy-five per cent of Nazi managers in business concerns with over one hundred employees.[37] As Justus Fürstenau notes, it was one of the paradoxes of the occupation that the French were the first of the Western Powers to include Germans in the denazification process, but also the last to give up true control of the overall system.[38]

Several other problems also exercised French concerns in 1946. First, GM decided to direct belated attention toward denazification of the economy. Although the French initially did little about economic denazification, Maurice Baumont was ordered to draft an appropriate directive. The result was CAB/C 2516, dated 31 October 1945, which ordered German *Land* officials to get busy in preparing measures, and *Land*-level branches of GM also issued further guidelines, aiming to start a programme early in the new year and wrap up matters by the spring of 1946. The entire effort was supposed to be carefully calibrated in order to minimize '[any] disturbance of economic life'. The French directives authorised the creation of two levels of committees, similar to the *Untersuchungsauschüsse* and the *Säuberungskommissionen*, which were designed to perform the same functions as these bodies. All owners, managers, directors, chief engineers and foremen in businesses employing over twenty workers or worth more than 500,000 Marks in common stock capital were supposed to bear investigation. After the introduction of the 'Württemberg model', three senior denazification committees per *Land* were also charged with the express task of handling economic denazification. Once the investigatory subcommittee of the National Assembly had reported, it also encouraged a rapid acceleration of economic denazification.

Unhappily, little was actually accomplished. The *Land* bureaucracies that were supposed to interpret and execute the French decrees were hesitant because they feared providing French military government with additional pretexts for requisitioning or dismantling German property, a source of major discord in the French zone. As a result, they threw down a long series of roadblocks. The instructions they provided to the *Kreis*-level investigation committees watered down the political nature of the process, substituting in its place a quasi-judicial inquiry with such a high standard of evidence for indictment that even 'active' Nazis and '*alte Kämpfer*' were difficult to charge, and which practically ensured that few of the economic abettors of Nazism would face confiscation of their property. After the economic denazification committees started operating, these bodies let major cases drag far beyond the original target date for completion of the programme. The French complained of a deliberate 'policy of obstruction' and ruefully noted in early 1947 that they had been given lists of denazified cleaning ladies, but nothing on key business owners or managers. Increasingly, the public resented seemingly arbitrary decisions and non-Nazi business-men refused to participate in the committees' work. German conservatives derided the entire process as an assault upon the capitalist system.[39] The British consul in Baden-Baden reported in 1947 'that ridiculously small fines are being inflicted on large ex-Nazi firms, while the small-time party man often gets severe treatment. It can be noted that part of the 20% of the shoe production in Pirmasens which is left to the manufacturers was being used until recently to corrupt de-nazification courts, on which Germans are now becoming afraid to sit.'[40] The French themselves were hardly absent of blame for the degeneration of the system, particularly since they con-nived in the retention of technical experts. At the vital I.G. Farben chemical works in Ludwigshafen, *Parteigenossen* who had already escaped the military draft during the Hitler regime, owing to their vital importance to the economy, continued to sail undisturbed through the French occupation.[41]

A second matter that interested the French, c.1946, involved restricting the civil rights of Nazi Party members. In May 1946, Koenig set the terms of reference for special bodies called Commissions of Electoral Revision, the duty of which was to draw up voter lists that restricted the franchise and eligibility of candidature enjoyed by *Parteigenossen*. Members of the denazification committees were appointed to these bodies. As a result of their work, 'major' Nazis were prohibited from voting and hold-ing elected positions, although lesser party comrades retained the franchise, if not the right to stand for office.[42] The short term result was also to strengthen the relative weight of the left-wing vote (which is perhaps not what all French officials wanted). The full civil rights of young ex-Nazis were restored in July 1947, as were those of 'nominal' party members in November 1947.[43]

Like the British and the Soviets, the French reacted to the introduction of CC Directive 38, particularly since there were still rumours in the other occupation zones about the alleged lack of rigour in the French programme, and the French Government was keen to deflect potential criticism at the forthcoming Moscow Conference. The French, as one British official noted, wanted to show '[that they] are in the hunt'. Directive 38 also provided a possible mechanism for the processing of internees, which was one of the chief remaining tasks in the French zone. Pierre Arnal began pushing for the inclusion of the CC Directive 38 provisions in *Land* denazification laws, which only Württemberg-Hohenzollern had adopted – every-where else, denazification was simply decreed by the French – and which differed between *Länder* only in details. Originally, Arnal had planned to encourage Baden and Rhineland-Palatinate to adopt South Württemberg's legislation, but working in close concert with Robert Schmelck, head of GM's Justice Section, he came up with an entirely new set of guidelines that he hoped to impose upon the *Länder* of the French zone.

This time the rural state of South Baden proved the catalyst behind zone-wide changes, although unlike the case with Württemberg-Hohenzollern's initiative in the spring of 1946, the French gave officials in South Baden little leeway. Unhappily, the attempt to adopt the 'Württemberg model' in South Baden had already proven largely abortive. In the spring of 1946, the French had permitted the creation of a Denazification Advisory Council and the appointment of a *Staatskommissar*, although the new denazification czar, *Staatsrat* Erwin Eckert, chairman of the Baden Communist Party, immediately claimed that the French had not awarded him with enough executive power. Following the example of South Württemberg, Eckert drafted a bill that would have been given Baden a fully legal denazification system, rather than a process based solely on the decrees of the occupying power. His proposal was built around a system of 'purge inspectors' who would have had considerable authority over the operations of *Untersuchungsauschüsse* and *Säuberungskommissionen* and would have acted as the functioning arms of a 'political control committee'. Eckert's project was then watered down in order to accomodate the objections of the local branch of the CDU, the Baden Christian Social People's Party (BCSV), which feared communisation of the denazification process, but the resulting scheme was then finally blocked by the French, who felt that Eckert had overreached himself by suggesting that his projected system should work only on a wholly autonomous basis, free of intervention from the occupiers. His ambitions checked, Eckert resigned in a huff on 25 October 1946.[44]

After the Eckert Affair, Arnal began to use *Land* Baden as a relatively clean slate upon which to impose French desires. On 5 November 1946, the head of South Baden's justice ministry was ordered to show up at the supreme headquarters of French military government in Baden-Baden. In an interview with officers of the *Direction Générale de la Justice*, he 'received the task of producing a draft law for the political cleansing of the entire French zone'. In addition, he was told to complete this job at the quickest possible pace. The French also provided a list of their 'relevant wishes' for the new legislation, which meant that the basic criteria were already in place, and that the role of the South Baden bureaucrats was to add finishing touches and provide the project with a German face. Indeed, Eckert's successor as *Staatskommissar*, Richard Streng, told *Land* premier Leo Wohleb that his mission was *not* to produce flourishes of original thought, but to reproduce in detailed form the broad outlines that had already been provided by the *Contrôle de la Justice*.

The eventual product of this discourse – the so-called 'Baden model' – provided for German denazification machinery that retained much of its previous character, although chairs and deputy chairs of the *Säuberungsauschüsse* were now required to have formal legal training, and the committees themselves were renamed *Spruchkammern*, which provided a nod to the U.S. zone precedent. As demanded by the French, the Baden bill included a definition of classifications of guilt that was identical with CC Directive 38, and the range of sanctions was similar to that specified in the U.S. zone 'Law for Liberation from National Socialism'. On the other hand, the drafters retained as much as possible of the original spirit of French zone denazification. 'Each case,' they proclaimed, 'shall be examined in terms of the personal responsibility of the individual judged... Simple membership of the NSDAP ... does not necessarily determine the classification of the individual proceeded against in one or other of the categories mentioned ... [although] non-membership ... cannot excuse responsibility if it is established that the accused has pursued an activity set forth in the present law.' The draft recommended especially severe judgements for individuals of independent means who had joined the Nazi Party and furthered its objectives or, worse yet, had served their own venal purposes through securing party membership. Brutal and tyrannical behavior, agitation against churches and trade unions, 'ridicul[ing], damag[ing] or destroy[ing] values of art or science', and 'poison[ing] the spirit and soul of the young' were all supposed to count more than possession of mere party rank or membership. Perhaps most importantly, the bill suggested narrow grounds for appeals. Only severe punishments could be appealed – that is, verdicts resulting in more than a year of imprisonment, the seizure of at least forty per cent of a respondent's property or the levying of a fine in excess of 15,000 Marks – and even then an appeal could be filed only on the claim that new evidence had come to light, that evidence produced in hearings had been false, or that verdicts had run contrary to law. In addition, there was no stay of sanctions while appeals were under consideration, and there was no separate level of tribunals for appeals, all appellate jurisdiction being vested in the same system of *Spruchkammern* that delivered the original verdicts.

Thus, the Baden journeymen faithfully provided the content desired by the *Contrôle de la Justice*, and French military government was so pleased with the result that they wanted Streng to start carrying out the bill's stipulations even before it had been approved by the South Baden *Land* cabinet or legislature. Perhaps the occupiers anticipated trouble. In any case, German grumbling started as soon as the draft law was brought to the floor of the South Baden Advisory Assembly in early March 1947. In particular, the legislators claimed that the bill's appellate mechanism was grossly insufficient and they immediately passed a supplementary declaration calling for consideration of 'the most extensive means for launching appeals'. The assembly's justice committee made the same point and submitted a proposal for revision of the bill, although such acts of resistance drew a tart response from the French. The *Land* military governor, Pierre Pène, told Wohleb that he had reviewed the German proposals but had concluded 'that their application would hinder court actions and would allow an unlimited submission of appeals'. More disturbingly, he accused the assembly's justice committee of plotting. Its proposal, he mused darkly, was 'not the reflection of momentary wishes expressed in the assembly, but rather the fruit of methodical work ... the purpose of which is to paralyze operation of the law'. Pène also wondered if the justice committee was trying to force the hand of GM, and he told Wohleb – menacingly – to provide him with the names of committee members. Finally, the military governor ordered Wohleb to report in person on 26 March, bringing with him three of his state secretaries, and it is clear that in this conclave, *Land* officials received their marching orders. Although the

South Baden cabinet was still adamantly opposed to passage of the draft legislation as late as 25 March, four days later the *Land* Assembly obediently passed the bill in its original form.

Aside from the doubts expressed in the South Baden, loud complaints also issued forth from the other *Land* governments. The French encouraged both Württemberg-Hohenzollern and Rhineland-Palatinate to adopt legislation based on the 'Baden model'. Unlike the case with the U.S.-supported 'Law for Liberation from National Socialism', each *Land* in the zone was not supposed to adopt identical pieces of legislation, but GM now became relatively less willing to entertain local variations of policy. Unfortunately, the influential 'Württemberg system' was already under fire. In particular, it had begun to provoke passive resistance among German civil servants, and Klaus-Dietmar Henke describes bureaucratic 'guerrilla warfare' dating from the fall of 1946. Moreover, the success of the CDU in local and *Land* elections in the autumn of 1946 marked the rise of a party that was relatively unenthusiastic about 'political'-style denazification, and the CDU dominated *Land* regimes that were built in the spring of 1947 on the basis of fully responsible government. Nonetheless, officials in Württemberg-Hohenzollern did put up a fight to save the 'Württemberg model', albeit in sharply altered form. In a paper submitted to the French in late 1946, Schmid and his cohorts argued that the existing system already produced sanctions equivalent to those prescribed by CC Law 38, except for the most serious punishments, such as death penalties and lengthy prison sentences, which had been meted out by French military courts. Schmid also admitted that he and Künzel saw the need for some quasi-judicial mechanism that could tackle the toughest denazification cases, as referred to it by the *Staatskommissar*, as well as handling appeals. Such difficult cases were believed to be limited in number, amounting to perhaps five per cent of the total. The answer, proposed Schmid, was not to abandon Württemberg-Hohenzollern's much-touted system, but to amend it in order to create a final body of appeal, a so-called '*Säuberungsgericht*', that would include representatives of political parties, trade unions and professional bodies, and would be run by a judge. In particular, many bureaucrats and CDU politicians were hoping to keep Künzel's earlier verdicts an open issue, mainly by allowing appeal of those decisions; their rationale was that the institutions of the new system would bear a firm legal character lacking in the original 'Württemberg model'. Schmid's scheme was backed by Widmer, but officials in Baden-Baden, particularly in the *Contrôle de la Justice*, feared a glut of appeals, and they also worried about creating the impression that denazification was operating in reverse, directly contrary to the image that they were seeking to promote. As a result, Schmid's proposal fell upon deaf ears. Schmid and his cohorts negotiated the right to bring their proposal to their floor of the *Land* assembly, but after a debate the French imposed legislation based on the 'Baden model', essentially as a *Diktat*.

Like the *Land* government of Württemberg-Hohenzollern, the leaders of Rhineland-Palatinate produced their own distinctive proposal. The existing system in Rhineland-Palatinate, it will be recalled, retained features outlined in the original

French directives of September–October 1945. Such ordinances, however, provided as little right of appeal as the 'Württemberg system', nor did the 'Baden model', which was suggested by the French, offer much more. As a result, the Rhineland-Palatinate Government also launched a campaign for an adequate appeals mechanism, and their draft legislation made even more provisions in this regard than its Württemberg-Hohenzollern equivalent. The Rhinelanders also wanted a system that was more transparent and they demanded full-scale hearings for all serious cases. As in Württemberg-Hohenzollern, the French allowed the Rhinelanders to bring their bill to the floor of the Rhineland-Palatinate assembly, where it won unanimous approval, but the occupiers disregarded the outcome of this vote and on 17 April forced the state government to adopt legislation based on the 'Baden model'.

It is true that at the turn of 1946/47, there was still some confusion in French military government about the degree to which the Länder should be allowed to pursue a quasi-independent course. As usual, Laffont and Koenig were not playing from the same score. In guidelines to the Länder governments issued in early 1947, Laffont said that new laws should incorporate the CC Directive 38 categories and should also use the Spruchkammer system as a model, but Laffont encouraged German bureaucrats to be flexible in arranging the categorisation of incriminated individuals and he urged officials not to be guided solely such rigid criteria as NSDAP rank or date of membership. Some officers in the regional GM headquarters, even officials in the *Contrôle de la Justice*, felt the same way, and they provided similar signals to the Germans. Klaus-Dietmar Henke contends, however, that the scheduling of the forthcoming Moscow Conference, which was set in mid-January 1947, provided an immediate advantage to hardliners within military government, since they could now argue that it was important to produce dramatic results quickly. Certainly, General Koenig's draft ordinance, *2ᵉ Projet GM*, was much less fluid than Laffont's guidelines. It also provided an obligatory acknowledgment of Land autonomy, but it was more insistent on CC Directive 38 as the framework for the new ordinances and it ordered German state governments to undertake 'necessary legislative or administrative measures within the scope fixed by this directive'. Only after some of the spirit of *2ᵉ Projet GM* was taken into account was a final French directive, Ordinance No. 79, issued to the Germans on 18 February 1947.[45]

Despite France's much-ballyhooed attempts to move denazification policy closer to the practices of its allies, the system in the French zone retained a number of distinctive characteristics. Since denazification of the civil service was almost finished, and the French were wary about hearing or re-hearing a huge number of cases, they favoured a limited expansion of denazification only to include persons who had previously sat beyond the parameters of the system, especially 17,000 repatriates and refugees, professional officers, returning PoWs and former members of Nazi youth movements and sports associations, although the burden of the latter task was lightened by the proclamation of a youth amnesty in May 1947. French denazification delegates in the *Kreise* soon found themselves busier than ever, particularly since the denazification of professional officers involved coordinating activity with members of the Disarmament Control Commission, and dealing with repatriates and refugees demanded the creation of screening centres. As was the case previously, however, French military government remained opposed to any collective measures or multiplication of inquiries that might cause 'needless apprehension' amongst the populace, instead preferring to narrow their sights upon a narrow number of cases in which the occupying power had an interest. They also limited the social shock waves from denazification by continuing to allow respondents to work at their regular jobs until (or unless) they received incriminating categorisations at their hearings. Categorisation, such as it was, focused mainly upon 'Major Offenders', whom the French believed were to be found largely within the ranks of present or former detainees. With particular regard to this group, the French intended to maintain a direct hand in prosecutions. Three French magistrates were posted to Lahr, Freiburg and Buhl, where all internees or ex-internees were directed for interrogation and processing. These magistrates undertook many of the functions usually performed by the *Untersuchungsauschüsse*, cooperating with French administrative officials and camp commandants in order to prepare files. After such preliminary steps, the cases were sent through the regular denazification system. Pushing the entire pool of internees and ex-internees through his initial vetting process took a year to complete.[46]

Meanwhile, opinion in Paris and Baden-Baden did not exist in a static state, particularly since the French, as much as the other occupying powers, were influenced by the gathering momentum of the Cold War. Although a few ex-Vichyite generals, such as Alphonse Juin, had already claimed that the weakening of Germany directly aided 'Russian Communism',[47] most French statesmen and military men only slowly came to see the USSR as a greater threat than the *Erbfeind* across the Rhine. Nonetheless, the start of sustained fighting with the Vietminh in far-off Indochina increased anti-communist sentiments amongst the French elite, and the French, as much as the other powers, failed to secure their objectives at the Moscow Conference, partly because of Soviet opposition to a decentralized form of government in Germany. In addition, Molotov embarrassed the French by rating them as the occupying power with the worst record on denazification. Alternately, the announcement of the Marshall Plan linked France more closely to the United States and it finally gave the country access to resources for recovery aside from coal systematically plundered from Germany. In addition, the May 1947 departure of the French Communist Party from the tripartite coalition government in Paris diminished the domestic sway of the communists and removed an institutional influence in favour of radical denazification, even as Paris became more actively involved in the planning and implementation of the purge.[48] At the same time, De Gaulle's momentary departure from politics weakened the revanchist school of thought, while the chief of the MRP, Georges Bidault, began to blame the unsuccessful irredentist policy on Gaullist influence and to admit that efforts to detach the Ruhr had been a mistake.[49] All these events conspired to reduce France's role as a third force in Germany and increasingly drove the country towards a conjunction with its traditional Anglo-American allies. Significantly, both America and Britain – it will be recalled – had begun the termination of their own denazification programmes by the end of 1947. As was the case in the U.S. and British zones of occupation, such factors also arose at a time when the natural impetus behind denazification had started to wane. A French military government spokesman warned as early as April 1947 that the most important Nazis had already been purged and that it was difficult to do more 'without dangerously affecting public life'.[50]

As for the 'Baden system', it underwent a steady pummeling throughout 1947. The French charged that mild verdicts by the *Spruchkammern* resulted in a 'veritable sabotage of the *épuration*', and they threatened that the allocation of any further governmental powers to the *Länder* might have to be limited or postponed. For their part, German bureaucrats continued to complain about the lack of an adequate appellate mechanism, and they also began to fret about the submersion of previously handled cases within the new categories, contending that the more advanced legal standards of the new system demanded a fresh review of all cases. In response, Laffont and other French officers dug in their heels. There was a particularly acrimonious confrontation in *Land* Württemberg-Hohenzollern, where French advocates of the 'Württemberg system', such as Georges Vigouroux, resented Baden-Baden's abandonment of the model and clashed repeatedly with Künzel's successor as *Staatskommissar*, Anton Traber, a conservative Catholic who – in sharp contrast to his predecessor – considered denazification 'a serious sickness in the body of our people'. Vigouroux and his cohorts realised that Künzel had already come close to completing denazification, and that as long as they denied Traber the power to revise existing verdicts, they could freeze the denazification process in a relatively advanced state, thus preserving much of what the 'Württemberg model' had accomplished. Württemberg-Hohenzollern, however, was not the only scene of discord: a British report suggested that 'the Spruchkammer set up in the Rhenish-Palatinate to deal with denazification are meeting with increased difficulties caused by the German authorities'. Meanwhile, as chaos and intrigue reigned at senior levels, members of the *Untersuchungsauschüsse* and *Spruchkammern* became progressively demoralised, making it impossible to recruit or retain personnel.[51]

This logjam eventually had to break, particularly since Baden-Baden admitted that the practical time and appetite for denazification was almost gone, and GM was also forced to concede that the German machinery responsible for the process was on the brink of collapse. In May 1947, Arnal's successor as denazification czar, Alain Radenac, suggested arranging a wide scale amnesty for people in the 'Follower' category, but Koenig was opposed because he feared the impact on French public opinion. However, when the Soviets announced the implementation of Order 201, which favoured the 'rehabilitation' of 'nominal' Nazis, Koenig changed his mind and asked Laffont to make arrangements for a similar measure. On 21 October 1947, Laffont told a meeting of *Land* premiers that the French authorities, rather than turning the *Spruchkammern* into '*Mitläuferfabriken*', were now preparing an effective amnesty for all '*Mitläufer*'. The official manifestation of this policy was Ordinance Number 133 (17 November 1947), in which Koenig ordered the cessation of denazification efforts against '*Mitläufer*', and he empowered the *Staatskommissar* to decide how far existing sanctions against such people should continue, although he had no objections to their full reinstatement or eligibility for public office. The military governor also instructed the *Länder* to expedite surviving denazification measures and to focus remaining efforts on Nazi 'activists' and members of the SS and Gestapo.

Meanwhile, GM's civilian masters in the State Secretariate for German and Austrian Affairs were becoming fed up with denazification (much like their counterparts in the British Control Office and the U.S. War Department). In March 1948, the state secretary, Pierre Schneiter, advised Koenig to wrap up the programme as soon as possible. However, it also became clear that Ordinance 133 was not having the desired effect in streamlining the process. Indeed, some '*Mitläufer*' continued paying fines, at least at the discretion of the *Staatskommissar*, and this fact actually slowed down operations of the *Spruchkammern* because 'minor' Nazis now had the right to launch appeals that the tribunals had to consider. As a result, Koenig modified Ordinance 133 in July 1948. He ordered cancellation of all small and moderate fines – those worth less than 15,000 Marks or the value of fifteen per cent of a respondent's property – and he revoked denazification measures against returning PoWs, except for men classified as 'Major Offenders'. In addition, Koenig ordered cancellation of the *Spruchkammer* sessions scheduled for 'Minor Offenders' at the end of their two or three year probation periods, all of which was supposed to leave the tribunals with the time and resources to judge 60,000 outstanding cases, many of them involving 'Major Offenders'.[52]

At the beginning of January 1949, French zone denazification authorities began the formal cessation of the programme, although it took more than a year for cases currently on the docket to pass through the system. In the Palatinate, for instance, the local *Spruchkammer* was still struggling with 200 cases as late as July 1949, and it was the early 1950s before the various *Länder* officially wrapped up the process and cancelled remaining sanctions.[53] The final figures – those of February 1950 – show that 669,000 cases had been examined, of which nearly half had been categorised. As late as July 1948, 133,000 respondents were still provisionally slotted into categories above the *Mitläufer* class, but this had led to complaints that French zone Nazis were facing inordinately harsher treatment than *Parteigenossen* in the other zones, and by 1950 most of these cases had been downgraded to 'Follower' status, leaving less than 18,000 people in the three higher categories of guilt. Moreover, because many *Mitläufer* escaped punishment, courtesy of Ordinance Number 133, Justus Fürstenau is probably right in concluding that the eventual outcome of French zone denazification was milder than in any other part of Germany.[54] As for the rate of dismissals in various government ministries, it fell between five and thirty per cent, although the range of this differentiation depended less on the particular character of a ministry than on the degree to which the French chose to examine its personnel.[55]

Overall, it must be admitted that the denazification of the French zone was far from perfect. The programme was unpopular, for which the French blamed German personnel, while the Germans concurrently blamed the French. More importantly, the French insistence on the importance of individual behavior, however laudable, often broke down. Indeed, Carlo Schmid noted at the height of denazification, as several thousand respondents passed through the system every week, that the process could hardly but be schematic. In particular, the denazification of police in the southern part of the French zone followed a strictly categorical formula, with all NSDAP members, and even members of party auxiliaries, systematically losing their jobs and benefits.[56] The system also produced the same discrepancies in punishment that we have seen in other zones, with 'lesser' Nazis often receiving disproportionally hard sentences while real villains were sometimes able to avoid or wait out the process.[57] In addition, even when the programme functioned in the intended fashion, any such process based on denunciations tended to elevate village feuds, vendettas and business rivalries into the subjects of official power, and indeed, there were complaints from the earliest days of the French occupation about the role of denunciations in provoking arrests and dismissals.[58] And finally, as Roy Willis notes, the heavy dependence of the system on fines, demotions and other forms of financial or bureaucratic punishments, rather than outright arrests or job dismissals, served administrative and economic needs, but it created the impression than simple amercement was sufficient to make amends for Nazism or to wipe away any responsibility for past behavior.[59] In the vital realm of economic cleansing, the denazification committees imposed the superficially impressive figure of 728 million Marks in financial penalties and property confiscations, at least by August 1947, but many of these fines went unpaid. Only a small number of businessmen and merchants were dropped from their jobs.[60]

On the other hand, many historians have claimed that the French made the most rational and reasonable attempt to denazify their zone, at least relative to their fellow occupying powers, and that the 'Württemberg system', in particular, found the golden mean between an excessive degree of severity and an inadequate standard of leniency. According to Klaus-Dietmar Henke, only such a bureaucratic approach could have accomplished denazification with the speed that both the French and German anti-fascists realised was necessary, at least before the momentary support of well-meaning forces eroded. Nonetheless, recent German research has concluded that despite the best efforts of the French and their German collaborators, the denazification drive was ultimately defeated by unfavorable forces of circumstance and by German bureaucratic opposition.[61]

And yet the very nature of the French approach was important because its humanism and recognition of the individual set the tone for a policy that would eventually take shape as Franco-German reconciliation. Although all the countries occupying Germany were partially thwarted in achieving their objectives, France – alone amongst the four – was able to reconfigure its German policy in way that supported the notion of a European union with a Franco-German axis at its core. More than any other factor, this eventual course provided France with a renewed claim to great power status.[62]

THE HOUSE OF LIES

How did Germans react to denazification? Unfortunately, the fact that the Allies came to Germany asking questions prompted many Germans to lie, or worse yet, to shade the truth to a point where a realistic sense of the past was lost even to the people who had experienced it. Whether a person had joined the Nazi Party, or had supported Hitler, or even had turned a blind eye to warmongering, abuse of foreign labour or outright genocide – all these matters involved subjective determinations that frequently went further than anything that could be conveyed by 'yes' or 'no' answers. This point was made most forcefully by Ernst von Salomon, a 'revolutionary conservative', *but* not a typical Nazi, who wrote a lengthy memoir as a literary response to his *Fragebogen*, in the process suggesting that the autobiographical details sought by the Allies often demanded an extensive and detailed accounting of one's own life. It is significant that von Salomon's tome, which was simply titled *Der Fragebogen*, became the best-selling book in early post-war Germany, achieving sales of 250,000 by 1955.[1]

Of course, from the perspective of the occupiers, matters looked far less ambiguous. Many Germans claimed to be 'apolitical', but the Allies soon learned that this was often code for a pattern of highly conservative and reactionary opinions. They also witnessed a steady parade of Nazi Party members who claimed to have always been 'stolid anti-fascists' at heart, but to have been unfortunate victims of circumstance. In the eastern zone, many Nazis claimed to have been secret communists. Often such elements described themselves as '*Mussnazis*', a term that was heard *ad nauseam* in 1945/46, and which signified that the claimant had supposedly been 'forced' to join the NSDAP, particularly after the Nazis had penetrated and reorganised the state bureaucracy. Of course, there was a fine line between advancing one's position and maintaining one's livelihood, but this distinction was rarely mentioned. A variation of the *Mussnazi* was the 'transient Nazi,' or *Maikäfer*, a so-called 'Mayfly' who had been drawn toward the movement at its high-water mark, but then had flown away. The 'anti-fascism' of such elements had inevitably been exercised in the private sphere: they had allegedly listened to the BBC or Radio Moscow, they had refused to give the Nazi salute, they had not paid party membership dues, or they had aided Jews – this last gambit an attempt to seek merit from protecting victims of a regime that they themselves had helped to organise. When Allied interrogators asked such people who had actually voted for Hitler or provided mass support, they were sometimes told 'the Germans', as if the respondents were speaking of some people far different from themselves, and even von Salomon conceded that few Nazis were willing to own up honestly. Indeed, if the occupiers encountered any single person brave enough to admit genuine and consistent support for the party, they joked that they had finally found the source of Hitler's constituency, letting off the hook millions of *Mussnazis* and *Maikäfer*. The Allies were particularly galled when party members, if engaged in serious conversation, slowly revealed that their main gripe with the Nazi regime was not that it had started the war, but that it had lost it. '*Man hat uns belogen und betrogen,*' they whined – 'They lied to us and deceived us.'[2] The occupiers were also annoyed by persistent use of the passive voice by people with something to hide. One Nazi, in noting that his parents had encouraged him to get party membership in 1933, explained that 'somehow this was done...' 'Somehow,' snapped his British interrogator. 'What is that supposed to mean. You applied for membership, completed and signed the application form and were accepted.'

While the occupiers saw the absolutes of black and white, ex-party members saw oceans of grey, and nearly always pleaded mitigating circumstances. Take, for instance, the case of Arnold Ziegfeld, a Berlin author and book publisher who was seeking a license to renew his business. Ziegfeld was a self-admitted 'German nationalist', who had a long record of association with the NSDAP and its aux-iliaries. He had joined the party in 1921, and after his membership lapsed, he had joined again in 1937, eventually coming to hold office in the Foreign Section of the party; he was a decade-long member of the SA and had spoken publi-cally on that organisation's behalf; and from 1941 to 1945, he had sent his son to an elite Nazi boarding school (a 'Napola'). However, Ziegler wanted complete exoneration in the denazification process and resented being classified even as a 'Follower'. For each of the lapses in his past he had a convenient excuse. He had originally joined the party in anti-Versailles spasm and had been interested mainly in the movement's sports wing. He had later rejoined in the 1930s because he had no choice if he wanted to keep publishing, and he became part of the SA when the right-wing German veterans' group, the *Stahlhelm*, transferred its members amass in 1934. In any case, he had allegedly decided to engage his lifelong antipa-thy toward militarism and Nazism by fighting the movement from within. He assumed party offices and speaking engagements because he needed camouflage for his secret campaign against National Socialism, limiting most of his involve-ment to comments on such 'harmless topics' as geography. He had enrolled his son in a Napola because it was the only school still open in Berlin and because the lad was a loner who supposedly required involvement in a community-oriented environment. After appealing his case to the occupying power, Ziegfeld was told – understandibly – that he had 'a somewhat confused image of himself'.[3]

How to deal with such people was one of the great conundrums of denazification. Many told boldfaced lies, others were dishonest even with themselves. Either way, a programme that encouraged the development of such falsehoods was perhaps not the optimal way to start a national '*Vergangenheitsbewältigung*', or 'coming to terms with the past', a necessary process if Germany was to move forward morally and intellectually. Moreover, as Helga Welsh notes, the character of the denazification system forced Nazis to think of themselves as members of proscribed groups, rather than pondering their own individual acts during the Third Reich. On the other hand, there is no doubt that there were many genuine *Mussnazis*. German dairy workers, for instance, were actually driven into the party under duress in 1937, and forest rangers, chimney sweeps and tradesmen were all subjected to similar treatment. Nurses were stampeded into the Nazi women's auxiliary, and gas station attendants and auto mechanics were forced to join the Nazi transport corps. Other Germans were involuntarily enrolled in the party individually, or were transferred from party auxiliaries to the main body of the party, often without giving their consent.[4] In addition, even *Mussnazis* who had joined the NSDAP from an overweening sense of conformism, rather than from true compulsion, were likely to continue bending in the face of prevailing political winds, even the democratic and socialist trends now encouraged by the occupation forces.[5] The main aim of conformists, after all, was to conform. Naturally, fellow Germans had more understanding of 'apoliticals', *Mussnazis*, *Maikäfer* and conformists than did the occupation forces, and German denazification commissions often accepted such claims as mitigating circumstances.[6]

In several instances, the Allies discovered organised or at least semi-coordinated attempts to lie on *Fragebogen*. In a school near Regensburg, which had a suspiciously large number of BdM leaders on its student roster, the schoolmaster was arrested for *Fragebogen* violations and AMG further discovered that only nineteen of thirty-five teachers had completed *Fragebogen*, and that even these documents had not been filed with the appropriate authorities. The school was temporarily closed and was only reopened under more stringent supervision.[7] Rather more blatant was the attempt to infiltrate SS men into the Wiesbaden municipal police, an operation organised by Willie Weber, a former member of the 4th *Waffen* SS Police *Panzer* Grenadier Division. In early 1946, Weber used a falsified *Fragebogen* to get hired as the personnel chief with the Wiesbaden constabulary, after which he was in a unique position to help his old friends, incuding eight colleagues from his own division. After a year on the job, Weber and his cohort were uncovered and then promptly brought to trial in a military court. Meanwhile, the AMG detachment in Wiesbaden was forced to undertake a painstaking review of the personnel files of 600 city policemen, detectives and jailers, a process that eventually turned up another one hundred cases with 'irregularities'. Of this group, forty-six men were eventually dismissed and tried in military court on charges of concealing previous NSDAP, SA or SS affiliations.[8]

In occupied Germany, believability could be a highly-charged political issue, as demonstrated especially by the treatment of anti-Nazis from *inside* the ranks of the NSDAP and the Nazi security apparatus. Although there were legions of *faux* infiltrators who later offered 'penetration' of the Nazi Party as an excuse for past behavior, there were a few legitimate members of the species,[9] particularly since the underground KPD had sent 'Trojan Horses' into Nazi ranks. The Allied criteria for accepting such claims was to demand *proof* that resisters had opposed the Nazi regime, either by providing documentation or producing witnesses. On such a basis the Allies would provide certificates allowing for the employability of the person in question, although these documents were issued only rarely. Under the terms of the Law for Liberation from National Socialism, as well as French denazification directive CAB/C 722 , former members of the NSDAP or Nazi security services could qualify as active anti-Nazis and thus be rewarded with full exoneration, but the criteria for such exemptions were narrowly defined.[10] In actuality, the handling of such cases often revealed the exercise of a double standard, as several examples from southern Germany will show.

The Catholic conservative elite in the Rhineland and Bavaria was more predisposed to accepting the claims of right-wing opponents of the Nazis – although there was some suspicion even of this group – while the claims of leftists were usually dismissed out of hand. One interesting case was that of Gustav Theuring, a former officer in the *Abwehr's* counter-intelligence bureau, which meant that he fit within an automatic removal category. Indeed, the Americans had captured Theuring in April 1945 and had interned him until August of the same year. Theuring was a veteran of the Cologne municipal police during the interwar period, and was again recruited by that force in January 1947, being reinstated as a senior officer. This appointment was approved by the Cologne municipal administration and Police Chief Winkler, who cited Theuring's splendid local reputation and longtime support of the Centre Party. Matters did not look so clear from a British perspective, and in February 1947 the Public Safety Branch began looking into the case, although Theuring eventually emerged with a clean bill of health. During the late 1920s and early 1930s, Theuring had been a member of the Political Police, in which he had fought the National Socialists, and although his services were retained after 1933, Nazi officials warned him that 'as a police official, it was unwise to practice one's religion so openly'. He had applied for membership in the NSDAP in 1938, but his application had been rejected on the grounds of his 'dubious political record and strong church convictions'. After being recalled to the German Army – he had been a reserve officer – he was posted with the *Abwehr*, but he had served on the staff of General Oster, who had been deeply involved in the 20 July conspiracy. Theuring later claimed to have been engaged in anti-Nazi activity until the SS security services purged Oster's office in 1943, whence he was transferred to another section. A German denazification panel, in reviewing the case, exonerated Theuring, and the British eventually arrived at much the same conclusion, noting that 'the Police Force can ill afford to lose his services at the present time'.[11]

A similar case involved Bavarian politician Josef Müller, nicknamed 'Cattleman Joe', who was chair of the CSU and a former *Wehrmacht* intelligence officer. As well as being an ex-member of the *Abwehr*, which was of concern to U.S. denazification officials, Müller was dogged by allegations of having participated in 1932 coalition talks between his old party, the BVP, and the NSDAP, and of having benefitted from the 'Aryanisation' of the property of German Jews. 'Cattleman Joe', however, had an effective retort, claiming that he had been connected with the 20 July plot and that he had secretly cooperated with the OSS station in Switzerland, although it was politically imprudent in the first post-war years – an era when the few survivors of 20 July were still trying to prove that they had not been traitors – to shout these facts from a rooftop. Thus, Müller, who generally regarded denazification as a 'national sorrow', had not deigned to clear his name before a *Spruchkammer*. There matters rested until Müller's enemies in the autonomist wing of the CSU cooperated with the communists and socialists to bring his errant denazification status to light, being aided in this endeavour by Special Branch officers who willingly provided information from Müller's *Fragebogen*. For several weeks in the fall of 1946, it looked as though Müller would lose the chairmanship of the CSU, even though he had just won an overwhelming vote of confidence at the party's annual convention. Eventually Clay and Dorn decided to let Müller keep his job, although he was prohibited from assuming the Bavarian premiership.[12]

On the other hand, KPD 'Trojan Horses' typically got much rougher treatment than right-wing resisters like Theuring and Müller. In one case, a KPD nominee for a cabinet post in the Hoegner government, Alfred Kroth, was adamantly blocked by AMG and by Bavarian Catholic conservatives, mainly with the rationale that he had been a member of the NSDAP and the Hitler Youth. Kroth could produce numerous witnesses to the fact that he had been instructed by the underground KPD to join the Nazi Party, and that he had consistently opposed the Hitler regime and protected German Jews, but to no avail. Kroth could also show that he had supported an anti-Nazi revolt near the end of the war, and had helped guide a U.S. Army unit into the Munich suburbs, but even this evidence failed to help his case. Rather, he was dropped from the Munich city council, blocked from access to his bank account, prohibited from any political activity and eventually arrested, although he was later acquitted of all charges.[13]

A similar case involved the control of the *Landratsamt* in the eastern Bavarian town of Wasserburg am Inn, although in this instance the occupiers took the opposite tack, backing a local communist, Josef Estermann, in order to balance the influence of the local Catholic conservative clique. Like Kroth, Estermann had participated in the 'Freedom Bavaria' revolt of 27/28 April, but local *Honoratioren* in Wasserburg noted that he had also served as a Gestapo informer after being released from a concentration camp. Estermann could plausibly contend that he had provided the Nazis with misinformation, although the clique wanted him judged only on the superficial facts of the case. The Americans staunchly supported Estermann until he was eventually beat in *Kreis* elections by the Catholic camarilla, whose first choice for the *Landrat's* office had been rejected by AMG on denazification grounds – his credentials had apparently not offended the coterie – although the group eventually recruited a second candidate, who then ran under the banner of the CSU. Upon his election, the new *Landrat* distinguished himself by providing special ration allotments to members of the Catholic clique, and by denouncing the regional UNRRA director as 'a filthy Jewish scoundrel', although this outrage bothered no one in the local elite.[14]

Despite differences of opinion about specific cases, there was originally a considerable appetite in occupied Germany for anti-Nazi purges. In late July 1945, 21st Army Group reported 'a general and increasing outcry against the retention of Nazis in office', even of so-called 'nominals', and reports from the American and French zones also indicated across-the-board support for denazification, with even elements of the CDU and the churches calling for a cleansing of German public life.[15] It is true that there was little popular acceptance of 'collective guilt'[16] – indeed, underground Nazi propaganda scored considerable successes in rejecting Allied accusations and atrocity publicity[17] – but neither was there much continuing tolerance of the NSDAP. The autocratic comportment of the Nazi Party's regional bosses, the *Gauleiter* and *Kreisleiter*, had long alienated many Germans, and the Nazis had further shamed themselves by the response of party officials to the enemy invasion of Germany, which was usually either self-annihilation or precipitate flight. 'They all sought escape,' remembered Helmut Gollwitzer, 'either in death or in an Alpine hut, but none of them died in the cause for which they had callously sacrificed millions, and had demanded the uttermost sacrifice from us all.'[18] One German general later remembered the disgust of his troops when the local *Kreisleiter* showed up at a hospital in Schwäbisch-Gmünd, taking time out from his run to the rear in order to tend a flesh wound: 'We don't want any "Kreisleiter" in here,' raged the soldiers.[19] A few anti-fascists launched a '*Fasenenjagd*', or hunt for 'golden pheasants' (that is, those clothed in fancy brown uniforms), in which they intended to pursue their own violent brand of denazification. Reports from occupied Berlin, for instance, suggest that secret avengers were claiming police powers to spirit away Nazis and then deal out vigilante justice.[20] The Allies, however, generally disapproved of such independent initiatives or methods. In the Hessian town of Kirchain, where an anti-fascist band led by a KPD member attacked a former Nazi *Bürgermeister* and threatened other

Parteigenossen, the local AMG detachment ordered the vigilante group to disband. Thus, there was no chance for the sort of radical self-cleansing carried out by anti-fascist Partisans in northern Italy.[21]

For the most part, Germans across the political and social spectrums were disenchanted with their former political masters. German conservatives had long been repelled by Nazi terror, anti-clericalism and disdain for the rule of law – they saw Nazism, like communism, as a troubling facet of 'mass society' – and prominent NSDAP members seemed like handy scapegoats for the involvement of a broader German elite in projects of national aggrandisement. Some members of polite society resented having been replaced or passed over by Nazi interlopers, who were often their educational and social inferiors, and denazification seemed a potential means of evening the score. In southern Germany, some regional elites saw a chance to get rid of Prussians who had taken up positions in local administration, and there were even demands for deporting northerners to the British and Soviet zones. However, most conservatives thought of purging only the most senior levels of the bureaucracy and the police, and they were concerned that even this imperative be achieved through discretionary means. Wholesale collapse of the administrative structure, they warned, would open the path to 'Bolshevisation', and they also resented the importation of the American 'spoils system' into German administrative culture. In Hesse, an influential memorandum by Werner Hilpert, the local founder of the CDU, portrayed denazification as a philosophical challenge that had already been largely met by the shock of capitulation, and he warned the Americans to keep their hands off the economy, which was necessary to 'the reconstruction of Western Europe'. Hilpert suggested forcing Nazis through a short re-education course based on Wendell Wilkie's internationalist tome *One World*.

The churches too were eager to see the end of a totalitarian force that had impinged upon their sphere, although the middle class origins of most of the episcopate meant that there was little sympathy for social revolution, and there was some worry that personnel purges would cause distress. Niemöller's influence led the Evangelical Church to issue the 'Stuttgart Declaration of Guilt', although this proclamation was not a full recognition of 'collective guilt', at least as the term was understood by the Americans, but rather an admission of Protestant failure to provide a spiritual basis for resistance to National Socialism. Moreover, the 'Stuttgart Declaration' blamed Nazism on the rise of secularism, which detached it from specifically German values and traditions, and which implied that the answer to the problems of the modern age was 're-Christianisation'. The declaration did provide the basis for a new concern with 'God-given human rights' and the importance of political engagement, but it did not support either class warfare or the style of personnel purging undertaken by the occupiers. Rather, guilt was supposedly an abstract problem to be spiritualised and internalised at the individual level. Instead of casting stones, Niemöller advised Christians to get their own houses in order. Talk of Christian charity and forgiveness also became a staple element of this dialogue, and Niemöller argued that 'young people who have lived through the closing months of the war will be healed of Nazism by events themselves'. It was obvious, however, there had to be penal sanctions for Nazis guilty of specific crimes.

The Catholic discourse was much the same. On 8 May 1945, Archbishop Gröber of Freiburg noted that true change had to come through acceptance of Christ and his message. Like Niemöller, he warned of the distinction between moral and legal responsibility, and while all criminal acts deserved punishment, he recalled the advice of St. Augustine, 'hate the sin, but love the sinner'. Of course, the fact that Gröber was an honorary chaplain in the SS might have blunted the impact of his message, but church fathers in other parts of the zone adopted the same tone. In the Upper Palatinate, the Bishop of Regensburg reminded local AMG that the people of his region were 'black', that is, loyal Catholics, and that they had been largely hostile to the Nazis. He also put in a good word for everybody individually innocent and 'not to be blamed for the great disaster because of personal cooperation with National Socialism'. Many Bavarian Catholics argued that had denominational schools been able to function unhindered, they might well have prevented the outbreak of the Second World War, and of the First World War as well. Some clerics worried about the impact of a prospective purge upon the parochial school system. The General-Vicar of Passau warned Fritz Schäffer that in the classroom, it was 'better [to have] a Nazi defector than ten Nazi haters … who understand barely anything of education'.

Not surprisingly, forces on the Left were possessed by relatively more severe attitudes. After being literally chased into exile, SPD leaders and theorists called for a revolution against Hitler, a supposedly millennial event that would have involved creating revolutionary tribunals and undertaking a sweeping purge of the state bureaucracy, at least as a way station on the path toward restoring a parliamentary republic. Some elements spoke of crushing 'the fascist ruling classes'. Socialist youth leader Willie Brandt, for instance, argued that the guilty included 'not only [Nazi] party leaders and Gestapo terrorists, but also Junkers, big industrialists, generals, bureaucrats and professors who were involved and who unleashed terror and war'. Elements on the Left of the SPD continued to promote such objectives as late as 1944/45, although this programme was increasingly contingent upon the occupiers allowing such a 'dependent revolution' to unfold. This was perhaps an unrealistic expectation, although socialists in Germany would later point out that the BBC had promised the vigorous elimination of all Nazis from both the government and the economy.

On the other hand, figures in the right-wing and centre of the SPD increasingly abandoned such assumptions as it became clear that Germany would be overrun and occupied before any prospective revolution could occur. With the dawn of such realisations, these elements increasingly assumed the mantle of 'the other Germany', partly in order to resist some of the more outlandish features of Allied occupation policy. They regarded denazification as a 'test case' through which the 'other Germany' could prove itself. Such an approach involved detaching the matter from the Allied realm of concerns, and rather handling it in German courts and in accordance with the rule of law. The moderates also revealed the same protective attitude toward the administrative structure that had limited social change during the German Revolution of 1918. In the first few weeks of the occupation, the occupiers consulted such SPD leaders as Carl Severing in Bielefeld and Wilhelm Keil in Ludwigsburg, but these men advised them *not* to destroy the German bureaucracy, but to tighten up the structure by using existing disciplinary procedures or by allowing newly-appointed SPD, *Zentrum* or Liberal officials to deal with Nazis. They minimised the disruptive effects of such measures by arguing that the Nazis had already bloated the size of the bureaucracy, thus creating a degree of slack, or by contending that the number of dismissals should be limited and that certain functions would be assumed by volunteer bodies, such as anti-fascist committees. In Krefeld, the secretary of the local SPD, *Herr* Hellenbock, advised penalising only the *Kreisleiter* and senior party leaders, while making rank-and-file Nazis perform a brief period of forced labour, which he interpreted as a rehabilitative device. [22]

Despite the fact that there was originally a considerable wave of German support for some form of denazification, this sentiment was undercut by a tectonic shift in opinion that began in the late summer and fall of 1945. Indeed, the percentage of Germans backing the programme steadily declined. Polling data in the U.S. zone reveals that the number of Germans content with the nature of the purge slipped from fifty-seven per cent in early 1946 to thirty-two per cent in 1947, and that by 1949 it had dwindled to seventeen per cent. By the turn of 1946/47, thirty per cent of Germans wanted the Americans to resume control of the programme, either because they wanted to see more firmness or because they wanted to thrust the responsibility upon American (rather than German) shoulders. [23] There was increasing popular resentment over the fact that 'technical experts' and businessmen appeared to be exempt from the programme, and the results produced by the purge seemed arbitrary and imprecise. In Bremen, Left-wing activist Friedrich Buschmann was aghast at how the Americans drew out English-speakers – all of them Nazis – from amongst the masses of Germans assembled to clear rubble at the municipal airport, and he noted how such elements became chummy with the occupation authorities, being given office jobs and supervisory positions. In Hamburg, trade unionists and leftists were angry about the lack of sufficiently severe punishments specified in Zonal Policy Instruction 54, especially for Nazis falling into category three, although there were also simultaneous complaints that British retention of control over denazification made the process little more than an Allied *Diktat*. From Lörrach came public complaints that many old Nazis had disguised themselves as communists or Francophiles and had thus evaded the hostile interest of the occupying power. Discrepancies of treatment between local military government detachments, and between the occupation garrisons in the various zones, were noticed by Germans and were the source of much adverse commentary.[24] Leftist activists and trade unionists were particularly disappointed that their gains in social or economic power seemed limited, and conservative mayors and *Land* officials claimed that German hopes for liberation were being smashed by the high-handedness and vengefulness of the occupying powers. Theodor Heuss, a future president of Germany who was then a cabinet minister in Württemberg-Baden, argued that schematic denazification was driving German youth toward nihilism and destroying the 'inner peace' of the country.[25] Such resentments existed even in the Russian zone, where there was an 'unmistakable change in the public mood'. From Zwickau came reports of 'state and [SED] party functionaries whor[ing] around with SS wives… Worker's wives see these [women] given preference in stores and driving luxury cars'. The *Oberlandrat* of Cottbus reported deep social divisions about the Soviet practice of stripping Nazis of commercial property, 'One segment of the population is of the opinion that only active PGs should be encroached upon, while another is in favour of making no exceptions even in regard to the so-called nominal members.'[26]

Unfortunately, by the time that German denazification tribunals began operating, the original wave of enthusiasm was over, replaced by a mood of increasing cynicism and disapproval.[27] Consequently, it was difficult to recruit personnel for the new bodies. In fact, the denazification boards often found that they could attract only the most committed anti-fascists, such as the secretary of the Cultural *Spruchkammer* in Berlin, a left-wing social democrat named Wolfgang Schmidt, whose zeal burned so bright that it scared even the British. Schmidt's interrogation technique was to scream abuse at his subjects, which reminded one British officer of Gestapo methods. Germans also worried about the quality of personnel serving in the denazification system, and in the U.S. zone the authorities eventually had to resort to drafting lawyers in order to man *Spruchkammern*, although most evaded this ploy by pleading issues of conscience, religious scruples or bad health. In several rural counties in Bavaria, where AMG tussled with obstructionist *Landräte*, the occupiers found it impossible to recruit several dozen *Spruchkammer* personnel from local populations numbering in the tens of thousands. In Starnberg, one prospective candidate told the Americans that such service would render him morally dead to the community: no workman would labour for him, no merchant would sell to him, and perhaps one night – on his way home – a Werewolf would accost him and bring an end to his life. Another kind of problem is suggested by the following Special Branch report from Steinach, dated 31 October 1946:

> The Spruchkammer of this Landkreis is one of the most incompetent
> Spruchkammern in the entire Land. The chairman and Public Prosecutors are

ordinary farmers who are practically illiterate. There is one young law student, who, until now, has carried by himself the entire responsibility for operations. Since neither the Public Prosecutor nor the Chairman are capable of drawing up anything approaching adequate charges or a decision, this man has alternated between writing charge sheets for the Public Prosecutor and decisions for the Chairman. Thus he has found himself in the peculiar position of first drafting up charges and then drafting a decision opposing his own charges. This legalistic 'Jekyll and Hyde' situation has been much of a strain and now, after four months of it, he is close to a nervous breakdown. In addition to his other duties, he has been in charge of all administrative matters.

Persons who did serve in the denazification system were generally treated as lepers, and many Germans eventually became convinced that such people were either opportunists or shirkers.[28]

Fear of retaliation also forced a crystallisation of popular attitudes toward denazification. As soon as it dawned on Germans that denazification might not fully translate into action, and that individual Nazis might be able to keep or regain their jobs, support for the programme began to decline.[29] The fact that the following joke was circulating among Germans as early as the summer of 1945 bears a sad testament to such anxieties:

– 'Do you know where I can apply for membership in the NSDAP?'
– 'Why? Do you want to become a Werewolf?'
– 'Ach, was! I want to apply for a job on the town council.'[30]

Indeed, fear of a Nazi 'come-back' remained tangible until the end of the occupation.[31] Potential witnesses for denazification hearings grew reluctant, and according to the chairman of the *Untersuchungsausschuss* in Horb, such people withdrew 'out of fear, making excuses by claiming illness'. In eastern Bavaria, such 'invalids' were sometimes spotted vigorously enjoying themselves in local pubs. In Nördlingen, the chairman of the denazification tribunal made an honest yet devastating estimate of the situation. The Germans, he claimed, should never have been given the opportunity to run the denazification programme, 'The German people have no sense of guilt. They think they are imposed upon. The Spruchkammer is too close to the people and knows them too well and it is protecting itself for the future, in the event the Americans leave.' Even in the Soviet zone, the labour force at the huge synthetics plant at Schwarzheide – 5,000 strong – could produce only five prosecution witnesses against forty-five suspect supervisors examined by a local Denazification Commission. Such episodes prompted grim talk about the continuing influence of 'German fascism', although many Germans simply wanted to avoid becoming part of a 'culture of denunciation', especially since the creation of a similar climate was one of the things they held against the Nazi regime itself.[32]

In addition to other forms of anti-denazification resentment, German bureaucrats and politicians began to complain about the administrative and economic
consequences of denazification. In the British zone, the finance minister of North-
Rhine Westphalia, Franz Blücher, claimed that 'the denazification panels were
robbing him of all his best men', and there were similar concerns in the American
and Russian zones, where 'a sort of mutual protective association' formed among
officials and managers.[33] In Greifswald, a brewery refused to release a chemist
who was proscribed by the local denazification commission, and who had already
been demoted from being the manager of a nearby dairy. Both management and
trade union officials rallied around their colleague, claiming that he had distinguished himself through overtime work and that he was socially integrated into
the firm – 'As far as the staff is concerned, his coworkers stand beside him in full
harmony… We have not found [him responsible] for any transgressions at all.'[34]
In Munich, the executive of a local brick works openly challenged Law Number
8, stating 'that he simply was not going to put party members out and point[ing]
out that nothing much could be done to him'. *Herr* Sörensen, manager of the
Machinenfabrik Augsburg *und* Nürnberg, told the Americans that he had resisted
previous Nazi pressure to sack Jews and non-Nazis, and he was not about to start
engaging in political firings, although AMG was asking for the release of 172
employees.[35] Worst of all, the headquarters of the Bavarian *Landpolizei* reportedly
told its subsidiary offices to hide documents related to Nazis in their ranks, and
in Weilheim the CIC discovered that *Landpolizei* officials were actively supporting the infiltration of Nazis back into the police force. In *Kreis* Wilhelm, nine of
twelve *Dienststellenleiter* posts were occupied by *Parteigenossen*.[36]

In many areas of Germany, local cliques worked to sabotage the denazification
programme, both from administrative considerations and because of the social
solidarity of regional elites. In Landsberg, for instance, local officials savaged the
district denazification prosecutor in reports to Munich, after which the latter
accused his own boss of abetting such elements and meddling in *Spruchkammer*
decisions. The prosecutor also described his superior – not unfairly – as 'extraordinarily corrupt and reactionary'. Not surprisingly, the prosecutor was then
sacked by the *Land* Denazification Ministry, and the deputy public prosecutor,
in sympathy with his colleague, also resigned. After this debacle, the Landsberg
Spruchkammer chair provided the ministry with a blistering assessment of local
officialdom. He said that relations with the CSU *Landrat* and mayor were not bad,
but that both were 'real dead weights' – 'The *Landrat* impresses me as a rubber
sponge. One can press without pause, and it then resumes its original shape.' The
Kreis chief of the SPD was not much better. Although he described himself as a
'bloodhound … on the attack against reactionaries', he had exploited the denazification process to use condemned Nazis to build his house.[37]

In Wolfratshausen, a rural Bavarian county where 8,000 of the 40,000 inhabitants had once been members of the NSDAP, a scandal erupted around the CSU

Landrat, Hans Thiemo. An AMG report described Thiemo as 'a man with Nazi connections, if not actually a Party member himself', and he was closely associated with thirty *Parteigenossen*, the '*Dreissiger-Auschuss*', who ran Wolfratshausen as a Nazi feifdom. He also owed his position as *Landrat* to a somewhat broader clique, the *Löwenbrauregierung*, who managed Wolfratshausen's affairs from their chairs in a local pub. Thiemo and his associates hindered denazification operations by stamping '*Nichts Nachteiliges bekannt*' ('nothing prejudicial known') on every *Fragebogen* that came to their attention, even those of the worst Nazi zealots, and they also appointed former army officers to senior civil service positions. In the village of Dingharting, Thiemo overturned the election of *Bürgermeister* Peter Seidel in order to install his friend, *Herr* Schlosser, even though Schlosser had previously served in the local Nazi *Kreisleitung* and his wife had headed the county chapter of the NSDAP farmers' organisation. Thiemo truly sealed his fate, however, by railing against the Americans, who were allegedly to blame for all problems in government and had the support only of 'a few parasites'. He also came to the attention of the occupying power by circulating an anti-Allied tract by the famous German writer Ernst Weichert, who lived in Wolfratshausen. In early 1946, Thiemo was sacked at the demand of AMG.[38]

One of the most organised cliques was the 'U-7' conspiracy in Regen, a small Bavarian market town where, as in Wolfratshausen, the U.S. occupiers were held in low esteem.[39] The 'U-7' was a highly coordinated group of individuals who met bi-weekly and included many figures of local renown, including the *Landrat*, Werner Haas; the mayor of Bodenmais, Johann Gurster; Regen town councilman and *Kreistag* member Baptist Zellner, who offered his restaurant and butcher shop as the group's meeting place; Josef König, owner of the largest contracting firm in *Kreis* Regen and source of the group's financial muscle; and Nicholas Hackl, a Catholic priest who used his prestige to encourage pro-Nazi sentiment and devised many methods used to foil denazification. Hackl was appointed as an assessor with the local *Spruchkammer*, where he worked assiduously to slot all incriminated Nazis into the 'Follower' category or to exonerate them completely. After Hackl was thrown off the *Spruchkammer* panel, he pursued his campaign into the local ranks of the CSU, using party meetings as a forum to pour vitriol upon the entire denazification process. All of the chief members of 'U-7' were notable for their willingness to issue *Persilscheine*, even in favour of the most notorious *Parteigenossen*, and Zellner threatened witnesses scheduled to appear in *Spruchkammer* hearings or he bribed them with meat from his shop. Such tactics were designed as subsidiary parts of a complicated strategy to convince the population that all administrative failures had occurred as a direct consequence of the purge. The ultimate hope was to provoke a popular outcry for 'renazification'. In addition, Haas and Zellner hid Nazi Party records from the authorities, and Zellner was also involved with 'Cell 9', a small group of Werewolves connected to Baumgartner, the ex-propaganda leader of the local NSDAP chapter, and *Ortsgruppenleiter* Eberhardt, who made periodic visits to Regen while on leave from the Moosburg Internment Camp. 'Cell 9' drew up blacklists of denazification officials and organised the withholding of grain and vegetables from *Land* officials, although this effort was defeated when AMG ordered trucks into the region in order to forcibly collect the harvest.

By the spring of 1947, 'U-7' leaders had become wary of CIC surveillance and they curtailed their most open activities, as well as increasing the security of their meetings. It was of no avail. On 7 July 1947, Zellner was arrested on Black Market charges, and a week later the CIC, fearing that Zellner's arrest might panic the remainder of the group into destroying evidence, conducted a raid against Regen, arresting nineteen people. Unfortunately, the CSU immediately rallied behind the prisoners – Haas, in particular, had been caught participating in a secret CSU intelligence network with anti-Allied inclinations – and CSU officials visited the detainees and promised legal assistance. Once the 'U-7' conspirators were released on bail, they quickly tracked down the individuals who had denounced them and began intimidating prosecution witnesses. The ultimate result was that almost all the charges were eventually dropped. Haas was brought before a military court because of his possession of a loaded pistol, but even his conviction was overturned by AMG. 'This decision,' noted a U.S. Constabulary report, 'has provoked a great deal of critical comment on the part of people in the vicinity', particularly since local anti-fascists had already risked their lives by calling attention to 'U-7' in the first place.[40]

Although there were multiple factors behind the increasingly hostile German tone toward denazification, four elements particularly stand out in causing the shift in public opinion. First, Germans gradually began to understand the consequences, in human terms, of by-the-book denazification, which resulted in millions of redundancies among 'nominal' NSDAP members and also caused the internment of hundreds of thousands of mid- and senior-echelon figures in the party. Most Germans already resented Allied accusations of 'collective guilt', and key aspects of that discourse seemed to lay behind the entire structure of the denazification programme. There was also a sense of popular wonder about the wisdom of shifting white-collar workers into skilled (or even unskilled) jobs that they were sometimes unable to master. As an official in the Palatinate noted, 'One could indeed make a shoemaker into a State Secretary without much further ado, but not the reverse!' A joke that made the rounds in Berlin presented the image of a street sweeper making a mess of his task as he advanced down the Kurfürstendamm. An onlooker comments on his performance, only to be told that the street sweeper yesterday was a bank clerk, but that he was a Nazi and this was his punishment. 'Well ha-bloody-ha,' exclaims his interlocutor, 'I lost my job too because I was in the party.' 'And what did you do?' asks the ex-teller, only to be told – 'I was the local road sweeper!'[41] As early as September 1945, Robert Murphy observed that, 'Germans usually feel that many persons who were only nominal Nazis are falling under the axe unjustly and that some active Nazis are being missed.'[42] Two months later, Eisenhower reported that 'there had been a marked reversal of public opinion regarding the denazification policy since its application, through Public Law No.8, to the 'little Nazis' in business and Government. In general, the Germans have checked earlier demands for more thorough denazification and are now actively criticising the policy for its severity.'[43] Hans Habe, writing in *Die Neue Zeitung* during the same period, noted that there was an emergent form of solidarity 'between the former enemies of National Socialism and the ex-supporters of Hitlerdom', a sentiment he attributed to a reawakening sense of German nationalism, itself informed by disappointment with Allied occupation, as well as a supposed German code of knightly values, which included extending a hand to defeated foes. And so we find cases like *Herr Rehbein*, who became police chief of Hanau in September 1945 and immediately began issuing a steady flow of *Persilscheine* to unquestioned Nazis. The local military government officer was aware of this practice, but summed up the situation as follows:

> Mr. Rehbein is an honest, kindly well meaning old man, unwilling to think evil, or to refuse a favour, to any of his old acquaintances. It might also be well to mention that as chief of police he is an administrative 'wash-out', retained in office solely on the basis of his political acceptability, the story of oppression which he has suffered leaving no doubt on this score.[44]

A second factor bearing upon public opinion involved the response of Nazi elements to denazification measures, including some largely effective modes of resistance. Nazis were often mystified about why an allegedly unjust form of legal pestilence had suddenly descended upon them. After all, they claimed, they had merely been good patriots doing their duty to their country, and they asked – pointedly – whether 'the party ever [would] have come to power on legal grounds if not ninety per cent of its members had ranked among the best Germans'. They generally stuck with stock Nazi explanations for the origin of the war: the Poles had been abusing ethnic Germans in Poland, said one young ex-*Führerin* of the BdM, hence 'we had to invade Poland'.[45] Robert Murphy noted in September 1945 that Nazis were already exploiting their 'network of connections', hoping that such links would tied them over until the Allies became concerned with other objectives, and a particularly sense of fraternity – the '*Kameradschaft*' – developed in internment facilities and PoW camps for SS men, some of which were still dominated by strident Nazis. In particular, the internment enclosures at Darmstadt and Platting were reported to be centres for the active dissemination of Nazi propaganda.[46] Outside camp wire, the Allies also noted the existence of numerous clusters of dispossessed Nazis. In the U.S. zone, one such group petitioned AMG to remove a communist *Bürgermeister*, and

the American authorities noted that such elements 'seem to be receiving support from antifascist organisations'.[47] In the British zone, a similar group had its
base in Eutin and drew members from Oldenburg and Schleswig-Holstein, the
latter of which generally served as a post-war gathering ground for ex-Nazis.[48]
There is no doubt that there were tensions among these marginalised National
Socialists – local Nazis (*Einheimischer*) were annoyed with their colleagues who
had become refugees, '*Alte Kämpfer*' tended to resent their post-1937 confreres,
and *Parteigenossen* took umbrage with Nazi military officers who were usually
unburdened with the formality of party membership – and a majority of Nazis
even believed that some form of denazification was desirable! However, such
elements were largely united in criticising the form and character of the existing programme. Kurt Tauber called this collectivity 'the fraternal lodge of the
disinherited, the denazified'; in the Nazi jargon of the era, it was the '*Schicksalsgem
einschaft*', or 'community of fate'.[49]

The essence of the Nazi response is encapsulated in an underground
leaflet circulated in *Kreis* Muhldorf in early 1947: 'The denazification law,' it asserts,
'violated an elementary legal principle … [because] any act committed cannot be
punished unless the law setting forth such punishment was in existence at the time of
commission.'[50] Aside from lecturing the Allies on the rule of law (which their own
regime had regularly transgressed), Nazis admitted that Hitler's treatment of Jews
had been evil, but contended that the new purge was 'a thousand times worse',
presumably because it targeted 'thousands of the best Germans'.[51] A number of
other arguments were also floated. The 'Union of Former *Ortsgruppenleiter*', which
had 2,400 members and was headquartered in the Moosburg Internment Camp,
claimed that the Allied measures against NSDAP district officials were wrongheaded because they were supposedly based on a handbook devised by Robert Ley,
the onetime organisational boss of the NSDAP. This book, claimed the union, was
unknown to most *Ortsgruppenleiter* and specified a degree of training and tasks that
most officials of this rank never undertook. Rather, *Ortsgruppenleiter* were allegedly
simple functionaries who had no control over state administration or auxiliary bodies of the party, and most were naive lovers of order who had been drawn to the
flame of Nazism before they realised what it would eventually consume.[52] Rather
than arguing with the nature of the process, some *Parteigenossen* contended that they
had been awarded unfair treatment within its parameters. Thus, former *Luftwaffe*
officer Arthur Dettweiler blamed all his his troubles on alleged 'scapegoating' by a
single Special Branch officer who had slotted him, plus his wife and daughter, in
the 'Offender' category. While Dettweiler was willing to admit that all three had
once been officials in the NSDAP or its auxiliaries, he managed to convince a
Spruchkammer to re-examine the three cases 'blind' (that is, with the names con-
cealed), a process that resulted in all the members of the family being assigned
to the 'Follower' category.[53] Multiplied into the thousands, such attempts to win
sympathy had a considerable impact on German public opinion.[54]

When appeals for sympathy failed to move fellow Germans, Nazis were willing to employ threats and intimidation, a propensity that was certainly suggested by the dark history of the party. In Schwetzingen, the chair of the denazification board was warned by letter that he '[had] committed a serious crime by cooperating with the denazification tribunal. Should an opportunity arise, you will have to bear the consequences of your actions. Think of your family.' Several similar notes were sent to *Spruchkammer* members and prosecutors in *Kreis* Lauterbach, 'When the hour comes, the whole of Germany will be in a trance of bloodshed… Gallows will be erected in the market place of Lauterbach, and all of you will hang there with heads down.' As a direct result, Special Branch reported that denazification personnel in Lauterbach were 'intimidated. Afraid to perform their duties. This LK is full of threatening rumors.' In Mainburg, the deputy chairman of the local tribunal resigned 'because he was afraid of [the] consequences'. Because of this unexpected departure, the *Spruchkammer* was delayed in starting operations. In Pfarrkirchen, even the commanding officer of the local AMG detachment was threatened, receiving through the mail a bullet with an attached note, 'There are more where this came from.' The American officer suspected confederates of Georg Schmidthuber, who had recently received a three year prison sentence from a *Spruchkammer*, largely on the basis of evidence provided by military government.[55]

The rising tide of opposition to denazification also seemed to legitimate direct action (at least in the opinion of threatened Nazis). By the end of 1946, *Spruchkammer* windows and lighting fixtures were being smashed and the vehicles of tribunal chairs and assessors were vandalized and their homes attacked. In Fiengen, the walls of the *Spruchkammer* building were defaced and members of the tribunal received letters adorned with swastikas and a crude sketch of a gallows. In Frankfurt and Bad Homburg, AMG ordered German police to provide guards for *Spruchkammer* members.[56] In Wertingen, the *Spruchkammer* building was burgled and the car of the denazification prosecutor was blown up, incidents that AMG investigators traced to several ex-members of the Hitler Youth, all from ardently Nazi families. In Gerolzhofen, the denazification prosecutor, one of the best in the U.S. zone, received abysmal treatment from his countrymen. According to Special Branch investigators, '[he] was threatened in one village and stoned while in another. The new directives of the Ministry for Liberation to discontinue classification of Nazi "activists" as "followers" were answered with hostility by the populace, which nicknamed the tribunal "the hangmen".'[57]

Small bands of Nazis also bombed denazification facilities in Stuttgart, Esslingen, Backnang and Nuremberg. The blasts in Württemberg were the handiwork of a ten-man group that was rounded up in November 1946, while they were actually in the process of fusing more bombs. There were two explosions in Nuremberg, the second of which was rated by CIC as an 'incident of exceptional importance' because it damaged the offices of Camille Sachs, chair of the *Spruchkammer* hearing the case of Hitler's onetime vice-chancellor, Franz von Papen. Typewritten leaflets warning Germans against the SPD and KPD – and signed 'HIUF' (Hitler *ist unser Führer*) – were also scattered around the scene of the second Nuremberg blast. AMG immediately ordered an around-the-clock guard for Nuremberg denazification facilities.[58] If the bombing was intended to deter Sachs, it failed: two days after the blast he revoked the defendant's bail, and on 24 February 1947 he sentenced von Papen to six and a half years in a labour camp, plus a fine of 416,000 Marks.[59]

Six weeks after the attempt to kill Sachs, Nazi arsonists in Schleuchtern wrecked a local *Spruchkammer* building, an outrage that prompted the American authorities to cancel leaves and other privileges for Nazis housed in nearby detainment camps. The Schleuchtern blaze destroyed files connected to the denazification of U.S. zone universities and high schools,[60] and suspicious fires also destroyed denazi-fication records in Munich, Nuremberg and Berlin, the last of these incidents occurring in 1953![61]

Perhaps most seriously, Reinhold Hub, a prominent communist and a prosecu-tor in the Freiburg am Breisgau denazification tribunal, was shot to death on 22 March 1947. Although suspicion momentarily hovered around the son of a for-mer Nazi *Kreisleiter*, who had already threatened to kill Hub, the German police eventually arrested two Polish refugees, who claimed that they had committed the crime while attempting to rob Hub's residence in Öhringen. The two Poles were quickly brought to trial and executed. *Frau* Hub, who had heard the assail-ants speaking in faultless Swabian dialect, continued to believe that the attack was politically motivated, noting that her husband had been a zealous prosecutor and had frequently received death threats. Whatever the truth, there is no doubt that the crime had a chilling effect, and that Allied authorities were 'deeply con-cerned', fearing that it would become impossible to recruit jurists or prosecutors for denazification boards.[62]

There were similar occurrences in Soviet-occupied Germany, another zone with a relatively tough denazification regime. In particular, the promulgation of Order 201 was accompanied by a spate of armed attacks against denazification officials, as well as threats against members of purge commissions. Conditions in Germany could yet change, such people were warned, '[and] then should the [new] masters have only themselves to worry about'. In October 1947, shots were fired at a denazification functionary in Rostock, although the police could not find the perpetrator of this incident. In Waren, a member of a denazification commission was stoned by a mob shouting 'Kill the denazification pig!' SED cadres responsible for coordinating denazification were also vulnerable to attack, as illustrated by a case involving an SED *Kreis* Secretary in Neubrandenburg. In this instance, the attacker was caught, but his membership in the CDU quickly turned the affair into a political issue.[63]

The broad impact of such resistance was to destroy an initial assumption – shared by many Germans – that Allied occupation would necessarily break the Nazis as a political force, or that the individual power and authority of *Parteigenossen* would be weakened. The fact that one's immediate or long-range security could now be imperilled by support for denazification naturally had a dampening effect on anti-fascist activism. By the end of 1947, however, even substantial numbers of Nazis were coming to recognize the rehabilitation aspect of denazification,[64] and violent resistance correspondingly diminished.

A third factor that tended to shift public opinion involves the role of German priests, pastors and bishops, who had enjoyed substantial moral and spiritual influence before 1945, but were now in an especially strong position because of the bankruptcy of National Socialism. It was turning away from religiosity, they warned, that had already brought an unprecedented disaster upon the nation. Moreover, in the absence of German civil government, at least at the national level, the churches were one of the few institutions capable of mediating between the victors and the German population. There was some debate among churchmen, however, about whether their new popularity owed to a genuine religious awakening amongst their countrymen, or if masses of ex-Nazis and supporters of Hitler were simply trying to whitewash themselves by claiming a new spirituality.

Many clergymen had originally expressed lukewarm support for a purge, but this attitude shifted as they became aware of the schematic nature of denazification and as they learned that the programme covered even wayward clerics, an extension of Allied authority that they deeply resented.[65] Churchmen also became convinced that the Russians were plotting the communisation of eastern Germany, and many believed that the latter intended to use denazification as a mechanism to serve this purpose. Naturally, they resisted this development. Not even the 'Stuttgart Declaration' went unopposed, and as Clemens Vollnhals notes, there were many Lutheran prelates who rejected what they saw as a one-sided admission of guilt; rather, they preferred to refocus on the injustices and abuses of power that they perceived in the denazification programme. Bishop Schöffel of Hamburg called Niemöller a 'dictator' who had subjected his colleagues to a 'terror'. Amongst Catholic clergy, there was even broader opposition to the idea of 'collective guilt'. Ironically, and from an Allied point of view, annoyingly, even supporters of the 'Stuttgart Declaration' felt free to criticise Allied policy because they could claim that they had freely accepted a great burden of guilt upon their own country, and should thus be at liberty to point out other injustices wherever they saw them. In fact, they noted that not speaking out against iniquities was precisely their failing during the Third Reich, and that they had no intention of repeating this mistake.

Within six months of the German capitulation, Catholic vicars were already running illegal mail services for SS and civilian internees; three priests were arrested for such activity in July 1945. While this practice could always be rationalised as an act of charity rather than a condemnation of denazification, a

revealing AMG canvass of clerical opinion in Darmstadt found evidence of clear
doubts about the nature of the purge. This survey, conducted in September 1945,
suggested that of thirteen prelates – four Catholic, seven Evangelical and two
Confessional – only one was in favour of the form of denazification undertaken
by the Allies. The president of the Evangelical Church of *Land* Hesse, Dr Thomas
Müller, who was based in Darmstadt, argued that discharged Nazis were crucial
to the reconstruction of the nation and would 'inevitably' have to be reappointed
to their jobs, at which time he hoped that the occupiers would seek the counsel of clergy. Müller was a right-wing liberal and a great admirer of Paul von
Hindenburg, who, he averred, had 'saved the Reich from the Marxists'.

It was Theophil Wurm, the Evangelical bishop of Württemberg, who led the
charge. A belated critic of the Nazis, Wurm was a profoundly conservative man
who worried about the 'grave danger [of Bolshevism] that menaces the world'.
His son was an SS officer and was therefore interned by the Allies, which also
gave Wurm a personal stake in the way that denazification was organised and
implemented. The bishop was initially willing to countenance a measure of 'collective guilt', but as early as June 1945 he was complaining about denazification,
'I feel that many of these former "Nazis" are indispensable because they cannot
be replaced. You are denazifying too quickly and putting people into positions
who can't know their jobs.' He also argued that many young men who had been
dragooned into the SS were still interned and that there was no sign of their
release. In September 1945, he warned the Allies that the publicity given to Nazi
atrocities was doing nothing to warm relations between the occupiers and their
German charges. A month later, Wurm complained about the arbitrariness of Law
Number 8, arguing that it posed 'a question of life and death' to the German
people, and contending that German bureaucrats had a reputation for apolitical incorruptibility, whether or not they were formally *Parteigenossen*. Most of
these men, he added, had been *Mussnazis*, and their release from employment was
not only unfair, but a breach of traditional German laws that guaranteed their
seniority. What Wurm omitted to say was that customary rights of tenure in the
German civil service no longer existed: the Nazis themselves had abrogated such
privileges through the Civil Service Law of 7 April 1933, mainly so that Hitler
could purge socialists and Jews.

What Wurm demanded of the Allies was 'Germanification' of denazification.
After the introduction of the 'Law for Liberation from National Socialism', however, he denounced the legislation and announced that 'the Christian Church'
could not support any measure that sacrificed the basic civil rights of those who
stood to be accused, particularly because it imposed *ex post facto* standards of
legality. He denounced the labour prohibition for defendants awaiting a hearing,
a practice which, he claimed, unfairly prejudiced the '*Mitläufer*' who made up
the likely mass of the system's targets; he railed against the artificial distinction
between pre- and post-1937 Nazis; he complained about the inclusion of low-

ranking officeholders in the NSDAP's various affiliates, such as the NS-*Lehrerbund*, the Nazi lawyers' association and the National Socialist Welfare Organisation; and he claimed that *Wehrmacht* officers should not be held to account for simply following the orders of political authorities, and that they should certainly not be included in the most serious categories of guilt. Many of these criticisms were valid, although it galled the Allies to have any German attempt to seize the moral high ground, and AMG became convinced that the elements in charge of the Evangelical Church were 'nationalistic and Junker-monarchial rather than international and liberal-democratic in ... political outlook.'

Other Lutheran and Catholic ecclesiarchs soon joined the chorus. In December 1945, Bishop Meiser of Bavaria, one of Niemöller's chief opponents, joined with Cardinal Faulhaber in calling for the U.S. authorities to act as quickly as possible in cases of political detainment, to loosen the rules for provision of pension payments to the ill and elderly, and to improve privileges for internees. Faulhaber made a pastoral visit to the Dachau Concentration camp, now used for the internment of SS men, and was deeply moved by the apparent faith of the inmates. In the spring of 1946, two Catholic bishops in the British zone issued a blistering declaration, calling upon the occupiers to respect the rule of law and condemning mass release of Nazi officeholders as 'a violation of God's law'. So severe was the tone of this epistle that AMG banned its circulation in the U.S. zone, although the British authorities – ever hesitant 'to interfere with the liberty of the church' – allowed its publication.[66]

The churches, alas, did not limit their efforts to polemics designed to shift the thinking of their flock. The Catholic Church also prohibited priests from serving on *Spruchkammern* or *Untersuchungsausschüsse*. In Obernburg, a local parish priest defied this ban and agreed to serve as *Spruchkammer* chair, although Special Branch was hardly impressed with his performance, noting '[that] many persons coming before tribunals hold letters of recommendation from Church sources, and the result is exoneration'. A few curates even worked actively to hinder denazification. In Marktheidenfeld, a town near Aschaffenburg, an AMG investigation revealed that local priests had proclaimed it a sin to provide damaging testimony in *Spruchkammer* hearings, while they themselves were happily providing *Persilscheine*, even to the worst Nazi scoundrels. Special Branch reported from Steinach that 'the mere word of the local priest is sufficient to exonerate most defendants before the Spruchkammer, or at least place them in the group of Followers'''. Perhaps this was a strategy intended to make amends: the previous parish priest in Steinach had been an '*Alte Kämpfer*' and had recruited an extraordinarily large proportion of the county's population into the NSDAP, which was now yielding denazification consequences. Eventually, the Protestant churches advised that their followers avoid serving upon denazification boards or appearing as witnesses in hearings, and in February 1948, even Niemöller reluctantly called upon Germans to refuse further cooperation with the process.[67] In a few cases, such as the town of Traunstein, Allied authorities believed that local Lutheran church structures had come under the influence of *Parteigenossen*, and many Protestant congregations resolutely refused to rid themselves of pastors with a history of NSDAP membership.[68]

A final factor that helped to sway public opinion involved the stance of the KPD, which shifted radically from 1945 to 1948. Although all the German political parties gradually lost patience with the denazification process, the changing position of the communists eventually denied the denazification system of its most eager proponents, at least in the Western zones of occupation. Despite pro-Allied directives from the KPD in Berlin, most communists had originally believed that the presence of foreign occupiers was regrettable. In its absence, they would supposedly have risen up and cleansed the German administration without benefit of legal or procedural niceties, although Lutz Niethammer rightly notes that this militant position undercut the KPD's much-stated desire for an anti-fascist coalition with more moderate parties. However, as long as the Allies proposed to do something about the problem of Nazi domination, most communists resolved to cooperate with the occupiers and to do so as enthusiastically as possible. During the summer of 1945, communist cadres eagerly purged Nazis at the municipal and *Kreis* level, often cooperating with the Allies in the arrest or dismissal of *Parteigenossen*. In September, Dorn lauded the KPD as 'the most reliable anti-Nazis', and a month later Clay noted that unlike most of the newly-minted German political parties, the communists were not critical of indiscriminate removals of Nazis, but only of the tentativeness and slowness of the process. When the denazification programme was devolved to the control of the German *Länder*, communists were disproportionately represented on the new denazification boards.[69]

In some parts of Germany, however, the communists' predominant position in the denazification machinery was relatively short-lived. In Bavaria, newly-appointed Denazification Minister Anton Pfeiffer swept communists out of his ministry and out of the *Spruchkammern*, claiming that many of them were barely literate or had criminal backgrounds. It is true that the denazification process was already bedeviled by corruption and by poorly-reasoned *Spruchkammer* decisions, but such problems continued even after Pfeiffer's house-cleaning. Meanwhile, scores of redundant ex-*Spruchkammer* chairs, prosecutors and investigators formed an unhappy – and increasingly surly – assembly under the leadership of two senior deposed communists, Max Holy and Heinrich Schmitt. Pfeiffer, they yelled, was 'watering down' denazification.

A similar process unfolded in the neighbouring *Land* of Hesse, where the senior communist in the Denazification Ministry, Dr Heckert, was characterised by AMG as 'an aggressive radical whose political enthusiasms often affect his judgement'. Under American pressure, the Hessian minister-president, Dr Geiler, transferred Heckert to a less sensitive post in the Interior Ministry, thus weakening the role of the KPD in the local denazification machinery. Concurrently, there was aggressive jockeying for position at lower levels. In Fritzlar-Homberg, an ex-German Army officer chairing the local *Spruchkammer* rejected assessor applications from five KPD members, claiming that they all possessed criminal records. Soon after, the chair received an anonymous letter promising that he would be 'hanged or buried' within three months, a warning that the authorities suspected of originating with communists rather than Nazis. By October 1946, KPD militants in Hesse were either spreading leaflets or organising '*Flusterpropaganda*' (underground rumours) attacking the composition and policies of the *Spruchkammer*. By the following year, they were openly accusing the Denazification Ministry of obfuscation and the coddling of senior Nazis, and the *Land* branch of the KPD opposed an April 1947 bill to force Hessians to serve on denazification panels. Around the same time they officially denounced the entire programme and withdrew their representatives from the tribunals.

In north-western Germany, the KPD organised a number of mass rallies in which the demonstrators called for accelerated denazification, amongst a range of other demands, and in the Zonal Advisory Council communist representatives tried (without effect) to overthrow *Herr* Schlange-Schöningen, the head of the British zone food distribution authority. The communists pointed out – not entirely without merit – that Schlange-Schöningen was a large estate owner and a former member of the German Nationalist Party, which had been allied to the NSDAP. Worse yet, they alleged that Schlange-Schöningen's zonal food office was only a modestly-reformed version of the Nazi-era 'Reich Food Estate', and that it employed inspectors who were frequently ex-*Wehrmacht* or SS officers.[70]

While the KPD loudly beat the drum about inadequate denazification, the party also began to evince an exaggerated concern for the fate of 'nominal' members. Although this policy appeared paradoxical, at least at a superficial level, it actually touched to the heart of the denazification problem, and the communists could provide a solid theoretical rationale by claiming that the mass incrimination of 'nominals' was driving 'small' and 'big' Nazis into a single camp and thus creating a more effective resistance movement. In truth, however, the KPD was moved to action by an increasing realisation that it had failed to re-energize much of the mass base that the party had enjoyed before 1933. As a result, KPD strategists increasingly began looking upon the mass of NSDAP 'Followers' as a discontented element that they might be able to draw to their own denuded ranks. As early as the fall of 1945, the American authorities cited reports from Munich suggesting that the Bavarian Communist People's Party was trying to recruit Nazis, and an AMG intelligence assessment suggested that the party was secretly delighted with the nature of the denazification programme: 'every day the purge continues, the ranks of the communists swell with new converts, and the American policy itself takes the place of any need for communist propaganda'.[71] Forced to rally a base for the various *Kreis* and *Land* elections held in 1946 and 1947, the KPD made sympathy for the '*Mitläufer*' a major part of its political discourse, and it seized upon every sign of inequity in treatment, claiming for instance, that working class people formerly in the NSDAP or the German Labour Front were being prohibited from holding political offices and trade union positions, whereas middle class *Parteigenossen* suffered no such restrictions. '*Die Grossen hängen, die Kleinen laufen lassen*' – 'Hang the "big shots", let the "small fry" walk' – became the new slogan of the party. With the KPD's impact on the denazification process already starting to shrink, some communist press organs began calling for a total cessation of the programme – 'an end to the Fragebogen war', as one newspaper described it – and on 10 August 1948, the KPD formally withdrew its remaining representatives from the denazification bodies still functioning in the three Western zones.[72] Thus came to an end the involvement of a party that, in a single swipe, had helped discredit denazification in the eyes of German centrists and right-wingers, but had also once provided the process with its most ardent advocates.[73]

By 1947, denazification was widely regarded by Germans as a fiasco. In some locations, the inmates had literally overrun the asylum. In a number of instances, *Parteigenossen* were appointed as denazification tribunal assessors or prosecutors. If uncovered, they were typically arrested and charged with *Fragebogen* falsification, although some cases were difficult to prove. In Uffenheim, Allied officials received four letters denouncing the local public prosecutor, *Herr* Schmidt, as an NSDAP member, although there was no documentary evidence substantiating this charge. At the very least, Schmidt was in a discretionary removal category, since he had been a captain in the *Wehrmacht* and an officer in a Nazi auxiliary.[74] Nazis also infiltrated other elements of the denazification machinery. In Arnsberg, Dietrich Hartmann, the local government official responsible for denazifying heavy industry, was exposed as an SS man who had acquired the identity papers of an ex-concentration camp inmate and had successfully presented himself to the authorities under this cover.[75] In *Land* Württemberg-Baden, Hermann Wedderkopf, chief of the Denazification Ministry's office for internees and labour camps, was charged with committing war crimes in France, where he had run a transit camp for political prisoners.[76] With each such disclosure came a corresponding slip in the popular level of confidence in the system.

Within *Land* denazification ministries and boards, morale was at an all-time low, and as the willingness of personnel declined, so did job performance. In South Württemberg, the representative of the *Staatskommissar* reported that members of the *Untersuchungsausschüsse* at Ravensburg and Hechingen 'more than ever lack the heart to do their jobs'.[77] In Bremen, purge officials sold evidence to defence lawyers, and a number of denazification prosecutors garnered reputations for defending the accused rather than presenting the state's case (although part of this problem derived from different views of the prosecutional function: in Anglo-American legal practice, it was to present an argument, while in continental law it was to seek the truth and obtain justice).[78] As the standing of denazification institutions sank even further, it became impossible to recruit people willing to keep their personal or political feelings out of the process. Some denazification officials allegedly sought such positions in order to attack their personal enemies, but they had little concern – and made little effort – beyond this level. In the *Spruchkammer* at the Darmstadt Internment Camp, the public prosecutor was accused of trading placement in lower categories of guilt in return for a promise by defendants to work in the Soviet zone, particularly if their original homes were in that region. In several instances, left-wing tribunal prosecutors charged industrialists or financiers as war profiteers, allegedly on anti-capitalist rather than anti-nazi grounds, but such manoeuvres were usually checked by the *Land* denazification ministries, and in Hesse, a *Berufskammer* ruled in August 1947 that employers who had reaped a 'normal' level of profit during the war could not be held liable.[79] Stories of businessmen or farmers bribing *Spruchkammer* members with butter or other commodities were legion. In Neumarkt, for instance, the local *Spruchkammer* chairman, *Herr* Beck, was accused of 'receiv[ing] gifts from wives of political internees in return for which he has used his influence to cause the release of these internees'.[80] An AMG detachment in Eichstätt noted that as time passed, the more capable *Spruchkammer* personnel left for jobs in the private sector or public administration, while the weaker elements, anticipating unemployment in the post-denazification era, worked to drag out the process.[81] In a belated recognition of this problem, the *Länderrat* passed a resolution in January 1948 promising denazification officials a job for three years and a salary at least sixty per cent of their highest wage for a period of eighteen months.[82] As for conditions in the Soviet zone, Timothy Vogt depicts denazification commissioners as being hopelessly divided between the desire to purge and the necessity to rehabilitate, performing a thankless task that put them at odds with the bulk of society.[83]

In Bavaria, the decomposition of the system reached almost spectacular levels, part of which was due to the comportment of Alfred Loritz, a populist demagogue with a knack for inspiring his particular brand of anti-Nazism with a distinctly fascist spirit. During the second half of 1946, Loritz built his splinter party, the Economic Reconstruction Union (WAV), into a major political force, especially by appealing to the anti-establishment resentments of refugees and other destabilised portions of the middle class. He particularly played upon the perception of such elements that the Catholic conservative elite was escaping responsibility for its long toleration of Nazism, while people in the lowest echelon of the NSDAP were paying an unfairly heavy price for their involvement. Like the communists, Loritz saw the Nazis as a front for the 'establishment', and he too adopted the motto, '*Die Grossen hängen, die Kleinen laufen lassen*'. After the CSU victory in the *Land* elections, the very Catholic hierarchs whom Loritz despised offered him control of the Denazification Ministry, mainly with the assumption that his penchant for shady deals and his potential for clashes with AMG would soon skewer him politically.

The conservative grandees were not disappointed. Loritz started his tenure by purging the administrative apparatus of his ministry, releasing scores of competent officials whose abilities were already at a premium. As a result, many *Spruchkammern* lost regular contact with the ministry and operations began grinding to a halt, forcing AMG to step in and assume support functions in order to prevent a total collapse. The ministry also failed to organise a sufficient *Berufskammern* to handle a flood of 400,000 denazification appeals, more than ten times the sum that was anticipated. As military government liaisons looked on in dismay, the tenor of the ministry's relations with AMG plummeted. The Special Branch had at least expected Loritz to be a strict denazifier, but with the exception of a few high-profile cases, such as the von Papen hearing, such hopes were washed away by Loritz's administrative incompetence. As central control over the *Spruchkammern* and *Berufskammern* diminished, their judgements got milder rather than more severe. Loritz's former supporters grew so disenchanted that the minister's retinue was nearly overrun by a crowd of unruly Munich anti-fascists during an appearance by the minister in early April 1947. Loritz barely reached the podium, where he then sat – ashen-faced and with his eyes shut – only to be shouted down when he rose to speak.

The final straw, however, was provided by Loritz's interest in internment camps, which had been transferred to *Land* control in 1946 and where chaos – escapes, unauthorised furloughs and bribery of guards – reigned unchecked. After the Nuremberg *Spruchkammern* bombings, which were widely blamed on conspirators in the internment centres, Loritz created a security force called the *Kontrolldienst* (KD), which was recruited largely among refugees in the WAV and the KPD and oversaw a crackdown in the camps. In typical Loritz fashion, the KD bore a disturbing resemblance to the SS *Sicherheitsdienst*, particularly in its freedom from normal bureaucratic and legal constraints, as well as in its members tendency to menace refractory prisoners (and guards) with the restoration of discipline through 'other measures'. Since AMG had already prohibited the formation of German secret police agencies, in May 1947 the American authorities ordered the Bavarian Government to dissolve the KD, particularly since a rash of negative stories was concurrently appearing in the press. The Bavarian premier, Hans Ehard, also launched an investigation into Loritz's role in creating the KD, but before any new information came to light, Loritz was overthrown in an intra-party putsch within the WAV. Within days, he was also fired as denazification minister and in July 1947 he was arrested on charges of black marketeering.[84] Not surprisingly, the reputation of the denazification programme sank to unprecedented levels of unpopularity.

Meanwhile, all the major political parties supported changes to denazification, at least in the western zones, and they slowly began to restrict their participation.[85] The various zonal chapters of the CDU, CSU and BCSV had long been caught in a difficult bind: they drew support from the same strata of society as the NSDAP, which tended to imply a lenient approach toward denazification; on the other hand, they also wanted to maintain passably good relations with the other political parties and with the occupiers. Some of the centrists behind the Christian parties accepted a limited form of schematic denazification – Adam Stegerwald, one of the founders of the CSU, is a good example – and in the French-occupied part of the Rhineland, the local CDU described denazification as 'the touchstone for the future of Germany', and vigorously backed denazification of the economy.[86] Generally, however, the stance of the Christian parties followed the same shift that occurred in overall public opinion. Certainly this change was tangible in the British zone. Adenauer and other CDU bosses had originally taken a starkly critical view of Nazism, but as time passed, they adopted a more pragmatic outlook. The CDU programme of March 1946 called for the punishment of outright criminal acts and 'responsibility for the war', but it also advised that the process be quick and that it advance through regular legal channels. Adenauer added that 'we finally should leave the followers in peace, those who did not oppress others, who did not enrich themselves, and who broke no laws'. Two months later, the party called for some middle ground between sheer economic ruin and a full reprieve for *Parteigenossen*, suggesting fines as a form of punishment that might limit the potential for social chaos.[87] In Bavaria, the CSU claimed a Christian repugnance of Nazism, but its leaders maintained that the 'Law for Liberation from National Socialism' was a recipe for the corruption of public life through denunciations and abuse of *Spruchkammer* processes for political purposes. In Hesse, Maria Sevenich shocked the American authorities with her shrill accusation – presented in front of CDU crowds – that the denazification process was the intellectual product of hate-filled German émigrés who had abandoned their country in its hour of need and had lost track of local conditions. In its present form, she declared, '[denazification] is intolerable [and] it lays the groundwork for the Bolshevisation of Germany'.[88] Like-minded spirits in the local *Ortsgruppen* of the Christian parties attempted to hinder denazification and several municipal chapters of the CDU and CSU were thus 'suspended' by the occupying powers, most notably in Würzburg and Schwarzenburg.[89] By 1947, the inclusion of Christian Democrats in denazification boards and *Land* ministries was diminishing, and in 1948 the parties officially withdrew their officials from all involvement in the programme.[90]

The SPD was not far behind. The boss of the Social Democrats in the western zones, Kurt Schumacher, planned to break the power of the economic forces behind Hitler, particularly through the wide scale nationalisation of industry, rather than fighting prolonged skirmishes with Nazis, whom he regarded as 'lumpen proletariat upstarts' working in service of monopoly capital. In any case, it might be difficult to distinguish Nazis, whom Schumacher defined not only as members of the NSDAP, but as anyone who had supported the Third Reich. Although Schumacher supported a purge of Nazi personnel, it was a subordinate strategy and he hoped to win over and re-educate substantial numbers of Nazis, a purpose for which he was willing to pursue a more nationalistic – and thus politically attractive – line vis-à-vis the occupying powers. Schumacher, most assuredly, did not believe in the doctrine of 'collective guilt'. Although the SPD supported the creation of denazification panels and *Land* ministries – in Bavaria, social democrats were still surging into such bodies as late as 1947 – there was a distinct lack of interest at the top of the party.[91] Walter Dorn noted in 1946 that Schumacher rarely spoke of denazification, and he provided only a lukewarm endorsement of Zonal Executive Directive 54. In a number of cases SPD members were caught giving help to ex-Nazis. In Wesermünde, a local SPD administrative official was arrested for providing such assistance, and in Reichenburg, the local SPD chief helped certify the existence of a local 'Antifa' – comprised entirely of high-profile Nazis – which had surrendered the town to American troops (although it continued to secretly stock weapons even afterwards). Membership in this august body was presented as a mitigating factor in denazification proceedings.[92] In a number of locations, local chapters of the SPD feared that enthusiastic support for denazification might scare away 'nominal' Nazis who could otherwise be enrolled under the party's banner. In the Rhineland, the SPD voted to withdraw its representatives from the denazification apparatus and a motion to censor the process as a deliberate sabotage of democracy only narrowly failed to win the support of a regional party convention. One of Schumacher's lieutenants, a longtime party functionary named Hasselbring, lost his 1948 bid for reelection to the party's central committee, partly because he had a reputation as an enthusiastic denazifier. Similarly, Willi Wendt, a career SPD official, was brought before a party court in 1948 because he had 'cooperated with communists over denazification'. Although exonerated, Wendt's standing in the party was ruined.[93]

As the interest and involvement of the major parties evaporated, hundreds of thousands of Nazis came flooding back into local government and the administrative apparatus of the *Länder*. Many of these reinstated *Parteigenossen* had passed through the '*Mitläuferfabriken*' and were ostensibly rehabilitated; others had been amnestied or had avoided the entire process through various means. Some Nazis with private resources, or with a willingness to accept public relief, had spent two or three years without working, but were still able to reclaim their old jobs and work their way back to a degree of social status. Those who could wait until they could pass through the denazification process in its final, farcical phase, reaped definite benefits: Wilhelm Shepmann, the former chief of the SA, was completely exonerated of serious involvement in National Socialism, while Hans Friedrich Blunck, a Nazi writer who was onetime president of the Reich Chamber of Literature, was ranked as a *Mitläufer*. In Darmstadt, Dr Kohler, president of the Chamber of Commerce and a liberal democrat legislator, was slotted into the 'Follower' category, even though he had abused forced labourers at his factory and in 1942 had directed that 'a foreign labourer who is lazy will be given confinement at reduced rations in a dark cell...' At Kohler's appeal hearing in 1948, the prosecution refused to swear in its own witnesses and called doubt on their credibility, while at the same time accepting an oath from a witness who testified in Kohler's favour. In any case, the prosecutor concluded that 'the Russian workers were not treated any worse than German workers are treated in Russia now'.

By September 1948, thirty-three per cent of the officials in the *Land* Württemberg-Baden government had been chargeable under the 'Law for Liberation from National Socialism', and at senior echelons of the state bureaucracy, the figure was fifty-six per cent. From Hesse came an AMG report suggesting that eighty-five per cent of persons earlier removed by American intervention were back at their jobs, including some leading *Land* officials. The report concluded that 'it is difficult to understand how we intend a democratic government to be built up by people who do not believe in democracy'. A survey of the Bavarian Government in May 1949 showed that the number of ex-Nazi officials (*Beamter*) in the *Land* ministries ranged between thirty to sixty per cent of the total number of functionaries, with the exception of the Transport Ministry, where only eight per cent of its personnel were comprised of former *Parteigenossen*. In the Bavarian state chancellery, more than one fifth of the staff were ex-Nazis. General Clay excused these numbers by explaining that most of the reintegrated Nazis were former 'nominals' who had been successfully denazified, and he explained that if Nazi 'activists' were installed in any key positions – such a reality was uncovered in the teaching staffs in a number of schools in Württemberg-Baden – American officials were still willing to intervene. Reinstatement provisions, however, allowed '*Mitläufer*' to serve as *Bürgermeister*, city counselors or *Landtag* deputies, and since even notorious Nazis were now classed as 'Followers', the doors were wide open.[94] In Württemberg-Baden, Frank Konrad, the former Nazi *Oberbürgermeister* of Schwäbisch-Gmünd, recaptured the mayoralty in a bitter municipal election in 1948, although not before his campaign team had threatened and attacked his rival's followers, belted out the 'Horst Wessel *Lied*' and smeared a Star of David on the town square (the latter a reference to the Jewish faith of Konrad's opponent). Only this outrageous behavior prompted the Director of AMG for Württemberg-Baden to prevent Konrad's accession, although this decision aroused great controversy. The responsible U.S. official, Charles La Follette, was one of the few senior figures in AMG who believed that it was still worth fighting 'renazification'.[95]

Such potential for Allied interventions diminished in 1949 with the promulgation of the Occupation Statute, which limited the powers of the occupiers, while at the same time Article 131 of the Federal Republic's new constitution, the Basic Law, suggested the expanded re-employment of *Beamter* who had compromised themselves during the Third Reich. After the first federal elections, the new coalition government, comprised of Christian Democrats, Christian Socialists, Free Democrats and representatives of the German Party, evinced attitudes toward denazification that ranged from indifferent to hostile. Such broad masses had been the target of the programme that none of the government parties showed any desire to further punish such persons, nor even to stigmatize or ostracize them in any meaningful way. Quite to the contrary, the new government took an almost adverse pleasure in flaunting questionable appointments in the face of foreign powers or the SPD.

A big part of the problem was that Adenauer had no intention of reforming the public service, the senior members of which (*Beamte*) were traditionally uni-versity-trained jurists of an upper-class background, and who had long regarded themselves as a social estate pledged to the highest values of national service. AMG and British military government attempts to arrange civil service reform had already been largely thwarted by German conservatives, and whatever ele-ments had been successfully implemented were undone by Adenauer's Federal Civil Service law of July 1953, which restored the traditionally hierarchical and undemocratic basis of German public service. Even before the promulgation of this statute, however, the flood gates had already been opened to former Nazis. In addition to their functional argument – that they possessed administrative abili-ties now at a premium – they also added a moral contention, namely, that they ought not to be held to different standards than private employees. As early as 1948, Hans Globke and a group of *Mussnazis* formerly in the Reich Ministry of Interior had been negotiating with Adenauer. In fact, this group supplied the future chancellor with a list of officials willing to re-enter the civil service, and the creation of the Federal Republic saw a wave of such appointments, partly based on Globke's lists. Even the SPD was willing to countenance the rehiring of '*Mussnazis*', at least in subaltern positions, but the standards for distinguishing '*Mussnazis*' from the more genuine variety of National Socialist were lax, and the positions to which '*Mussnazis*' could aspire did not always remain in subordinate categories. As early as August 1950, a quarter of all ministerial department heads were already ex-Nazis, and this proportion had shot up to sixty per cent by 1953. The Foreign Office, which was run directly by Adenauer, was the cause of a pub-lic scandal in 1951/52, when it was revealed that former *Parteigenossen* had been hiring each other as a matter of preference, as a result of which the percentage of NSDAP members in the ministry – sixty-six per cent – was higher in 1952 than it had been in 1940! Adenauer threatened all critics with legal action and denounced the practice of 'sniffing around for Nazis'.

At the most senior level of government, Adenauer definitely cared whether or not his officials had a Nazi taint, but this consideration was trumped by his concern for administrative efficiency. Hans Globke, leader of the ex-Interior Ministry clique, was the classic case in kind. By all accounts, Globke was a highly capable functionary: he had started his career in the 1920s as a Prussian *Beamter*, and was then transferred to the Reich Ministry of Interior in 1934. While in the latter post he had helped to write the gloss for the Nuremberg Race Laws, instructing German bureaucrats on the practical policy implications of segregat-ing and disinheriting German Jews or saving the 'Aryan race' from the horrors of miscegenation. Globke had never joined the NSDAP – he had applied in 1940, although his application was blocked by Martin Bormann – but he was an archetypical case of the bureaucratic 'fellow traveler', willing to undertake any enterprise for the powers-that-be. Shockingly, Adenauer appointed Globke as the boss of his state chancellery, a position that gave Globke an impact on broad aspects of policy formation and personnel decisions. There is no doubt that Globke was no longer a Nazi, if he ever had been, and Globke still has his defenders, such as Hans-Peter Schwarz and Manfred Kittel, who point out that he had done his best to moderate the race law commentaries and that he had served as an agent of the Catholic bishops within the bureaucracy of the Third Reich. On the other hand, Globke had enjoyed the option of shifting to a job in private business, c. 1934/35 – he had married the daughter of an industrialist – so that unlike many of his colleagues, he had an alternate means of support that he refused to exploit. The Allies had been undecided about Globke: the British regarded him as an anti-fascist and he was also acceptable to the Americans, although the French had sufficient reason to deny him a cabinet position in the regional government of Rhineland-Hesse-Nassau. In any case, Adenaur's appointment of Globke was a major source of embarrassment for the new government. Günter Grass called it the shame of the republic and it was a propaganda bonanza for the rival regime in the East. Worse yet, evidence has recently come to light suggesting that West German intelligence officers were long aware of the location and alias of Adolf Eichmann, chief architect of the Final Solution, but that they avoided extraditing Eichmann because of fear about what he might say about Globke. Thus, one of the indirect implications of hiring a 'mild' Nazi was to shield the worst surviving villain of the Third Reich.

The Adenauer government also had to address Article 131 of the Basic Law, which promised redress for anyone who had lost a job in public or military service as a result of the war. Data collected in the late 1940s suggested that of the 345,000 people qualified for potential recompensatory hiring under Article 131, the so-called '131ers', nearly twenty-nine per cent had fallen under categories one to four of denazification proscription, and a somewhat higher number had actually held membership in the NSDAP or had been spiritual Nazis (mostly ex-professional soldiers who had never joined any political party). The 'Article 131 Law' of May 1951 can hardly be characterised as anything but generous to this group. Through this ordinance, Adenauer promised '131ers' with ten years or more of service a job 'equivalent' to the one that they had held in 1945. This commitment was to be met by reserving twenty per cent of all regular appointments in public enterprises – federal, *Land* and municipal – to '131ers'. Any agency falling short of the twenty per cent mark was forced to pay a 'compensation fee' to the Federal Government. Moreover, all persons awaiting placements through the scheme qualified for a 'transitional payment', which was usually financed by the 'Federal Compensation Agency'. For appearance's sake, existing denazification penalties were 'unaffected' by the new law, although most demotions and salary cuts imposed in the 1940s were limited to five years and were about to lapse in the period 1950–52. As for 55,000 civil servants who had actually been fired under denazification provisions, they were not supposed to be eligible for specific reappointment under the 'Article 131 Law', although a clever loophole was inserted within the legislation in order to encourage the hiring of such people. This group did qualify for 'transitional payments', although these transfers had to be funded from the individual budgets of agencies that had formerly employed members of this group, *without* support from the 'Federal Compensation Agency', which naturally had the effect of encouraging such bodies, particularly *Land* and municipal governments, to rehire personnel for whom they were already bearing a financial cost. The final result of this policy was not only to partially 'renazify' the public service, but to skew its demographic character toward middle aged employees – '131ers' hired in preference to younger applicants. Agencies such as the post office and federal railways were also forced to provide 'compensation jobs' to many older workers who lacked experience in these particular fields.

By the mid-1950s, however, there were two groups that did remain effectively segregated from positions of power. Neither the 'Article 131 Law' nor the Federal Civil Service Law covered appointees who had been brought into the public service from 1933 to 1945, specifically on the strength of their National Socialist convictions, nor did they provide compensation for persons who had held no other public post than in the Gestapo or the *Waffen*-SS. Thus, militant *Parteigenossen* remained out of state service, although many of them were able to build handsome careers in private business.[96] Ironically, the other group that lost status because of denazification was comprised of the German denazifiers themselves. Ten years after the heyday of denazification, former denazification prosecutors, assessors and tribunal chairs frequently found themselves ostracized and suffering from either unemployment or underemployment.[97]

Finally, it should be noted that the new Adenauer government, barely out of its swaddling clothes, presided over the hasty wrap up of denazification proceedings, although the fact that nearly all the *Länder* were already tying up loose ends made this federal initiative more symbolic than real. The German Party, the WAV and the Free Democrats – all parties containing a high proportion of *Parteigenossen* – had been pushing for action since September 1949, when the Federal Republic was founded. Hans Joachim von Merkatz of the German Party had already called denazification 'a modern witch hunt' and 'a monstrous birth engendered by totalitarian thinking and an orientation toward class warfare'. As Norbert Frei notes, it was the smaller parties that increasingly dominated the debate over denazification, in the process further influencing the public's already negative assessment. They got most of what they wanted, particularly because the CDU/CSU depended on the Free Democrats and the German Party to maintain their hold on power. Tom Bower, in a typically blunt appraisal of the situation, argues that Adenauer depended on ex-Nazis in order to stay in office, which in turn demanded the reciprocal delivery of favours. Adenauer's final denazification bill encouraged the abandonment of all pending procedures against Nazis slated in the lesser categories of guilt, as well as the cessation of employment restrictions against such people. The legislation also removed property ownership restrictions and restored the right to vote to all categories of guilt. At the insistence of both the CDU and the SPD, however, proceedings and sanctions against the two most senior categories of guilt continued, although the pervasive practice of downgrading Nazis into lower classes of guilt meant that there were only minuscule numbers remaining in the two highest categories.[98]

In considering the overall German reaction to denazification, several points bear mentioning. By 1947, there was certainly a wide scale revulsion against the programme, which laid the psychological basis for the Federal Republic to later undo most of what had been accomplished, at least in the bulk of Germany that it governed. Indeed, as John Montgomery notes, there was a much broader rejection of denazification than had ever manifested itself against Nazism, a perverse reality that tended to infuriate the occupiers.[99] Whether this turn of sentiment was driven by elites or by the unguided oscillations of mass opinion is unclear, although there are several indicators suggesting that it was the latter. If so, perhaps this was a good thing: at least it showed Germans thinking as individuals, although there is no doubt that the nefarious influence of Nazi intimidation crept into many peoples' thinking. As Jeffrey Herf notes, 'daring more democracy' eventually involved empowering voters who had come to oppose denazification and simply wanted to forget the past. Thus, Adenauer's version of democracy was built upon the principle of justice deferred.[100] The final result was a Germany in which the most senior echelons were cleansed of 'active' Nazis, at least in government, although the great mass of hangers-on and '*Mussnazis*' muddled through the occupation and into the new era.

THE RECKONING

As this narrative suggests, denazification failed. Nearly all historians have arrived at the same conclusion, and even Lutz Niethammer and his acolytes, who see the rehabilitation of '*Mitläufer*' as a means of securing denazification objectives, set a rather low threshold for success: the programme 'succeeded', in a fashion, because it eventually addressed the problems caused by its own over-extension. Indeed, all historians have agreed about the overly wide scope of denazification, which resulted in a vast purge of minor Nazis, while many 'big shots' simultaneously escaped censure or punishment. Depending on the historians' own predilections, they have tended to emphasize either one of these problems or the other. Figures on the Right have frequently concentrated on the former; those from the Left on the latter. Certainly, both kinds of problems have become abundantly apparent in the course of this text. Too much was attempted; too little succeeded. Moreover, in each occupation zone, denazification had costs. As Timothy Vogt notes, '[it] turned into a bureaucratic nightmare that bedeviled occupation authorities, hindered reconstruction, and gained the enmity of the German people'.[1] Klaus-Dietmar Henke bemoaned 'the nonsensical and impractical spread of the American denazification programme, with all its serious consequences for the political cleansing of Germany'.[2] And as Henke implies, it is not just that the fates were unkind; a proposition had been put forward that was almost bound to fail.

Given this reality, and the nature of the literature that reflects it, it is a surprise that denazification has nonetheless been used by modern-day statesmen and opinion-makers as a positive point of reference, or even worse, as a model, for recent exercises in the purging of totalitarian bureaucracies. With the fall of the Berlin Wall, it became fashionable to compare denazification to the 'destasification' of the German Democratic Republic, particularly since totalitarianism theory – the contention that fascist and communist dictatorships shared essential similarities – flourished in the period around the end of the Cold War. Several German historians wisely advised their countrymen not to draw hasty conclusions:

the imperative for denazification, they claimed, was not as pressing in the case of 'destasification,' and in any case a purge was likely to be handled far differently if it was a matter between Germans, rather than an imposition by outside forces.[3]

More troubling was the fact that the 'debaathification' of Iraq – the final fruit of yet another American moral crusade – closely followed the schematic model of denazification, although the latter was already widely considered to have been a fiasco. One wonders what books were read by policy-makers in the U.S. Defense Department and the Iraqi Provisional Authority? One of the most famous accounts of the purge in Germany, Constantine FitzGibbon's *Denazification*, notes that 'if ever similar circumstances should arise, and the Government of the United States finds itself in a position to exercise its will upon the citizens of another defeated totalitarian state, the same blueprint will not be produced again'.[4] Indeed, Douglas Porch, an analyst at the Naval Postgraduate School who had read FitzGibbon's book and the other historical accounts, advised purging only a few of Saddam's most senior officials, but leaving the bulk of one and a half million Baathists in place.[5] But alas, the most key members of the political and bureaucratic elite drew a different conclusion. In May 2003, the Lucius Clay of the Iraqi occupation, L. Paul Bremer, released from public service *all* Baath Party members with the ranks of regional commander, branch member, section member or group member, and he also allowed Shiite Iraqis allied to the United States – most particularly Ahmed Chalabi – to form a 'De-Baathification Committee', which was devoted to helping in this process and extending it to trade associations and private enterprise. As in Germany, thousands of minor officials and teachers were forced out of their jobs and were prevented from working while their appeals were pending, a development that eventually came to concern even Bremer. Unlike the case in Germany, however, the purge was not just a division of 'spoils'; it was part of a true revolution wrought by democratisation – a genuine transfer of power from one section of society to another, Sunni Iraqi to Shiite Arab and ethnic Kurd. Such a process had never occurred in occupied Germany and the final result was a development that had only barely flickered to life in Germany, but which fully bared its ugly head in Iraq: a violent counterrevolution. By the time that the inevitable backpedaling began in 2004, it was already too late to avoid the worst sort of outcome.[6]

The only rationale for using denazification as a model for anything comes from the assumption that Germany successfully democratised in the long run, so denazification must have played a positive role in that transition. Unfortunately, this is a rather simplistic view of historical causation. Many historians have argued that the moral denazification of Germany actually began during the Second World War, and that below the surface, the deepest currents of social life and opinion had begun to shift even while Hitler still stood at the helm. Ironically, the Third Reich itself broke down traditional class and confessional barriers that had supported more traditional forms of German authoritarianism, and it thus helped create the

soil in which a party like the CDU could eventually take root. Bombing, ration-
ing and enemy occupation also produced an effect of class leveling. At the same
time, the paternalism of German family structures began to erode as the Nazi
regime itself encouraged youth autonomy, or at least the association of youth with
rival forms of authority, such as the Hitler Youth, while the impact of the war
forced wives and mothers to fall back upon their own resources, rather than relying on absent males. Moreover, as has often been observed, mass support for Hitler
began to erode after the debacle at Stalingrad, although the regime could still rally
substantial popular support at the time of the 20 July Putsch, and even after the
end of the war, many Nazi ideas remained intact, even while the structure of the
party disappeared.[7] At the height of the denazification drive, opinion polling of
Germans sometimes produced shocking results. In 1946/47, more Germans still
rated Nazism 'a good idea badly carried out' than those who thought the entire
ideology wrongheaded, and only twenty per cent thought that the recent war
was Germany's fault. An assessment by the U.S. occupation garrison (November
1947) concluded that 'Germans have forgotten their war guilt … and a tendency
to reminisce about "the glory of the Third Reich" is frequently observed'. As
late as 1954, less than half the population had a negative impression of Hitler.[8]
Nonetheless, developments in the 1950s and 1960s reinforced earlier currents of
change, particularly an economic boom that fostered the rise of consumer culture;
by the late 1950s, the rate of social mobility had nearly matched that of American
society. Social scientists began talking about 'a leveled-out middle-class society'.
The 'economic miracle' was also closely connected to integration within the
Common Market, which encouraged Germans to develop a more pan-European
sense of identity. In addition, family life continued to change; the legal right of
husbands to dominate family decisions was formally abrogated in 1957.[9] While the
Adenauer Republic still maintained a staid and patriarchal political climate, militarism had been largely discredited – a process aided by the isolation of the Prussian
heartland in the socialist east – and popular concerns about the formation of the
Bundeswehr (1956) comprised perhaps the first sign of a significant change in the
popular mood. In the 1960s, the 'Spiegel Affair', in which the government made
heavy-handed use of the police to suppress dissent, helped foster an increasingly
broad recognition of the need for political engagement, and the 1968 Student
Revolt – the ultimate 'denazification' of higher education – as well as the electoral
rise of a more centrist SPD, also signaled a new beginning. Meanwhile, detente
with the DDR suggested the end of a virulent strain of anti-communism that
had resembled its Nazi forebear, and beginning with the Eichman Case, Germans
were increasingly in a mood to look at their past, however painful that experience.
Few other European countries had gone through such a rapid or thorough transformation. Denazification had little or nothing to do with this process.

Despite this reality, denazification may continue to be used as a basic pattern
for the purge of totalitarian administrative structures, which rather forces us to

deal with its function as a model. Thus, while historians are usually expected to maintain a sense of detachment from their topics, in this case it may be appropriate to study denazification in the same way that general staff officers approach an historic battle or campaign – that is, as an analytical subject capable of providing lessons for the future. Regarded in such a sense, the nub of the matter is not only what went wrong, but what could have been done to have secured a more favourable outcome. It is possible, as Michael Balfour claims, that something much different than schematic denazification was impossible within the climate that existed in 1945,[10] but here are several suggestions that are rather shamelessly offered with the advantage of hindsight.

First, it is clear that the programme was too big. Denazification bore a metaphorical resemblance to carpet bombing – another product of the 'collective guilt' mentality – because it emphasized raining down a scattered series of blows rather than focusing on a limited target, in this case perhaps the 200,000 officials most deserving of dismissal or arrest. Thus, the programme should not have included ordinary members of the party, but only the senior categories of leadership, plus lists based on active and enthusiastic supporters of the regime, including those in the economy, whether or not they held party membership.[11] An stress on individual investigations would have negated the heavy emphasis on categories of guilt so central to the Allied programme, and would have encouraged Allied investigators to move beyond party ranks in the search for the real facilitators of Nazi aggression and brutality. Perhaps the lists of people to be removed from their jobs could have been identical with the automatic arrest cases; if the process was limited to the worst of the worst, those worth dismissing were probably also worth interning. Such categories and lists could have been supplemented by denunciations, and social democrats, centrists, communists and surviving German Jews should have been more encouraged to step forward and provide the information for such a process. It is true that limiting the size of the purge would have meant keeping many Nazis in office, particularly 'nominals', but many *Parteigenossen* eventually returned to positions of considerable power and authority anyway. Failing the concession of this larger point, the Americans at least should have avoided blocking the employment of 'nominal' Nazis before they passed through the denazification system. This practice forced the adoption of numerous subterfuges that enjoyed wide scale assent and did more than anything to discredit the entire system.

Obviously, a process based on individual investigations would have required a considerable diversion of manpower by the occupiers, although perhaps no more than the task of scouring millions of *Fragebogen*. In any case, if the occupiers really felt that the Second World War was a battle of ideas, rather than just a fight for geopolitical dominance, then it might have made sense to have devoted large scale resources to the defeat of Nazism as a political force as well as a military threat. Each of the great powers in the anti-Nazi coalition had access to such large numbers of German-speakers – Jewish and anti-Nazi refugees, émigré communists, German-Americans, re-educated PoWs, Alsatians – that it would have been possible to set up a massive denazification machine capable of functioning in Germany and carrying out requisite investigations and identity checks. A Special Branch staffed with such elements would have constituted a powerful instrument for the occupation forces. Such a system would also have signaled a true Allied commitment to the purge process and would have been infinitely better than hurriedly sloughing off denazification responsibilities upon domestic Germans. Unless the Western Allies wished to assist in a true social revolution – which they most assuredly did not – any means of keeping the process in their own hands would have been preferable to handing over a faulty system to demoralised Germans.

As for the matter of replacement personnel, instead of allowing Allied field commanders to follow individual preferences and rules of thumb in making appointments, it might have made sense to have provided each combat and military government detachment with data about the last free municipal, *Kreis* and *Land* elections and to have encouraged the distribution of posts based on the proportion of the vote won by the various parties in each locality near the end of the Weimar era. Naturally, the Nazi vote would have been counted out and redistributed proportionally to the other parties. This process might have given a particular boost to the KPD, which had been much stronger in 1932 than it was in 1945, but it would have also limited the strength of establishmentarian elements that were relatively more willing to accommodate Nazi or pro-Nazi personnel.

Of course, it is easy to be wise after the event, and there is certainly much that the occupiers did right. Barbara Marshall argues that the Allies created an overall framework that allowed the Germans' own process of social and political change to move forward, and that they also absorbed much of the negativity that was bound to accompany enemy occupation, rather than have such feelings refract upon the German political parties. Indeed, many Nazis were removed from the political process long enough for new forces to redefine it, and once *Parteigenossen* individually returned to their jobs, they usually accepted the new standards developed in their absence.[12] Allied information and cultural exchange policies in Germany also served the country well, and the publicity campaigns surrounding concentration camps, while they repulsed many Germans at the time, had a beneficial long range effect, providing details about Nazism's sins that were difficult for later apologists to either reject or ignore.[13] However, while such policies complemented denazification, they were not at the heart of that draconian idea. The purge itself suffered from a fundamental problem that often bedevils large scale social engineering projects: while such measures frequently fail to produce the desired effect, they do often produce unintended byproducts (in this case, broad sympathy for *Parteigenossen*, eventual 'renazification' of the bureaucracy) that are far from what the planners had originally intended.

LIST OF
ABBREVIATIONS

Readers should note that, for simplicity's sake, I have avoided using some of the most technical terms for military government in the four occupation zones. U.S. Group Control Council (USGCC), Office of Military Government U.S. (OMGUS), and Control Council (British Element) (CC(BE)) were all synonyms for 'military government', or as Wolfgang Friedmann points out, they were 'the main instrument[s] of military government'. To further confuse matters, American terminology shifted during the early phase of the occupation. In preference to any of the formal U.S. acronyms, I have employed the term 'American Military Government' (AMG). I have also used the standard English-language translation for Russian military government, that is 'Soviet Military Administration' (SMA), and instead of the official French title of '*Gouvernement Militaire en Zone Française d'Occupation en Allemagne*' (GMZFOA), I have employed the simpler designation of '*Gouvernement Militaire*' (GM).

ACAO – Official Committee on Armistice Terms and Civil Administration
AMG – American Military Government
APW – Armistice and Post-War Committee
BBC – British Broadcasting Corporation
BdM – German Girls' Federation
BVKP – Bavarian People's Communist Party
BVP – Bavarian People's Party
CC – Control Council
CCS – Combined Chiefs of Staff
CDU – Christian Democratic Union
CIA – Central Intelligence Agency
CIC – Counter Intelligence Corps
COSSAC – Chief of Staff, Supreme Allied Commander
CSU – Christian Social Union
DAF – German Labour Front

DDR – German Democratic Republic
FDP – Free Democratic Party
FIAT – Field Information Agency, Technical
FORD – Foreign Office Research Department
GCU – German Country Unit
GM – *Gouvernement Militaire*
HJ – Hitler Youth
JCS – Joint Chiefs of Staff
KD – *Kontrolldienst*; Control Service
KPD – Communist Party of Germany
NDP – National Democratic Party
NGCC – North German Coal Control
NKGB – People's Commissariat for State Security
NLP – Lower Saxony Party
NSDAP – National Socialist German Workers' Party; Nazi Party
OSS – Office of Strategic Services
PoW – Prisoner of War
PW – Psychological Warfare
PWE – Political Warfare Executive
R&A – Research and Analysis Branch (of the OSS)
RC – Reconstruction Committee
RWCS – Rhenish-Westphalian Coal Syndicate
SA – *Sturmabteilung*; Storm Troopers
SD – SS Security Service
SED – Socialist Unity Party
SHAEF – Supreme Headquarters, Allied Expeditionary Force
SMA – Soviet Military Administration
SPD – Social Democratic Party of Germany
SS – 'Guard Corps'; elite 'order' of the Nazi Party
UNRRA – United Nations Relief and Rehabilitation Administration
UPC – University Planning Committee
WAV – Economic Reconstruction Union

List of Foreign Terms

Abwehr – defense; German military intelligence
'*Alte Kämpfer*' – 'old fighters'; pre-1933 members of the Nazi Party
Amtsträger – office holder in the Nazi Party or its affiliates
Angestellte – salaried employees
Apparat – apparatus
Arbeiter – workers
Arbeitsamt – Employment Bureau
Auschüsse zur Durchführung der Directive 24 – Commissions for the Implementation of Directive 24
Beamte (pl. *Beamter*) – civil servant
Berufskammer (pl. *Berufskammern*) – appeals panel
Blockleiter – Nazi block leader
Bundeswehr – army of the German Federal Republic
bürgerlich – middle class
Bürgermeister – mayor
Cinquième Bureau – Fifth Bureau
Comité interministérial des Affairs allemandes et autrichiennes – Inteministerial Committee for German and Austrian Affairs
Contrôle de la Justice – Inspectorate for Justice
curators de l'université – university officers
Deuxième Bureau – Second Bureau
Dienstellenleiter – section leader
Diktat – command
Direction Générale de la Justice – General Directorate for Justice
Directives pour notre action en Allemagne – Directives for Our Action in Germany
Direktorium – board of directors
'*Dreissiger-Auschuss*' – 'Commission of Thirty'
écoles normales – teachers' colleges
École Nationale d'Administration – National School of Administration
Einheimischer – locals
épuration – cleansing
Erbfeind – archenemy

'*Fasenenjagd*' – hunt for 'golden pheasants'; search for Nazi bosses
Finanzamt – Finance Department
'*Flusterpropaganda*' – 'whisper propaganda'
Fragebogen – denazification questionnaire
Frontoviki – Red Army combat troops
Führerprinzip – leadership principle
Gastwirter – restaurant proprietors
Gauleiter – Nazi region leader
Gefolgschaften – workforce, retinue
Gleichschaltung – coordination
Hansestadt – Hanseatic city
Hochschule – college
Honoratioren – local notables
Kameradschaft – comradeship
Kampfgruppen – battle groups
Kommandatura – town commandant
Kommandos – labour task groups
Kreis (pl. *Kreise*) – county
Kreisleiter – Nazi county leader
Kreistag – county council
Kulturpolitik – cultural policy
Land (pl. *Länder*) – German state
Länderrat – Council of States
Landpolizei – state police
Landrat (pl. *Landräte*) – local government official
Landtag – state assembly
Luftwaffe – air force of the Third Reich
'*Maikäfer*' – 'Mayfly'
Meldebogen – denazification questionnaire
mission civilisatrice – civilising mission
Mitläufer – follower; fellow traveler
'*Mitläuferfabrik*' – 'Follower' factory
'*Mussnazi*' – Nazi by obligation
Oberpräsident – provincial president
Ortsgruppenleiter – Nazi district leader
NS-*Frauenschaft* – Nazi women's auxiliary
NS-*Lehrerbund* – Nazi-affiliated teachers' organisation
NS-*Zeit* – National Socialist era
Oberst – colonel
Oberbürgermeister – lord mayor
'*Ohne mich*' – 'without me'
Opergruppe (pl. *Opergruppy*) – Operations Group
'*Ordnungszelle*' – centre of order
Parteigenosse (pl. *Parteigenossen*) – 'party comrade'
Persilschein (pl. *Persilscheine*) – written testimonial to the 'good character' of a Nazi
Rechtswahrerbund – Nazi affiliated lawyers' organisation
Reichsbahn – German National Railway
Reichsbank – German National Bank
Reichspost – German Post Office
Rektor – rector
Regierungspräsident – local government president
Reichsleiter – Reich leader

Reichswehr – Weimar-era German Army
'*Säuberungsgericht*' – 'cleansing' court
Säuberungskommission (pl. *Säuberungskommissionen*) – cleansing commission
'*Schicksalsgemeinschaft*' – 'community of fate'
schnell – fast
'*Schweinerei*' – 'dirty dealing'
Service de l'Épuration – Cleansing Service
Sonderweg – special path
Sowjetische Aktiengesellschaft – Soviet Joint Stock Company
Speziallager – Special Camp; internment compound
Spruchgericht (pl. *Spruchgerichte*) – denazification court
Spruchkammer (pl. *Spruchkammern*) – denazification panel
Staatskommissar für die politische Säuberung – State Commissioner for Political Cleansing
Staatsrat – state counselor
Stadt – city
Stahlhelm – steel helmet; German veterans' organisation
Ständestaat – corporate state
Sûreté – security; police
Untersuchungsauschuss (pl. *Untersuchungsauschüsse*) – investigatory committee
Vergangenheitsbewältigung – 'struggling with the past'
Volksschulen – basic schools
Volkssturm – German mass militia
Waffen-SS – Armed SS
Wehrmacht – armed forces of the Third Reich
'*wilde Säuberung*' – 'wild purges'
Zentrum – Centre Party
Zwangsmassnahmen – compulsion measures

LIST OF
ILLUSTRATIONS

NA = USA National Archives

1 A German illustration (1946) parodies the new 'Germanised' version of the denazification system: black wolves are dumped into the machinery and emerge as white sheep. Source: Clemens Vollnhals, ed., *Entnazifizierung. Politische Säuberung und Rehabilitirung in den vier Besatzungszonen* 1945–1949, p.331 (Munich, 1991).

2 A political cartoon from *Die Neue Zeitung*, 16 September 1948. A Nazi 'big shot' stands complacently next to the sleeping dragon of denazification. 'He won't do anything to me,' he gloats. 'He's long since satiated with "small fry".' Source: Clemens Vollnhals, ed., *Entnazifizierung. Politische Säuberung und Rehabilitirung in den vier Besatzungszonen* 1945–1949, p.305 (Munich, 1991).

3 The *Oberbürgermeister* of Koblenz alerts townspeople to the fact that new *Fragebogen* were being distributed, and that they must be filled out and returned within forty-eight hours. Most of the earlier *Fragebogen* handed out in July 1945 had supposedly been completed incorrectly or incompletely. Source: Franz Josef Heyen, ed., *Rheinland-Pfalz entsteht: Beiträge zu den Anfängen des Landes Rheinland-Pfalz in Koblenz* 1945–1951, p.263 (Boppard, 1984).

4 A denazification form used by the Special Branch of U.S. military government. Source: NA.

5 U.S. military government graphs on denazification rates show most cases being slotted in the 'Follower' category, January 1947. Source: NA.

6a and b SHAEF G-2 'Arrest Categories Handbook', April 1945. Source: NA.

7 American officers and reporters at Furstenhagen look at a collection of captured Nazi personnel documents, 15 November 1945. This set included the names of most *Wehrmacht* intelligence and counter-intelligence agents, all of whom ranked highly on Allied black lists. Source: NA.

8 Nazi Party members in Duisberg are forced to exhume the bodies of Russian and other foreign labourers murdered by the Nazi security police shortly before the Allied advance. Source: NA.

9 Germans in München-Gladbach read Allied proclamation No.1, as posted by the U.S. authorities on 5 March 1945. This proclamation included the initial denazification stipulations presented to Germans. Source: NA.

10 *Bürgermeister* Dr Levie of Nuremberg speaks to a visiting delegation from the American

Veteran's Committee. Levie, who had been held in Auschwitz, argued that Germans interpreted American goodwill as weakness and that *Spruchkammern* were dealing with Nazis much too leniently. Source: NA.

11 Civilians caught in a joint Franco-American swoop operation, codenamed 'Fox', on 26 August 1946. The elderly man on the right is shown holding a copy of *Mein Kampf*, possession of which had led to his arrest. Source: NA.

12a, b and c Three photographs showing operations of the Steglitz Denazification Board, March 1946. Steglitz is in the southern part of Berlin. Photograph 12a shows a former Nazi Party member handing in his papers to the secretary of the board; 12b shows the board in weekly session; 12c shows the representative of the Liberal Democrats on the board, Dr Faust, listening to a witness tell about the past of a former party member.

13a and b Schema explaining the denazification process in Bavaria under the 'Law for Liberation from National Socialism and Militarism'. 13a is a pictorial representation of the denazification process; 13b is a chart showing the denazification system. Source: NA.

14 A regional government is installed at Neustadt after U.S. military government officials had screened 200 prospective candidates for their Nazi affiliations. This government controlled part of Westmark and southern Hesse. Source: NA.

15 Major General Horace McBride, representing the U.S. Third Army, inspects the Moosberg Civilian Internment Enclosure prior to its transfer to Bavarian officials on 10 October 1946. Moosberg was the first internment camp turned over to control of a German Land government. Source: NA.

16 Bavarian Denazification Minister Pfeiffer (left) and Minister-President Högner (right) sign for the transfer of Moosberg Internment Camp on 10 October 1946. Source: NA.

17 Civilians in München-Gladbach line up for security screening and registration at the headquarters of U.S. military government, 21 March 1945. Source: NA.

18 Eduard Houdremont in Allied custody, July 1947. Houdremont, although a Nazi Party member, had received American permission to run the Krupp concern for several months after the end of the Second World War. Source: NA.

19 Lucius Clay in August 1947. Clay was the chief proponent and executor of U.S. zone denazification. Source: NA.

20 Marshall Zhukov and his staff, June 1945. Zhukov was the first military governor of the Soviet zone and believed that the Soviets should rapidly denazify (although not Bolshivise) the territory that they controlled in Germany. Source: NA.

21 General Clay and his senior officers at a meeting of the *Länderrat* on 5 July 1946. From left to right: Jim Pollock, Lucius Clay, Walter Muller (director of military government in Bavaria) and James Newman (director of military government in Hesse). Source: NA.

22 James Riddleberger, a U.S. State Department official, was one of the main figures involved in the 1944/45 debate over the direction of American occupation policy in Germany. Source: NA.

23 A hearing in the Denazification Tribunal at Zehlendorf, Berlin, 26 March 1946. This was the first full session of the board. Until a March 1946 law passed by the Allied *Kommandatura*, a denazification respondent had been questioned by a single interrogator and then sentenced, but the new regulations allowed for the respondent to appear before the board and provide a defence of his/her conduct. Source: NA.

24 The 'Big Three', Attlee, Truman and Stalin, at the Potsdam Conference. Basic decisions about the nature of denazification were made at this meeting. Source: NA.

25 Former members of the NSDAP are forced to tend a Jewish graveyard in Bergheim, July 1945. Their former party comrades had once desecrated the site. Source: NA.

26 Following the denazification debacle in Bavaria, George Patton addresses troops of the U.S. Third Army in a transfer-of-command ceremony, 7 October 1945. To Patton's right

NOTES

The Denazification Debate

1 Constantine FitzGibbon, *Denazification* (London, 1969), p.133; and Clay to Commanding General, USFET, 26 Dec. 1946, OMGUS – Office of the Adjutant General: General Correspondence (Decimal File) 1945–49, Record Group (RG) 260, U.S. National Archives (NA).

2 Bergmann to Greenbaum, 17 Nov. 1943, CAD 014 Germany, RG 165, NA. Elmer Plischke errs in suggesting that the term 'denazification' was first used by the political staff in Eisenhower's high command. See Elmer Plischke, 'Denazification in Germany: A Policy Analysis', in Robert Wolfe, ed., *Americans as Proconsuls: United States Military Government in Germany and Japan, 1944–52* (Carbondale, 1984), p.207.

3 See, for instance, Jérôme Vaillant, 'La Dénazification: un problème culturel', in Jérôme Vaillant, ed., *La Dénazification par les Vainqueurs* (Lille, 1981), p.12.

4 *Foreign Relations of the United States: The Conferences at Washington and Quebec, 1943* (Washington, 1970), pp.104, 114; *Foreign Relations of the United States: The Conferences at Malta and Yalta, 1945* (*FRUS: Malta and Yalta*) (Washington, 1955), pp.147–49; *Foreign Relations of the United States: The Conference at Berlin (the Potsdam Conference), 1945* (*FRUS: Potsdam*) (Washington, 1960), ii, pp.498–99; Plischke, 'Denazification in Germany', p.211; Roy Willis, *The French in Germany, 1945–1949* (Stanford, 1962), pp.152–53; William Griffiths, 'The Denazification Program in the United States Zone of Germany', Ph.D. Dissertation, Harvard University, April 1950, pp.64–5; and Lutz Niethammer, *Entnazifizierung in Bayern: Säuberung und Rehabilitierung unter amerikanischer Besatzung* (Frankfurt, 1972), p.12.

5 *Foreign Relations of the United States, 1945* (*FRUS, 1945*) (Washington, 1966), v, p.662; Tom Bower, *The Pledge Betrayed: America and Britain and the Denazification of Post-war Germany* (New York, 1982), pp.127–28; Julian Bach, *America's Germany: An Account of the Occupation* (New York, 1947), pp.225–26; and Lothar Ketternacker, *Krieg zur Friedenssicherung. Die Deutschlandplannung der britischen Regierung während des Zweiten Weltkrieges* (Göttingen, 1989), pp.353–54.

6 *Weser-Kurier*, 29 Nov. 1945; and 12 Dec. 1945.

7 Justus Fürstenau, *Entnazifizierung. Ein Kapitel deutscher Nachkriegspolitik* (Neuwied, 1969), p.6; Rainer Möhler, *Entnazifizierung in Rheinland-Pfalz und im Saarland unter französischer Besatzung von 1945 bis 1952* (Mainz, 1992), p.5; Ian Turner, 'The British Occupation and

its Impact on Germany', in Ian Turner, ed., *Reconstruction in Post-War Germany: British Occupation Policy and the Western Zones, 1945–55* (Oxford, 1989), pp.3–4; and Helga Welsh, *Revolutionärer Wandel auf Befehl? Entnazifizierungs- und Personalpolitik in Thüringen und Sachsen (1945–1948)* (Munich, 1989), p.10.

8 See, for instance, the observation in Niethammer, *Entnazifizierung in Bayern*, p.14.

9 Eugene Davidson, *The Death and Life of Germany* (New York, 1959), pp.13–14, 61–64, 77–78, 128–29, 160, 189–91, 276–77; Harold Zink, *The United States in Germany, 1944–1955* (Princeton, 1957), pp.2–3, 87–91, 92, 94–99, 167–68, 252–55, 356–57; Fürstenau, *Entnazifizierung*; Wolfgang Friedmann, *The Allied Military Government of Germany* (London, 1947), chapter 7; FitzGibbon, *Denazification*; and Michael Balfour, 'Four-Power Control in Germany, 1945–1946', in *Four-Power Control in Germany and Austria, 1945–1946* (London, 1956), pp.62–64, 180–83, 258–59.

10 John D. Montgomery, *Forced to Be Free: The Artificial Revolution in Germany and Japan* (Chicago, 1957).

11 Ernst von Saloman, *Fragebogen* (New York, 1955); and Caspar von Schrenk-Notsing, *Charakterwäsche* (Stuttgart, 1965).

12 Niethammer, *Entnazifizierung in Bayern*, p.48.

13 John Gimbel, *The American Occupation of Germany: Politics and the Military, 1945–1949* (Stanford, 1968), pp.9–13, 108–10; Earl Ziemke, 'The Formulation and Initial Implementation of U.S. Occupation Policy in Germany', in Hans Schmitt, ed., *U.S. Occupation in Europe after World War II* (Lawrence, 1978), p.42; and Earl Ziemke, *The U.S. Army in the Occupation of Germany* (Washington, 1975), pp.345–46, 380–90, 445–46, 448–49. In much the same spirit of scholarship, see also Paul Hammond, 'Directives for the Occupation of Germany: The Washington Controversy', in Harold Stein, ed., *American Civil Military Decisions* (Birmingham, 1963), pp.432–33, 436–38.

14 John Gimbel, 'The Artificial Revolution in Germany', *The Political Science Quarterly* 76, no.1 (March 1961), pp.88–89, 91, 93, 104; and John Gimbel, *A German Community under American Occupation: Marburg 1945–52* (Stanford, 1961), pp.201–05, 208.

15 George Stein, review of Lutz Niethammer's *Entnazifizierung in Bayern*, in *The American Historical Review* 78 (Oct. 1973), p. 1095; and Timothy Vogt, *Denazification in Soviet-Occupied Germany: Brandenburg, 1945–48* (Cambridge, 2000), p.13.

16 Niethammer, *Entnazifizierung in Bayern*, pp.17, 18, 27.

17 *Ibid.*; quote from p.178.

18 Bower, *The Pledge Betrayed*, pp.161–62, 166–74, 176–81, 183–89, 193, 206–07, 452–57.

19 Edward Peterson, *The American Occupation of Germany: Retreat to Victory* (Detroit, 1977), pp.10, 54, 154, 341, 351; and James Tent, *Mission on the Rhine: Re-education and Denazification in American-Occupied Germany* (Chicago, 1982), pp.10, 41, 83, 107–08, 312–13, 316–17, 318.

20 Curt Garner, 'Public Service Personnel in West Germany in the 1950s: Controversial Policy Decisions and their Effects on Social Composition, Gender Structure, and the Role of Former Nazis', *The Journal of Social History* 29, no.1 (Fall 1995), pp.25, 66; and Anselm Doering-Manteuffel, 'Deutsche Zeitgeschichte nach 1945. Entwicklung und Problemlagen der historischen Forschung zur Nachkriegszeit', *Vierteljahrshefte für Zeitgeschichte* 41 (1993), pp.10–29.

21 S.F.V. Donnison, *Civil Affairs and Military Government, North-West Europe, 1945–1946* (London, 1961).

22 Ian Connor, 'Denazification in Post-War Germany', *European History Quarterly* 21 (1991), p.398.

23 Jill Jones, 'Eradicating Nazism from the British Zone of Germany: Early Policy and Practice', *German History* 8, no.2 (1990); Ian Turner, 'Denazification in the British Zone', in Turner, ed., *Reconstruction in Post-War Germany*; and Barbara Marshall, *The*

Origins of Post-War German Politics (London, 1988).

24 Wolfgang Krüger, *Entnazifiziert! Zur Praxis der politischen Säuberung in Nordrhein-Westfalen* (Wuppertal, 1982).

25 Möhler, *Entnazifizierung in Rheinland-Pfalz und im Saarland*, pp.6–7; and Cornelia Rauh-Kühne,' Forschungen zur französischen Zone. Geschichte der Besatzungspolitik oder Geschichte der Besatzungszeit?', *Informationen zur Modernen Stadtgeschichte* 2 (1994), p.16.

26 Klaus-Dietmar Henke, *Politische Säuberung unter französischer Besatzung* (Stuttgart, 1981); Möhler, *Entnazifizierung in Rheinland-Pfalz und im Saarland*; and Reinhard Grohnert, *Die Entnazifizierung in Baden 1945–1949. Konzeptionen und Praxis der 'Epuration' am Beispiel eines Landes der französischen Besatzungzone* (Stuttgart, 1991).

27 Welsh, *Revolutionärer Wandel auf Befehl?*; Vogt, *Denazification in Soviet-Occupied Germany*; Damian van Melis, 'Denazification in Mecklenburg-Vorpommern', *German History* 13, no.3 (1995); and Damian van Melis, *Entnazifizierung in Mecklenburg-Vorpommern. Herrschaft und Verwaltung 1945–1948* (Munich, 1999).

Chapter 1: A Perfectionist's Plan

1 Fürstenau, *Entnazifizierung*, pp.220–21; Richard Merritt, 'American Influences in the Occupation of Germany', *The Annals of the American Academy of Political and Social Science* 428 (Nov. 1976), p.92; Leslie Lipson, 'European Responses to the American Revolution', *The Annals of the American Academy of Political and Social Science* 428 (Nov. 1976), pp.24–28; Balfour, 'Four-Power Control in Germany', pp.25–26; and Thomas Hill, 'Morality in Foreign Policy: An Expression of American Idealism', *Contemporary Review* 232, no.1344 (Jan. 1978), 23–24.

2 Niethammer, *Entnazifizierung in Bayern*, p.32.

3 J. Samuel Walker, *Henry A. Wallace and American Foreign Policy* (Westport, 1976), pp.7–8, 70–71; Henry Wallace, 'Veblen's "Imperial Germany and the Industrial Revolution"', *The Political Science Quarterly* 55 (Sept. 1940), pp.435–45; John Morton Blum, ed., *The Price of Vision: The Diary of Henry A. Wallace, 1942–1946* (Boston, 1973), pp.123, 184, 638; Hermann Fromm, *Deutschland in der öffentlichen Kriegszieldiskussion Grossbritanniens 1939–1945* (Frankfurt a.M., 1982), p.211; *Prefaces to Peace* (New York, 1943), pp.405, 410–411; and U.S. Memoranda No.161, 18 March 1943, *Review of the Foreign Press, 1939–1945* (Munich, 1980), p.3.

4 Robert Dallek, *Franklin D. Roosevelt and American Foreign Policy, 1932–1945* (Oxford, 1979), pp.8–13, 15–20, 421, 438–39, 536, 538; and James MacGregor Burns, *Roosevelt: The Soldier of Freedom, 1940–1945* (New York, 1970), pp.vii–viii. From his youth, Roosevelt was a confirmed Germanophobe, partly because he had developed a negative view of the Wilhelmine Reich while visiting Germany as a student. While serving as assistant secretary of the navy during the First World War, Roosevelt had thundered against 'Prussianism' and 'Kaiserism', and had encouraged the total subjugation of Germany, with the nation prospectively 'cut down and purged'. As Rexford Tugwell notes, the mature FDR transformed his bigotries to fit a liberal-progressive mold, at least superficially, but 'his undisguised chauvinism and eagerness to punish the Germans did not die out'. Klaus Dietmar Henke, *Die amerikanische Besetzung Deutschlands* (Munich, 1995); Michael Beschloss, *The Conquerors: Roosevelt, Truman and the Destruction of Hitler's Germany, 1941-1945* (New York, 2002), pp.9–11; and Rexford Tugwell, *The Democratic Roosevelt* (Baltimore, 1969), p.105.

5 Bradley Smith, *The Road to Nuremberg* (London, 1981), pp.13–14; Balfour, 'Four-Power Control in Germany', p.15; Beate Ruhm von Oppen, ed. *Documents on Germany under*

Occupation, 1945–1954 (London, 1955), p.1; and *Foreign Relations of the United States: The Conferences at Washington, 1941–1942, and Casablanca,* 1943 (Washington, 1968).

6 Warren Kimball, *Swords or Ploughshares? The Morgenthau Plan for Defeated Nazi Germany, 1943–1946* (Philadelphia, 1976), pp.10–11, 12; Beschloss, *The Conquerors,* pp.20–21; David Dilks, ed., *The Diaries of Sir Alexander Cadogan, 1938–1945* (New York, 1972), p.506; Robert Sherwood, *The White House Papers of Harry L. Hopkins* (London, 1949), pp.708–09; *Foreign Relations of the United States,* 1943 (Washington, 1966), p.542; *Foreign Relations of the United States: The Conferences at Cairo and Tehran (FRUS; Cairo-Tehran),* (Washington, 1961), pp.253–54, 256–310, 532–33; William Leahy, *I Was There* (New York, 1950), p.187; Cordell Hull, *The Memoirs of Cordell Hull* (New York, 1948), pp.1265–66, 1284–85; Beatrice Bishop Berle, ed., *Navigating the Rapids, 1918–1971: From the Papers of Adolf A. Berle* (New York, 1973), pp.4833–34; and Winston Churchill, *The Second World War: Closing the Ring* (London, 1952), pp.354–56.

7 *FRUS: Cairo-Tehran,* pp.511, 513, 553–55, 600–04, 879–80, 882.

8 Kimball, *Swords or Ploughshares?* pp.93–94; and *Morgenthau Diary* (Germany) (Washington, 1967), pp.414–15.

9 Lucius Clay, *Decision in Germany* (Garden City, 1950), p.8; Dwight D. Eisenhower, *Crusade in Europe* (New York, 1948), pp.104–11, 191–92, 433–34; Dallek, *Franklin D. Roosevelt and American Foreign Policy,* pp.364–65; Stephen Ambrose, *Eisenhower the Soldier, 1890–1952* (London, 1984), pp.204–10; and F.S.V. Donnison, *Civil Affairs and Military Government Central Organisation and Planning* (London, 1966), pp.63–64.

10 Smith, *The Road to Nuremberg,* pp.14–15; and Griffiths, 'The Denazification Program', pp.2–3.

11 Ziemke, *The U.S. Army in the Occupation of Germany,* pp.3–5; Earl Ziemke, 'Erwin L. Hunt, Henry J. Morgenthau and German-American Relations after Two Wars', in Hans Trefouss, ed., *Germany and America: Essays on Problems of International Relations and Immigration* (New York, 1980), pp.229, 235–36; Conrad Latour and Thilo Vogelsang, *Okkupation und Wiederaufbau. Die Tätigkeit der Militärregierung in der amerikanischen Besatzungszone Deutschlands 1944–1947* (Stuttgart, 1973), p.132; Kimball, *Swords to Ploughshares?* pp.4–5; S.K. Padover, L.F. Gittler and P.R. Sweet, 'The Political Situation in Aachen', in Daniel Lerner, ed., *Propaganda in War and Crisis* (New York, 1972), pp.445–46; Bower, *The Pledge Betrayed,* p.124; Griffiths, 'The Denazification Program', pp.5, 37–8; Niethammer, *Entnazifizierung in Bayern,* pp.53–54; Marshall, *The Origins of Post-War German Politics,* pp.5,7; Harold Zink, *American Military Government in Germany* (New York, 1947), pp.138–39; Zink, *The United States in Germany,* p.153; and School of Military Government 'Suggested Draft for Directive from CCS for Military Government of the German Reich', *c.*Oct. 1943, CAD 014 Germany, Record Group (RG) 165, U.S. National Archives (NA).

12 Enclosure 'A', 'CCAC Problems of the Occupation of Germany', 21 Feb. 1944, RG 165, CAD 014 Germany, NA. Although printed under a CCAC heading, this was a COSSAC-prepared document.

13 *Handbook for Military Government for Germany,* sect. x, sect. xii and sect. viii; DCA 'Comments on SHAEF Handbook edition of 1 Sept., 1944', 25 Sept. 1944; War Office comments on SHAEF *Military Government Handbook for Germany* (4th draft), 12 Sept. 1944; FO notes on part i of SHAEF *Handbook for Military Government in Germany* – 5th edition, 20 Sept. 1944, all in FO 945/869, National Archives of the United Kingdom (NAUK).

14 Troutbeck to Peake, 29 Aug. 1944, FO 945/869, NAUK. For doubts about the *Handbook* in the British Government, see 'Conference between M/Gen. Hilldring & Col. Sherman', 28 Aug. 1944, CAD 014 Germany, RG 165, NA.

15 Zink, *The United States in Germany,* pp.151–52, 154; Zink, *American Military Government*

in Germany, pp.130–31; Niethammer, *Entnazifizierung in Bayern*, p.58; Griffiths, 'The Denazification Program', pp. 6–8, 10–16; and SHAEF G-5 'Annex IV: Section I – Political and General', 11 Aug. 1944, CAD 014 Germany, RG 165, NA.

16 Griffiths, 'The Denazification Program', pp.6, 12–13, 16.

17 Niethammer, *Entnazifizierung in Bayern*, pp.58–59; Zink, *The United States in Germany*, pp.151–52; and Karl Leebrick, SHAEF Special Staff – CA German Section Historical Subsection 'Monthly Report for April 1944', 30 April 1944, WO 219/3469, NAUK.

18 Barry Katz, *Foreign Intelligence: Research and Analysis in the Office of Strategic Services, 1942–45* (Cambridge, 1989), pp.29–41; Barry Katz, *Herbert Marcuse & the Art of Liberation* (London, 1982), pp.114–16; R. Harris Smith, *OSS: The Secret History of America's First Central Intelligence Agency* (Berkeley, 1972), p.217; and Bradley Smith, *The Shadow Warriors: O.S.S. and the Origins of the C.I.A.* (New York, 1983), pp.360–64.

19 OSS R&A Branch 'R&A No.1477: The Process of German Collapse', in *OSS/State Department Intelligence and Research Reports: Germany and Its Occupied Territories during World War II* (Washington, 1977), reel 11; Franz Neumann, *Behemoth: The Structure and Practice of National Socialism* (New York, 1963), pp.462–76; Klaus-Dietmar Henke, *Die amerikanische Besetzung Deutschlands* (Munich, 1995), pp.574–77; and Niethammer, *Entnazifizierung in Bayern*, pp.48–50.

20 Montgomery, *Forced to Be Free*, p.11; and Henke, *Die amerikanische Besetzung Deutschlands*, pp.631–34.

21 'Comments on Mr. Warburg's proposals re surrender and post-surrender policy toward Germany', 23 March 1944, CAD 014 Germany, RG 165, NA.

22 For Neumann's comments on Wilsonianism and the New Deal, see Franz Neumann, 'The Social Sciences', in *The Cultural Migration: The European Scholar in America* (New York, 1961), p.18. Neumann opposed the division or 'enslavement' of Germany and he also noted that his historicist and theoretical training had bred a skepticism about social engineering that he often did not encounter in Americans: 'To me, and to many others, the extraordinary optimism about the potentialities of social science to change the world cannot be shared. Our expectations are far more modest; the limits to social science presented by the historical process are far narrower'. *Ibid.*, p.24; and Neumann, *Behemoth*, p.475.

23 Niethammer, *Entnazifizierung in Bayern*, pp.50–51.

24 Henke, *Die amerikanische Besetzung Deutschlands*, pp.577–78; Griffiths, 'The Denazification Program', pp8–9; Bower, *The Pledge Betrayed*, pp.146–47; Tent, *Mission on the Rhine*, p.53; Smith, *The Road to Nuremberg*, p.17; Montgomery, *Forced to Be Free*, pp.21–22; Franz Neumann, *The Democratic and the Authoritarian State* (Glencoe, 1957), p.viii; Douglas Kellner, *Herbert Marcuse and the Crisis of Marxism* (Berekey, 1984), p.149; Niethammer, *Entnazifizierung in Bayern*, pp.55, 148; Katz, *Foreign Intelligence*, pp.35, 46–47; Katz, *Herbert Marcuse*, p.117; Donnison, *Civil Affairs and Military Government North-West Europe*, pp.363–64; and Plischke, 'Denazification in Germany', p.214. For German Masons escaping the denazification net, see excerpt from 'XV Corps Intelligence Bulletin', 31 July 1945, OB 28993, RG 226, NA.

25 FitzGibbon, *Denazification*, p.165; Bower, *The Pledge Betrayed*, p.146; Kurt Tauber, *Beyond Eagle and Swastika: German Nationalism since 1945* (Middletown, 1967), I, pp.28, 880; and Henke, *Politische Säuberung*, p.7.

26 Balfour, 'Four-Power Control in Germany', pp.52, 171–72; Griffiths, 'The Denazification Program', p.17; Marshall, *Origins of Post-War German Politics*, pp.48–49; and Youmans to Hiscock, 21 June 1944, CAD 014 Germany, RG 165, NA. For the size of the German civil service, see Garner, 'Public Service Personnel in West Germany in the 1950s', p.26.

27 To be fair to the R&A Germanists, Lutz Niethammer points out that they were not the only Germans who explored the idea of schematic denazification. The Kreisau

Circle, an anti-Hitler German resistance group, also developed plans for mandatory and discretionary arrest categories, which extended far down the administrative pyramid. Such planning was meant to facilitate purge operations by a prospective post-Nazi German government brought to power after the overthrow of Hitler. Niethammer, *Entnazifizierung in Bayern*, pp.77–79.

28 Katz, *Foreign Intelligence*, pp.41, 43.

29 *Foreign Relations of the United States: The Conference at Quebec, 1944 (FRUS: Quebec)* (Washington, 1972), p.72; and *FRUS: Malta and Yalta*, pp.182–83.

30 Alain Martineau, *Herbert Marcuse's Utopia* (Montreal, 1986), p.17; and Alastair MacIntyre, *Marcuse* (London, 1970), pp.67–69.

31 MacIntyre, *Marcuse*, pp.87–89; and Kellner, *Herbert Marcuse and the Crisis of Marxism*, pp.371–372, 374.

32 Katz, *Foreign Intelligence*, pp.45–47.

33 Felix Gilbert, *A European Past: Memoirs, 1905–1945* (New York, 1988), p.189; Niethammer, *Entnazifizierung in Bayern*, p.60; and Smith, *The Road to Nuremberg*, pp.16–17.

34 Troutbeck to Peake, 29 Aug. 1944; and FO notes on Part iii, SHAEF Handbook for Germany, 5th Edition, 19 Sept. 1944, both in FO 945/869, NAUK. For the final disposition of the list of 1800 key financial and industrial leaders, see Nixon to Bowie, 2 Jan. 1946, OMGUS – Office of the Adjutant General: General Correspondence (Decimal File) 1945–49, RG 260, NA.

35 Jones, 'Eradicating Nazism from the British Zone of Germany', p.154.

36 Barbo Eberan, *Luther? Friedrich 'der Grosse'? Wagner? Nietzsche? ...? ...? Wer war an Hitler schuld? Die Debatte um die Schuldfrage 1945–1949* (Munich, 1983), pp.32–34, 74–75, 177–81; FitzGibbon, *Denazification*, pp. 67–68, 97; and Claudia Koonz, *Mothers in the Fatherland* (New York, 1987), pp.xxxiv, 385.

37 Jones, 'Eradicating Nazism from the British Zone of Germany', pp.161–62.

38 Clemens Vollnhals, *Evangelische Kirche und Entnazifizierung 1945–1949* (Munich, 1989), p.36; and Balfour, 'Four-Power Control in Germany', p.61.

39 FitzGibbon, *Denazification*, pp.11, 26, 98.

40 Reinhold Niebuhr, 'The Germans and the Nazis', *The Nation* (4 April 1942), p.398.

41 For a discussion of 'German collective guilt' and the impact of this idea, see Friedmann, *The Allied Military Government of Germany*, pp.223–25, 230–31; Josef Foschepoth, 'German Reaction to Defeat and Occupation', in Robert Moeller, ed., *West Germany under Construction: Politics, Society and Culture in the Adenauer Era* (Ann Arbor, 1997), pp. 75–76; and Fürstenau, *Entnazifizierung*, pp.23–24, 25–26.

42 Fromm, *Deutschland in der öffentlichen Kriegszieldiskussion Gossbritanniens*, pp.134–35, 139–40; and Aaron Goldman, 'Germans and Nazis: The Controversy over "Vansittartism" in Britain during the Second World War', *The Journal of Contemporary History* 14 (1979), pp.165–66.

43 Henke, *Die amerikanische Besetzung Deutschlands*, pp.74–75.

44 Eberan, *Wer war an Hitler schuld?*, pp.30–32; Kurt Keppler, *Tod über Deutschland. Der Morgenthauplan. Vorgeschichte – Geschichte – Wesen – Hintergründe* (Tübingen, 1971), pp.29–35. For specific details, see Louis Nizer, *What to Do with Germany* (Chicago, 1944), chapter 1; and William Ziff, *The Gentlemen Talk of Peace* (New York, 1944), chapter 18.

45 D.D. Eisenhower, *At Ease: Stories I Tell to Friends* (London, 1967), p.311.

46 *FRUS: Cairo-Tehran*, pp.254–56.

47 Max Hastings, *Armageddon: The Battle for Germany, 1944–1945* (New York, 2004), pp.14–16; JIC 208/1 'German Plans for Underground Operations Following Surrender', 16 Aug. 1944, *Records of the Joint Chiefs of Staff, Part I – 1942–1945: European Theatre* (Frederick, 1981), reel 10; and 'Weekly Summary of Psychological Warfare' 25, 19 March 1945, FO 371/46894, NAUK.

48 SHAEF G-5 'Planning for Germany', 31 July 1944, WO 219/3488, NAUK.

49 Alfred Chandler and Louis Galambos, eds., *The Papers of Dwight David Eisenhower – The War Years* (Baltimore, 1978), iv, p.2107; and Ambrose, *Eisenhower the Soldier*, pp.331–332, 421–22.

50 Fred Smith, 'Rise and Fall of the Morgenthau Plan', *U.N. World* i (1947), 32; *New York Post*, 24 Nov. 1947); Dwight D. Eisenhower, *Crusade in Europe* (Garden City, 1949), p.287; and Bradley Smith, *The Road to Nuremburg* (London, 1981), p.21.

51 Niethammer, *Entnazifizierung in Bayern*, p.57; Kettenacker, *Krieg zur Friedenssicherung*, pp.336–37; Holmes to Hilldring, 21 Aug. 1944, included on CAD Historical Section analysis sheet, 10 Nov. 1944, WO 219/3761A, NAUK; and SCAF to AGWAR for CCS, 23 Aug. 1944, CAD 014 Germany, RG 165, NA. In March 1944, SHAEF requested the issue of a 'pre-surrender directive', which was then prepared by the U.S. War Department and took the eventual form of CCS 551. 'Problems of the Occupation of Germany', CCAC 25th Meeting, 9 March 1944; and CCAC 26th Meeting, 16 March 1944, both in CCAC 014 Germany, RG 218, NA.

52 Holmes to Hilldring, 11 Sept. 1944, CAD 014 Germany, RG 165, NA.

53 J.W. Pehle, 'Memorandum for the Files', 24 Aug. 1944, Office of the Secretary of the Treasury, Records of the Assistant Secretary John W. Pehle, Chronological Series, RG 56, NA; and *Foreign Relations of the United States, 1944* (Washington, 1965), p.839.

54 *Morgenthau Diary (Germany)*, p.424; and Smith, *The Road to Nuremberg*, p.21.

55 Beschloss, *The Conquerors*, p.73.

56 *New York Post*, 24 Nov. 1947; *The New York Times*, 14 Nov. 1953; and Smith, 'Rise and Fall of the Morgenthau Plan', 32.

57 *Morgenthau Diary (Germany)*, p.445.

58 Holmes to Hilldring, 11 Sept. 1944, CAD 014 Germany, RG 165, NA; and *Morgenthau Diary (Germany)*, p.453.

59 *Morgenthau Diary (Germany)*, p.484; and Smith, *The Road to Nuremberg*, pp.25–26.

60 Smith, *The Road to Nuremberg*, pp.26–27; Balfour, 'Four-Power Control in Germany', pp.19–20; Bower, *The Pledge Betrayed*, pp.124–25; and *FRUS: Quebec*, p.110.

61 Kimball, *Swords or Ploughshares?*, pp.3–4, 29–31, 37–41, 44, 47; John Chase, 'The Development of the Morgenthau Plan through the Quebec Conference', *The Journal of Politics* xvi (1954), 349–59; John Snell, *Wartime Origins of the East-West Dilemma over Germany* (New Orleans, 1959), p.89; Balfour, 'Four-Power Control in Germany', p.21; *FRUS: Cairo-Tehran*, p.884; *FRUS: Quebec*, pp.325, 327; and letter to the author from John McCloy, c.31 Oct. 1982.

62 *The Washington Post*, 21 Sept. 1944.

63 After the scandal over the Charlottesville school and the 'Darlan Deal', Marshall told Hilldring to protect the army against 'unjust accusations' and avoid further damage to the military's reputation. Hilldring regarded this mission as 'a sacred trust'. Forrest Pogue, *George C. Marshall: Organiser of Victory, 1943–1946* (New York, 1973), p.458. In 1944, Hilldring maintained that the greatest success of overseas military government officers was 'to crowd government agencies for policies and decisions', and he told Eisenhower's chief of staff, Walter Bedell Smith, that 'nothing is further from my mind than to cause you trouble or irritation, no matter how slight'. McCloy affirmed that 'we always try to lean over backwards' to meet Eisenhower's needs. Notes by USGCC historian, 21 Oct. 1944, WO 219/3652, NAUK; Peterson, *The American Occupation of Germany*, p.33; and *Morgenthau Diary (Germany)*, p.543. According to one of Hilldring's subordinates, the guideline provided by the general was 'to avoid orders to the occupation forces which would impede the wholly unnatural and undesirable task of military rule over civilians'. Letter to the author from Ernest Gross, 1 Nov. 1982.

64 Hilldring to Asst. CoS, G-2, 26 Aug. 1944, CAD 091.412, RG 165, NA. Both McCloy

and Hilldring impressed Treasury representatives as 'ready to do a tough job' and neither bothered to deny that GCU planners had planned to use military government for New Deal-style public works projects in Germany. *Morgenthau Diary (Germany)*, pp.424, 428.

65 Henry Stimson and McGeorge Bundy, *On Active Service in Peace and War* (London, 1949), pp.325–26; and letter to the author from John McCloy, *c*.31 Oct. 1982.

66 Niethammer, *Entnazifizierung in Bayern*, pp.34–36, 39, 40; and Smith, *The Road to Nuremberg*, pp.32–33.

67 Bower, *The Pledge Betrayed*, p.124; Kimball, *Swords or Ploughshares?*, pp.4, 5–6, 10, 22–23, 68–70; Balfour, 'Four-Power Control in Germany', pp.15, 17; Griffiths, 'The Denazification Program', pp.3–4; Niethammer, *Entnazifizierung in Bayern*, pp.54–55; and *FRUS: Quebec*, pp.49–53.

68 *Morgenthau Diary (Germany)*, p.500.

69 Draft telegram to the JSM in Washington, annex ii to note by the Secretariate, APW, 29 Aug. 1944, CAB 87/68, NAUK; 'Occupation Policy and Control of Germany (CCAC 122)', 15 Sept. 1944; Hilldring to SHAEF, 15 Sept. 1944, both in CAD 014 Germany, RG 165, NA; and CAD Historical Section analysis sheet, 10 Nov. 1944, WO 219/3716A, NAUK.

70 *Morgenthau Diary (Germany)*, pp.460–61, 464–67, 484, 492, 590, 610. It may or may not be germane that during this period, White was illegally providing intelligence to the Soviet secret service, and that he expressed himself 'ready for any self-sacrifice', although it is not clear that he was being ordered to influence policy in favour of Soviet objectives. The Soviet heavy industry commissariats, presumably, preferred to get access to German industrial assets rather than having them obliterated pell-mell. David Rees, *Harry Dexter White: A Study in Paradox* (New York, 1973), pp.212, 214; and http://www.nsa.gov:8080/ docs/v …aug44/04_aug_1944_r3-m3_p1.gif, as of 25 Feb. 1997.

71 *The Presidential Diaries of Henry Morgentha, Jr.: (1938-45)*, p.587.

72 *The Papers of Dwight D. Eisenhower*, iv, pp.2589–90; SHAEF G-4 to SHAEF G-5, 28 Dec. 1944; Eisenhower to Hilldring, 31 Dec. 1944; and McLean to SHAEF G-5 Supply and Economics Branch, 3 Feb. 1945, all in WO 219/3512, NAUK.

73 *Morgenthau Diary (Germany)*, pp.539, 543, 547, 558, 561, 564.

74 Donnison, *Civil Affairs and Military Government North-West Europe*, p.363; Turner, 'Denazification in the British Zone', p.246; *Morgenthau Diary (Germany)*, pp.535, 538, 540–41, 561, 567; AGWAR to SHAEF Main, 13 Sept. 1944; memorandum by DCA for consideration for the ACAO, 11 Sept. 1944; JSM Washington to AMSSO, 15 Sept. 1944; 16 Sept. 1944; minute sheet 124/Germany/44, 17 Sept. 1944, all in FO 945/869, NAUK; and 'Proposed Cable to the Supreme Commander, Allied Expeditionary Forces', CAD 014 Germany, RG 165, NA.

75 Donnison, *Civil Affairs and Military Government North-West Europe*, p.359; ECAD 'General Intelligence Bulletin' no.23, 2 Nov. 1944; Analysis Sheet, 6 Nov. 1944 (Holmes to Chief of Staff, 5–7 Sept. 1944), both in WO 219/3761A, NAUK; JSM Washington to AMSSO, 16 Sept. 1944; JSM Washington to War Office, 16 Sept. 1944, both in FO 945/869, NAUK; OSS R&A 'European Political Report', 20 Oct. 1944, WO 219/3761A, NAUK; and Thompson to Doob, 18 Sept. 1944, CAD 014 Germany, RG 165, NA.

76 Arthur Kahn, *Experiment in Occupation: Witness to the Turnabout, Anti-Nazi War to Cold War, 1944–1946* (University Park, 2004), p.14.

77 SHAEF Directive for Military Government of Germany prior to Defeat or Surrender, WO 219/1634, NAUK; and Grasset to CoS, SHAEF, WO 219/3498, NAUK.

78 Henke, *Die amerikanische Besetzung Deutschlands*, p.635; and Kahn, *Experiment in Occupation*, pp.14, 18–19.

79 Barbara Marshall, 'The Democratisation of Local Politics in the British Zone of Germany: Hanover 1945-47', *Journal of Contemporary History* 21 (1986), p.436; and

Balfour, 'Four-Power Control of Germany', pp.61–62.

80 Stimson and Bundy, *On Active Service in Peace and War*, p.327; *FRUS: Quebec*, p.90; and
    FRUS: Malta-Yalta, p.160.

81 *FRUS: Quebec*, p.91.

82 *Ibid.*, pp.52, 69, 77, 83–84, 88, 106–07, 112–13, 140; *Foreign Relations of the United States,
    1944 (FRUS, 1945)* (Washington, 1966), i, pp.108, 220–221, 305, 336; Griffiths, 'The
    Denazification Program', pp.31; and White to Hilldring, 13 June 1944, CAD 014
    Germany, RG 165, NA.

83 *Morgenthau Diary (Germany)*, p.564.

84 Kellner, *Herbert Marcuse and the Crisis of Marxism*, pp.149–50; and Gilbert, *A European Past*,
    p.189.

85 *FRUS: Quebec*, pp.69, 109; *FRUS: Malta-Yalta*, p.182; and *FRUS, 1944*, i, pp.322, 325.

86 *Morgenthau Diary (Germany)*, pp.567–68.

87 Kimball, *Swords or Ploughshares?*, pp.42–44, 45, 54; Snell, *Wartime Origins of the East-West
    Dilemma over Germany*, pp.177, 180–81; Hammond, 'Directives for the Occupation of
    Germany', p.375; John Backer, *Priming the German Economy* (Durham, 1971), pp.22–30,
    36–38, 58–59, 83, 127, 198–99, 201; Balfour, 'Four-Power Control in Germany', p.21;
    FRUS: Malta-Yalta, pp.155, 158–59, 175–76; *FRUS, 1944*, i, p.358; and letter to the author
    from John McCloy, c.31 Oct. 1982. For language in CCS 551 that proposed aid to the
    German people 'to the minimum extent necessary to prevent disease and unrest', see
    'Appendix 'D' to CCAC 69/5: Economic and Relief Guide for Germany', CCAC 014
    Germany, RG 218, NA.

88 Walter Dorn, 'the Debate over American Occupation Policy in Germany in 1944–1945',
    Political Science Quarterly 72, no.4 (Dec. 1957), pp.491–500; *FRUS: Malta-Yalta*, pp.145–47,
    156, 162; *FRUS, 1944*, i, pp.344, 420; *Foreign Relations of the United States, 1945 (FRUS,
    1945)* (Washington, 1968), iii, pp.375, 381–83, 413, 432; Hull to Stimson, 23 Sept. 1944;
    Col. William Chanler 'Directive to SCAEF for the administration of post-defeat
    military government in Germany', 28 Sept. 1944, both in CAD 014 Germany, RG
    165, NA; and letter to the author from John McCloy, c.31 Oct. 1982. In late September
    1944, McCloy informally provided an initial draft of JCS 1067 to SHAEF. Since it
    allowed the option of ignoring the German economy, SHAEF officers were delighted.
    Eisenhower's chief of staff, Walter Bedell Smith, called it 'the most encouraging and
    helpful document that we have seen in a long time...' SHAEF to War Dept., 27 Sept.
    1944, CAD 014 Germany, RG 165, NA.

89 James Byrnes, *Speaking Frankly* (New York, 1947), pp. 186–87; Kimball, *Swords or
    Ploughshares?*, p.55; Niethammer, *Entnazifizierung in Bayern*, pp.65–67; Fürstenau,
    Entnazifizierung, pp.24–29; Balfour, 'Four-Power Control in Germany', p.173; *FRUS,
    1944* i, p.420; *FRUS, 1945*, i, pp.373–74, 433, 435, 437, 451, 457, 459, 460, 464, 467, 469,
    471–72, 487–89; and von Oppen, *Documents on Germany under Occupation*, p.17.

90 *FRUS: Malta-Yalta*, p.970; Fürstenau, *Entnazifizierung*, pp.20–22; Krüger, *Entnazifiziert!*,
    p.20; Griffiths, 'The Denazification Program', pp.52, 56; and *Zwischen Befreiung und
    Besatzung* (Wuppertal, 1976), pp.181–82.

91 *FRUS: Potsdam*, ii, pp.73–74, 284, 751, 776, 784–86, 1482, 1502–03; Balfour, 'Four-Power
    Control in Germany', p.177; Krüger, *Entnazifiziert!*, pp.27–28; Möhler, *Entnazifizierung
    in Rheinland-Pfalz und im Saarland*, pp.86–87; Friedmann, *Allied Military Government*,
    p.111; Fürstenau, *Entnazifizierung*, pp.45–47; and Byrnes, *Speaking Frankly*, p.187.

92 *FRUS, 1945*, iii, p. 979.

93 Turner, 'Denazification in the British Zone', p.251–52, 254–55; Niethammer,
    Entnazifizierung in Bayern, pp.298–99; Willis, *The French in Germany*, p.156; von Oppen
    ed., *Documents on Germany under Occupation*, pp.102–107, 168–79; Latour and Vogelsang,
    Okkupation und Wiederaufbau, p.137; Friedmann, *Allied Military Government*, pp.51–52,

112, 115–17; Griffiths, 'The Denazification Program', pp.129–30, 148, 176–77, 317; Möhler, *Entnazifizierung in Rheinland-Pfalz und im Saarland*, pp.87–88, 90–92, 238–44; Krüger, *Entnazifiziert!*, pp.28–31; Balfour, 'Four-Power Control in Germany', p.177; Montgomery, *Forced to Be Free*, pp.25–26; Fürstenau, *Entnazifizierung*, pp.47–48, 104; FitzGibbon, *Denazification*, pp.108–113, 130; Vogt, *Denazification in Soviet-Occupied Germany*, pp.82–83; Plischke, 'Denazification in Germany', p.223; Donnison, *Civil Affairs and Military Government North-West Europe*, pp.361, 364–65; Gimbel, *The American Occupation of Germany*, p.104; 'Appendix 'A' to SCD/P (46) 53 dated 18 September 1946—Interpretation of Paragraphs 5 and 8(b) of Control Council Directive No.24', WO 311/634, NAUK; and Berlin (Military Governor) to FO, 4 July 1947, FO 371/64744, NAUK.

94 Jones, 'Eradicating Nazism from the British Zone of Germany', pp.161–62. One of General Clay's advisors, Henry Parkman, made a similar point: the Allies, he claimed, had never distinguished the idea of punishment from a wider political strategy designed to remove Nazis in order to allow the growth of democracy. OMGUS IA&C Division 'Plan for Resumption of Military Government Responsibility for Denazification', 2 Dec. 1946, OMGUS – Records of the CAD, Public Safety Branch: Law for Liberation from National Socialism and Militarism, 1945–49, RG 260, NA.

95 Alasdair MacIntyre, *Marcuse* (London, 1970), pp.21–22, 59, 61, 87–88, 91–92; Alain Martineau, *Herbert Marcuse's Utopia* (Montreal, 1986); and Douglas Kellner, *Herbert Marcuse and the Crisis of Marxism* (Berkeley, 1984), 371–72, 374.

96 Balfour, 'The Four-Power Control of Germany', p.26.

Chapter 2: From Idea to Reality

1 *FRUS: Potsdam*, ii, p.762; Zink, *American Military Government in Germany*, pp.137–38; Zink, *The United States in Germany*, p.157; Bower, *The Pledge Betrayed*, p.128; and Tent, *Mission on the Rhine*, p.53.

2 *The New York Times*, 2 Oct. 1944; 5 Oct. 1944; and Morgenthau to Stimson, 6 Oct. 1944, CAD 014 Germany, RG 165, NA. Stimson responded by saying that he realised 'the necessity of eternal vigilance'. He also promised to forward Morgenthau's letter to the appropriate authorities. Stimson to Morgenthau, 9 Oct. 1944, CAD 014 Germany, RG 165, NA.

3 Zink, *American Military Government in Germany*, pp.133–35; Griffiths, 'The Denazification Program', pp.38–41; Irmgard Lange, ed., *Entnazifizierung in Nordrhein-Westfalen. Richtlinien, Anweisungen, Organisation* (Seiburg, 1976), pp.13, 20–21; Saul Padover, *Experiment in Germany: The Experience of an Intelligence Officer* (New York, 1946), pp.31– 48, 53, 55, 78–79, 80, 87, 99–100, 120–24, 157–63, 173–74, 184, 218, 220, 221, 222–260; Padover, Gittler and Sweet, 'The Political Situation in Aachen', pp.434–456; FitzGibbon, *Denazification*, pp.87–91; Kahn, *Experiment in Occupation*, p.36; Bower, *The Pledge Betrayed*, pp.125–26; Henke, *Die amerikanische Besetzung Deutschlands*, pp.259–61, 262–63, 268–69, 276–85; Fürstenau, *Entnazifizierung*, pp.35–36; and Vollnhals, *Evangelische Kirche und Entnazifizierung*, pp.9, 10–11.

4 Henke, *Die amerikanische Besetzung Deutschlands*, pp.284, 285–86, 288–95; Niethammer, *Entnazifizierung in Bayern*, pp.65, 151; Turner, 'Denazification in the British Zone', p. 246; Bower, *The Pledge Betrayed*, p.128–29; Latour and Vogelsang, *Okkupation und Wiederaufbau*, p.133; Zink, *American Military Government in Germany*, p.145; Clemens Vollnhals, ed., *Entnazifizierung. Politische Säuberung und Rehabilitierung in den vier Besatzungszone 1945–1949* (Munich, 1991), pp.121–22; Vollnhals, *Evangelische Kirche*

und Entnazifizierung, pp.10–11; Tent, *Mission on the Rhine*, pp.50, 326; Griffiths, 'The Denazification Program', pp.42–46, 47, 61; Balfour, 'Four-Power Control in Germany', pp.183, 256–57; *FRUS*, 1945, iii, pp.932–33; Hilldring to McSherry, 4 Feb. 1945; Grassett to Bedell-Smith; SHAEF to army groups, 23 Feb. 1945; Heyman to various SHAEF agencies, 23 Feb. 1945; Byard to G-5 Legal Branch, 10 March 1945; Newman to army groups, 24 March 1945; Tarr to Patch and de Lattre de Tassigny, 30 March 1945, all in WO 219/3498, NAUK; Horton to Martin, 21 Feb. 1945; Sheen to AcoS. 12th AG, 1 March 1945, both in WO 219/1648A, NAUK; and 9th U.S. Army 'Inclosure 2, to Annex No.4, to Letter of Instructions Number Twenty One', 21 April 1945. Padover was willing to accept that AMG detachments lacked political direction and that they had been issued confusing directives. In the absence of 'a clear policy', he warned, 'MG will continue to flounder in a mess of contradictions, and MG officers will improvise policies according to their temperament, convictions and personal prejudices.' Padover, *Experiment in Germany*, p.251.

5 Padover, *Experiment in Germany*, pp.282, 318–26, 331–32; Henke, *Die amerikanische Besetzung Deutschlands*, pp.287, 295, 367, 376; Henke, *Politische Säuberung*, p.22; Raymond Ebsworth, *Restoring Democracy in Germany: The British Contribution* (London, 1960), pp.8–9; and Tent, *Mission on the Rhine*, p.52. For Svoboda's eventual promotion, see John Maginnis, *Military Government Journal: Normandy to Berlin* (Amherst, 1971), pp.340, 343, 344.

6 Niethammer, *Entnazifizierung in Bayern*, pp.231–32.

7 Maginnis, *Military Government Journal*, p.242. James Tent notes that whenever the press became quiescent, AMG officers interpreted denazification orders in a less draconian fashion. Tent, *Mission on the Rhine*, pp.50–51.

8 Henke, *Die amerikanische Besetzung Deutschlands*, pp.365, 367–75; Helmuth Pütz, ed., *Konrad Adenauer und die CDU der britischen Besatzungszone 1946–1949* (Bonn, 1975), pp.4–5; Henning Köhler, *Adenauer. Eine politische Biographie* (Berlin, 1994), pp.323–25, 330–32, 340, 342–73; Konrad Adenauer, *Erinnerungen 1945–1953* (Stuttgart, 1965), i, pp.19–23, 27–29, 34–37; Charles Williams, *Adenauer* (New York, 2000), pp.288–90, 293–95, 296–05; and Balfour, 'Four-Power Control in Germany', p.175.

9 Henke, *Die amerikanische Besetzung Deutschlands*, pp.695–96, 698–701; and Bradley to Eisenhower, 3 April 1945, WO 219/2587, NAUK.

10 Edward Peterson, *Russian Commands and German Resistance: The Soviet Occupation, 1945–1949* (New York, 1999), pp.145–46, 171, 307–09, 333–34, 336, 380.

11 Kehm to AcoS, SHAEF G-2, 28 May 1945, WO 219/1651, NAUK.

12 SHAEF G-5 Minutes of the 3rd Military Government Conference, 12 April 1945, WO 219/3499, NAUK.

13 HQ 6th AG MG Circular no.1, 2 May 1945, WO 219/3498, NAUK; Griffiths, 'The Denazification Program', p.46; and Henke, *Politische Säuberung*, pp.22–23.

14 Niethammer, *Entnazifizierung in Bayern*, pp.138–43; and Henke, *Die amerikanische Besetzung Deutschlands*, pp.365–67.

15 Kahn, *Experiment in Occupation*, pp.42–44, 46, 47, 57–58, 66, 191.

16 *Ibid.*, p. 139; Niethammer, *Entnazifizierung in Bayern*, pp.131–34, 181; *Die Neue Zeitung*, 8 Nov. 1945; and 'Consolidation of OMGUS Denazification Field Inspector's Reports Received since 1 November 1946', OMGUS – Office of the Adjutant General: General Correspondence (Decimal File) 1945–49, RG 260, NA.

17 Kahn, *Experiment in Occupation*, pp.59–60, 62–63, 64, 66–67, 80, 84, 86, 87, 108, 115, 118, 123, 124, 125, 142, 144, 149; W. Dettelbacher, *Würzburg. Ein Gang durch seine Vergangenheit* (Würzburg, 1974), p.181; Niethammer, *Entnazifiziering in Bayern*, pp.166–67, 175, 181, 231; *Zwischen Befreiung und Besatzung*, pp.151–52; Percy Knauth, 'The German People', *Life* xviii, no.19 (7 May 1945), pp.74, 76; *The New York Times*, 30 Sept. 1945; *The Stars and Stripes*, 1 Oct. 1945; and *Deutsche Volkszeitung*, 27 March 1946.

18 Kahn, *Experiment in Occupation*, pp.81–90, 107–09, 201, 203–04; Niethammer, *Entnazifizierung in Bayern*, pp.123–25, 160–65, 170–71, 173–198; Griffiths, 'The Denazification Program', pp.73–81, 85; Tent, *Mission on the Rhine*, p.51; Ladislas Farago, *The Last Days of Patton* (New York, 1981), pp.75–78, 143–44, 213; Bower, *The Pledge Betrayed*, pp.135–36, 143; Volnhals, *Evangelische Kirche und Entnazifizierung*, p.136; Vollnhals, ed., *Entnazifizierung*, p.150; *FRUS, 1945*, iii, pp.945–49, 952, 973, 983–85; and MGB Office of the Director 'Fritz Schäffer', 28 March 1946, OMGUS – Office of the Adjutant General: General Correspondence (Decimal File) 1945–49, RG 260, NA.

19 Niethammer, *Entnazifizierung in Bayern*, pp.231–36; Griffiths, 'The Denazification Program', pp.81–93; Farago, *The Last Days of Patton*, pp.68, 89, 97–98, 100–01, 134–37, 141–42, 143, 146–47, 156, 163–65, 174, 175–194, 197–200, 202–217; Bower, *The Pledge Betrayed*, pp.136–37; FitzGibbon, *Denazification*, pp.91–94; Ambrose, *Eisenhower the Soldier*, pp.423–424; Davidson, *The Death and Life of Germany*, p.77; Kahn, *Experiment in Occupation*, pp.110–12; *FRUS, 1945*, iii, pp.971–73; Patton Diary, entries for 22 and 31 August, *Papers Relating to the Allied High Command, 1943/45* (East Ardsley, Wakefield, 1983), reel 4; Garde, Adcock, Dorn to Clay, 14 April 1946, OMGUS – Office of the Adjutant General: General Correspondence (Decimal File) 1945–49, RG 260, NA.

20 Eberan, *Wer war an Hitler schuld?*, p.22; Bower, *The Pledge Betrayed*, p.139; Griffiths, 'The Denazification Program', p.81; FitzGibbon, *Denazification*, pp.12, 95–96; Kahn, *Experiment in Occupation*, pp.80, 144, 212; and Farago, *Last Days of Patton*, p.5. When Clay was first posted as chief of AMG, his appointment was 'generally interpreted as a victory for the partisans of a firm policy regarding Germany'. 'French Ambassador, Washington, Comments on Appointment of General Clay', 13 April 1945, HW 12/313, NAUK.

21 Niethammer, *Entnazifizierung in Bayern*, pp.147–56, 195; Fürstenau, *Entnazifizierung*, p.39; Gimbel, *The American Occupation of Germany*, p.101; Frank Horvay, 'Military Government and Denazification in Ansbach, 1945–1946', in Michael Ermarth, ed., *America and the Shaping of German Society, 1945–1955* (Oxford, 1993), pp.169–70; Griffiths, 'The Denazification Program', pp.49–50, 57–63; Latour and Vogelsang, *Okkupation und Wiederaufbau*, pp.134–35; Henke, *Die amerikanische Besetzung Deutschlands*, p.254; Henke, *Politische Säuberung*, pp.27–30; Kahn, *Experiment in Occupation*, p.199; Tent, *Mission on the Rhine*, pp.51–52; Hans Woller, *Gesellschaft und Politik in der amerikanischen Besatzungszone. Die Region Ansbach und Fürth* (Munich, 1986), p.95; Vollnhals, *Evangelische Kirche und Entnazifizierung*, pp.46–47; George Dyer, *XII Corps: Spearhead of Patton's Third Army* (Baton Rouge, 1947), p.461; *The Stars and Stripes*, 1 Oct. 1945; E. Wendt 'Report on a Trip to Mannheim on July 23rd to Determine Nature and Extent of the Denazification Program', 31 July 1945, State Dept. Decimal File 1945–49, 740.00119 Control (Germany), RG 59, NA; Wilson to Smith, 10 Dec. 1945; Clay to Hilldring, 8 Dec. 1945, both in OMGUS – Records of the CAD, Public Safety Branch: Law for Liberation from National Socialism and Militarism, 1945–49, RG 260, NA; and SHAEF G-5 to G-2 (Counter Intelligence), 11 July 1945, WO 219/3501, NAUK.

22 Lutz Niethammer, 'Alliierte Internierungslager in Deutschland nach 1945: Ein Vergleich und offene Fragen', in Peter Reif-Spirek and Bodo Ritscher, eds., *Speziallager in der SBZ. Gedenkstätten mit 'doppelter Vergangenheit'* (Berlin, 1999), p.104; Lange, ed., *Entnazifizierung in Nordrhein-Westfalen*, p.12; and Niethammer, *Entnazifizierung in Bayern*, pp.255–59. AMG interned one of every 142 inhabitants in the U.S. zone. In the Russian zone the ratio was one to every 144 persons; in the French zone it was one to 263; and in the British zone it was one to 284.

23 Maginnis, *Military Government Journal*, p.345; *The Stars and Stripes*, 6 Aug. 1945; 7 Nov. 1945; and USFET G-2 'Weekly Intelligence Summary' no.26, 1 Jan. 1946, State Dept. Decimal File 1945–49, 740.00119 Control (Germany), RG 59, NA.

24 Tent, *Mission on the Rhine*, pp.51, 54, 56.

25 Fürstenau, *Entnazifizierung*, pp.39–41; Griffiths, 'The Denazification Program', pp.82–3,
94–108; Latour and Vogelsang, *Okkupation und Wiederaufbau*, pp.135–36; Vollnhals,
Evangelische Kirche und Entnazifizierung, pp.47–48; Ziemke, 'U.S. Occupation Policy
in Europe', p.34; Vollnhals, ed., *Entnazifizierung*, pp.100–05; *Zwischen Befreiung und
Besatzung*, p.180; Beschloss, *The Conquerors*, p.273; Niethammer, *Entnazifizierung in
Bayern*, pp.157–58, 240–44; Bower, *The Pledge Betrayed*, pp.148–49; Davidson, *The Death
and Life of Germany*, p.130; Montgomery, *Forced to Be Free*,
pp.101–02; Tent, *Mission on the Rhine*, p.56; Zink, *American Military Government in
Germany*, p.140; Plischke, 'Denazification in Germany', p.215; *FRUS*, 1945, iii, pp.993–94;
Stars and Stripes, 7 Nov. 1945; USFET G-2 'Weekly Intelligence Summary' no.14, 18
Oct. 1945; no.16, 1 Nov. 1945; and no.19, 21 Nov. 1945, all in State Dept. Decimal Files
1945–49, 740.00119 Control (Germany), RG 59, NA.

26 Latour and Vogelsang, *Okkupation und Wiederaufbau*, p.136; Griffiths, 'The Denazification
Program', pp. 67–69, 112–114; Bower, *The Pledge Betrayed*, p.135; Montgomery, *Forced to
Be Free*, pp.101–02; *FRUS*, 1945, iii, pp.975–76, 978–79, 988, 1002–03; Whipple to Chief,
17 Oct. 1945; CoS OMGUS to Lee, 19 Oct. 1945; Whipple to Hughes and Wilson, 3
Nov. 1945; CoS OMGUS to Director, OMGUS, 3 Nov. 1945; USFET 'Removal of
Nazis and Militarists in the German Reichspost', 20 Nov. 1945; and USFET 'Removal
of Nazis and Militarists in the German Reichsbahn and Other Fields of Transport', 26
Nov. 1945, all in OMGUS – Office of the Adjutant General: General Correspondence
(Decimal File) 1945–49, RG 260, NA.

27 Zink, *The United States in Germany*, pp.158–60; Zink, *American Military Government in
Germany*, pp.141, 143, 145; Balfour, 'Four-Power Control in Germany', pp.104, 175–76,
178; Niethammer, *Entnazifizierung in Bayern*, p.248; Griffiths, 'The Denazification
Program', pp.141–42; Fürstenau, *Entnazifizierung*, p.38; Peterson, *The American Occupation
of Germany*, p.90; Friedmann, *Allied Military Government*, p.114; Bower, *The Pledge
Betrayed*, p.151; Horvay, 'Military Government and Denazification in Ansbach', p.170;
George Clare, *Berlin Days* (London, 1989), p.112; Davidson, *The Death and Life of
Germany*, p.127; FitzGibbon, *Denazification*, p.140; Tent, *Mission on the Rhine*, pp.53–54;
Latour and Vogelsang, *Okkupation und Wiederaufbau*, pp.134–35; *The New York Times*, 13
Oct. 1945; 21 Oct. 1945; and OMGUS Public Safety Branch 'Denazification Report',
31 Dec. 1945, OMGUS – Office of the Adjutant General: General Correspondence
(Decimal File) 1945–49, RG 260, NA.

28 Maginnis, *Military Government Journal*, p.315.

29 Friedmann, *Allied Military Government*, pp.117–18; Griffiths, 'The Denazification Program',
pp.142–53, 160–88, 308–09, 311 112, 314, 320, 322; Niethammer, *Entnazifizierung in
Bayern*, pp.60, 260–332, 341–42, 350, 351–52, 354–55, 437–41; Tauber, *Beyond Eagle and
Swastika*, I, pp.29–31, 32; Zink, *American Military Government in Germany*, pp.143–44;
Zink, *The United States in Germany*, pp.160–62; Bower, *The Pledge Betrayed*, pp.149,
151–53, 162–63; FitzGibbon, *Denazification*, pp.130–32, 140, 179; Latour and Vogelsang,
Okkupation und Wiederaufbau, pp.134, 136–39, 141, 142; *Zwischen Befreiung und Besatzung*,
pp.179–81; Fürstenau, *Entnazifizierung*, pp.54–69, 83; Davidson, *The Death and Life of
Germany*, p.130; Balfour, 'Four-Power Control in Germany', pp.177–78; Tent, *Mission on
the Rhine*, pp.83, 98–99; Gimbel, *The American Occupation of Germany*, pp.36–37, 102–06;
Vollnhals, ed., *Entnazifizierung*, pp.262–72; Plischke, 'Denazification in Germany', p.218;
FRUS, 1945, iii, p.1032; *Foreign Relations of the United States, 1946* (Washington, 1969)
(*FRUS*, 1946), v, pp.667–71; *The Stars and Stripes*, 8 July 1945; 'Monthly Report of the
Military Governor, U.S. Zone – No.6: Denazification and Public Safety', 20 Jan. 1946,
FO 371/55659, NAUK; SHAEF G-5 to G-2 (Counter Intelligence), 11 July 1945, WO
219/3501, NAUK; ACC Coordinating Committee 'Report to the Council of Foreign

Ministers', Section ii – Denazification, 21 Feb. 1947, FO 371/64352, NAUK; Hilldring
to Smith, 2 April 1945, CAD 014 Germany, RG 165, NA; Clay to Echols, 15 Dec. 1946;
Parkmann to Legal Division, 14 Jan. 1947, both in OMGUS – Records of the CAD,
Public Safety Branch: Law for Liberation from National Socialism and Militarism, 1945–
49, RG 260, NA; Meade to CoS, 19 Oct. 1945; Robinson to Fahy, 3 Jan. 1946; OMGUS
'Report of the Denazification Policy Board', 15 Jan. 1946; Pollock to Clay, 15 Feb. 1946;
23 Feb. 1946; Clay to Minister Presidents of Bavaria, Wuerttemberg-Baden, Greater
Hesse, 5 March 1946; OMGUS Special Branch – Public Safety 'Explanation of German
Denazification Law Charts', 2 April 1946; 'Progress Report no.3 on Carrying Out the
Denazification Law', 8 May 1946; Sewall to CoS, 15 Aug. 1946; Clay to Commanding
General, USFET, 26 Dec. 1946, all in OMGUS – Office of the Adjutant General:
General Correspondence (Decimal File), 1945–49, RG 260, NA; USGCC/G Acting
Director to CG. ASF, 27 July 1945; USGCC/G to WD (G-2), 1 Aug. 1945, both in CAD
334, RG 165, NA; and USFET G-2 'Weekly Intelligence Summary' no.18, 15 Nov. 1945,
State Dept. Decimal File 1945–49, 740.00119 Control (Germany), RG 59, NA.

30 *PM*, 3 July 1946.

31 Clay to Clark, 8 Aug. 1946, OMGUS – Office of the Adjutant General: General
Correspondence (Decimal File) 1945–49, RG 260, NA.

32 Tent, *Mission on the Rhine*, pp.61–68, 74–76, 79–102, 104–106, 277–78; Vollnhals,
Evangelische Kirche und Entnazifizierung, pp.123, 170–79; Vollnhals, ed., *Entnazifizierung*,
pp.155–56; James Tent, 'Edward Y. Hartshorne and the Reopening of German
Universities, 1945–1946: His Personal Account', *Pedagogica Historica* xxxiii, no.1 (1997),
pp.85, 190–91, 194, 197–99; Geoffrey Giles, 'Re-education at Heidelberg University',
Pedagogica Historica xxxiii, no.1, (1997), pp.205–06, 208,213–14; Bower, *The Pledge
Betrayed*, pp. 165–66; Kahn, *Experiment in Occupation*, pp.153, 207–08; *The New York Times*,
18 Feb. 1946; 22 April 1946; 23 April 1946; *Die Neue Zeitung*, 15 Dec. 1945; 1 Feb. 1946;
18 Feb. 1946; 26 Feb. 1946; 8 March 1946; 22 March 1946; 1 April 1946; 27 May 1946;
USFET 'Weekly Intelligence Summary' no.31, 14 Feb. 1946; no.45, 24 May 1946; no.56,
8 Aug. 1946; OMGUS Public Relations Office press release, 13 Nov. 1946, all in State
Dept. Decimal File 1945–49, 740.00119 Control (Germany), RG 59, NA; ADMG to
Public Safety Branch, 28 May 1946; Adcock to Sibert, 14 June 1946; ADMG to IA&C
Division, 27 June 1946; OMGUS Office of Military Governor 'Disciplinary Measures
against Managing and Administrative Staffs of Educational Institutions, Teaching Staff
and Students Guilty of Militarist, Nazi or Anti-Democratic Propaganda', 16 July 1946;
'DANA Report', 17 July 1946; 'Topical Commentary by Herbert Gassner', 18 July 1946;
OMGUS CAD, Policy Enforcement Branch 'Denazification of Institutions of Higher
Learning', 10 Oct. 1946; OMGUS CAD Policy Enforcement Branch 'Denazification of
University of Munich', 15 Nov. 1946; 'Denazification of Heidelberg University', 15 Nov.
1946; CAD to PE Branch, 6 Dec. 1946; and CAD to PE Branch, 11 Dec. 1946 'Report
on Denazification of Erlangen University', all in OMGUS – Office of the Adjutant
General: General Correspondence (Decimal File) 1945–49, RG 260, NA.

33 Tent, 'Edward Y. Hartshorne', pp.198–99; USFET 'Weekly Intelligence Summary' no.63,
26 Sept. 1945, State Dept. Decimal File 1945–49, 740.00119 Control (Germany), RG
59, NA; party membership card – Johann Detterbeck, Berlin Document Center files,
Bundesarchiv (BA); *The New York Times*, 1 Sept. 1946; 6 Sept. 1946; *The Washington Post*,
pp.4 Sept. 1946; 5 Sept. 1946; *Die Neue Zeitung*, 2 Sept. 1946; and 9 Sept. 1946.

34 Gailey to Director, CAD, Sept. 1946, OMGUS – Office of the Adjutant General: General
Correspondence (Decimal File) 1945–49, RG 260, NA.

35 Niethammer, *Entnazifizierung in Bayern*, pp.335–39, 354–86, 388–89, 407–30, 567–617;
Griffiths, 'The Denazification Program', pp.187–95, 238–9, 245, 256, 260, 266, 305,
307, 310, 316, 317–19, 320, 321, 322–330, 332–33, 334–5, 337–47, 353–55; Zink, *The*

United States in Germany, pp.162–63; Zink, *American Military Government in Germany*, p.143; Vollnhals, ed., *Entnazifizierung*, pp.281–84; Fürstenau, *Entnazifizierung*, pp.70–85, 100–01, 164–65, 174–77, 194–96; FitzGibbon, *Denazification*, pp.165–66, 179; Latour and Vogelsang, *Okkupation und Wiederaufbau*, pp.139–42; Gimbel, *The American Occupation of Germany*, pp.105–10, 159; Friedmann, *Allied Military Government*, pp.119–20; Montgomery, *Forced to Be Free*, pp.23, 63–64, 193–94; Bower, *The Pledge Betrayed*, pp.153–54, 163–65; Tent, *Mission on the Rhine*, pp.95, 98; Balfour, 'Four-Power Control in Germany', pp.178–79; Kahn, *Experiment in Occupation*, p.173; *FRUS*, 1946, v, p.696; *Frankfurter Rundschau*, 11 March 1947; *Stars and Stripes* Weekend Supplement, 23 Feb. 1947; *Die Neue Zeitung*, 5 July 1946; OMGUS Public Safety Branch 'Observer's Report: First Proceeding under the Law for Liberation from National Socialism and Militarism', 21 May 1946; 'Consolidation of Findings by OMGUS Field Interrogators for Week 10 to 17 August 1946'; 'Consolidation of Findings by OMGUS Field Inspectors for Week 17 to 24 August 1946'; 'Consolidation of OMGUS Denazification Field Inspector's Reports Received since 1 November 1946', all in OMGUS – Office of the Adjutant General: General Correspondence (Decimal File), 1945–49, RG 260, NA; 'Progress Report no.3 on Carrying Out the Denazification Law', 8 May 1946; Koenig to Clay, 26 July 1946; OMGB 'Completion of German Denazification', 22 Aug. 1946; OMGUS Office of the Military Governor 'Correction of Denazification Defeciencies', 27 Aug. 1946; Public Safety Branch, IA&C Division to ADMG, 24 Oct. 1946; Reese to Hoegner, 24 Oct. 1946; Regional Govt. Coordinating Office 'Speech of Lt. General Lucius Clay Delivered at the Fourteenth Meeting of the Laenderrat', 5 Nov. 1946; OMGUS Office of Military the Governor 'Resumption of Denazification Responsibility by the Military Governor', Dec. 1946; OMGUS IA&C Division 'Plan for resumption of Military Government responsibility for Denazification', 2 Dec. 1946; 22 Jan. 1947; 'Non-Concurrence of Chief, Denazification Section, Public Safety Branch, IA&C Division'; ICD Report no.55 'Public Attitudes toward Denazification', 15 April 1947, all in OMGUS – Records of the CAD, Public Safety Branch: Law for Liberation from National Socialism and Militarism, 1945–49, RG 260, NA; and USFET G-2 'Weekly Intelligence Summary' no.69, 7 No.1946, State Dept. Decimal Files 1945–49, 740,00119 Control (Germany), RG 59, NA.

36 Montgomery, *Forced to Be Free*, pp.104–05, 114–15; Gimbel, *The American Occupation of Germany*, pp.171–72; and Niethammer, *Entnazifizierung in Bayern*, p.546.

37 Niethammer, *Entnazifizierung in Bayern*, pp.12-13, 25, 193, 244, 272–79, 617–25.

38 *FRUS*, 1946, v, pp.517–20; and vi, pp.696–709.

39 V.M. Molotov, *Problems of Foreign Policy* (Moscow, 1949), pp.352–53; *Foreign Relations of the United States, 1947* (*FRUS,* 1947) (Washington,), ii, pp.249–51, 403, 427–28, 462; Vogt, *Denazification in Soviet-Occupied Germany*, p.95; Gimbel, *The American Occupation of Germany*, pp.98–100, 116–21, 123–24, 126–28, 150–51, 158, 163–69; John Backer, *The Decision to Divide Germany: American Foreign Policy in Transition* (Durham, 1978), pp.166–67; *Foreign Relations of the United States, 1947* (*FRUS,* 1947) (Washington, 1972), ii, pp.249–51, 403, 427–28, 462; and Vogt, *Denazification in Soviet-Occupied Germany*, p.95.

40 'Barbie's Recruitment and Use by the U.S. Army, 1947–1950', in Allan Ryan, *Klaus Barbie and the United States Government* (Frederick, 1984), pp.13–21; and Tom Bower, *Klaus Barbie: Butcher of Lyons* (London, 1985), pp.68–76, 159–60, 162–190, 196–222.

41 Timothy Naftali, 'Berlin to Baghdad: The Pitfalls of Hiring Enemy Intelligence', in *Foreign Affairs* 83, no.4 (July/Aug. 2004), pp.128–29.

42 John Gimbel, 'German Scientists, United States Denazification Policy, and the Paperclip Conspiracy', *International History Review* xii, no.3 (Aug. 1990), pp.441–65; and Linda Hunt, 'U.S. Coverup of Nazi Scientists', *Bulletin of the Atomic Scientists* 41, no.4 (April 1985), pp.16–21.

43 Vollnhals, ed., *Entnazifizierung*, pp.298–302; Griffiths, 'The Denazification Program',
    pp.333–34; Davidson, *The Death and Life of Germany*, pp.157–58; Gimbel, *The American
    Occupation of Germany*, pp.160–61; FitzGibbon, *Denazification*, p.176; *The New York Times*,
    2 March 1947; *Stars and Stripes*, 10 March 1947; and Burress to CoS, 21 Nov. 1946,
    OMGUS – Office of the Adjutant General: General Correspondence (Decimal File)
    1945–49, RG 260, NA.

44 Gimbel, *The American Occupation of Germany*, pp.158, 163–69; and John Backer, *The
    Winds of History: The German Years of Lucius DiBignon Clay* (New York, 1983), pp.172–77,
    181–83, 186, 289–90.

45 Plischke, 'Denazification of Germany', p.208.

46 Gimbel, *The American Occupation of Germany*, pp.161–62, 171–74; Fürstenau,
    Entnazifizierung, pp.87–99; Latour and Vogelsang, *Okkupation und Wiederaufbau*,
    pp.142–44; Zink, *The United States in Germany*, p.163; FitzGibbon, *Denazification*, p.135;
    Griffiths, 'The Denazification Program', pp.269, 271, 472–73, 475, 478–508, 514; Tent,
    Mission on the Rhine, pp.99, 277; *Foreign Relations of the United States*, 1948 (*FRUS*, 1948),
    ii, p.1302; 'Memorandum to Proposals of the Ministers for Political Liberation for
    Revision of the Law of 5 March 1946'; and Noble and Teitelbaum to Director, CAD,
    OMGUS, 28 April 1948, OMGUS – Records of the CAD, Public Safety Branch: Law
    for Liberation from National Socialism and Militarism 1945–49, RG 260, NA.

47 Tent, *Mission on the Rhine*, p.107; FitzGibbon, *Denazification*, pp.135, 140, 167–68, 171, 179;
    and Davidson, *The Death and Life of Germany*, pp.277–78.

48 Jürgen Weber, *Germany, 1945–1990: A Parallel History* (Budapest, 2004), pp.6–7; Merritt,
    'American Influences in the Occupation of Germany', pp.94–95; and *FRUS*, 1948, ii,
    pp.1302–03.

49 Balfour, 'Four-Power Control in Germany', pp.181; Hans Woller, 'Germany in Transition
    from Stalingrad (1943) to Currency Reform (1948)', in Michael Ermarth, ed.,
    America and the Shaping of German Society, 1945–1955 (Oxford, 1993), p.30; and Turner,
    'Denazification in the British Zone', p.266.

50 FitzGibbon, *Denazification*, pp.129, 132, 134–35; and Griffiths, 'The Denazification
    Program', pp.527–28.

51 FitzGibbon, *Denazification*, pp.133–34; Plischke, 'The Denazification of Germany', pp.216–
    17; Zink, *The United States in Germany*, p.163; Davidson, *The Death and Life of Germany*,
    p.131; and ICD Report no.80 'Opinions on Denazification', 26 Nov. 1947, OMGUS
    – Records of CAD, Public Safety Branch: Law for Liberation from National Socialism
    and Militarism, 1945–49, RG 260, NA.

52 Zink, *American Military Government in Germany*, p.145; Zink, *The United States in Germany*,
    p.164; Tent, *Mission on the Rhine*, p.316; Balfour, 'Four-Power Control in Germany',
    p.183; and Montgomery, *Forced to Be Free*, pp.196–97.

53 Niethammer, *Entnazifizierung in Bayern*, p.336.

Chapter 3: A Modest Purge

1 Ebsworth, *Restoring Democracy in Germany*, pp.xii–xiii; Trevor Davies, 'A British View of
    Education in Berlin', in Arthur Hearnden, ed., *The British in Germany: Educational
    Reconstruction after 1945* (London, 1978), p.218; W.D. Halls, 'The "German Question" and
    Post-War University Reform in Germany: A Comparative Note', in David Phillips, ed.,
    *German Universities after the Surrender: British Occupation Policy and the Control of Higher
    Education* (Oxford, 1983), p.31; Marshall, *Origins of Post-War German Politics*, pp.22–23;
    Kurt Jürgensen, 'British Occupation Policy after 1945 and the Problem of "Re-

Educating Germany"', *History* 68 (1983), pp.231–32; Clare, *Berlin Days*, p.146; Turner, 'The British Occupation and its Impact on Germany', p.6; Bower, *The Pledge Betrayed*, p.132; Donnison, *Civil Affairs and Military Government Central Organisation and Planning*, pp.12, 18; and FitzGibbon, *Denazification*, p.19.

2 Marshall, 'The Democratisation of Local Politics', p.437; Bower, *The Pledge Betrayed*, pp.121, 123; FitzGibbon, *Denazification*, p.120; Stephen Spender, *European Witness* (New York, 1946), pp.21–22; Folke Bernadotte, *Instead of Arms* (London, 1949), pp.175–76; Murphy to Secretary of State, 23 Oct. 1945, State Dept. Decimal File 1945–49, 740.00119 Control (Germany), RG 59, NA; and CSDIC(UK) GG Report, SRGG 1343, 12 Aug. 1945, WO 208/4170, NAUK. Unfortunately, memories of the British role in occupying the Rhineland from 1918 to 1930 provided few guideposts for policy formation. The earlier experience had been motivated largely by the desire to restrain Britain's own ally, France, and thus to allow Germany the chance to recover in a relatively unmolested condition, while in 1945 it was obvious that the impact of foreign rule in Germany would have to be more profound than anything previously envisioned, although German economic rehabilitation was still regarded as a principal goal. In addition, Britain was now trying to restore France as a great power, although strident French Germanophobia soon occasioned a revival of anti-French sentiments. The official historian of British military government, F.S.V. Donnison, refused to even regard the earlier British presence in the Rhineland as a genuine military government, calling it 'an ineffectual attempt to exercise indirect control over a part of the German administration'. David Williamson, *The British in Germany, 1918–1930: The Reluctant Occupiers* (Oxford, 1991), pp.2–5, 346, 348–49; and Donnison, *Civil Affairs and Military Government Central Organisation and Planning*, pp.17–18, 84.

3 Fromm, *Deutschland in der öffentlichen Kriegszieldiskussion Grossbritanniens*, pp.45–46, 48–49, 69–84, 120–29, 137–38, 169–70, 174–88, 197–220, 226–38; Eberan, *Wer war an Hitler schuld?*, pp.18–20; Kettenacker, *Krieg zur Friedenssicherung*, pp.28–34, 198–200, 206–07, 271, 363–64, 381, 447–48, 483–84, 491; Goldman, 'Germans and Nazis', pp.155–58, 176, 181–82; Balfour, 'Four-Power Control in Germany', pp.27–30, 34–35; Jürgensen, 'British Occupation Policy after 1945', pp.226–28; Turner, 'The British Occupation and its Impact on Germany'; David Welch, 'Priming the Pump of German Democracy: British Re-Education Policy in Germany after the Second World War'; Barbara Marshall, 'British Democratisation Policy in Germany', all in Turner, ed., *Reconstruction in Post-War Germany*, pp.4–6, 190, 216–17; Marshall, *Origins of Post-War German Politics*, pp.2–3; Niethammer, *Entnazifizierung in Bayern*, pp.41–44; FitzGibbon, *Denazification*, p.115; Friedmann, *Allied Military Government*, p.19; Lothar Kettenacker, 'The Planning of "Re-Education" during the Second World War', in Nicholas Pronay and Keith Wilson, *The Political Re-Education of Germany & Her Allies After World War II* (London, 1985), pp.59–62; Snell, *Wartime Origins*, p.2; and Lord Vansittart, *Lessons of My Life* (New York, 1943), p.25.

4 Jones, 'Eradicating Nazism from the British Zone of Germany', pp.146–48; and Turner, 'Denazification in the British Zone', p.242.

5 Donnison, *Civil Affairs and Military Government Central Organisation and Planning*, pp.34–39, 41; and Kettenacker, *Krieg zur Friedenssicherung*, pp.159–60.

6 David Carlton, *Anthony Eden: A Biography* (London, 1981), p.225; Llewellyn Woodward, *British Foreign Policy in the Second World War* (London, 1972), pp.438–39, 473–74; George Murray, 'The British Contribution', in Hearnden, *The British in Germany*, pp.65–67; Josef Foschepoth, 'British Interest in the Division of Germany after the Second World War', *Journal of Contemporary History* 21 (1986), pp.393–94; D.C. Watt, *Britain Looks to Germany* (London, 1965), pp.34–35, 37–38; T. D. Burridge, *British Labour and Hitler's War* (London, 1976), p.131, 134–35; Snell, *Wartime Origins*, p.21; Bower, *Blind Eye to Murder*,

pp.81, 122–23; Kettenacker, 'The Planning of "Re-Education"', pp.63, 71; Balfour, 'Four-Power Control in Germany', pp.30–31; Donnison, *Civil Affairs and Military Government Central Organisation and Planning*, pp.124–29; and Weber, *Germany, 1945–1990*, p.8.

7 Nicholas Pronay, 'To Stamp Out the Whole Tradition …'; Kettenacker, 'The Planning of "Re-Education"'; Kurt Koszyk, 'The Press in the British Zone of Germany', all in *The Political Re-Education of Germany & Her Allies*, pp.1–2, 63–70, 108–11; Kettenacker, *Krieg zur Friedenssicherung*, pp.151–52, 157, 365–72, 374–75; Welch, 'Priming the Pump of German Democracy', pp.217–19; and Jürgensen, 'British Occupation Policy after 1945', pp.229–31, 234.

8 Kettenacker, *Krieg zur Friedenssicherung*, pp.157, 320–21, 349–53; Jones, 'Eradicating Nazism from the British Zone of Germany', pp.148–51; Marshall, 'The Democratisation of Local Politics', p.415; Marshall, *Origin of Post-War German Politics*, p.7; and George Murray, 'The British Contribution', in Hearndon, ed., *The British in Germany*, p.71.

9 Watt, *Britain Looks to Germany*, pp.34, 37–38; Kenneth Harris, *Attlee* (London, 1982), pp.208–13; Hugh Dalton, *The Fateful Years: Memoirs, 1931–1945* (London, 1957), pp.424, 431–32; Burridge, *British Labour and Hitler's War*, pp.24, 29, 43, 56–57, 59–67, 94–95, 104–07, 114–23, 126–32, 136–38, 157, 168–69; Kettenacker, *Krieg zur Friedenssicherung*, pp.136, 171–72, 193, 321–22, 348–49, 359, 396; Fromm, *Deutschland in der öffentlichen Kriegszieldiskussion Grossbritanniens*, pp.44, 140–41, 170; *The Second World War Diary of Hugh Dalton 1940–1945*, ed. Ben Pimlott (London, 1986), p.770; *FRUS, 1944* i, p.143; and Troutbeck to Peake, 29 Aug. 1944, FO 945/869, NAUK. For Dalton's relationship to Vansittart, see *The Second World War Diary of Hugh Dalton*, p.368.

10 Jones, 'Eradicating Nazism from the British Zone of Germany', p.151.

11 Harris, *Attlee*, p.49; Jones, 'Eradicating Nazism from the British Zone of Germany', p.145; Balfour, 'Four-Power Control in Germany', p.31; and *The Second World War Diary of Hugh Dalton*, p.521.

12 *FRUS: The Quebec Conference*, pp.325–27, 342–43, 361–62; Anthony Eden, *The Eden Memoirs: The Reckoning* (London, 1965), pp.370, 552; Woodward, *British Foreign Policy*, pp.442, 450, 471, 473–79; Balfour, 'Four-Power Control in Germany', p.33; John Wheeler-Bennett and Anthony Nicholls, *The Semblance of Peace: The Political Settlement after the Second World War* (London, 1972), pp.175, 181–86; Keppler, *Tod über Deutschland*, pp.131–39; Kimball, *Swords or Ploughshares?*, pp.3–4, 35–40, 47–49; Excerpt from conclusions of the 122nd meeting of the War Cabinet, 14 Sept. 1944, FO 945/869, NAUK; and copy of cable from FO to Eden, 14 Sept. 1944, CAB 87/58, NAUK.

13 Donald C. Watt, 'Hauptprobleme des britischen Deutschlandpolitik 1945–1949', in Claus Scharf and Hans-Jürgen Schröder, eds., *Deutschlandpolitik Grossbritanniens und die britischen Zone 1945–1949* (Wiesbaden, 1979), p.16.

14 Bower, *The Pledge Betrayed*, p.147.

15 French, DCA, comment on SHAEF Civil Affairs Handbook for Germany, 13 July 1944; McSherry to DCA, War Office, 10 Aug. 1944; and 'Extract from the Minutes of the 39th Meeting of the ACAO, 20th September 1944', all in FO 945/869, NAUK.

16 Draft telegram to the JSM in Washington, annex ii to note by the APW Secretariate, 29 Aug. 1944, Cabinet Office Records [CAB] 87/68, NAUK; CAD to SHAEF 'Occupation Policy and Control of Germany (CCAC 122)', 15 Sept. 1944; Hilldring to SHAEF, 15 Sept. 1944, both in CAD 014 Germany, RG 165, NA; CAD Historical Section analysis sheet, 10 Nov. 1944, WO 219/3761A, NAUK; and memorandum by DCA for consideration of the ACAO, 11 Sept. 1944, FO 945/869, NAUK.

17 *FRUS: The Conferences at Malta and Yalta*, pp.164, 174.

18 Appendix 'A', 'Comparison of JCS 1067 the British Draft Directives to EAC', filed under SHAEF G-5 staff study on Post-Defeat MG Planning, Dec. 1944, WO 219/3868, NAUK; and *FRUS, 1945*, iii, pp.420, 422. In general, the Americans carped that British planning

put an excessive premium on 'administrative convenience', that it was inadequate in dealing with the numbers of Nazis facing internment, and that it provided 'too much political freedom' to the Germans. *FRUS: The Conferences at Malta and Yalta*, pp.164–65.

19 McCloy to Macready, 27 Oct. 1944, CAD 014 Germany, RG 165, NA.

20 *FRUS*, 1945, iii, p.522.

21 Jones, 'Eradicating Nazism from the British Zone of Germany', pp.151, 153–54, 156–59; Turner, 'Denazification in the British Zone', pp.246–48; Lange, ed., *Entnazifizierung in Nordrhein-Westfalen*, pp.14–15; Zink, *American Military Government in Germany*, pp.144–45; Zink, *The United States in Germany*, pp.166–67; and Fürstenau, *Entnazifizierung*, pp.30, 43.

22 Bower, *The Pledge Betrayed*, pp.130–32, 147–48; Lange, ed., *Entnazifizierung in Nordrhein-Westfalen*, pp.14, 16; Krüger, *Entnazifiziert!*, pp.24–27; Donnison, *Civil Affairs and Military Government Northwest Europe*, p.228; Friedmann, *Allied Military Government*, pp.17, 45–46, 124; Turner, 'Denazification in the British Zone', p.245; FitzGibbon, *Denazification*, pp.87, 119–20; Marshall, *Origins of Post-War German Politics*, p.8; Marshall, 'The Democratisation of Local Politics', pp.415–16, 429; Clare, *Berlin Days*, p.28; and Fürstenau, *Entnazifizierung*, pp.43–44.

23 Clare, *Berlin Days*, pp.25–27.

24 Turner, 'Denazification in the British Zone', p.244; Bower, *The Pledge Betrayed*, p.156; Balfour, 'Four-Power Control in Germany', p.171; and Robertson to Jenkins, 7 March 1947, FO 371/64352, NAUK.

25 Jones, 'Eradicating Nazism from the British Zone of Germany', pp.155–57; Turner, 'Denazification in the British Zone', p.245; Ebsworth, *Restoring Democracy in Germany*, pp.9, 180; Bower, *The Pledge Betrayed*, pp.169–70; Donnison, *Civil Affairs and Military Government Central Organisation and Planning*, 276–77, 279; Caffney to Deputy Comm. (Military), Norfolk House, 18 April 1945; and SHAEF G-5 'Minutes of Third Military Government Conference', 12 April 1945, both in WO 219/3499, NAUK. For the background of British policy toward the German police, see Kettenacker, *Krieg zur Friedenssicherung*, pp.354–57.

26 *The Times*, 9 April 1945; 12 April 1945; and Eisenhower to Montgomery for Mil Gov, 17 April 1945, WO 219/3513, NAUK.

27 CCG(BE) Intelligence Division 'Summary' no.3, 13 Aug. 1945, FO 1005/1702, NAUK.

28 Chief, IA&C Division to DcoS (Exec), Office of Deputy Military Governor, 5 June 1946; HQ Military Government, North Rhine Region 'Denazification of German Police', 29 May 1946; and IA&C Division, Intelligence Section, CCG(BE) 'Denazification of German Police – Aachen', 5 June 1946, FO 1032/639, NAUK.

29 Ebsworth, *Restoring Democracy in Germany*, pp.8–9; Murray, 'The British Contribution', p.74; Turner, 'Denazification in the British Zone', pp.256–57; Bower, *The Pledge Betrayed*, pp.140, 157; Marshall, *Origins of Post-War German Politics*, p.48; and Donnison, *Civil Affairs and Military Government North-West Europe*, p.371. In Schwerin, a British investigation of the municipal regime exonerated 95 employees and found 24 Nazis who were worth retaining, although 37 *Parteigenossen* were also released. Peterson, *Russian Commands and German Resistance*, p.438.

30 Marshall, 'The Democratisation of Local Politics in the British Zone', pp.416–17, 419–23, 424–25, 428–29; Marshall, *Origins of Post-War German Politics*, pp.25–26, 28–29, 34–35, 36–39, 43, 45, 49–51, 52–53, 56; Jones, 'Eradicating Nazism from the British Zone of Germany', p.155; Donnison, *Civil Affairs and Military Government Northwest Europe*, p.218; and Theodore Draper, *The 84th Infantry Division in the Battle of Germany* (New York, 1946), p.225.

31 Bower, *The Pledge Betrayed*, pp.168–169, 171; Marshall, *Origins of Post-War German Politics*, pp.37–38; Concomb to Troopers, 11 May 1946; 13 May 1946; Troopers to Concomb, 18

May 1946; Concomb to Confolk, 26 May, 1946; Wilberforce to Balfour, 28 June 1946; Balfour to Wilberforce, 22 July 1946; 'Memorandum on Conditions in the German Police Force at Hannover'; Wilberforce to Balogh, 11 Sept. 1946, all in FO 945/95, NAUK; Public Safety Branch, HQ Military Government, Hannover Region 'De-Nazification of German Police'; and Robertson to Hynd, 21 Aug. 1946, both in FO 1032/639, NAUK.

32 Robert Birley, 'British Policy in Retrospect'; Murray, The British Contribution'; George Murray, 'The Training of Teachers'; Fritz Borinski, 'The British Influence on German Adult Education', all in Hearnden, ed., *The British in Germany*, pp. 52, 75, 131–32, 139, 233; Marshall, *Origins of Post-War German Politics*, p. 51; Krüger, *Entnazifiziert!*, pp. 22–23; Lange, ed., *Entnazifizierung in Nordrhein-Westfalen*, p. 29; Tent, *Mission on the Rhine*, pp. 201–02, 220; and Donnison, *Civil Affairs and Military Government North-West Europe*, p. 373.

33 Lutz Niethammer, 'Privat-Wirtschaft. Erinnerungsfragmente einer anderen Umerziehung', in Lutz Niethammer, ed., *'Hinterher merkt man, dass es richtig war, dass es schiefgegangen ist.' Nachkriegserfahrungen im Ruhrgebiet* (Berlin, 1983), ii, p. 49.

34 Falk Pingel, 'Attempts at University Reform in the British Zone', in Phillips, ed., *German Universities after the Surrender*, p. 23.

35 David Phillips, 'The Re-opening of Universities in the British Zone: The Problem of Nationalism and Student Admissions', pp. 6, 9; L.H. Sutton, 'Shuffling Feet: A Discourse on the University of Göttingen', pp. 109–10, 112, 116, both in Phillips, ed., *German Universities after the Surrender*; Bower, *The Pledge Betrayed*, pp. 167–68; Birley, 'British Policy in Retrospect', p. 55; Tent, *Mission on the Rhine*, pp. 313–14; Robert Ericksen, 'Religion und Nationalsozialismus im Spiegel der Entnazifizierungsakten der Göttinger Universität', *Kirchliche Zeitgeschichte* 7, no. 1 (1994), pp. 83–101; Klaus Hentschel and Gerhard Rammer, 'Kein Neuanfang: Physiker an der Universität Göttingen 1945–1955', *Zeitschrift für Geschichtswissenschaft* 48, no. 8 (2000), pp. 718–41; MI-14 'Mitropa', 15 Dec. 1945, FO 371/55630, NAUK; OSS Report from Germany L-983, 24 Nov. 1945, XL 31521, Entry 19, RG 226, NA; and USFET 'Weekly Intelligence Summary' no. 19, 21 Nov. 1945, State Dept. Decimal Files 1945–49, 740.00119 Control (Germany), RG 59, NA.

36 *Weser-Kurier*, 16 March 1946.

37 *Stars and Stripes*, 25 Jan. 1946; 30 Jan 1946; and USFET 'Weekly Intelligence Summary' no. 32, 21 Feb. 1946, State Dept. Decimal Files 1945–49, 740.00119 Control (Germany), RG 59, NA.

38 *Die Neue Zeitung*, 10 March 1947.

39 A.W.J. Edwards, 'Technical Education and the 'Zweiter Bildungsweg'', in Hearnden, ed., *The British in Germany*, p. 177; Lange, ed., *Entnazifizierung in Nordrhein-Westfalen*, p. 34; Pingel, 'Attempts at University Reform in the British Zone', pp. 23–25; Phillips, 'The Re-opening of Universities in the British Zone', pp. 7, 10–15; and Harry Beckhough, 'The Role of the British University Control Officer in Post-War Germany', in Phillips, ed. *German Universities after the Surrender*, p. 77.

40 Bower, *The Pledge Betrayed*, pp. 171–75; Ebsworth, *Restoring Democracy in Germany*, pp. 9–10; Friedmann, *Allied Military Government*, p. 8; and 'Appendix 'A' to SCD/P(46)60 dated 28 Sept. 1946', WO 311/634, NAUK.

41 Vollnhals, ed. *Entnazifierung*, p. 330.

42 *Ibid.*, pp. 138–41; Henke, *Die amerikanische Besetzung Deutschlands*, pp. 496–98, 500–03, 510–12, 518–19, 523, 537–43; and William Manchester, *The Arms of Krupp, 1587–1968* (New York, 1970), pp. 674–78.

43 Marshall, 'The Democratisation of Local Politics in the British Zone', p. 423.

44 Donnison, *Civil Affairs and Military Government North-West Europe*, pp. 366–67, 371; Turner, 'Denazification in the British Zone', pp. 246–47, 257; Henke, *Die amerikanische Besetzung Deutschlands*, pp. 512, 540–45, 562; Marshall, *Origins of Post-War German Politics*, p. 53;

Bower, *The Pledge Betrayed*, pp.296–98, 303; and 'Extract from CoS(BZ)/M/(45)9 of 1.8.45', FO 1032/628, NAUK.

45 Bower, *The Pledge Betrayed*, pp.148–49.

46 Manchester, *The Arms of Krupp*, pp.689–90, 696; Lange, ed., *Entnazifizierung in Nordrhein-Westfalen*, pp.18, 19, 22; Turner, 'Denazification in the British Zone', p.257; Montgomery, *Forced to Be Free*, p.101; and Henke, *Die amerikanische Besetzung Deutschlands*, pp.555–56, 562–67.

47 Appendices 'A' and 'B' to HQ/06101/6/Sec. Political, May 1946, FO 1032/628, NAUK.

48 Niethammer, 'Privat-Wirtschaft', pp.70–71.

49 Friedmann, *Allied Military Government*, p.113; Marshall, *Origins of Post-War German Politics*, p.13; and Balfour, 'Four-Power Control in Germany', p.256.

50 Mark Roseman, 'The Uncontrolled Economy: Ruhr Coal Production, 1945–48', in *Reconstruction in Post-War Germany*, pp.94–100, 102–04, 115–18; and Robert Carden, 'Before Bizonia: Britain's Economic Dilemma in Germany, 1945–46', *Journal of Contemporary History* 14, no.3 (July 1979), pp.542–47, 549. For figures on production in the British zone, see Friedmann, *Allied Military Government*, p.32.

51 Donnison, *Civil Affairs and Military Government North-West Europe*, pp.410–11; Roseman, 'Uncontrolled Economy', pp.100–01; Turner, 'Denazification in the British Zone', p.258; Henke, *Die amerikanische Besetzung Deutschlands*, pp.547–50, 561; 'Extract from CoS(BZ)/M/(45)9 of 1.8.45'; 'Note for Chief of Staff (British Zone) for a Meeting to Be Held in the Main Conference Room at 1700 Hours on Wednesday, 8 August 1945'; CCG(BE) 'Minutes of a Meeting held in Room 35, Tax House, Lübbecke'; Concomb to Troopers, 9 Aug. 1945; 'Denazification of the Coal Industry', Feb. 1946; Robertson to Permanent Secretary, CO, Feb. 1946, all in FO 1032/628, NAUK; CCG(BE) Standing Committee on Denazification (Policy) 'Denazification of German Industry', 15 March 1946, WO 311/634, NAUK; and NGCC 'Denazification of the Coal Industry in the British Occupied Zone of Germany', 10 Oct. 1946, FO 945/784, NAUK.

52 *The Times*, 21 Feb. 1945; 22 Feb. 1945; 23 Feb. 1945; 25 Feb. 1945; NCGG 'Preliminary Report on the Disaster at Monopol Grimberg III/IV, Wednesday, 20 February, 1946', FO 1037/20, NAUK; NGCC 'Safety in Mines as Affected by the Denazification Policy', March 1946, FO 1032/628, NAUK; and Erskine to Street, 2 April 1946, FO 945/784, NAUK.

53 Ralph Uhlig, ed., *Confidential Reports des Britischen Verbindungsstabes zum Zonenbereit der britischen Besatzungszone in Hamburg (1946–1948)* (Frankfurt a.M., 1993), p.77.

54 '22/2/46 Signal CCLB/BM/G/723 for Gen. Robertson from Sir Arthur Street', FO 945/784, NAUK.

55 Interview with Sir Edgar Williams, 8 May 1986.

56 Concomb to Bercomb, 12 July 1946, FO 1032/638, NAUK.

57 Bower, *The Pledge Betrayed*, pp.298–99; Lange, ed., *Entnazifizierung in Nordrhein-Westfalen*, pp.31, 40; Vollnhals, ed., *Entnazifizierung*, pp.142–49; Fürstenau, *Entnazifizierung*, pp.112–14; Turner, 'Denazification in the British Zone', p.258; ACoS (EXEC) 'Note for the Secretariat', 2 May 1946; COALCO to Confolk, 5 June 1946; T&I Division 'Denazification of the Coal Industry', 6 June 1946; Concomb to Bercomb, 7 June 1946; Legal Division, CCG(BE) 'Denazification of the Coal Industry', 18 June 1946; Office of the Deputy Military Governor, CCG(BE) 'Denazification of the Coal Industry', 21 June 1946; Tjaden to British Liaison Staff, ZAC, 8 July 1946; NGCC 'Denazification of the German Coal Industry', 23 Aug. 1946; 20 Sept. 1946; 26 Sept. 1946, all in FO 1032/628, NAUK; Wilberforce to Erskine, 16 April 1946; Erskine to Wilberforce, 23 April 1946; 9 June 1946; 'Extract from ZAC 67', 29 May 1946; 'Denazification of the Coal Industry', both in FO 1060/1213, NAUK; Office of the Deputy Military Governor, CCG(BE) 'Denazification of the Coal Industry', 11 July 1946; NGCC 'Denazification of the Coal Industry in the British Occupied Zone of Germany', 10 Oct. 1946; and J. Wiefels

'Report on the Activities of the Special Coal Advisory Denazification Commission', 10 Oct. 1946, all in FO 945/784, NAUK.

58 Friedmann, *Allied Military Government*, p.125; and CCG(BE) 'Statement on Denazification of the Coal Mining Industry', 6 Nov. 1946, FO 371/64744, NAUK.

59 Bower, *The Pledge Betrayed*, pp.8–13; Henke, *Die amerikanische Besetzung Deutschlands*, pp.565, 567; Jones, 'Eradicating Nazism from the British Zone of Germany', p.160; and 'Observations on British Draft Directive covering Finance and Property in Germany for the Post-Surrender Period', CAD 014 Germany, RG 165, NA.

60 Uhlig, ed., *Confidential Reports des Britischen Verbindungsstabes*, p.77; Henke, *Die amerikanische Besetzung Deutschlands*, pp.533, 568, 569–71; Krüger, *Entnazifiziert!*, pp.149–50; Griffiths, 'The Denazification Program', pp.537-38; Bower, *The Pledge Betrayed*, pp.13, 299, 324–28, 331, 340–42, 349; Turner, 'Denazification in the British Zone', pp.250, 258; Manchester, *The Arms of Krupp*, pp. 713–70; CCG(BE) Standing Committee on Denazification (Policy) 'Denazification of German Industry', 15 March 1946; 'Release of Interned Industrialists', 12 July 1946, both in WO 311/634, NAUK; Land Public Safety Dept., Special Branch, Land North Rhine/Westphalia to HQ Denazification Section, Lübbecke, 28 April 1948; and Concomb Lübbecke to FO (German Section), 5 May 1948, both in FO 1032/635, NAUK. For the Carp case, see FO (German Section) to Concomb, Lübbecke, 17 Nov. 1947; Concomb Lübbecke to FO (German Section), 16 Dec. 1947; Broomfield to Marsden-Smedley, 7 Feb. 1948; and Sampson to Control Secretariate, Zonal Executive Offices, HQ CCG Lübbecke, all in FO 1032/635, NAUK.

61 Marshall, 'The Democratisation of Local Politics in the British Zone', p.423; Marshall, *Origins of Post-War German Politics*, p.54; Bower, *The Pledge Betrayed*, p.309; and Balfour, 'Four-Power Control in Germany', p.257.

62 CCG(BE) Standing Committee on Denazification (Policy) 'Registration and Screening of Owners, Partners and Directors of Industrial and Commercial Undertakings', 26 Sept. 1946, WO 311/634, NAUK.

63 Welch, 'Priming the Pump of German Democracy', pp.219–20; Balfour, 'Four-Power Control in Germany', p.50; PWE 'Political Warfare Directive (European Theatre)', 18 April 1945; 26 April 1945; 1 June 1945; 8 June 1945, all in FO 371/46790, NAUK; Steel to Troutbeck, 3 May 1945; note by O'Neill on file cover of C2049, 10 May 1945; Sargent to Steel, 22 May 1945; and Steel to FO, 27 May 1945, all in FO 371/46894, NAUK.

64 Donnison, *Civil Affairs and Military Government North-West Europe*, p.238.

65 Welch, 'Priming the Pump of German Democracy', pp.220–221.

66 *Ibid.*, pp.360–62; Balfour, 'Four-Power Control in Germany', pp.174, 179–80, 180–81; Krüger, *Entnazifiziert!*, pp.72–73; Donnison, *Civil Affairs and Military Government in North-West Europe*, pp.360–62; Friedmann, *Allied Military Government*, pp.120–21, 231, 238; Fürstenau, *Entnazifizierung*, pp.106–07; Turner, 'Denazification in the British Zone', p.255; Norbert Frei, *Adenauer's Germany and the Nazi Past: The Politics of Amnesty and Integration* (New York, 2002), p.9; Heiner Wember, 'Entnazifizierung nach 1945: Die deutschen Spruchgerichte in der britischen Zone', *Geschichte in Wissenschaft und Unterricht* 43, no.7 (1992), pp.405–26; *Die Neue Zeitung*, 3 Feb. 1947; 24 March 1947; 28 March 1947; 21st AG 'Counter-Intelligence Instruction No.4: Occupation of Germany', WO 205/1086, NAUK; 'Draft: Outline Instructions for the Organisation and Administration of Internment Camps in Germany'; 21st AG to 1st Canadian Army and 2nd British Army, 12 May 1945, both in WO 205/388, NAUK; FO (German Section) 'Progress Report', 10 Feb. 1946, FO 371/70660, NAUK; 'Appendix 'A' to SCD/P (46) 38 (Revise) dated 28 June 1946—Downgrading of Categorised Persons: Draft Instructions for British Review Boards', WO 311/634, NAUK; 'United Kingdom Delegation Brief for CFM: Denazification Z—Release of SS Personnel on Parole', FO 371/64353, NAUK; and ACC Coordinating Committee 'Report to the Council of

Foreign Ministers', Section ii – Denazification, 21 Feb. 1947, FO 371/64352, NAUK.

67 Birley, 'British Policy in Retrospect', p.53; Krüger, *Entnazifiziert!*, p.19; and Chief, Legal Division to HQ Intelligence Division, 13 July 1947, FO 1060/1213, NAUK.

68 Donnison, *Civil Affairs and Military Government North-West Europe*, pp.367–68; Turner, 'Denazification in the British Zone', p.253; Jones, 'Eradicating Nazism from the British Zone of Germany', p.154; Marshall, *Origins of Post-War German Politics*, p.50; FitzGibbon, *Denazification*, pp.121–22 and interview with Noel Annan, 29 April 1986. Interestingly, Montgomery was convinced that 60 per cent of the population in the British zone were 'out-and-out Nazis'. FitzGibbon, *Denazification*, p.121.

69 Fürstenau, *Entnazifizierung*, pp.104–06; Krüger, *Entnazifiziert!*, pp.12, 20, 23-24, 31-35, 44-50, 153-54; Lange, ed., *Entnazifizierung in Nordrhein-Westfalen*, pp.15, 24-27, 28, 34, 37-40; Turner, 'Denazification in the British Zone', pp.252–57; Ebsworth, *Restoring Democracy in Germany*, pp.5–6, 10–13, 29–30, 32; Friedmann, *Allied Military Government*, p.118; Marshall, *Origins of Post-War German Politics*, p.48; Donnison, *Civil Affairs and Military Government North-West Europe*, pp.368, 371, 375; Balfour, 'Four-Power Control in Germany', p.179; Bower, *The Pledge Betrayed*, pp.157–58; Pütz, ed., *Konrad Adenauer und die CDU*, pp.54–55; Uhlig, ed., *Confidential Reports des Britischen Verbindungsstabes*, p.83; MI-14 'Mitropa' no.15, 9 Feb. 1946; No.23, 5 June 1946, both in FO 371/55630, NAUK; ACC Coordinating Committee 'Report to the Council of Foreign Ministers', Section ii – Denazification, 21 Feb. 1947; DPD 'General Bishop Explains Aims of New Denazification Order', 7 Feb. 1947, both in FO 371/64352, NAUK; CCG(BE) Standing Committee on Denazification (Policy) 'Zone Policy Instruction No.3 (Revise)', 8 April 1946; 'Annexures 1, 2 and 3 to Appendix 'C' to SDC/P (46) 13 dated 16 March '46 – Denazification Measures in the British Zone'; CCG(BE) Standing Committee on Denazification (Policy) 'ZPI No.3 Press Releases', 12 April 1946; 'Speeding Up of Denazification', 28 June 1946, all in WO 311/634, NAUK; and 'Zone Executive Instruction No.54', 30 Nov. 1946, FO 371/64352, NAUK.

70 J.M. Troutbeck, 5 June 1946, file sheet C7154, FO 371/55615, NAUK; Robertson to Jenkins, 7 March 1947, FO 371/64352, NAUK; and Gen. McCreery, untitled paper on the security situation in occupied Germany, 11 June 1947, FO 371/64878, NAUK.

71 Donnison, *Civil Affairs and Military Government North-West Europe*, p.376.

72 Uhlig, ed., *Confidential Reports des Britischen Verbindungsstabes*, p.106.

73 Friedmann, *Allied Military Government*, pp.231, 233; and Marshall, *Origins of Post-War German Politics*, p.48.

74 Marshall, *Origins of Post-War German Politics*, pp.21–23; Ebsworth, *Restoring Democracy in Germany*, pp.128–32; Balfour, 'Four-Power Control in Germany', pp.68, 102; Clare, *Berlin Days*, pp.146–47; Friedmann, *Allied Military Government*, pp.36, 38–39; and Fürstenau, *Entnazifizierung*, p.103.

75 Friedmann, *Allied Military Government*, p.120; Turner, 'Denazification in the British Zone', p.259; Fürstenau, *Entnazifizierung*, pp.107–08; Marshall, *Origins of Post-War German Politics*, pp.54–55; and CCG(BE) Standing Committee on Denazification (Policy) 'Responsibilities of Denazification Panels and Committees', 18 Sept. 1946, WO 311/634, NAUK.

76 Krüger, *Entnazifiziert!*, pp.37-38; Turner, 'Denazification in the British Zone', p.250; and Ebsworth, *Restoring Democracy in Germany*, p.17.

77 Clare, *Berlin Days*, p.72.

78 MI-14 'Mitropa' no.23, 5 June 1946, FO 371/55630, NAUK; and ACC Coordinating Committee 'Report to the Council of Foreign Ministers', Section ii – Denazification, 21 Feb. 1947, FO 371/64352, NAUK.

79 Donnison, *Civil Affairs and Military Government North-West Europe*, p.376.

80 Turner, 'Denazification in the British Zone', pp.261–64, 266; Krüger, *Entnazifiziert!*,

pp.55–57; Lange, ed., *Entnazifizierung in Nordrhein-Westfalen*, pp.52–53; Fürstenau,
Entnazifizierung, pp.108, 109–10, 114–29; Turner, 'The British Occupation and its Impact
on Germany', p.9; Balfour, 'Four-Power Control of Germany', p.179; Robertson to
Jenkins, 7 March 1947; Confolk to Bercomb, 3 Jan. 1947; 'Denazification in the British
Zone of Germany', all in FO 371/64352, NAUK; Berlin to Control Office, 5 March
1947; 7 March 1947; 'Record of a Meeting held in the Chancellor's Room on Thursday
12th June, to Discuss the Future of De-Nazification'; Berlin to FO (German Section),
18 June 1947; FO (German Section) to Berlin, 19 June 1947; Berlin to FO (German
Section), 2 July 1947; Berlin (Military Governor) to FO, 4 July 1947; FO (German
Section) to Berlin, 11 July 1947, all in FO 371/64744, NAUK; and 'Denazification', FO
371/64353, NAUK.

81 Jürgensen, 'British Occupation Policy after 1945', p.226; and Marshall, *Origins of Post-War
German Politics*, p.16.

82 Fürstenau, *Entnazifizierung*, pp.127–33; Krüger, *Entnazifiziert!*, pp.58–63, 67–69, 77,
144–45, 154–55; Lange, ed., *Entnazifizierung in Nordrhein-Westfalen*, pp.54–55; Turner,
'Denazification in the British Zone', pp.264–65; and Garner, 'Public Service Personnel
in West Germany in the 1950s', pp.45, 74

83 Turner, 'Denazification in the British Zone', pp.266–67.

84 *Ibid*, p.244; and Balfour, 'Four-Power Control in Germany', p.259.

85 Friedmann, *Allied Military Government*, pp.39–41, 42–48, 122–23, 228–29, 231. For the tendency
of the Germans to judge Allied shortcomings against the conquerors' proclamations of
moral superiority, see Balfour, 'Four-Power Control in Germany', pp.63, 112.

86 FitzGibbon, *Denazification*, p.165; Turner, 'Denazification in the British Zone', pp.248–49,
266; Marshall, *Origins of Post-War German Politics*, p.48; Krüger, *Entnazifiziert!*, pp.14–15,
38, 156–59; and Jones, 'Eradicating Racism from the British Zone', p.162.

87 Marshall, *Origins of Post-War German Politics*, p.57; Krüger, *Entnazifiziert!*, pp.157; and
Turner, 'Denazification in the British Zone', p.239

Chapter 4: The Red Broom

1 Alexei Filitov, 'Stalins Deutschlandplanung und politik während und nach dem zweiten
Weltkrieg', in V.I. Dashichev, Boris Meisner and Alfred Eisfeld, *50 Jahre soujetische und
russische Deutschlandpolitik sowie ihre Auswirkung auf das gegenseitige Verhälnis* (Berlin, 1999),
pp.43, 51; and Vogt, *Denazification in Soviet-Occupied Germany*, pp.4, 14, 153, 234. For examples,
see FitzGibbon, *Denazification*, p.100; Davidson, *The Life and Death of Germany*, pp.77–78;
Fürstenau, *Entnazifizierung*, pp.9–10, 22–23, 167; Lange, ed., *Entnazifizierung in Nordrhein-
Westfalen*, p.11; Barbara Ann Chotiner and John Atwell, 'Soviet Occupation Policy toward
Germany, 1945–1949', in Hans Schmitt, ed., *U.S. Occupation in Europe after World War II*
(Laurence, 1978), p.56; and Plischke, 'Denazification in Germany', pp.219–220. Among
recent scholars, Helga Welsh, Damian van Melis and R.C. Raack tend to continue seeing
denazification as part of a larger Bolshevisation scheme intended by the Soviets from
the outset. See Welsh, *Revolutionärer Wandel auf Befehl?*, pp.7–9, 167; Damian van Melis,
'Denazification in Mecklenburg-Vorpommern', pp.355, 369–70; van Melis, *Entnazifizierung
in Mecklenburg-Vorpommern*, pp.3, 67, 321, 330–31; and R.C. Raack, 'Stalin Plans his Post-
War Germany', *Journal of Contemporary History* 28, no.1 (1993), pp.60–61. Welsh claims to
be undecided about whether the Soviets had a 'master plan' for the occupation, and she
admits that in the early phase of the exercise, their actions were disorganised and often
reactive. Welsh, *Revolutionärer Wandel auf Befehl?*, pp.171–72. As for van Melis, he admits that

the particular focus of his study, the largely agrarian *Land* of Mecklenburg-Vorpommern, provided an environment where German communists were able to seize power more quickly than elsewhere in the Soviet zone, partly because the region lacked a large middle class or a significant Social Democratic milieu, either of which could have stood in the path of rapid communisation. Nonetheless, he regards Mecklenburg-Vorpommern *not* as a deviation from the general pattern, but as 'an early model for the rearrangement of Soviet zone society'. van Melis, *Entnazifizierung in Mecklenburg-Vorpommern*, pp.322, 332

2 Gavriel Ra'anan, *International Policy Formation in the USSR: Factional 'Debates' during the Zhdanovschina* (Hamden, 1983), pp.4–5; William McCagg, *Stalin Embattled, 1943–1948* (Detroit, 1978), pp.15, 372; and Aleksei Filitov, 'The Soviet Union and the Grand Alliance: The Internal Dimension of Foreign Policy', in *Soviet Foreign Policy, 1917–1991: A Retrospective* (London, 1994), p.97. For an example, see Chotiner and Atwell, 'Soviet Occupation Policy toward Germany', p.46.

3 Vogt, *Denazification in Soviet-Occupied Germany*, pp.4–5, 176, 196–97, 230–32, 234–37, 239–40; Norman Naimark, *The Russians in Germany: A History of the Soviet Zone of Occupation, 1945–1949* (Cambridge, 1995), pp.24–25; Vojtech Mastny, *The Cold War and Soviet Insecurity: The Stalin Years* (New York, 1996), p.19; Ulrich Pfeil, 'Antifascism et Dénazification en Zone d'Occupation Soviétique (SBZ), 1945–1948', *Revue d'Allemagne et des Pays de langue allemande* 32, no.1 (2000), pp.14–15; and Peterson, *Russian Commands and German Resistance*, p.491.

4 Silvio Pons, 'In the Aftermath of the Age of Wars: The Impact of World War II on Soviet Security Policy', in Silvio Pons and Andrea Romano, eds., *Russia in the Age of Wars, 1914–1945* (Milan, 2000), pp.278–80, 307; Arnold Sywottek, *Deutsche Volksdemokratie: Studien zur politischen Konzeption der KPD 1935–1946* (Düsseldorf, 1971), pp.23–51; Jeffrey Herf, *Divided Memory: The Nazi Past in the Two Germanys* (Cambridge, 1997), pp.17–19, 27–32; Welsh, *Revolutionärer Wandel auf Befehl?*, p.7; Niethammer, *Entnazifizierung in Bayern*, pp.106–12; Vogt, *Denazification in Soviet-Occupied Germany*, pp.18–22; Teddy Ulricks, 'Soviet Security Policy in the 1930s', in Gorodetsky, *Soviet Foreign Policy*, pp.65–73; Alexander Dallin and F.I. Firsov, *Dimitrov and Stalin, 1934–1943: Letters from the Soviet Archives* (New Haven, 2000), pp.8–14, 33–34, 143, 189–92; and Jonathan Adelman and Deborah Anne Palmieri, *The Dynamics of Soviet Foreign Policy* (New York, 1989), pp.73–80, 104. For Koestler's observation, see Arthur Koestler, *Darkness at Noon* (Hammondsworth, Middlesex, 1977), p.31.

5 Wolfgang Leonhard, *Child of the Revolution* (London, 1979), pp.238–39, 243–45, 255–61, 266–68, 272–79; Sywottek, *Deutsche Volksdemokratie*, pp.124–47; Niethammer, *Entnazifizierung in Bayern*, pp.112–14; Chotiner and Atwell, 'Soviet Occupation Policy toward Germany', p.46; Herf, *Divided Memory*, pp.23–24; and Vogt, *Denazification in Soviet-Occupied Germany*, pp.22–23.

6 McCagg, *Stalin Embattled*, p.38.

7 Filitov, 'Stalins Deutschlandplanung', pp.44–46, 47; Aleksei Filitov, 'Problems of Post-War Construction in Soviet Foreign Policy Conceptions during World War II', in Francesca Gori and Silvio Pons, eds., *The Soviet Union and Europe in the Cold War, 1943–1953* (New York, 1996), pp.6–8, 16–21; Wilfried Loth, *Stalin's Unwanted Child: The Soviet Union, the German Question and the Founding of the GDR* (New York, 1998), p.6; Vladimir Volkov, 'Die deutsche Frage aus Stalins Sicht (1947–1952)', *Zeitschrift für Geschichtswissenschaft* 48, no.1 (2000), p.24; Horst Duhnke, *Die KPD von 1933 bis 1945* (Cologne, 1972), pp.394–95; Mastny, *The Cold War and Soviet Insecurity*, pp.18–19; Peterson, *Russian Commands and German Resistance*, pp.9–12, 14–15, 479–80; Herf, *Divided Memory*, pp.37, 74; Friedmann, *Allied Military Government*, pp.25–26, 41; Sywottek, *Deutsche Volksdemokratie*, pp.148–49; Balfour, 'Four-Power Control in Germany', pp.43–44; Pons, 'In the Aftermath of the Age of Wars', pp.280–81, 283, 285–86, 296–98; Ra'anan, *International Policy Formation in the USSR*, pp.22, 85–89, 91, 93–94; Antony Beevor, *The Fall of Berlin, 1945* (New York, 2003), pp.25, 36, 169–70; 194, 197; McCagg, *Stalin Embattled*, pp.136–37, 156; Vogt, *Denazification in Soviet-Occupied Germany*, pp.9, 11, 234, 239;

van Melis, *Entnazifizierung in Mecklenburg-Vorpommern*, p.23; Leonhard, *Child of the Revolution*,
pp.281, 337, 348–49; Naimark, *The Russians in Germany*, pp.9–10, 18–19, 20, 22, 26, 143, 167,
179–81, 183, 258–59, 319–20, 322–26, 332–33, 465–66, 470; Chotiner and Atwell, 'Soviet
Occupation Policy toward Germany', pp.55–56; Raack, 'Stalin Plans', pp.54–55, 60–68;
Vladimir Rudolph, 'The Administrative Organisation of Soviet Control, 1945–1948', in
Robert Slusser, ed., *Soviet Economic Policy in Post-war Germany: A Collection of Papers by Former
Soviet Officials* (New York, 1953), pp.18–24, 27–28, 41; Clare, *Berlin Days*, p.60; and *FRUS: The
Conferences at Malta and Yalta*, pp.176–77.

8 Welsh, *Revolutionärer Wandel auf Befehl?*, pp.23–24; Naimark, *The Russians in Germany*, pp.13–14,
21–22, 467; Loth, *Stalin's Unwanted Child*, p.23; Friedmann, *Allied Military Government of
Germany*, pp.35–36; Padover, *Experiment in Germany*, p.385; Peterson, *Russian Commands
and German Resistance*, p.15; *The Times*, 7 March 1945; and APW (44) 105 'Effect of
Disintegration of Central German Administration', 20 Oct. 1944, CAB 87/68, NAUK.

9 Leonhard, *Child of the Revolution*, pp.283–84; van Melis, *Entnazifizierung in Mecklenburg-
Vorpommern*, pp.19–20, 28–30, 39, 89; Vollnhals, ed., *Entnazifizierung*, pp.172, 174; Vogt,
Denazification in Soviet Occupied Germany, pp.23–24, 33; Naimark, *The Russians in Germany*,
pp.252–53; Sywottek, *Deutsche Volksdemokratie*, 182–84, 187, 192, 198; Duhnke, *Die KPD*,
p.399; and Ernst-Joachim Krüger, 'Zur Arbeit der Initiativgruppe Sobottka in Mecklenburg',
Wissenschaftliche Zeitschrift der Ernst-Moritz-Arndt-Universität Greifswald 13 (1964), pp.105–07.

10 Bower, *The Pledge Betrayed*, pp.132–33.

11 For instance, see the remarks of Heinrich Fomferra cited in Naimark, *The Russians in
Germany*, pp.43–44.

12 Wilfried Loth, 'Stalin's Plans for Post-War Germany'; Loth, *Stalin's Unwanted Child*, pp.5–12;
Volkov, 'Die deutsche Frage aus Stalins Sicht', p.26; Filitov, 'Problems of Post-War
Construction', both in Gori and Pons, eds., *The Soviet Union and Europe in the Cold War*,
pp.19–20, 24–27; Mastny, *The Cold War and Soviet Insecurity*, pp.19, 24; Balfour, 'Four-Power
Control in Germany', p.44; Peterson, *Russian Commands and German Resistance*, pp.8,
14, 19–20; Filitov, 'Stalins Deutschlandpolitik', pp.46–47, 49–51, 54; Sywottek, *Deutsche
Volksdemokratie*, pp.150–56, 174–80; Ra'anan, *International Policy Formation in the USSR*,
pp.89–91; Niethammer, *Entnazifizierung in Bayern*, pp.114–15; Naimark, *The Russians in
Germany*, pp.251-52, 319–20, 325, 334, 467; Leonhard, *Child of the Revolution*, pp.280–83,
297, 308, 346–50; Geoffrey Roberts, 'Stalin and Soviet Foreign Policy', in Melvin Leffler
and David Painter, eds., *Origins of the Cold War: An International History* (New York, 1994),
pp.50–51; Dallin and Firsov, *Dimitrov and Stalin*, p.256; Vogt, *Denazification in Soviet Occupied
Germany*, pp.24, 27–28, 34, 234; Erich Gniffke, *Jahre mit Ulbricht* (Cologne, 1966), pp.192–93,
233; Friedmann, *Allied Military Government*, p.25; Speech, 13 May 1945; and KPD Org Büro
'Politische Fragen', 20 May 1945, both in NY 4182/851a, Stiftung Archiv der Parteien und
Massenorganisationen der DDR im Bundesarchiv (SAPMO).

13 Loth, *Stalin's Unwanted Child*, p.13; Sywottek, *Deutsche Volksdemokratie*, p.161; Eberan, *Wer
war an Hitler schuld?*, p.22; Raack, 'Stalin Plans', pp.58–59; McCagg, *Stalin Embattled*,
pp.173–75, 371; Beevor, *The Fall of Berlin*, pp.197–98, 413; Maginnis, *Military Government
Journal*, p.259; Balfour, 'Four-Power Control in Germany', pp.41–42; Friedmann, *Allied
Military Government*, pp.25, 34; Goldman, 'Germans and Nazis', p.179; FitzGibbon,
Denazification, p.97; Gilbert, *A European Past*, p.203; Chotiner and Atwell, 'Soviet
Occupation Policy toward Germany', pp.49, 56; Clare, *Berlin Days*, p.95; Kahn,
Experiment in Occupation, p.212; *FRUS*, 1944, iii, 11; Robert Slusser, 'Soviet Policy and
the Division of Germany, 1941–1945', in Susan Linz, ed., *The Impact of World War II
on the Soviet Union* (Totowa, 1985), p.120; *FRUS*, 1945 v, pp.829–31; von Oppen, ed.,
Documents on Germany under Occupation, pp.37–38; Con O'Neill, note on file cover of
C2049, 10 May 1945, FO 371/46894, NAUK; and MI-14 'Mitropa' no.1, 29 July 1945,
FO 371/46967, NAUK.

14 Filitov, 'Problems of Post-War Construction', p.8; and *FRUS: The Conferences at Malta and Yalta*, p.177.

15 Loth, 'Stalin's Plans for Post-War Germany', p.33; Vogt, *Denazification in Soviet Occupied Germany*, pp.12, 19, 23–24, 35–36, 47, 91, 239; van Melis, *Entnazifizierung in Mecklenburg-Vorpommern*, pp.168–69; and FitzGibbon, *Denazification*, p.101.

16 ACC Coordinating Committee 'Report to the Council of Foreign Ministers', Section ii – Denazification, 21 Feb. 1947, FO 371/64352, NAUK.

17 Horvay, 'Military Government and Denazification in Ansbach', p.170; FitzGibbon, *Denazification*, pp.40–41, 82–83; Niethammer, *Entnazifizierung in Bayern*, pp.115–17; *FRUS, 1945*, iii, p.1040; *FRUS, 1946*, v, pp.535–36; and Public Safety Branch 'Evolution of Denazification in the Soviet Zone', 14 Feb. 1947, OMGUS – Public Safety Branch: Law for Liberation from National Socialism & Militarism 1945–49, RG 260, NA.

18 Naimark, *The Russians in Germany*, pp.11–16; and Friedmann, *Allied Military Government*, pp.60–61.

19 Zink, *American Military Government in Germany*, p.144; and Padover, *Experiment in Germany*, p.387.

20 van Melis, *Entnazifizierung in Mecklenburg-Vorpommern*, pp.38–39.

21 *Ibid.*, pp.69–70; and van Melis, 'Denazification in Mecklenburg-Vorpommern', pp.355, 357, 359.

22 *Pogranichnye Voiska SSSR Mai 1945–1950* (Moscow, 1976), p.112.

23 Peterson, *Russian Commands and German Resistance*, pp.174, 195; 'Vertraulicher Bericht über die Bezirkskonferenz der Provinz Sachsen am 20.7.1945'; 'Bericht aus dem Unterbezirk Rochlitz', 9 Aug. 1945, both in NY 4182/855, SAPMO; and 'Bericht aus Quedlinburg am Harz', 1 Aug. 1945, NY 4182/854, SAPMO.

24 FitzGibbon, *Denazification*, p.100; Vollnhals, ed., *Entnazifizierung*, pp.180–86; Peterson, *Russian Commands and German Resistance*, p.266; and *Thüringer Volkszeitung*, 5 Aug. 1945. For the heavy Nazification of the administrative apparatus in Thuringia, particularly in rural districts, see 'Bericht über die Mitgliederwerbung des Bez. Thüringen', NY 4182/856, SAPMO. Many of the replacements for Thuringian officials came from Silesia, which ensured that their backgrounds were difficult to trace, although it did not guarantee that they were not Nazis. Peterson, *Russian Commands and German Resistance*, p.292.

25 Welsh, *Revolutionärer Wandel auf Befehl?*, pp.171–72. See, for instance, Wolfgang Meinecke, 'Die Entnazifizierung in der sowjetischen Besatzungszone 1945 bis 1948', *Zeitschrift für Geschischtswissenschaft* 32 (1984), p.970.

26 Vogt, *Denazification in Soviet-Occupied Germany*, pp.29, 31–32; Naimark, *The Russians in Germany*, pp.256, 259–60, 271; Raack, 'Stalin Plans', pp.60–61; and Leonhard, *Child of the Revolution*, pp.318–26.

27 Naimark, *The Russians in Germany*, pp.268–69.

28 *Ibid.*, p.355; van Melis, *Entnazifizierung in Mecklenburg-Vorpommern*, p.68; Balfour, 'Four-Power Control in Germany', pp.67–68, 176; Peterson, *Russian Commands and German Resistance*, pp.19–20; and Vogt, *Denazification in Soviet-Occupied Germany*, pp.39, 44–45, 52–53, 59, 205–06.

29 KPD-Betriebsgruppe der Bergwitzer Braunkohlenwerke AG 'Bergwitzer Braunkohlenwerke AG', 26 Feb. 1946, NY 4182/1197, SAPMO.

30 Peterson, *Russian Commands and German Resistance*, p.407.

31 Naimark, *The Russians in Germany*, p.13; and van Melis, 'Denazification in Mecklenburg-Vorpommern', pp.356, 358–59.

32 Naimark, *The Russians in Germany*, pp.15, 266, 275; Peterson, *Russian Commands and German Resistance*, pp.459–60; Pfeil, 'Antifascisme et Dénazification', 19–20, 22; Vogt, *Denazification in Soviet-Occupied Germany*, pp.6, 38, 60, 66, 74; and Balfour, 'Four-Power Control in Germany', pp.68, 176.

33 Peterson, *Russian Commands and German Resistance*, pp.224, 233–37.

34 Sywottek, *Deutsche Volksdemokratie*, pp.184–85; van Melis, 'Denazification in Mecklenburg–Vorpommern', p.359; and Krüger, 'Zur Arbeit der Initiativgruppe Sobottka', p.112.

35 Beevor, *The Fall of Berlin*, pp.298, 300, 307–08, 310–16, 326–27, 340, 344–46, 355, 363, 366, 370, 392–95, 409–14, 417–19; Ernst-Günther Schenk, *Ich Sah Berlin Sterben* (Herford, 1970), p.109; and Leonhard, *Child of the Revolution*, p.298.

36 Gniffke, *Jahre mit Ulbricht*, pp.23–25; Leonhard, *Child of the Revolution*, pp.297, 301–07, 309, 315–16, 330; Naimark, *The Russians in Germany*, p.15; Beevor, *The Fall of Berlin*, pp.307–08, 320–21; 'Bezirk Köpenick Bericht über die Funktionärversammlung am 5.6.45', NY 4182/851a, SAPMO; and 'Preliminary Interrogation Report on Ove Leif Guidperd', Entry 119A, RG 226, NA.

37 Pfeil, 'Antifascism et Dénazification', pp.16–17; Maginnis, *Military Government Journal*, p.262; and Abtlg. Landespolitik 'Entnazifizierung in Gross-Berlin', 17 Feb. 1948, NY 4182/1197, SAPMO.

38 Maginnis, *Military Government Journal*, pp.277, 288, 290, 298, 302, 304, 345. The chief exception to Berlin's denazification involved Ulbricht's retention of the infamous NS *Blockleiter* system, which the KPD's 5 April instructions permitted. Ulbricht cleansed this structure of its most unregenerate Nazis and kept it in place. After some nasty exchanges between the Western Allies and the Russians, the Americans (in August) and the British (in October) disbanded the *Blockleiter* system in their sectors of the city.

39 *Manchester Guardian*, 27 Aug. 1945

40 *FRUS*, 1946, v, pp.704–06.

41 Niethammer, 'Allierte Internierungslager in Deutschland nach 1945', pp.102, 105–10, 113–16; van Melis, *Entnazifizierung in Mecklenburg-Vorpommern*, pp.25–27; Beevor, *The Fall of Berlin*, pp.415–16; Naimark, *The Russians in Germany*, pp.376–86, 394–95; Peterson, *Russian Commands and German Resistance*, pp.25, 63, 85; Jan Lipinsky, 'Häftlingsstruktur im Speziallager Bautzen aus sowjetischer Sicht', in Alexander Plato, ed., *Sowjetische Speziallager in Deutschland 1945 bis 1950: Studien und Berichte* (Berlin, 1998), pp.497, 500; and van Melis, 'Denazification in Mecklenburg-Vorpommern', p.358.

42 Peterson, *Russian Commands and German Resistance*, pp.19, 113; van Melis, 'Denazification in Mecklenburg-Vorpommern', p.357; and Naimark, *The Russians in Germany*, p.62. The Mayor of Leipzig complained that he had the texts of only twenty of 148 orders issued by the Soviets, and the minister-president of Saxony claimed that he lacked an archive of such instructions. Many Soviet orders were communicated only orally.

43 van Melis, *Entnazifizierung in Mecklenburg-Vorpommern*, p.105.

44 *Ibid.*, pp.71–76, 80–111, 116–17, 119–21, 125, 323, 332; Peterson, *Russian Commands and German Resistance*, pp.18, 194–95, 203, 256, 350; van Melis, 'Denazification in Mecklenburg-Vorpommern', pp.356, 360–63; Vollnhals, ed. *Entnazifizierung*, pp.178–80; Pfeil, 'Antifascisme et Dénazification', p.21; Vogt, *Denazification in Soviet-Occupied Germany*, pp.49–52, 53–55, 60–61, 144–45, 165; Naimark, *The Russians in Germany*, pp.62–63, 289; and 'Order No.0128 – Implementation of Control Council Law No.10', 23 Dec. 1945, OMGUS – Public Safety Branch: Law for Liberation from National Socialism & Militarism 1945–49, RG 260, NA.

45 Vogt, *Denazification in Soviet-Occupied Germany*, pp.63–68; Vollnhals, ed., *Entnazifizierung*, p.191; Chotiner and Atwell, 'Soviet Ocupation Policy toward Germany', p.59; van Melis, 'Denazification in Mecklenburg-Vorpommern', pp.367–68; van Melis, *Entnazifizierung in Mecklenburg-Vorpommern*, pp.323–24; Peterson, *Russian Commands and German Resistance*, pp.18, 108–09, 112–13, 117, 118, 127, 129, 152, 154, 176–81, 195, 203, 211, 239, 240, 279, 319, 385, 407, 443, 489; Naimark, *The Russians in Germany*, pp.170–72, 183–86, 191–92, 452–57; KPD Org Büro 'Politische Fragen', 20 May 1945, NY 4182/851a, SAPMO; DVZI/6032/Pf/Wa 'Allgemeiner Überblick über den Stand der Entnazifizierung der Verwaltung

und Wirtschaft in der Industrie und dem Handwerk innerhalb der sowjetischen Besatzungszone', 28 April 1947, NY 4182/1197, SAPMO; SED Zentralsekretariat to all Landesvorstände der SED, 10 Sept. 1947, DY 30/IV 2/2.022/5, SAPMO; and memo by Political Division, CCG(BE), 15 April 1947, FO 371/64353, NAUK.

46 Welsh, *Revolutionärer Wandel auf Befehl?*, pp.94–114; Naimark, *The Russians in Germany*, pp.27, 66, 441–46, 448; Peterson, *Russian Commands and German Resistance*, pp.25–26, 243, 324, 342; Vogt, *Denazification in Soviet-Occupied Germany*, pp.160–62; van Melis, *Entnazifizierung in Mecklenburg-Vorpommern*, pp.126–27, 167–68; Marion Klewitz, 'Allied Policy in Berlin', pp.199, 203; Trevor Davies, 'A British View of Education in Berlin', both in Hearndon, ed., *The British in Germany*, p.219; and Tent, *Mission on the Rhine*, pp.238–39. In *Land* Thuringia, a school board conference instructed teachers to purge schools of the children of Nazi Party members. This radical measure was blocked by the Thuringian education minister on 10 January 1947. Minister of Interior, *Land* Thuringia to Ulbricht, 12 March 1947, NY 4182/1197, SAPMO.

47 Helga Welsh, 'Entnazifizierung und Wiederöffnung der Universität Leipzig 1945–1946', *Vierteljahrshefte für Zeitgeschichte* 33 (1985), pp.343–54, 359–72; Peterson, *Russian Commands and German Resistance*, pp.151; 157–58, 416; van Melis, *Entnazifizierung in Mecklenburg-Vorpommern*, pp.126–27; Tent, *Mission on the Rhine*, p.66; Phillips, 'The Reopening of Universities in the British Zone', pp.12, 15; Pingel, 'Attempts at University Reform in the British Zone', p.23, both in Phillips, ed., *German Universities after the Surrender*; and Naimark, *The Russians in Germany*, pp.36, 66.

48 Peterson, *Russian Commands and German Resistance*, pp.52–53; Balfour, 'Four-Power Control in Germany', p.105; and Naimark, *The Russians in Germany*, pp.17, 30–31. If one recalls the horrendous scale of wartime casualties in the USSR, as well as the pressing demands of domestic reconstruction, the reason for manpower shortages becomes apparent. The Soviet garrison in Germany shrank by a million men from May 1945 to February 1947, eventually settling at a level between 350,000 to 500,000 troops. In 1946, 5000 SMA cadres were sent back to Russia, leaving 10,000 of 41,000 positions in the SMA unfilled.

49 While municipal institutions in Berlin had been effectively cleansed in 1945, there was still room for a broader denazification programme, albeit organised on a four-power basis. In March 1946, the Berlin *Kommandatura* decreed Law 101a, which required the dismissal of all persons belonging to the mandatory removal categories of CC Directive 24. The law also mandated the creation of seven-person denazification committees, which had the power to entertain appeals and forward cases to the Sector Commandants for final resolution. All decisions by the denazification boards had to be unanimous. Naturally, appeals came mainly from 'nominal' Nazis. According to opinion polling conducted by the Americans, Berliners had an appetite for a relatively harsh form of denazification, at least in comparison to public attitudes in other parts of Germany. MI-14 'Mitropa' no.18, 23 March 1946, FO 371/55630, NAUK; Demoth to Fahy, 19 March 1946, OMGUS – Office of the Adjutant General: General Correspondence (Decimal File) 1945–49, RG 260, NA; ICD Report no.55 'Public Attitudes toward Denazification', 15 April 1947, OMGUS – Records of CAD, Public Safety Branch: Law for Liberation from National Socialism and Militarism, 1945–49, RG 260, NA; and Abtlg. Landespolitik 'Entnazifizierung in Gross-Berlin', 17 Feb. 1948, NY 4182/1197, SAPMO.

50 Welsh, *Revolutionärer Wandel auf Befehl?*, p.18, 66–67; Vollnhals, ed., *Entnazifizierung*, pp.191–93, 200–01; Vogt, *Denazification of Soviet-Occupied Germany*, pp.48–49, 55, 72, 77–78, 79, 80–82, 111, 183; van Melis, *Entnazifizierung in Mecklenburg-Vorpommern*, pp.146–49, 167–87; Naimark, *The Russians in Germany*, p.275; Peterson, *Russian Commands and German Resistance*, p.44; Leonhard, *Child of the Revolution*, pp.357–58; *FRUS*, 1947, ii,

p.140; *Neue Zeit*, 4 Nov. 1945; Parteivorstandes der SED 'Zur Frage der ehemaligen nominellen Mitgleider der NSDAP', 20 June 1946; DZVI/6032/Pf/Wa 'Allgemeiner Überblick über den Stand der Entnazifizierung der Verwaltung und Wirtschaft in der Industrie und dem Handwerk innerhalb der sowjetischen Besatzungszone', 28 April 1947, both in NY 4182/1197, SAPMO; 'Directives for the Punishment and Expiation of Hitler Criminals and Nazi Activists', 3 Aug. 1945; Public Safety Branch 'Evaluation of Denazification in the Soviet Zone', 14 Feb. 1947, both in OMGUS – Public Safety Branch: Law for Liberation from National Socialism & Militarism 1945–49, RG 260, NA; and ACC Coordinating Committee 'Report to the Council of Foreign Ministers', Section ii – Denazification, 21 Feb. 1947, FO 371/64352, NAUK.

51 Naimark, *The Russians in Germany*, pp.16, 328–29.

52 Vogt, *Denazification in Soviet-Occupied Germany*, pp.5, 58, 85–89, 116–17, 119, 123–24, 127, 132, 164–68, 177, 181–90, 224, 237, 447; Peterson, *Russian Commands and German Resistance*, pp.34–35; van Melis, 'Denazification in Mecklenburg-Vorpommern', pp.364–65; van Melis, *Entnazifizierung in Mecklenburg-Vorpommern*, pp.116–17, 189–94, 196, 199; Friedmann, *Allied Military Government*, pp.118–19; Pfeil, 'Antifascisme et Dénazification', pp.22–23; Vollnhals, ed., *Entnazifizierung*, pp.203–05; ACC Coordinating Committee 'Report to the Council of Foreign Ministers', Section ii – Denazification, 21 Feb. 1947, FO 371/64352, NAUK; Fechner and Ulbricht to the *Land* central committees of the SED, 31 Jan. 1947; DZVI/6032/Pf/Wa 'Stand der Säuberung in Wirtschaft und Verwaltung von Industrie und Handwerk des Landes Sachsen von nazistischen Elementen…', 24 April 1947; DVZI/6032/Pf/Wa 'Allgemeiner Überblick über den Stand der Entnazifizierung der Verwaltung und Wirtschaft in der Industrie und dem Handwerk innerhalb der sowjetischen Besatzungszone', 28 April 1947; FDGB Bundesvorstand 'Anwendung des Befehls Nr. 201 in der Bertrieben', 19 Sept. 1947; A. Plenkowski 'Über den Stand der Entnazifizierung in der Sowjetischen Besatzungszone', 30 April 1947, all in NY 4182/1197, SAPMO; and Public Safety Branch 'Evaluation of Denazification in the Soviet Zone', 14 Feb. 1947, OMGUS – Public Safety Branch: Law for Liberation from National Socialism & Militarism 1945–49, RG 260, NA.

53 Vogt, *Denazification in Soviet-Occupied Germany*, pp.169–70.

54 *Ibid.*, pp.6, 9, 88, 91–93, 95–96, 129, 154–55, 164, 233; Volkov, 'Die deutsche Frage aus Stalins Sicht', pp.27–29; Vollnhals, ed., *Entnazifizierung*, pp.197–99, 202; van Melis, *Entnazifizierung in Mecklenburg-Vorpommern*, pp.195–97; Peterson, *Russian Commands and German Resistance*, pp.64–65, 358; 'Extract from Digest for Germany and Austria no.476 of Feb. 28th', FO 371/64352, NAUK; W. Pieck 'Der Sinn der Entnazifizierung', 21 Feb. 1947; DZVI/6032/Pf/Wa 'Allgemeiner Überblick über den Stand der Entnazifizierung der Verwaltung und Wirtschaft in der Industrie und dem Handwerk innerhalb der sowjetischen Besatzungszone', 28 April 1947; A. Plenikowski 'Über den Stand der Entnazifizierung in der Sowjetischen Besatzungszone', 30 April 1947, both in NY 4182/1197, SAPMO; and Director of Intelligence 'PGs in Official Positions in Province Saxony', 28 Feb. 1947, OMGUS – Public Safety Branch: Law for Liberation from National Socialism & Militarism 1945–49, RG 260, NA. For the formation of the NPDP, see Loth, *Stalin's Unwanted Child*, p.98.

55 Herbst to Landesregierung Sachsen-Anhalt, Minister für Wirtschaft v. Verkehr, Abt. Wasserwirtschaft, 12 July 1947; and Abt. Landespolitik 'Über den Stand der Entnazifizierung in der sowjetischen Besatzungszone', 4 Aug. 1947, both in NY 4182/1197, SAPMO.

56 Leonhard, *Child of the Revolution*, pp.326–28, 350–51; Naimark, *The Russians in Germany*, pp.143, 258, 386–87; and Loth, *Stalin's Unwanted Child*, p.25. For the official re-founding of the KPD, see *Deutsche Volkszeitung*, 13 June 1945.

57 Loth, 'Stalin's Plans for Post-War Germany', pp.32–33; Loth, *Stalin's Unwanted Child*, pp.25–26; Peterson, *Russian Commands and German Resistance*, pp.21, 483–84; Chotiner

and Atwell, 'Soviet Occupation Policy toward Germany', pp.56–57; van Melis, *Entnazifizierung in Mecklenburg-Vorpommern*, p.34; and Naimark, *The Russians in Germany*, pp.65, 274–76.

58 Naimark, *The Soviets in Germany*, pp.277–84, 309, 320, 323–24, 331–35, 468; Loth, *Stalin's Unwanted Child*, pp.26–34; and Peterson, *Russian Commands and German Resistance*, pp.40–43, 79–80.

59 Vogt, *Denazification in Soviet-Occupied Germany*, p.90.

60 Rudolph, 'The Administrative Organisation of Soviet Control', pp.32–33, 41–42, 52–53; Ra'anan, *International Policy Formation in the USSR*, pp.22–23, 93; Peterson, *Russian Commands and German Resistance*, pp.30–32, 152–53, 261–62; McCagg, *Stalin Embattled*, pp 136–37; Loth, *Stalin's Unwanted Child*, pp.44–45; Beevor, *The Fall of Berlin*, p.407; Naimark, *The Russians in Germany*, pp.180–83; Leonhard, *Child of the Revolution*, p.361; and J.P. Nettle, *The Eastern Zone and Soviet Policy in Germany* (London, 1951), p.201.

61 Ra'anan, *International Policy Formation in the USSR*, pp.91–92; Naimark, *The Russians in Germany*, pp.24, 44–45, 68, 336–41; and Peterson, *Russian Commands and German Resistance*, pp.29, 42, 480–81.

62 Loth, 'Stalin's Plans for Post-War Germany', pp.29–33; Loth, *Stalin's Unwanted Child*, pp.24, 72, 95–110, 181–82; Peterson, *Russian Commands and German Resistance*, pp.51–52, 71, 82, 475, 484; Naimark, *The Russians in Germany*, pp.299–313, 332–35, 340–42, 344–46, 352; and Gniffke, *Jahre mit Ulbricht*, pp.248–59, 255–66, 271–76.

63 Naimark, *The Russians in Germany*, pp.350–52, 466–69; Loth, 'Stalin's Plans for Post-War Germany', p.33; Loth, *Stalin's Unwanted Child*, pp.24; and Mastny, *The Cold War and Soviet Insecurity*, p.25.

64 For the change in the tenor and nature of the SED, see Leonhard, *Child of the Revolution*, pp.360–64.

65 Vogt, *Denazification in Soviet-Occupied Germany*, pp.96–99, 103–05, 108, 110, 113, 116, 130–31, 170, 186, 210, 219, 224, 235–36; van Melis, *Entnazifizierung in Mecklenburg-Vorpommern*, pp.201–32, 237–45, 251–76; Vollnhals, ed., *Entnazifizierung*, pp.206–11; Niethammer, 'Alliierte Internierungslager in Deutschland nach 1945', p.111; von Melis, 'Denazification in Mecklenburg-Vorpommern', pp.356, 365–66; Pfeil, 'Antifascisme et Dénazification', pp.23–24; Naimark, *The Russians in Germany*, p.361; *Neues Deutschland*, 17 Aug. 1947; 23 Aug. 1947; *Tägliche Rundschau*, 20 Aug. 1947; 'Richtlinien zur Durchführung der Direktiven 24 und 38 des Alliierten Kontrollrats', 4 Aug. 1947; 'Vorschläge zum Befehl Nr. 201 bei der Besprechung im Sekretariat Ulbricht-Fechner am Sonnabend, dem 23.8.47'; 'Entnazifizierung der Deutschen Zentralverwaltung des Verkehrs', 25 Aug. 1947, both in NY 4182/1197, SAPMO; and SED Zentralsekretariat to all Landesvorstände der SED, 10 Sept. 1947, DY 30/IV 2/2.022/5, SAPMO.

66 Naimark, *The Russians in Germany*, pp.52–56, 163–66; Gniffke, *Jahre mit Ulbricht*, pp.197–99, 280–82; and Peterson, *Russian Commands and German Resistance*, pp.73–75.

67 Vogt, *Denazification in Soviet-Occupied Germany*, pp.3, 99, 100–07, 111–12, 131, 142, 218–30; van Melis, *Entnazifizierung in Mecklenburg-Vorpommern*, pp.232–33, 235–37; Peterson, *Russian Commands and German Resistance*, p.85; Friedmann, *Allied Military Government*, p.125; A. Plenikowski, 'Über den Stand der Entnazifizierung in der Sowjetischen Besatzungszone', 30 April 1947; and Referat P5 'Bericht', 24 Jan. 1948, both in NY 4182/1197, SAPMO.

68 Naimark, *The Russians in Germany*, pp.54–55; and van Melis, *Entnazifizierung in Mecklenburg-Vorpommern*, pp.211–12.

69 Naimark, *The Russians in Germany*, pp.65–66, 304, 306–07, 366–67, 386, 394–95; Vollnhals, ed., *Entnazifizierung*, pp.212–20; van Melis, *Entnazifizierung in Mecklenburg-Vorpommern*, pp.198–99, 245–49; Vogt, *Denazification in Soviet-Occupied Germany*, pp.3, 107–11, 116–17, 122–23, 127–28, 130–31, 155, 165, 168, 170–71, 184, 228–29, 231, 235–36; Pfeil,

'Antifascisme et Dénazification', pp.17, 24; Peterson, *Russian Commands and German Resistance*, pp.85, 209, 212–13, 247, 363; van Melis, 'Denazification in Mecklenburg-Vorpommern', p.366; Referat P5 'Bericht', 24 Jan. 1948; 'Gute und schlechte Biespiele bei der Durchführung der Befehls 201', 7 Feb. 1948; Plenikowski to Ulbricht, 12 Feb. 1948; Abt. Landespolitik 'Auswertung der Entnazifizierung nach Befehl 201 nach dem Stand vom 25.1.48 in der Sowjetische Besatzungzone', 18 Feb. 1948; Abteilung Landespolitik 'Strukturplan für die Errichtung und den Betrieb von Häftlingslagern gemäss Befehl 201', 11 March 1948; 'Durchführung des Magistrats von Gross-Berlin v. 23.2.1949 über den Abschluss der Entnazifizierung'; 'Entwurf – Verordnung', 3 Aug. 1949; 'Entwurf – Beschluss des Volksrates'; Landesvorstand SED Saxony, Sekretariat und PPA to Mückeberger and Schliebe, 3 Aug. 1949, all in NY 4182/1197, SAPMO; and SED Zentralsekretariat to all Landesvorstände, 10 Sept. 1947, DY/30/IV 2/2.022/5, SAPMO.

70 Vogt, *Denazification in Soviet-Occupied Germany*, pp.3, 14; Pfeil, 'Antifascisme et Dénazification', pp.13, 25; Herf, *Divided Memory*, p.72; and Peterson, *Russian Commands and German Resistance*, p.85. The Soviets themselves claimed that 520,000 Nazis were denazified in 1947/48. Vollnhals, ed., *Entnazifizierung*, p.220.

71 Peterson, *Russian Commands and German Resistance*, pp.119, 129, 362, 483.

72 Welsh, *Revolutionärer Wandel auf Befehl?*, p.168.

73 Vogt, *Denazification in Soviet-Occupied Germany*, pp.2–3, 15, 126–27, 165; Vollnhals, ed., *Entnazifizierung*, pp.222–24; Pfeil, 'Antifascisme et Dénazification', pp.15–16, 25–26; and Welsh, *Revolutionärer Wandel auf Befehl?*, pp.168–69.

74 Vogt, *Denazification in Soviet-Occupied Germany*, p.240.

75 *Ibid.*, pp.62–70; and Loth, *Stalin's Unwanted Child*, p.35.

76 Peterson, *Russian Commands and German Resistance*, p.491; and van Melis, 'Denazification in Mecklenburg-Vorpommern', p.355.

Chapter 5: Tough but Sensitive

1 Angelika Ruge-Schatz, *Umerziehung und Schulpolitik in der französischen Besatzungszone 1945–1949* (Frankfurt a.M., 1977), pp.34–35; Möhler, *Entnazifizierung in Rheinland-Pfalz und im Saarland*, pp.14, 54, 403; Grohnert, *Die Entnazifizierung in Baden*, pp.11-13, 57; Charles Muller, 'Les premiers mois de l'occupation', in Joseph Jurt, ed., *Von Besatzungszeit zur deutsch-französischen Kooperation/De la période d'occupation à la coopération franco-allemande* (Freiburg, 1993), pp.190–91; Rainer Hudemann, 'Kulturpolitik im Spannungsfeld der Deutschlandpolitik. Frühe Direktiven für die französische Besatzung in Deutschland', in Franz Knipping, Jacques le Rider, Karl Mayer, eds., *Frankreichs Kulturpolitik in Deutschland 1945–1950* (Tübingen, 1987), p.19; Klaus-Dietmar Henke, 'Politik der Widersprüch. Zur Charakteristik der französischen Militärregierung in Deutschland nach dem Zweiten Weltkrieg', in Claus Scharf and Hans-Jürgen Schröder, eds., *Die Deutschlandpolitik Frankreichs und die Französische Zone 1945–1949* (Wiesbaden, 1983), p.56; Willis, *The French in Germany*, pp.71–73; and MI-14 'Mitropa' no.5, 22 Sept. 1945, FO 371/46967, NAUK.

2 Balfour, 'Four-Power Control in Germany', pp.36–37; Willis, *The French in Germany*, pp.8–14; and *FRUS: The Conferences at Malta and Yalta*, pp.297–98.

3 FitzGibbon, *Denazification*, p.107; Plischke, 'Denazification in Germany', p.219; Henke, *Politische Säuberung*, pp.23, 40; Möhler, *Entnazifizierung in Rheinland-Pfalz und im Saarland*, p.71; Willis, *The French in Germany*, pp.96, 105–06, 108; Volker Rödel, 'Die Entnazifizierung in Nordteil der französischen Zone', in Franz-Josef Heyen, ed., *Rheinland-Pfalz ensteht: Beiträge zu den Anfängen des Landes Rheinland-Pfalz in Koblenz*

1945–1951 (Boppard, 1984), pp.263–64; Perry Biddiscombe, *Werwolf!* (Cardiff, 1998), p.260; and MI-14 'Mitropa' no.5, 22 Sept. 1945, FO 371/46967, NAUK.

4 *FRUS: The Conferences at Malta and Yalta*, pp.307–09; Friedmann, *Allied Military Government*, pp.27–29; Möhler, *Entnazifizierung in Rheinland-Pfalz und im Saarland*, pp.14-15, 18, 21-25; Grohnert, *Die Entnazifizierung in Baden*, pp.9–10; Elmar Krautkrämer, 'Das Rhénanieprojekt und die Frage der territorialen Gestaltung der französischen Besatzungszone', in Jurt, ed., *Von Besatzungszeit zur deutsch-französischen Kooperation/De la période d'occupation à la coopération franco-allemande*, pp.62–65, 73–76; Eberan, *Wer war an Hitler schuld?*, pp.24–25; Fürstenau, *Entnazifizierung*, pp.42, 135; Hellmuth Auerbach, '"Que faire l'Allemagne?"' Diskussionsbeitrage Französischer Deutschlandexperten 1944–1950', *Cahiers de l'institut d'histoire du temps présent* 13–14 (1989), pp.290–92; Jérôme Vaillant, 'La Dénazification: un problème culturel', in Jérôme Vaillant, ed., *La dénazification par les vainqueurs* (Lille, 1981), pp.9–10; Raymond Poidevin, 'Die Französische Deutschlandpolitik 1943–1949'; Wilfried Loth, 'Die Franzosen und die deutsche Frage 1945–1949', both in Scharf and Schröder, eds., *Die Deutschlandpolitik Frankreichs und die Französische Zone*, pp.15–21, 27–36; FitzGibbon, *Denazification*, pp.101–03; Balfour, 'Four-Power Control in Germany', pp.38–39; Willis, *The French in Germany*, pp.30–33, 36–39, 93–94;148–49; Hudemann, 'Kulturpolitik im Spannungsfeld der Deutschlandpolitik', p.17; Rainer Hudemann, 'Französischer Besatzungszone 1945–1952', *Neue politische Literatur* 26 (1981), pp.327, 330–32; Ruge-Schatz, *Umerziehung und Schulpolitik*, pp.30–31; and W.D. Halls, 'The 'German Question' and Post-War University Reform in Germany: A Comparative Note', David Phillips, ed., *German Universities after the Surrender – British Occupation Policy and the Control of Higher Education* (Oxford, 1983), pp.33–34.

5 Willis, *The French in Germany*, pp.71, 149.

6 Hudemann, 'Kulturpolitik im Spannungsfeld der Deutschlandpolitik', pp.15–16, 18, 30–31; Möhler, *Entnazifizierung in Rheinland-Pfalz und im Saarland*, pp.2–4; and Rauh-Kühne, 'Forschungen zur französischen Zone, pp.16–17.

7 Ruge-Schatz, *Umerziehung und Schulpolitik*, pp.22–23, 36–38; Möhler, *Entnazifizierung in Rheinland-Pfalz und im Saarland*, pp.27-28; FitzGibbon, *Denazification*, p.102; Balfour, 'Four-Power Control in Germany', p.39; Hudemann, 'Kultirpolitik im Spannungsfeld der Deutschlandpolitik', p.18; Willis, *The French in Germany*, pp.149–50; Raymond Betts, *Assimilation and Association in French Colonial Theory, 1890–1914* (Lincoln, 2005), pp.x-xi, 12–32, 43; Laird Boswell, 'From Liberation to Purge Trials in the "Mythic Provinces": Recasting French Identities in Alsace and Lorraine, 1918–1920', *French Historical Studies* 23, no.1 (Winter 2000), pp.141, 153–54; Stephen Harp, *Learning to Be Loyal: Primary Schooling as Nation Building in Alsace and Lorraine, 1850–1940* (Dekalb, 1998), pp.186–92; and minutes on File C 10529, 11 Aug. 1947, FO 371/64351, NAUK.

8 Willis, *The French in Germany*, pp.94–95, 167–77, 188; Vollnhals, ed., *Entnazifizierung*, p.154; Grohnert, *Die Entnazifizierung in Baden*, pp.108-16; FitzGibbon, *Denazification*, pp.107–08; Friedmann, *Allied Military Government*, pp.23, 30, 42; Hudemann, 'Französischer Besatzungszone', pp.351–52; Jean Moreau, 'Les aspects particuliers de la politique d'occupation française dans les domaines de la jeunesse et de l'éducation populaire'; Angelika Ruge-Schatz, 'Le revers de la médaille: Contradictions et limites de l'apport culturel du gouvernement militaire français en Allemagne', both in Vaillant, ed., *Le dénazification par les vainqueurs*, pp.20–22, 105–07; Halls, 'The "German Question" and Post-War University Reform in Germany', p.34; Tent, *Mission on the Rhine*, p.313; and Robert Birley, 'British Policy in Retrospect', in Arthur Hearnden, ed., *The British in Germany* (London, 1978), pp.46–47.

9 Hudemann, 'Kulturpolitik im Spannungsfeld der Deutschlandpolitik', pp.19–21, 24–25; Hudemann, 'Französischer Besatzungszone', p.327; Ruge-Schatz, *Umerziehung und Schulpolitik*, pp.40–41; Auerbach, '"Que faire l'Allemagne?"', pp.291–92; Henke, *Politische*

Säuberung, p.36; Henke, 'Politik der Widersprüch', pp.56–57, 62–63; Möhler, *Entnazifizierung in Rheinland-Pfalz und im Saarland*, pp.15-16, 18-19, 20-21, 22, 23, 69, 406; Grohnert, *Die Entnazifizierung in Baden*, pp.15, 57–58; Moreau, 'Les aspects particuliers de la politique d'occupation française', p.20; Rauh-Kühne, 'Forschungen zur Französischen Zone', p.17; Muller, 'Les premiers mois de l'occupation', pp.192–93; and Willis, *The French in Germany*, pp.67–70, 73, 89–91. In a new version of the 'deprussianisation' idea, Rainer Hudemann admits a degree of tension between the 'soft' and 'hard' elements of French policy, but argues that they were actually two sides of 'a double-sided security policy'. Rainer Hudemann, 'Frankreichs Besatzung in Deutschland: Hindernis oder Auftakt der deutsch-französischen Kooperation?', in Jurt, ed., *Von Besatzungszeit zur deutsch-französischen Kooperation / De la période d'occupation à la coopération franco-allemande*, pp.241–43.

10 Rödel, 'Die Entnazifizierung in Nordteil der französischen Zone', p.263; Möhler, *Entnazifizierung in Rheinland-Pfalz und im Saarland*, pp.403; Henke, *Politische Säuberung*, p.25; FitzGibbon, *Denazification*, pp.102–04, 139; Plischke, 'Denazification in Germany', p.219; Clare, *Berlin Days*, pp.106–07; Ruge-Schatz, *Umerziehung und Schulpolitik*, p.71; Balfour, 'Four-Power Control in Germany', p.176; and Willis, *The French in Germany*, pp.95, 150, 182.

11 Hudemann, 'Kulturpolitik im Spannungsfeld der Deutschlandpolitik', p.26; and Auerbach, '"Que faire l'Allemagne?"', p.292.

12 Laffont to Directors General and Directors (CAB/C No.722), 19 September 1945, OMGUS – Records of the Civil Administration Division, Public Safety Branch: Law for Liberation from National Socialism & Militarism 1945–49, RG 260, NA.

13 Henke, *Politische Säuberung*, p.43; and Fürstenau, *Entnazifizierung*, p.42.

14 Balfour, 'Four-Power Control in Germany', pp.105, 177. In denazification matters that came up at the Control Council, the French often supported the British position. 'Denazification: Progress since the Meeting of the Council of Foreign Ministers in Moscow', FO 371/64353, NAUK.

15 Hudemann, 'Kulturpolitik im Spannungsfeld der Deutschlandpolitik', p.24; Möhler, *Entnazifizierung in Rheinland-Pfalz und im Saarland*, pp.54-57, 403; Grohnert, *Die Entnazifizierung in Baden*, pp.13-14, 17-23; Fürstenau, *Entnazifizierung*, pp.30, 135–37; Henke, *Politische Säuberung*, pp.20–21, 23, 34–37; Rödel, 'Die Entnazifizierung in Nordteil der französischen Zone', p.263; Peter Brommer, ed., *Quellen zur Geschichte von Rheinland-Pfalz während der französischen Besatzung* (Mainz, 1985), pp.39, 55; and Willis, *The French in Germany*, pp.73–74, 76. For an example of a French officer citing the Potsdam decisions, see Vollnhals, ed., *Entnazifizierung*, pp.105, 107.

16 Georges Ferber, 'Vicissitudes ou les débuts de la presse à Constance en 1945-1946', in Vaillant, ed., *La dénazification par les vainqueurs*, pp.65–66; Willis, *The French in Germany*, p.71; Perry Biddiscombe, *The Last Nazis* (Stroud, 2004), pp.238–39; Biddiscombe, *Werwolf!*, pp.260–61; Henri Amouroux, *La page n'est pas encore tourneé* (Paris, 1993), p.274; Grohnert, *Die Entnazifizierung in Baden*, pp.27-28; *Temps Présent*, 27 April 1945; *The Observer*, 29 April 1945; *Neue Zürcher Zeitung*, 12 July 1945; 6th Army Group G-5 Mission 'Alleged Sanctions at Freiburg and Freudenstadt', 26 June 1945, State Dept. Decimal Files 1945–49, 740.00119 Control (Germany), RG 59, NA; and Swiss press excerpts on Germany, 26 July 1945, FO 371/46933, NAUK. The occupying power's arrogance and the excesses of the initial occupation period did much to create a negative impression of French occupation, which remains popular in southwestern Germany even today. Rainer Hudemann, 'Zur Politik der französischen Besatzungsmacht', in Heyen, ed., *Rheinland-Pfalz ensteht*, pp.31, 41; and Henke, 'Politik der Widersprüch', p.55.

17 Niethammer, 'Allierte Internierungslager in Deutschland nach 1945', p.112; and ACC Coordinating Committee 'Report to the Council of Foreign Ministers', Section ii – Denazification, 21 Feb. 1947, FO 371/64352, NAUK.

18 Henke, *Politische Säuberung*, pp.40–41; Möhler, *Entnazifizierung in Rheinland-Pfalz und im Saarland*, pp.358-60, 403; Fürstenau, *Entnazifizierung*, p.45; Willis, *The French in Germany*, p.155; Montgomery, *Forced to Be Free*, p.137; Rödel, 'Die Entnazifizierung in Nordteil der französischen Zone', pp.266, 278; Ruge-Schatz, *Umerziehung und Schulpolitik*, p.71; Einstein to de Caquaray, 31 Dec, 1944; Furnival-Jones to intelligence staffs at army groups, ETOUSA and AFHQ, 12 Jan. 1945, both in WO 219/1578, NAUK; 'Statement by the French member on procedure – the French Zone and Sector'; and Koenig to the Military Governors and General/Senior Delegates, 9 April 1948, both in OMGUS – Records of the Civil Administration Division, Public Safety Branch: Law for Liberation from National Socialism & Militarism 1945–49, RG 260, NA.

19 Henke, *Politische Säuberung*, p.36; Grohnert, *Die Entnazifizierung in Baden*, pp.54-56; Willis, *The French in Germany*, pp.71–72, 80, 82–86, 149; and FitzGibbon, *Denazification*, p.139.

20 Möhler, *Entnazifizierung in Rheinland-Pfalz und im Saarland*, pp.207-08, 213-18; and Rödel, 'Die Entnazifizierung im Nordteil der französischen Zone', p.266.

21 Montgomery, *Forced to Be Free*, pp.135–38; and Möhler, *Entnazifizierung in Rheinland-Pfalz und im Saarland*, p.207.

22 Henke, *Politische Säuberung*, pp.23–27, 35–36, 38–39, 74, 116; Vollnhals, ed., *Entnazifierung*, pp.127, 130; Willis, *The French in Germany*, p.155; Grohnert, *Die Entnazifizierung in Baden*, pp.33-46; and Brommer, ed., *Quellen zur Geschichte von Rheinland-Pfalz*, pp.44–45, 52.

23 Vollnhals, ed., *Entnazifierung*, pp.105–06; and Muller, 'Les premiers mois de l'occupation', pp.193–94.

24 Ruge-Schatz, *Umerziehung und Schulpolitik*, pp.71–74; Möhler, *Entnazifizierung in Rheinland-Pfalz und im Saarland*, p.81-83, 112-13, 196–97; Grohnert, *Die Entnazifizierung in Baden*, pp.129-35; Willis, *The French in Germany*, pp.168–69; Rödel, 'Die Entnazifizierung im Nordteil der französischen Zone', p.266; Hudemann, 'Französischer Besatzungszone', p.357; and Hudemann, 'Kulturpolitik im Spannungsfeld der Deutschlandpolitik', p.19.

25 Willis, *The French in Germany*, p.173; and René Cheval, 'L'Université de Tübingen pendant la période d'occupation', in Vaillant, ed., *La dénazification par les vainqueurs*, p.56.

26 Gilbert, *A European Past*, p.206; Grohnert, *Die Entnazifizierung in Baden*, pp.136-43; Corine Defrance, 'L'Enseignement supérieur en zone française d'occupation en Allemagne, 1945–1949: une étude comparative', *Francia* 22, no.3 (1995), pp.43–64; and Vollnhals, ed., *Entnazifizierung*, pp.154–55.

27 Hugo Ott, 'Martin Heidegger und die Universität Freiburg nach 1945: Ein Bespiel für die Auseinandersetzung mit der politischen Vergangenheit', *Historisches Jahrbuch* 105, no.1 (1985), pp.95–128; and Vollnhals, ed., *Entnazifizierung*, p.157.

28 Defrance, 'L'Enseignement supérieur en zone française', pp.43–64; Cheval, 'L'Université de Tübingen', pp.56, 58–59; Stefan Zauner, 'Universität Tübingen und Leibniz-Kolleg in der französischen Besatzungszeit 1945–1949. Aspekte des Akademischen Nuebeginns im Nachkriegsdeutschland', *Historisches Jahrbuch* 119 (1999), pp.209–231; and OMGUS – Director of Information Control, Intelligence Branch 'Daily Intelligence Digest' no.190, 20 June 1946, OMGUS – Office of the Adjutant General: General Correspondence (Decimal File) 1945–49, RG 260, NA.

29 Willis, *The French in Germany*, pp.175–76; Vollnhals, ed., *Entnazifizierung*, p.157; Möhler, *Entnazifizierung in Rheinland-Pfalz und im Saarland*, p.169-70; FORD 'Germany: Weekly Background Notes' no.106, 4 Sept. 1947, FO 371/64392, NAUK; and British Consulate General, Baden Baden to Political Division, Berlin, 20 Oct. 1947, FO 371/64276, NAUK.

30 Willis, *The French in Germany*, pp.76–77.

31 Hudemann, 'Kulturpolitik im Spannungsfeld der Deutschlandpolitik', p.19.

32 Willis, *The French in Germany*, pp.27–29, 83–84, 150, 156–59, 161, 176; Grohnert, *Die Entnazifizierung in Baden*, pp.62-63, 69–70, 73–77, 80–94; Möhler, *Entnazifizierung in Rheinland-Pfalz und im Saarland*, p.8-9, 71–73, 76–79, 88–93, 97–99, 105–06, 143–44, 145,

151–56, 164–67, 192–96, 231, 404–05, 406, 407; Fürstenau, *Entnazifizierung*, pp.42, 137–38; Henke, *Politische Säuberung*, pp.47–52, 55, 56–59, 61, 64–72, 80–111, 115–16, 126, 131, 137; Rödel, 'Die Entnazifizierung in Nordteil der französischen Zone', pp.266, 271–74, 276; Hudemann, 'Französischer Besatzungszone', p.354; Rauh–Kühne, 'Forschungen zur französischer Zone', p.19; FitzGibbon, *Denazification*, pp.103, 114; Friedmann, *Allied Military Government*, p.29; Loth, *Stalin's Unwanted Child*, p.36; 'Statement by the French member on procedure – the French Zone and Sector'; Public Safety Branch 'Denazification in the French Zone of Occupation', 15 August 1947; Laffont to Directors General and Directors (CAB/C No.722), 19 September 1945, all in OMGUS – Records of the Civil Administration Division, Public Safety Branch: Law for Liberation from National Socialism & Militarism 1945–49, RG 260, NA; and ACC Coordinating Committee 'Report to the Council of Foreign Ministers', Section ii – Denazification, 21 Feb. 1947, FO 371/64352, NAUK.

33 Fürstenau, *Entnazifizierung*, pp.140–43; Möhler, *Entnazifizierung in Rheinland-Pfalz und im Saarland*, p.187–89; and Public Safety Branch 'Denazification in the French Zone of Occupation', 15 August 1947, OMGUS – Records of the Civil Administration Division, Public Safety Branch: Law for Liberation from National Socialism & Militarism 1945–49, RG 260, NA.

34 FitzGibbon, *Denazification*, p.139.

35 Henke, *Politische Säuberung*, pp.88, 96, 120.

36 *Ibid.*, pp.84, 116–117; Willis, *The French in Germany*, pp.158, 279; Möhler, *Entnazifizierung in Rheinland-Pfalz und im Saarland*, p.69–70, 94, 106-08, 193–94, 408; Grohnert, *Die Entnazifizierung in Baden*, p.61; Public Safety Branch 'Denazification in the French Zone of Occupation', 15 August 1947; and Laffont to Directors General and Directors (CAB/C No.722), 19 September 1945, both in OMGUS – Records of the Civil Administration Division, Public Safety Branch: Law for Liberation from National Socialism & Militarism 1945–49, RG 260, NA. For numbers of French military government personnel in 1946, see Balfour, 'Four-Power Control in Germany', p.106. French military government cadres numbered 18 to every 100,000 German civilians. In the British zone, the proportion was ten to 100,000; in the U.S. zone, three to 100,000.

37 Henke, *Politische Säuberung*, pp.69–71; and Rödel, 'Die Entnazifizierung im Nordteil der französischer Zone', p.273.

38 Fürstenau, *Entnazifizierung*, p.134.

39 Henke, *Politische Säuberung*, pp.72–79, 80, 88–89, 95, 110–13, 115, 121; Rauh–Kühne, 'Forschungen zur französischen Zone', pp.19–20; Möhler, *Entnazifizierung in Rheinland-Pfalz und im Saarland*, p.29–30, 73-74, 79-81, 109-12, 175–77, 198–201; Grohnert, *Die Entnazifizierung in Baden*, pp.62, 152, 159; Ruge-Schatz, *Umerziehung und Schulpolitik*, p.44; Hudemann, 'Französischer Besatzungszone', p.355; and Montgomery, *Forced to Be Free*, p.135.

40 British Consulate General, Baden Baden to Political Division, Berlin, 20 Oct. 1947, FO 371/64276, NAUK.

41 Möhler, *Entnazifizierung in Rheinland-Pfalz und im Saarland*, p.174-75; and Rödel, 'Die Entnazifizierung im Nordteil der französischer Zone', p.278.

42 Willis, *The French in Germany*, p.195; and ACC Coordinating Committee 'Report to the Council of Foreign Ministers', Section ii – Denazification, 21 Feb. 1947, FO 371/64352, NAUK.

43 Montgomery, *Forced to Be Free*, p.135; 'Ordinance No.92 on Youth Amnesty', 2 May 1947; and 'Ordinance No.133 on Denazification', 17 Nov. 1947, both in OMGUS – Records of the Civil Administration Division, Public Safety Branch: Law for Liberation from National Socialism & Militarism 1945–49, RG 260, NA.

44 Grohnert, *Die Entnazifizierung in Baden*, pp.153, 172–79; Möhler, *Entnazifizierung in*

Rheinland-Pfalz und im Saarland, p.247-49; 250 British Liaison Mission 'Report' no.6, Dec. 1946, FO 1005/1615, NAUK; and comments by M. Reddaway on file C4225/185/18, FO 371/64352, NAUK.

45 Henke, *Politische Säuberung*, pp.98–111, 114, 118, 126–46, 148, 158–59; Rödel, 'Die Entnazifizierung im Nordteil der französischer Zone', pp.274–76; Hudemann, 'Französischer Besatzungszone', p.355; FitzGibbon, *Denazification*, pp.108–14; Fürstenau, *Entnazifizierung*, pp.139–40, 143–44; Willis, *The French in Germany*, pp.156, 159; 'Ordinance No.79 of the Commander-in-Chief of French Forces in Germany concerning the Application of Control Council Directive No.38', 18 Feb. 1947; 'Baden Law implementing Directive 38'; Public Safety Branch 'Denazification in the French Zone of Occupation', 15 August 1947, all in OMGUS – Records of the Civil Administration Division, Public Safety Branch: Law for Liberation from National Socialism & Militarism 1945–49, RG 260, NA; and Livingston to Bevin, 5 March 1947, FO 371/64352, NAUK.

46 Rödel, 'Die Entnazifizierung im Nordteil der französischer Zone', p.277; Henke, *Politische Säuberung*, p.147; Möhler, *Entnazifizierung in Rheinland-Pfalz und im Saarland*, p.279-80, 291-92; 'Baden Law implementing Directive 38'; 'Ordinance No.92: Youth Amnesty', 2 May 1946; Public Safety Branch 'Denazification in the French Zone of Occupation', 15 August 1947; Koenig to the Military Governors and General/Senior Delegates, 9 April 1948, all in OMGUS – Records of the Civil Administration Division, Public Safety Branch: Law for Liberation from National Socialism & Militarism 1945–49, RG 260, NA; and 'Denazification: Progress since the Meeting of the Council of Foreign Ministers in Moscow', FO 371/64353, NAUK.

47 Patton Diary, entry for 18 April 1945, in *Papers Relating to the Allied High Command, 1943/45*, reel 4.

48 Willis, *The French in Germany*, pp.42–44, 49; Henke, *Politische Säuberung*, p.140; and Hudemann, 'Französischer Besatzungszone', pp.328–29.

49 *FRUS*, 1946, v, p.596.

50 Willis, *The French in Germany*, p.160; and Möhler, *Entnazifizierung in Rheinland-Pfalz und im Saarland*, p.406.

51 Rödel, 'Die Entnazifizierung im Nordteil der französischer Zone', pp.276–77; Henke, *Politische Säuberung*, pp.156–75; Fürstenau, *Entnazifizierung*, p.145; Möhler, *Entnazifizierung in Rheinland-Pfalz und im Saarland*, p.284-85, 286-87, 408; Hudemann, 'Französische Besatzungszone', pp.355–56; and Livingston to Political Division, 4 Nov. 1947, FO 371/64351, NAUK.

52 Rödel, 'Die Entnazifizierung im Nordteil der französischer Zone', pp.277, 279; Grohnert, *Die Entnazifizierung in Baden*, pp.201-04; Möhler, *Entnazifizierung in Rheinland-Pfalz und im Saarland*, p.292-98; Fürstenau, *Entnazifizierung*, pp.145–46; Henke, *Politische Säuberung*, pp.171, 174–87; 'Ordinance No.133 on Denazification', 17 Nov. 1947; Internal and Religious Affairs 'Implementation of Ordinance No.133', 6 July 1948, both in OMGUS – Records of the Civil Administration Division, Public Safety Branch: Law for Liberation from National Socialism & Militarism 1945–49, RG 260, NA.

53 Rödel, 'Die Entnazifizierung im Nordteil der französischer Zone', p.279.

54 Henke, *Politische Säuberung*, pp.171–72; Fürstenau, *Entnazifizierung*, pp.146–47, 228–30; and 'Statistiques relatives à l'Épuration au 1.7.48', OMGUS – Records of the Civil Administration Division, Public Safety Branch: Law for Liberation from National Socialism & Militarism 1945–49, RG 260, NA.

55 Montgomery, *Forced to Be Free*, pp.77–78; and Möhler, *Entnazifizierung in Rheinland-Pfalz und im Saarland*, p.409.

56 Montgomery, *Forced to Be Free*, pp.64–65, 89, 92; Grohnert, *Die Entnazifizierung in Baden*, pp.144-48; Möhler, *Entnazifizierung in Rheinland-Pfalz und im Saarland*, p..409

57 Rödel, 'Die Entnazifizierung im Nordteil der französischer Zone', pp.277–78, 280.

58 Swiss press excerpts on Germany, 26 July 1945, FO 371/46933, NAUK.

59 Willis, *The French in Germany*, p.163.

60 Henke, *Politische Säuberung*, pp.121, 123–24; Möhler, *Entnazifizierung in Rheinland-Pfalz und im Saarland*, p.405; and Public Safety Branch 'Denazification in the French Zone of Occupation', 15 August 1947, OMGUS – Records of the Civil Administration Division, Public Safety Branch: Law for Liberation from National Socialism & Militarism 1945–49, RG 260, NA.

61 Willis, *The French in Germany*, pp.151, 155; FitzGibbon, *Denazification*, p.107; Henke, *Politische Säuberung*, pp.7–8, 118, 123; Möhler, *Entnazifizierung in Rheinland-Pfalz und im Saarland*, p.405, 409-10; and Rauh-Kühne, 'Forschungen zur Französischen Zone', p.19. Henke emphasizes French hypocrisy and failure to transfer power as part of the reason for the failure of the 'Württemberg model', noting that the French sought not denazification, but the *image* of denazification. On the other hand, Rainer Hudemann suggests that the historical record can be interpreted in a way that also shows the French in a more positive light. Hudemann rightly notes that French military government experimented with an approach in Württemberg-Hohenzollern that exceeded the concurrent bounds of devolution in any other zone. Henke, *Politische Säuberung*, pp.147–48; Hudemann, 'Frankreichs Besatzung in Deutschland', pp.249–50; and Hudemann, 'Französischer Besatzung', pp.356–58.

62　FitzGibbon, *Denazification*, pp.106–07.

Chapter 6: The House of Lies

1 von Salomon, *Fragebogen*. For the commercial success of *Fragebogen*, see FitzGibbon, *Denazification*, pp.42, 168; Möhler, *Entnazifizierung in Rheinland-Pfalz und im Saarland*, p.146; and http://www.time.com/time/magazine/printout/0,8816,861117,00.html, as of 1 April 2007.

2 Padover, *Experiment in Germany*, pp.36–37, 61, 91, 97, 117–18; Willis, *The French in Germany*, p.160; Pfeil, 'Antifascisme et Dénazification', pp.16–17; Vogt, *Denazification in Soviet-Occupied Germany*, p.223; Beevor, *The Fall of Berlin*, p.430; Plischke, 'Denazification in Germany', p.218; Clare, *Berlin Days*, p.38; and FitzGibbon, *Denazification*, p.41.

3 Clare, *Berlin Days*, pp.116–20.

4 Vogt, *Denazification in Soviet-Occupied Germany*, pp.211–12, 215; and DZVI/6032/Pf/ Wa 'Allgemeiner Überblick über den Stand der Entnazifizierung der Verwaltung und Wirtschaft in der Industrie und dem Handwerk innerhalb der sowjetischen Besatzungszone', 28 April 1947, NY 4182/1197, SAPMO.

5 Bower, *The Pledge Betrayed*, p.144.

6 Vogt, *Denazification in Soviet-Occupied Germany*, pp.209–11, 215–18.

7 USFET G-2 'Weekly Intelligence Summary' no.42, 2 May 1946, State Dept. Decimal Files 1945–49, 740.00119 Control (Germany), RG 59, NA.

8 *Stars and Stripes*, 24 Jan. 1947; and Eucom 'Intelligence Summary' no.8, 22 May 1947, State Dept. Decimal Files 1945–49, 740.00119 Control (Germany), RG 59, NA.

9 For examples, see Tent, *Mission on the Rhine*, p.52; Gniffke, *Jahre mit Ulbricht*, pp.69–70; and Friedmann, *Allied Military Government of Germany*, pp.8, 113.

10 Horvay, 'Military Government and Denazification in Ansbach', pp.170–71; Griffiths, 'The Denazification Program', pp.212-13; Möhler, *Entnazifizierung in Rheinland-Pfalz und im Saarland*, p.79.

11 Cologne Intelligence Section to Public Safety, 808 Mil Gov, 24 April 1947; Nottingham

to Public Safety Branch, Zonal Executive Offices, 23 June 1947; Halland to Prain, 30 June 1947; Denazification and Liaison (Internal Affairs) Section 'Kriminalrat Gustav Theuring of the Cologne RB Police Force', July 1947; Bishop to Director, Denazification and Liaison, 16 July 1947; and Young to Steel, 14 July 1947, all in FO 1032/639, NAUK.

12 Niethammer, *Entnazifizierung in Bayern*, pp.369–70, 431–32; Frei, *Adenauer's Germany and the Nazi Past*, p.8; and *FRUS*, 1946, v, pp.695–700. For early attempts by the few survivors of July 20th to prove the legitimacy of the coup, see Klaus-Jürgen Müller and Hans Mommsen, 'Zur Historiographie der Widerstandes', in Klaus-Jürgen Müller, ed., *Der deutsche Widerstand 1933–1945* (Paderborn, 1986), pp.13–14. In conservative Bavaria, Müller's participation in the anti-Nazi resistance actually eroded his reputation and may have contributed to his deposition as party chairman in late 1949.

13 Kahn, *Experiment in Occupation*, p.125; and Niethammer, *Entnazifizierung in Bayern*, p.207.

14 Niethammer, *Entnazifizierung in Bayern*, pp.207, 390–91. For death threats against anti-Nazi activists in Wasserburg, see *Weser-Kurier*, 6 Feb. 1946.

15 Donnison, *Civil Affairs and Military Government in North-West Europe*, p.371; Grohnert, *Die Entnazifizierung in Baden*, pp.30-31; Jones, 'Eradicating Nazism from the British Zone', p.157; Fürstenau, *Entnazifizierung*, p.165; and Vollnhals, ed., *Entnazifizierung*, pp.319–20.

16 Montgomery claims that Allied moral reproaches 'hindered rather than helped the revolutionary outlook … [and] only increased the net supply of resentment and self-justification'. *Forced to Be Free*, p.31. In mid-May 1945, a study by the U.S. First Army summed up the German civilian attitude as follows: 'We always have been, and are, good and decent citizens. Whether stories from the camps are true or not, we have had nothing to do with it and are not responsible for it.' Rather, the predominant popular tendency was to blame everything on the SS. SHAEF G-5 'Weekly Journal of Information' no.13, 16 May 1945, WO 219/3918, NAUK. See also Beschloss, *The Conquerors*, p.273. The 'collective guilt' thesis was especially insulting to the few anti-fascists who had actively fought National Socialism and resented being lumped together with Nazis. Rödel, 'Die Entnazifizierung in Nordteil der französischer Zone', pp.261–62.

17 OSS Report from Stuttgart, 20 Sept. 1945, XL 22487, Entry 19, RG 226, NA; and OSS Report from Duisberg, 15 Oct. 1945, XL 33758, Entry 19, RG 226, NA.

18 Hellmut Gollwitzer, *Unwilling Journey* (Westport, 1974), p.22.

19 CSDIC(UK) G.G. Report SRGG 1189(C), 3 May 1945, WO 208/4169, NAUK.

20 *The Manchester Guardian*, 27 Aug. 1945.

21 Gimbel, *A German Community under American Occupation*, p.53; and Fürstenau, *Entnazifizierung*, p.133.

22 Niethammer, *Entnazifizierung in Bayern*, pp.73, 75, 83, 87, 88–89, 95–100, 102–05, 165–71, 212–13, 216–17, 281–82, 388; Fürstenau, *Entnazifizierung*, pp.10–14; Eberan, *Wer war an Hitler schuld?*, pp.168–75; Padover, *Experiment in Germany*, pp.230, 309–13; Balfour, 'Four-Power Control in Germany', p.249; Bower, *The Pledge Betrayed*, p.137; Vollnhals, *Evangelische Kirche und Entnazifizierung*, pp.15, 30–31, 33–35, 41–44, 136; Adrian Tillmanns, 'Die Erklärung von Stuttgart und ihre Interpretationen: Versuch einer psychoanalytischen Kritik', *Kirchliche Zeitgeschichte* 7, no.1 (1994), pp.59–82; and *Manchester Guardian*, 4 Sept. 1945.

23 Fürstenau, *Entnazifizierung*, pp.85–86; Montgomery, *Forced to Be Free*, pp.34, 129; Frei, *Adenauer's Germany and the Nazi Past*, p.xiii; ICD report no.55 'Public Attitudes toward Denazification', 15 April 1947, OMGUS – Records of CAD, Public Safety Branch: Law for Liberation from National Socialism and Militarism, 1945–49, RG 260, NA.

24 Donnison, *Civil Affairs and Military Government in North-West Europe*, p.371; Fürstenau, *Entnazifizierung*, p.107; Grohnert, *Die Entnazifizierung in Baden*, pp.30-31; Turner,

'Denazification in the British Zone', p.255; and Friedrich Buschmann, 'Dienstlicher Bericht über die Entnazifizierung in Bremen', in Wiltrud Ulrike Drechsel and Andreas Röpke, eds., *'Denazification' zur Entnazifizierung in Bremen* (Bremen, 1992), pp.21–22.

25 Marshall, 'The Democratisation of Local Politics in the British Zone', p.414; Niethammer, *Entnazifizierung in Bayern*, pp.176–77, 289; and LB-80 'Germany (Russian Zone): Political – Reactions to Denazification Policy', 5 Nov. 1946, OMGUS – Office of the Adjutant General: General Correspondence (Decimal File) 1945–49, RG 260, NA.

26 Peterson, *Russian Commands and German Resistance*, pp.118, 344; and Vogt, *Denazification in Soviet-Occupied Germany*, p.75.

27 Friedmann, *Allied Military Government of Germany*, p.120.

28 Donnison, *Civil Affairs and Military Government in North-West Europe*, p.372; Griffiths, 'The Denazification', pp.304, 307; Möhler, *Entnazifizierung in Rheinland-Pfalz und im Saarland*, p.409; Niethammer, *Entnazifizierung in Bayern*, pp.386, 392–93; Marshall, *The Origins of Post-War German Politics*, p.55; Montgomery, *Forced to Be Free*, p.63; FitzGibbon, *Denazification*, p.178; Clare, *Berlin Days*, pp.73–74, 108–10, 126–29; Bower, *The Pledge Betrayed*, p.153; and Montgomery to Steel, 29 May 1947, FO 371/64744, NAUK.

29 Vollnhals, ed., *Entnazifizierung*, p.320; Friedmann, *Allied Military Government of Germany*, p.120; and Bower, *The Pledge Betrayed*, p.155.

30 21st Army Group 'Weekly Political Intelligence Summary' no.6, 11 Aug. 1945, FO 371/46934, NAUK.

31 Donnison, *Civil Affairs and Military Government in North-West Europe*, pp.377–78; USFET G-2 'Weekly Intelligence Summary' no.54, 25 July 1946, State Dept. Decimal Files 1945–49, 740.00119 Control (Germany), Rg 59, NA; and 'Bulletin de Renseignements', 20 June 1949, OMGUS ODI General Correspondence 91 (French Zone), RG 260, NA.

32 Henke, *Politische Säuberung*, p.115; Niethammer, *Entnazifizierung in Bayern*, p.391; Bower, *The Pledge Betrayed*, p.155; Vogt, *Denazification in Soviet-Occupied Germany*, pp.179–80, 190–91, 192, 223; and 'Consolidation of OMGUS Denazification Field Inspector's Reports Received since 1 November 1946', OMGUS – Office of the Adjutant General: General Correspondence (Decimal File) 1945–49, RG 260, NA.

33 Uhlig, ed., *Confidential Reports des Britischen Verbindungsstabes zum Zonenbeirat*, p.111; Niethammer, *Entnazifizierung in Bayern*, p.287; Tauber, *Beyond Eagle and Swastika*, i, p.31; and Peterson, *Russian Commands and German Resistance*, p.344.

34 Van Melis, *Entnazifizierung in Mecklenburg-Vorpommern*, p.234.

35 USFET G-2 'Weekly Intelligence Summary' no.16, 1 Nov. 1945, State Dept. Decimal Files 1945–49, 740.00119 Control (Germany), RG 59, NA; and MAN 'Concerning Denazification Program', 27 Oct. 1945, OMGUS – Office of the Adjutant General: General Correspondence (Decimal File) 1945–49, RG 260, NA.

36 USFET G-2 'Weekly Intelligence Summary' no.74, 12 Dec. 1946, State Dept. Decimal Files 1945–49, 740.00119 Control (Germany), RG 59, NA.

37 Niethammer, *Entnazifiziering in Bayern*, pp.389–90.

38 Kahn, *Experiment in Occupation*, pp.141, 149; *Die Neue Zeitung*, 11 March 1946; and USFET 'Weekly Intelligence Summary' no.63, 26 Sept. 1946, State Dept. Decimal Files 1945–49, 740.00119 Control (Germany), RG 59, NA.

39 Constabulary G-2 'Weekly Intelligence Summary' no.62, 15 Aug. 1947, WWII Operations Reports 1940–48, RG 407, NA.

40 USFET 'Weekly Intelligence Summary' no.70, 14 Nov. 1946; Eucom ' Intelligence Summary' no.6, 28 April 1947; no.12, 17 July 1947; no.13, 29 July 1947; no.15, 2 Sept. 1947, all in State Dept. Decimal Files 1945–49, 740.00119 Control (Germany), RG 59, NA; Constabulary G-2 'Weekly Intelligence Summary' no.59, 25 July 1947; and no.88, 9 Feb. 1948, WWII Operations Reports 1940–48, RG 407, NA.

41 Clare, *Berlin Days*, p.72; Bower, *The Pledge Betrayed*, p.153; Möhler, *Entnazifizierung in*

Rheinland-Pfalz und im Saarland, p.151; Willis, *The French in Germany*, pp.160–61; van Melis, *Entnazifiziering in Mecklenburg-Vorpommern*, p.235; and ICD Report no.55, 'Public Attitudes toward Denazification', 15 April 1947, OMGUS – Records of CAD, Public Safety Branch: Law for Liberation from National Socialism and Militarism, 1945–49, RG 260, NA.

42 *FRUS,* 1945, iii, pp.960–61.

43 'Monthly Report of the Military Governor, U.S. Zone' no.4, 20 Nov. 1945, State Dept. Decimal Files 1945–49, 740.00119 Control (Germany), RG 59, NA.

44 *Die Neue Zeitung*, 30 Nov. 1945; and Turner to Director, Office of MG for Greater Hesse, 21 June 1946, OMGUS – Office of the Adjutant General: General Correspondence (Decimal File) 1945–49, RG 260, NA. For the sympathy of liberal German elements, see Tauber, *Beyond Eagle and Swastika*, i, p.35; and USFET G-2 'Weekly Intelligence Summary' no.16, 1 Nov. 1945, State Dept. Decimal Files 1945–49, 740.00119 Control (Germany), RG 59, NA.

45 Donnison, *Civil Affairs and Military Government in North-West Europe*, p.371; Kahn, *Experiment in Occupation*, p.145; Padover, *Experiment in Germany*, p.116; and Eucom 'Intelligence Summary' no.6, State Dept. Decimal Files 1945–49, 740.00119 Control (Germany), RG 59, NA.

46 Bower, *The Pledge Betrayed*, pp.162–63; Montgomery, *Forced to Be Free*, p.140; Niethammer, *Entnazifizierung in Bayern*, p.458; *FRUS,* 1945, iii, p.986; USFET G-2 'Weekly Intelligence Summary' no.42, 2 May 1946; no.53, 18 July 1946; no.56, 8 Aug. 1946, all in State Dept. Decimal Files 1945–49, 740.00119 Control (Germany), RG 59, NA; and LB-80 'Germany (Russian Zone): Political – Reactions to Denazification Policy', 5 Nov. 1945, OMGUS – Office of the Adjutant General: General Correspondence (Decimal File) 1945–49, RG 260, NA.

47 USFET G-5 'Bi-Weekly Political Summary' no.3, 29 Sept. 1945, XL 20917, Entry 19, RG 226, NA.

48 MI-14 'Mitropa' no 12, 29 Dec. 1945, FO 371/55630, NAUK.

49 Niethammer, *Entnazifizierung in Bayern*, pp.387; Tauber, *Beyond Eagle and Swastika*, i, pp.30–31, 34; and ICD Report no.80 'Opinions on Denazification', 26 Nov. 1947, OMGUS – Records of the CAD, Public Safety Branch: Law for Liberation from National Socialism and Militarism, 1945–49, RG 260, NA.

50 Montgomery, *Forced to Be Free*, p.30; and *Stars and Stripes*, 28 Jan. 1947.

51 Eucom 'Intelligence Summary' no.6, 28 April 1947, State Dept. Decimal Files 1945–49, 740.00119 Control (Germany), RG 59, NA.

52 Huber to Muller, 27 April 1947, OMGUS – Public Safety Branch: Law for Liberation from National Socialism and Militarism, 1945–49, RG 260, NA.

53 Marsh to Director, OMG Bavaria, 1 July 1946, OMGUS – Office of the Adjutant General: General Correspondence (Decimal File) 1945–49, RG 260, NA.

54 Tauber, *Beyond Eagle and Swastika*, i, pp.36–37.

55 USFET G-2 'Weekly Intelligence Summary' no.44, 16 May 1946; OMGUS Information Control 'Intelligence Summary' no.57, 31 Aug. 1946; Eucom 'Intelligence Summary' no.4, 31 March 1947; no.5, 14 April 1946; no.6, 28 April 1947, all in State Dept. Decimal Files 1945–49, 740.00119 Control (Germany), RG 59, NA; 'Consolidation of Findings by OMGUS Field Inspectors for Week 10 to 17 August 1946'; and 'Consolidation of Findings by OMGUS Field Inspectors for Week 17 to 24 August 1946', both in OMGUS – Office of the Adjutant General: General Correspondence (Decimal File) 1945–49, RG 260, NA.

56 USFET 'Weekly Intelligence Summary' no.69, 7 Nov. 1946; no.74, 12 Dec. 1946; Eucom 'Intelligence Summary' no.17, 29 Sept. 1947, all in State Dept. Decimal Files 1945–49, 740.00119 Control (Germany), RG 59, NA; and Constabulary G-2 'Weekly Intelligence Summary' no.66, WWII Operations Reports 1940–48, RG 407, NA.

57 Constabulary G-2 'Weekly Intelligence Summary' no.86, 26 Jan. 1948, WWII Operations
   Reports 1940–48, RG 407, NA; and 'Consolidation of Findings by OMGUS Inspectors
   for Week 10 to 17 August 1946', OMGUS – Office of the Adjutant General: General
   Correspondence (Decimal Files) 1945–49, RG 260, NA.

58 Biddiscombe, *The Last Nazis*, p.203; *Die Neue Zeitung*, 25 Oct. 1946; 22 Nov. 1946; 6 Jan.
   1947; 10 Jan. 1947; 3 Feb. 1947; 7 Feb. 1947; *Stars and Stripes*, 9 Jan. 1947; 22 Jan. 1947; 3
   Feb. 1947; 5 Feb. 1947; *The New York Times*, 21 Oct. 1946; 29 Oct. 1946; 2 Feb. 1947; 3
   Feb. 1947; *The Times*, 3 Feb. 1947; USFET G-2 'Weekly Intelligence Summary' no.68,
   31 Oct. 1946; Eucom 'Intelligence Summary' no.1, 13 Feb. 1947; USFET 'Theatre
   Commander's Weekly Staff Conference' no.2, 14 Jan. 1947; no.5, 4 Feb. 1947; all in State
   Dept. Decimal Files 1945–49, 740.00119 Control (Germany), RG 59, NA; Constabulary
   G-2 'Weekly Intelligence Report' no.20, 25 Oct. 1946; 'Weekly Intelligence Summary'
   no.21, 1 Nov. 1946; no.24, 22 Nov. 1946; no.31, 11 Jan. 1947, all in WWII Operations
   Reports 1940–48, RG 407, NA; and *History of the Counter Intelligence Corps* (Baltimore,
   1959), xxvii, pp.56–60, NA.

59 FitzGibbon, *Denazification*, pp.154–55.

60 *Die Neue Zeitung (Berliner Blatt)*, 25 March 1947; *Stars and Stripes*, 18 March 1947; FORD
   'Weekly Background Notes' no.86, 28 March 1947; and no.88, 17 April 1947, both in
   FO 371/64390, NAUK.

61 *Stars and Stripes*, 24 Jan. 1947; 30 Jan. 1947; and *The New York Times*, 15 March 1953.

62 Willis, *The French in Germany*, p.280; *Stars and Stripes*, 23 March 1947; 27 March 1947;
   30 March 1947; 31 March 1947; 2 April 1947; 1 May 1947; and FORD 'Weekly
   Background Notes' no.86, 28 March 1947, FO 371/64390, NAUK.

63 Van Melis, *Entnazifizierung in Mecklenburg-Vorpommern*, p.234.

64 ICD Report No.80 'Opinions on Denazification', OMGUS – Records of CAD, Public
   Safety Branch: Law for Liberation from National Socialism and Militarism, 1945–49,
   RG 260, NA.

65 Vollnhals, *Evangelische Kirche und Entnazifizierung*, pp.134–35; Vogt, *Denazification in
   Soviet-Occupied Germany*, p.86; Bower, *The Pledge Betrayed*, p.150; Kahn, *Experiment
   in Occupation*, p.103; and OMGUS 'Weekly Information Bulletin' no.67, 11 Nov.
   1946, State Dept. Decimal Files 1945–49, 740.00119 Control (Germany), RG 59,
   NA. Even Martin Niemöller argued that 'conflicts must arise if the order of the
   Protestant Church, that is, the order to preach, is abrogated by an authority outside
   the church'. For treatment of clergymen by denazification authorities, see Griffiths,
   'The Denazification Program', pp. 117-18; 'Progress Report no.3 on Carrying Out the
   Denazification Law', 8 May 1946, OMGUS – Office of the Adjutant General: General
   Correspondence (Decimal File) 1945–49, RG 260, NA; and 'Annexure 'A' to SCD/P
   (46) 17—Appendix 'B' to Zone Policy Instruction 3 (Revise): Application of Control
   Council Directive 24 to Ordained Priests', WO 311/634, NAUK.

66 Clemens Vollnhals, 'Die Hypothek des Nationalprotestantismus: Entnazifizierung und
   Strafverfolgung von NS-Verbrechen nach 1945', *Geschichte und Gesellschaft* 18, no.1
   (1992), pp.51–69; Vollnhals, *Evangelische Kirche und Entnazifizierung*, pp.16–20, 31, 34,
   36–40, 52–120; Fürstenau, *Entnazifizierung*, pp.160–63; Griffiths, 'The Denazification
   Program', pp. 115-117; Vollnhalls, ed., *Entnazifizierung*, pp.292–96; Niethammer,
   Entnazifizierung in Bayern, pp.171, 459; Kahn, *Experiment in Occupation*, pp.101–03, 105,
   156–59; Balfour, 'Four-Power Control in Germany', pp.249–53; Bower, *The Pledge
   Betrayed*, pp.137–38, 149–51, 162; and Chairman of the Vorsitzende, the Supreme
   Council of the Evangelical Church in Germany to U.S. Military Government in
   Germany, 26 April 1946, OMGUS – Records of the CAD, Public Safety Branch: Law
   for the Liberation from National Socialism and Militarism, 1945–49, RG 260, NA.

67 Willis, *The French in Germany*, p.162; Bower, *The Pledge Betrayed*, pp.154–55, 162; Griffiths,
   'The Denazification Program', pp. 509-10; Vollnhals, ed., *Entnazifizierung*, p.316;

Henke, *Politische Säuberung*, p.54; Fürstenau, *Entnazifizierung*, pp.204–05; 'Consolidation
of Findings by OMGUS Field Inspectors for Week 17 to 24 August 1946'; and
'Consolidation of OMGUS Denazification Field Inspector's Reports Received since
1 November 1946', both in OMGUS – Office of the Adjutant General: General
Correspondence (Decimal File) 1945–49, RG 260, NA.

68 Bower, *The Pledge Betrayed*, p.150; and USFET G-2 'Weekly Intelligence Summary' no.76,
26 Dec. 1946, State Dept. Decimal Files 1945–49, 740.00119 Control (Germany), RG
59, NA.

69 Niethammer, *Entnazifizierung in Bayern*, pp.116–17, 206–09, 398–99; Kahn, *Experiment in
Denazification*, p.122; and *FRUS*, 1945, iii, p.981.

70 Niethammer, *Entnazifizierung in Bayern*, pp.398–99; Vollnhals, ed., *Entnazifizierung*, pp.318–
19; Uhlig, ed., *Confidential Reports des Britischen Verbindungsstabes*, pp.43–45; Montgomery,
Forced to Be Free, pp.64–65; *Frankfurter Rundschau*, 17 April 1947; FORD 'Germany:
Weekly Background Notes' no.87, 2 April 1947, FO 371/64390, NAUK; 'Progress
Report no.3 on Carrying Out the Denazification Law', 8 May 1946, OMGUS – Office
of the Adjutant General: General Correspondence (Decimal File) 1945–49, RG 260,
NA; USFET G-2 'Weekly Intelligence Summary' no.67, 24 Oct. 1946; and no.69, 7
Nov. 1946, both in State Dept. Decimal Files 1945–49, 740.00119 Control (Germany),
RG 59, NA.

71 Vollnhals, ed., *Entnazifizierung*, p.319; *FRUS*, 1945, iii, pp.984–85; and USFET G-2
'Weekly Intelligence Summary' no.11, 27 Sept. 1945, State Dept. Decimal Files 1945–49,
740.00119 Control (Germany), RG 59, NA.

72 Montgomery, *Forced to Be Free*, pp.64–65; Willis, *The French in Germany*, p.162;
Möhler, *Entnazifizierung in Rheinland-Pfalz und im Saarland*, p.191-92; Niethammer,
Entnazifizierung in Bayern, p.388; and Information EF – 'Die grossen und die kleinen
Pgs. Ein Beitrag zur Entnazifizierungspraxis im Westen', ZK der SED, Sekretariat Paul
Merker, Befehle der SMAD, DY 30/IV 2/2002/5, SAPMO.

73 Bower, *The Pledge Betrayed*, p.153.

74 *Ibid.*, p.154; 'Consolidation of Findings by OMGUS Field Inspectors for the Week 10 to
17 August 1946'; 'Consolidation of Findings by OMGUS Field Inspectors for Week
17 to 24 August 1946'; USMG W/B 'Correction of Denazification Deficiencies', 19
Sept. 1946; and 'Consolidation of OMGUS Denazification Field Inspector's Reports
Received since 1 November 1946', all in OMGUS – Office of the Adjutant General:
General Correspondence (Decimal File) 1945–49, RG 260, NA.

75 *Weser-Kurier*, 28 Aug. 1947.

76 *Die Neue Zeitung*, 30 June 1947.

77 Henke, *Politische Säuberung*, p.115.

78 Bower, *The Pledge Betrayed*, p.155; Griffiths, 'The Denazification Program', pp.347-49;
'Consolidation of Findings by OMGUS Field Inspectors for Week 17 to 24 August
1946'; and 'Consolidation of OMGUS Denazification Field Inspector's Reports
Received since 1 November 1945', both in OMGUS – Office of the Adjutant General:
General Correspondence (Decimal File) 1945–49, RG 260, NA.

79 Ebsworth, *Restoring Democracy*, p.11; Henke, *Politische Säuberung*, pp.59–61; Griffiths, 'The
Denazification Program', pp.203; and Constabulary G-2 'Weekly Intelligence Summary'
no.88, 9 Feb. 1948, WWII Operations Reports 1940–48, RG 407, NA.

80 Niethammer, *Entnazifizierung in Bayern*, p.388; and 'Consolidation of OMGUS
Denazification Field Inspector's Reports Received since 1 November 1945', OMGUS
– Office of the Adjutant General: General Correspondence (Decimal File) 1945–49,
RG 260, NA.

81 Niethammer, *Entnazifizierung in Bayern*, p.393.

82 Griffiths, 'The Denazification Program', pp. 548-49; and Tauber, *Beyond Eagle and
Swastika*, i, p.36. A draft of this legislation was prepared by the labour committee of

Spruchkammer and Denazification Ministry employees in September 1947. They noted that without such protections, Nazis returning to the job market were likely to edge them out of available spots. 'Conclusion Concerning Securing the Future of Personnel Active with the Ministry for Political Liberation', 13 Nov. 1947, OMGUS – Records of the CAD, Public Safety Branch: Law for Liberation from National Socialism and Militarism, 1945–49, RG 260, NA.

83 Vogt, *Denazification in Soviet-Occupied Germany*, p.115.

84 Niethammer, *Entnazifizierung in Bayern*, pp.399–400, 431, 434, 441–69; Bower, *The Pledge Betrayed*, p.153; *Die Neue Zeitung*, 5 May 1947; 21 June 1947; 24 June 1947; 25 June 1947; *Weser-Kurier*, 2 April 1947; and 31 May 1947.

85 Montgomery, *Forced to Be Free*, pp.62–63, 64–65; Gimbel, *The American Occupation of Germany*, p.160; and Niethammer, *Entnazifizierung in Bayern*, pp.506–07.

86 Niethammer, *Entnazifizierung in Bayern*, pp.219–21; and Willis, *The French in Germany*, p.161.

87 Pütz, ed. *Konrad Adenauer und die CDU*, pp.17–18; Frei, *Adenauer's Germany and the Nazi Past*, pp.29–30; Herf, *Divided Memory*, p.217; and Montgomery, *Forced to Be Free*, pp.62, 66.

88 Niethammer, *Entnazifizierung in Bayern*, p.371; Kahn, *Experiment in Germany*, pp.150–52; and *Die Neue Zeitung*, 5 July 1946.

89 Vollnhals, ed., *Entnazifizierung*, p.197; and *Die Neue Zeitung*, 7 June 1946. As early as the spring of 1946, Adenauer argued that 'nominal' Nazis and ex-soldiers should be allowed to enter the CDU, 'though at first they cannot assume any functions in it'. Anything less, he suggested, would drive such elements toward 'a growing and extreme nationalism'. Herf, *Divided Memory*, p.217. This policy soon led to problems. AMG charged that a group of Nazis and '*Deutsch National*' sympathizers in *Kreis* Frankenburg 'reputably exerts considerable influence in the Christian Democratic Union'. USFET G-2 'Weekly Intelligence Summary' no.56, 8 Aug. 1946, State Dept. Decimal Files 1945–49, 740.00119 Control (Germany), RG 59, NA. For reports of Nazis filtering into the CDU, see USFET G-2 'Weekly Intelligence Summary' no.37, 28 March 1946, State Dept. Decimal Files, 740.00119 Control (Germany), RG 59, NA. For allegations about influence within the CSU by post-1937 Nazis and the wives of *Parteigenossen*, see *The New York Times*, 22 April 1946.

90 Willis, *The French in Germany*, p.155; Montgomery, *Forced to Be Free*, p.65; and Pütz, ed., *Konrad Adenauer und die CDU*, p.18.

91 Montgomery, *Forced to Be Free*, pp.59–61; Fürstenau, *Entnazifizierung*, pp.167–68; Niethammer, *Entnazifizierung in Bayern*, pp.214–15, 454; Frei, *Adenauer's Germany and the Nazi Past*, pp.28–29; Herf, *Divided Memory*, pp.244–46; and Ebsworth, *Restoring Democracy*, p.19.

92 Bower, *The Pledge Betrayed*, p.153; *Die Neue Zeitung*, 31 May 1946; USFET G-2 'Weekly Intelligence Summary' no.69, 7 Nov. 1946, State Dept. Decimal Files 1945–49, 740.00119 Control (Germany), RG 59, NA; 'Consolidation of Findings by OMGUS Field Inspectors for Week 17 to 24 August 1946'; 'Consolidation of OMGUS Denazification Field Inspector's Reports since 1 November 1945', both in OMGUS – Office of the Adjutant General: General Correspondence (Decimal File) 1845–49, RG 260, NA; and 'Dr. Schumacher's Views on New Denazification Directive', FO 371/64352, NAUK.

93 Montgomery, *Forced to Be Free*, pp.61, 65–66; and Marshall, *The Origins of Post-War German Politics*, p.56.

94 Ebsworth, *Restoring Democracy*, pp.13, 17; Griffiths, 'The Denazification Program', p.540; Tauber, *Beyond Eagle and Swastika*, i, pp.32, 33–34; Bower, *The Pledge Betrayed*, pp.272–73; Montgomery, *Forced to Be Free*, pp.79–80; FitzGibbon, *Denazification*, pp.136–37;

Vollnhals, ed., *Entnazifizierung*, p.329; Gontard to Raffaeli, 27 April 1948; and OMGH Denazification Division 'Denazification as it Affects Public Employment', 28 April 1948, both in OMGUS – Records of the CAD, Public Safety Branch: Law for Liberation from National Socialism and Militarism, 1945–49, RG 260, NA.

95 Griffiths, 'The Denazification Program', p.541; and Eucom 'Intelligence Summary' no.33, 11 May 1948, State Dept. Decimal Files 1945–49, 740.00119 Control (Germany), RG 59, NA.

96 Hans-Peter Schwarz, *Geschichte der Bundesrepublik Deutschland. Die Ära Adenauer 1949–1957* (Wiesbaden, 1981), ii, pp.38–39; Ebsworth, *Restoring Democracy*, pp.18–19, 153–56, 210; Turner, 'Denazification in the British Zone', pp.264–65; Manfred Kittel, *Die Legende von der 'Zweiten Schuld'. Vergangenheitsbewältigung in der Ära Adenauer* (Berlin, 1993), pp.80–86; Möhler, *Entnazifizierung in Rheinland-Pfalz und im Saarland*, p.185–86; Herf, *Divided Memory*, pp.183–85, 289–91; Frei, *Adenauer's Germany and the Nazi Past*, pp.41–66; Bower, *The Pledge Betrayed*, pp.355–59; Montgomery, *Forced to Be Free*, pp.34–35, 67, 73, 76–83, 113, 181; FitzGibbon, *Denazification*, pp.171–74, 180–83; and Garner, 'Public Service Personnel in West Germany in the 1950s', pp.28–37, 38–46, 50–52, 63. For the Eichmann story, see *The New York Times*, 7 June 2006.

97 Griffiths, 'The Denazification Program', p.549; Krüger, *Entnazifiziert!*, p.159; FitzGibbon, *Denazification*, pp.138, 145–46, 174; Bower, *The Pledge Betrayed*, p.286; and Tauber, *Beyond Eagle and Swastika*, i, p.36.

98 Frei, *Adenauer's Germany and the Nazi Past*, pp.27–39; Fürstenau, *Entnazifizierung*, pp.152–59; Bower, *The Pledge Betrayed*, pp.360–61; Herf, *Divided Memory*, p.7; FitzGibbon, *Denazification*, p.135; and Turner, 'Denazification in the British Zone', p.265.

99 Montgomery, *Forced to Be Free*, p.63.

100 Herf, *Divided Memory*, pp.7, 266.

The Reckoning

1 Vogt, *Denazification in Soviet-Occupied Germany*, p.2.

2 Henke, *Die amerikanische Besetzung Deutschlands*, p.295.

3 Vogt, *Denazification in Soviet-Occupied Germany*, pp.15–16.

4 FitzGibbon, *Denazification*, p.170.

5 Douglas Porch, 'Germany, Japan and the 'De-Baathification' of Iraq', 7 March 2003, http://www.ciaonet.org.ezproxy.library.uvic.ca/olj/si/si_2_3/si_2_3_pod01.pdf, as of 28 Feb. 2006.

6 *The Times*, 20 May 2004; *The Guardian*, 22 April 2004; *The Scotsman*, 23 April 2004; and *The Sunday Times*, 25 July 2004. Crane Brinton defined a revolution as the sudden substitution of one group in power for another. *Anatomy of a Revolution* (New York, 1952), p.2.

7 Turner, 'The British Occupation and its Impact on Germany', pp.11–12; Charles Frye, 'The Third Reich and the Second Republic', *Western Political Quarterly* 21 (1968), pp.670–80; Ralf Dahrendorf, *Society and Democracy in Germany* (Garden City, 1967), pp.408–11, 416–18, 438; and CCG(BE) 'Intelligence Review' no.5, 6 Feb. 1946, FO 371/55807, NAUK.

8 Kahn, *Experiment in Occupation*, p.143; Bower, *The Pledge Betrayed*, p.139; FitzGibbon, *Denazification*, p.181; Wolfgang Glatzer, Karl Otto Hondrich, Heinz-Herbert Noll, Karin Stiehr and Barbara Wörndl, *Recent Social Trends in West Germany 1960–1990* (Frankfurt a.M., 1992), p.540; USFET 'Weekly Intelligence Summary' no.26, 10 Jan. 1946; Eucom 'Intelligence Summary' no.20, 6 Nov. 1947, both in State Dept. Decimal Files 1945–49,

740.00119 Control (Germany), RG 59, NA; and ICD Report no.55 'Public Attitudes toward Denazification', 15 April 1947, OMGUS – Records of the CAD, Public Safety Branch: Law for Liberation from National Socialism and Militarism, 1945–49, RG 260, NA.

9 Glatzer, et al, *Recent Social Trends in West Germany*, pp.61, 120.

10 Balfour, 'Four-Power Control in Germany', p.170.

11 *Ibid.*, p.182; Friedmann, *The Allied Military Government of Germany*, pp.121, 123; and Clare, *Berlin Days*, p.73.

12 Marshall, 'The Democratisation of Local Politics', pp.414, 447; Möhler, *Entnazifizierung in Rheinland-Pfalz und im Saarland*, pp.409–10; Fürstenau, *Entnazifizierung*, p.22; and Turner, 'The British Occupation and its Impact on Germany', p.11.

13 Kahn, *Experiment in Occupation*, p.180; FitzGibbon, *Denazification*, p.12; and Merritt, 'American Influences in the Occupation of Germany', pp.94–95.

BIBLIOGRAPHY

Archives

Bundesarchiv
National Archives of the United Kingdom
U.S. National Archives

Microfilm and Published Document Collections

Ralph Uhlig, ed., *Confidential Reports des Britischen Verbindungsstabes zum Zonenbereit der britischen Besatzungszone in Hamburg (1946–1948)*, Franfurt a.M., 1993.

Wiltrud Ulrike Drechsel and Andreas Röpke, eds., *'Denazification' zur Entnazifizierung in Bremen*, Bremen 1992.

Beate Ruhm von Oppen, ed., *Documents on Germany under Occupation, 1945–1954*, London, 1955.

Clemens Vollnhals, ed., *Entnazifizierung. Politische Säuberung und Rehabilitierung in den vier Besatzungszone 1945–1949*, Munich, 1991.

Irmgard Lange, ed., *Entnazifizierung in Nordrhein-Westfalen. Richtlinien, Anweisung, Organisation*, Siegburg, 1976.

Ruth-Kristin Rössler, ed., *Die Entnazifizierungspolitik der KPD/SED 1945–1948. Dokumente und Materialien*, Goldbach, 1994.

Foreign Relations of the United States series, Washington, 1955, 1960, 1961, 1965, 1966, 1968, 1970, 1972.

Morgenthau Diary (Germany), Washington, 1967.

OSS/State Department Intelligence and Research Reports: Germany and its Occupied Territories during World War II, Washington, 1977.

Papers Relating to the Allied High Command, 1943/45 East Ardsley, Wakefield, 1983.

Alexander Plato, ed., *Sowjetische Speziallager in Deutschland 1945 bis 1950: Studien und Berichte*, Berlin, 1998.

Newspapers

Deutsche Volkszeitung
Frankfurter Rundschau
Manchester Guardian
Die Neue Zeitung
Neue Zürcher Zeitung
Neues Deutschland
New York Times
The Observer
PM
Stars and Stripes
Tägliche Rundschau
The Times (London)
Washington Post
Weser-Kurier

Principal Secondary Sources

Balfour, Michael, 'Four-Power Control in Germany, 1945–1946', in *Four-Power Control in Germany and Austria, 1945–1946,* London, 1956.

Bower, Tom, *The Pledge Betrayed: America and Britain and the Denazification of Post-war Germany,* New York, 1982.

Clare, George, *Berlin Days,* London, 1989.

Davidson, Eugene, *The Death and Life of Germany,* New York, 1959.

Donnison, S.F.V., *Civil Affairs and Military Government, North-West Europe, 1945–1946,* London, 1961.

Ebsworth, Raymond, Ebsworth, *Restoring Democracy in Germany: The British Contribution,* London, 1961.

Ericksen, Robert, 'Religion und Nationalsozialismus im Spiegel der Entnazifizierungsakten der Göttingen Universität', *Kirchliche Zeitgeschichte 7,* no.1 (1994).

FitzGibbon, Constantine, *Denazification,* London, 1969.

Frei, Norbert, *Adenauer's Germany and the Nazi Past: The Politics of Amnesty and Integration,* New York, 2002.

Friedmann, Wolfgang, *The Allied Military Government of Germany,* London, 1947.

Fürstenau, Justus, *Entnazifizierung. Ein Kapitel deutscher Nachkriegspolitik,* Lüchterhand, 1969.

Gimbel, John, *The American Occupation of Germany: Politics and the Military, 1945–1949,* Stanford, 1968.

Gimbel, John, *A German Community under American Occupation: Marburg 1945–52,* Stanford, 1961.

Gimbel, John, 'German Scientists, United States Denazification Policy, and the Paperclip Conspiracy.' *International History Review* xii, no.3 (Aug. 1990).

Griffiths, William, 'The Denazification Program', Ph.D. Dissertation, Harvard University, April 1950.

Grohnert, Reinhard, *Die Entnazifizierung in Baden 1945–1949. Konzeptionen und Praxis der 'Epuration' am Biespiel eines Landes der französischen Besatzungzone,* Stuttgart, 1991.

Henke, Klaus-Dietmar, *Die amerikanische Besetzung Deutschlands,* Munich, 1995.

Henke, Klaus-Dietmar, *Politische Säuberung unter französischer Besatzung*, Stuttgart, 1981.

Henke, Klaus-Dietmar, 'Die Trennung von Nationalsozialismus. Selbszerstörung, politische Säuberung, "Entnazifizierung", Strafverfolgung', in Klaus-Dietmar Henke and Hans Woller, eds., *Politische Säuberung in Europa. Die Abrechnung mit Faschismus und Kollaboration nach dem Zweiten Weltkrieg*, Munich, 1991.

Herf, Jeffrey, *Divided Memory: The Nazi Past in the Two Germanys*, Cambridge, 1997.

Horvay, Frank, 'Military Government and Denazification in Ansbach, 1945–1946', in Michael Ermarth, ed., *America and the Shaping of German Society, 1945–1955*, Oxford, 1993.

Jones, Jill, 'Eradicating Nazism from the British Zone of Germany: Early Policy and Practice', *German History* 8, no.2 (1990).

Kahn, Arthur, *Experiment in Occupation: Witness to the Turnabout, Anti-Nazi War to Cold War, 1944–1946*, University Park, 2004.

Krüger, Wolgang, *Entnazifiziert! Zur Praxis der politischen Säuberung in Nordrhein-Westfalen*, Wuppertal, 1982.

Latour, Conrad and Vogelsang, Thilo, *Okkupation und Wiederaufbau. Die Tätigkeit der Militärregierung in der amerikanischen Besatzungszone Deutschlands 1944–1947*, Stuttgart, 1973.

Marshall, Barbara, 'The Democratisation of Local Politics in the British Zone of Germany: Hanover 1945–47', *Journal of Contemporary History* 21 (1986).

Marshall, Barbara, *The Origins of Post-War German Politics*, London, 1988.

Melis, Damian van, 'Denazification in Mecklenburg-Vorpommern', *German History* 13, no.3 (1995).

Melis, Damian van, *Entnazifizierung in Mecklenburg-Vorpommern. Herrschaft und Verwaltung 1945–1948*, Munich, 1999.

Möhler, Rainer, *Entnazifizierung in Rheinland-Pfalz und im Saarland unter französischer Besatzung von 1945 bis 1952*, Mainz, 1992.

Montgomery, John D., *Forced to Be Free: The Artificial Revolution in Germany and Japan*, Chicago, 1957.

Naimark, Norman, *The Russians in Germany: A History of the Soviet Zone of Occupation, 1945–1949*, Cambridge, 1995.

Niethammer, Lutz, *Entnazifizierung in Bayern: Säuberung und Rehabilitierung unter amerikanischer Besatzung*, Frankfurt, 1972.

Padover, Saul, *Experiment in Germany: The Experience of an American Intelligence Officer*, New York, 1946.

Peterson, Edward, *The American Occupation of Germany: Retreat to Victory* Detroit, 1977.

Peterson, Edward, *Russian Commands and German Resistance: The Soviet Occupation, 1945–1949*, New York, 1999.

Pfeil, Ulrich, 'Antifascism et Dénazification en Zone d'Occupation Soviétique (SBZ), 1945–1948', *Revue Allemagne et des Pays de langue allemande* 32, no.1 (2000).

Plischke, Elmer, 'Denazification in Germany: A Policy Analysis', in Robert Wolfe, ed., *Americans as Proconsuls: United States Military Government in Germany and Japan*, Carbondale, 1984.

Rödel, Volker, 'Die Entnazifizierung in Nordteil der französichen Zone', in Franz-Josef Heyen, ed., *Rheinland-Pfalz entsteht: Beiträge zu den Anfängen des Landes Rheinland-Pfalz in Koblenz 1945–1951*, Boppard, 1984.

Salomon, Ernst von, *Fragebogen*, New York, 1955.

Schrenk-Notsing, Caspar von, *Charakterwäsche* Stuttgart, 1965.

Tauber, Kurt, *Beyond the Eagle and the Swastika: German Nationalism since 1945*, Middletown, 1967.

Tent, James, *Mission on the Rhine: Re-education and Denazification in American-Occupied Germany*, Chicago, 1982.

Turner, Ian, 'Denazification in the British Zone', in Ian Turner, ed., *Reconstruction in Post-War Germany: British Occupation Policy and the Western Zones, 1945–55*, Oxford, 1989.

Vaillant, Jérôme, *La dénazification par les vainqueurs*, Lille, 1981.

Vogt, Timothy, *Denazification in Soviet-Occupied Germany: Brandenburg, 1945–1948*, Cambridge, 2000.

Vollnhals, Clemens, *Evangelische Kirche und Entnazifizierung 1945–1949*, Munich, 1989.

Vollnhals, Clemens, 'Die Hypothek des Nationalprotestantismus: Entnazifizierung und Strafverfolgung von NS-Verbrechen nach 1945', *Geschichte und Gesellschaft* 18, no.1 (1992).

Wember, Heiner, 'Entnazifizierung nach 1945: Die deutschen Spruchgerichte in der britischen Zone', *Geschichte in Wissenschaft und Unterricht* 43, no.7 (1992).

Welsh, Helga, 'Entnazifizierung und Wiedereröffnung der Universität Leipzig 1945–1946', *Vierteljahrshefte für Zeitgeschichte 33* (1985).

Welsh, Helga *Revolutionärer Wandel auf Befehl? Entnazifizierungs- und Personalpolitik in Thüringen und Sachsen (1945–1948)*, Munich, 1989.

Willis, Roy, *The French in Germany, 1945–1949*, Stanford, 1962.

Woller, Hans, *Gessellschaft und Politik in der amerikanischen Besatzungszone. Die Region Ansbach und Fürth*, Munich, 1986.

Ziemke, Earl, *The U.S. Army in the Occupation of Germany*, Washington, 1975.

Zink, Harold, *American Military Government in Germany*, New York, 1947.

Zink, Harold, *The United States in Germany, 1944–1955*, Princeton, 1957.

Interviews and Correspondence

Lord Noel Annan, 29 April 1986

Ernest Gross, 1 November 1982

John McCloy, c.31 October 1982

Sir Edgar Williams, 8 May 1986

INDEX